Charlotte Perkins Gilman

Charlotte Perkins Gilman

OPTIMIST REFORMER

Edited by Jill Rudd & Val Gough

University of Iowa Press Iowa City

University of Iowa Press, Iowa City 52242
Copyright © 1999 by the University of Iowa Press
All rights reserved
Printed in the United States of America
http://www.uiowa.edu/~uipress
Printed on acid-free paper

Library of Congress Cataloging-in-Publication Data
Charlotte Perkins Gilman: optimist reformer / edited by Jill
Rudd and Val Gough.
p.   cm.
Includes bibliographical references (p.   ) and index.
ISBN 0-87745-695-X, ISBN 0-87745-696-8 (paper)
1. Gilman, Charlotte Perkins, 1860–1935—Political and social
views.   2. Feminism and literature—United States—History—19th
century.   3. Women and literature—United States—History—19th
century.   4. Social problems in literature.   5. Optimism in
literature.   I. Rudd, Jill.   II. Gough, Val.
PS1744.G57Z62   1999
818'.409—dc21   99-29216

99 00 01 02 03 C 5 4 3 2 1
99 00 01 02 03 P 5 4 3 2 1

CONTENTS

ACKNOWLEDGMENTS

The editors would like to thank the British Academy for their
generous support of the conference "Charlotte Perkins Gilman:
Optimist Reformer," Liverpool University, June 1995, which
provided the basis for this volume, and to acknowledge Opus
Technology for their sponsorship of that event. We are also
grateful to Professor Miriam Allot and the English Department
of the University of Liverpool for their help and support. Special
thanks are also due to Lisa Leslie for her sterling work in
helping prepare the manuscript for publication. All remaining
errors are the responsibility of the editors, as is the decision to
use "Wallpaper" rather than "Wall-paper" throughout.

JILL RUDD & VAL GOUGH

Introduction

In the final entry of her 1890 diary Charlotte Perkins Gilman records the year as one of "great growth and gain. My whole literary reputation dates within it – mainly from 'Similar Cases.' Also the dawn of my work as lecturer."[1] Although she had received a sporadic income from other pursuits, such as teaching or painting, from this date Gilman made her modest living from her abilities to lecture in a way which not only entertained and educated her audiences but also challenged them. Known to her contemporaries as a fervent advocate of reform on social, economic, and religious fronts, and designated an "optimist reformer" by William Dean Howells (*Living*, 182), Gilman produced a vast array of writing on a wide variety of topics across a range of genres: the poem "Similar Cases" to which she refers in her diary epitomizes the reputation she held during her lifetime, being a sharp satire of social expectations delivered in swift-moving verse.[2] Now, in a late-twentieth-century resurgence, she is remembered and celebrated more as a writer of novels and short stories, particularly *Herland* and "The Yellow Wallpaper," than as the author of the social and political essays which originally made her name.

This trend is reflected in the many readers and collections of critical essays which highlight Gilman's novels and short stories and often make only passing reference to the rest of her work.[3] However, the range is gradually widening as current articles are taking increasing account of her poetry, her lectures, and her essays, as well as her letters and diaries. The recent volume of critical essays edited by Joanne B. Karpinski (*Critical Essays on Charlotte Perkins Gilman*) is an indication of this process, as it contains contributions on Gilman's views on religion, her relation to feminism, and her poetry as well as a chapter dealing with Walter

Stetson's letters. Nevertheless, the general bias is still toward her creative work. While this is likely to continue to be the case as long as readers are more able to find Gilman's fictional work available in published form (and indeed as long as our own reading tastes continue to prefer fiction to essay) and while critical studies of her fiction continue to shed new and interesting lights on such texts, there is also room for more rounded appreciations of Gilman's oeuvre which remind us that the main focus and purpose of writing for her was reform.

This book aims to reflect in one volume this wider scope of Gilman's writing. The essays contained here discuss themes or individual texts not only in the light of their original context and Gilman's own preoccupations, but also in terms of the continued relevance of her arguments for feminism today. Individually and as a whole this collection provides direct engagement with Gilman and her views, regarding her not solely as a mother of feminism, but as someone who rewards critical attention and appraisal. A constant theme is the recognition of her unwavering belief that things could be changed for the better and surprisingly quickly, by dint of individual effort. It is this persistent optimism which made her a vociferous and forceful voice for reform, rather than a social satirist. Reading the essays here, it is clear that it is also this optimism which continues to inspire her audiences today.

The legacy for feminism which she has left us, expressed variously in essays, poems, and short stories, is not always a comfortable one. For instance, it is disconcerting to acknowledge that there is still a presumption that women must choose between marriage and work in terms that often represent no choice at all. This is a dilemma Gilman treated in several ways, including dramatizing it in *Three Women*, where the protagonist, Alena, seeks advice on the matter from two older women, her mother and her aunt, each of whom accepted the opposition of marriage and work and chose accordingly, and both of whom voice their regrets about the choice they made. Having listened to each of them, Alena elects to carve her own way, informed by the opinions of the previous generation, but not bound by them. It is perhaps in a similar way that we should now regard Gilman herself. If we treat her as one of our foremothers, we are bound to listen to what she says, but are not therefore obliged to follow uncritically in her footsteps. The line trod by this collection is the one between recognizing

what is less acceptable to us in her opinions yet nevertheless celebrating her forthright articulation of many of the issues which
confront us today. Throughout, her reputation for straight talking remains: regardless of genre, Gilman's direct voice speaks clearly from the
page, asserting views and arguing points in a way which demands
attention and expects concurrence. While that concurrence may
not always be entirely forthcoming, the impact of her writing on
successive generations of readers is undeniable. Having faded into
comparative obscurity in the second quarter of the twentieth century, her reputation has grown again steadily since the 1970s to
the point where she is once again a widely recognized figure in
the 1990s. Hand in hand with this resurgence has come an interest
in, and indeed respect for, the woman herself and the life she led
and tried to lead. Thus biographies and editions of her diaries and
letters have been as gladly received as the collections of short stories or editions of *Herland* which have made her more generally
available to a public eager to rediscover this figure of female resistance and reform.[4]

An example of the kind of reaction Gilman elicits is to be found
in Lynne Sharon Schwartz's introduction to *The Yellow Wallpaper
and Other Writings by Charlotte Perkins Gilman*, which is a powerful testament to the respect Gilman engenders in many of her
twentieth-century readers. In it Gilman's strong will and resolute
independence are admired and presented as patterns to inspire
imitation, while the continuing relevance of her recommendations
for reform is recognized in the tacit call to arms of Schwartz's final
sentence: "the succeeding generations she longed to reach have yet
to summon the wits and resilience to follow where she led" (xxvi).

Rhetorically effective as this is, some may take issue with
Schwartz. Reading Gilman's diaries and her articles in the *Forerunner*, it is clear that the people "she longed to reach" were not
"succeeding generations" but her own contemporaries. Her calls
to action are genuine and immediate: she hoped, even expected,
to see great changes as people in general, and women in particular,
altered their ways of life and thought. Her disappointment toward
the end of her life is almost palpable when she saw that women
had shaken off some forms of repression only to engage in others
which Gilman regarded as little better. "I did expect better things
of women than they have shown," she remarks in the penultimate

chapter of her autobiography, *The Living of Charlotte Perkins Gilman* (371), and it is a salutary reminder of the kind of almost belligerent optimism for reform that she possessed, which led her to expect much and regard more as possible. It may also serve to show that we are often like her contemporaries in choosing to ignore some aspects of her calls to reform, while enthusiastically espousing others.

However, as Judith Allen argues in her essay, some of the reforms for which Gilman called vociferously may no longer be relevant or even acceptable. As feminism has developed and subdivided, it is possible to assess Gilman's views diachronically as well as synchronically and to come to different evaluations of them as a result. As Ann J. Lane puts it in her chapter, "Now that we know for the first time in history in a substantial way something of what we were not allowed to know until these last few years, we must move beyond retrieval of that history to incorporating and using that new knowledge, not just paying obeisance to its existence." There is an echo here of another widely respected but problematic voice in feminism, that of Simone de Beauvoir, who asserted, "I think one must be able to say, 'No: no, that won't do! . . . Set higher standards for yourselves! Being a woman is not enough.'"[5]

Nonetheless, the very fact that Gilman's work continues to be in print, the existence of books about her, and the success of conferences devoted to her are proof that she has reached the succeeding generations mentioned by Schwartz. This volume looks in particular at Gilman's legacy for the women of the later twentieth century and in so doing allows us to reassess both her reformist ideas and our own views on latter-day feminism. Gilman scholarship has indeed moved on from the straightforward and much needed recovery of her work (such as that supplied by the Lane and Ceplair readers) to more critical treatments which allow us to acknowledge elements of her writing which are now regarded as unacceptable.[6] As a result, the analyses offered here are not uncritical of their subject; rather they seek to reappraise Gilman's views and writings in a way which allows us to address directly issues which are often overlooked or cause disquiet, such as her racism, her almost willful blindness to issues of class, and her broadly essentialist view of women, thereby creating room for just assessment of how much there is to be valued.

The effect of this collection is thus twofold: Gilman and her works are reassessed in the light of current feminist thought (as in the essay by Lisa Ganobcsik-Williams, which tackles the questions of Gilman's racism, classism, and ethnocentrism, and in Sandra Gilbert and Susan Gubar's contribution, which reassesses the effect of Gilman's views while also offering an appraisal of current feminist thought) and also presented in the context of Gilman's own time (as in the cases of Katharine Cockin's essay, which places Gilman's drama *Three Women* in the context of Pioneer plays performed in drawing rooms, and Karen Stevenson's contribution, which sets Gilman's advocacy of short hair against a background of an overview of the history of hairstyling). Over and again these essays demonstrate that engagement with Gilman's views is still pertinent for feminist debate today.

Ann J. Lane begins this volume with a consideration of Gilman's legacy for latter-day feminism in which she presents the case for not only reading but also acting upon Gilman's ideas and for seeking a historical root for women's studies. In particular Lane reminds us of Gilman's assertion that one of the effects of suppression, especially suppression in the form of lack of access to education, is an impoverished achievement. She argues both for the need to recognize our intellectual heritage for what it is and for Gilman's place in that heritage. Lisa Ganobcsik-Williams follows Lane's suggestion and seeks a widened evaluation of Gilman which gives her a place in the history of ideas. Taking up the views expressed by Lane in her introduction to *The Charlotte Perkins Gilman Reader* concerning the decision to omit the less creditable aspects of Gilman's life and thought ("not from the desire to hide that side of her thought but from the belief that her valuable ideas better deserve remembering and repeating" [xxx]), Ganobcsik-Williams discusses Gilman's views on race, class, and ethnicity. To an extent her racism can be seen as part of the social climate of the times and it is possible to describe her views as representing the best of intentions expressed in terms which are only now regarded as patronizing and white-centered, but Ganobcsik-Williams challenges this attitude as she deals openly with Gilman's racism. She also cautions against simplified readings of Gilman, which tend to result in lumping accusations of classism with those of racism. This essay reminds us not to "limit the scope of our research on Gilman and class by assuming that since she was a well-known, white, female figure at the turn of the century, she was representing and advocating some monolithic class perspective."

Lane's comments about the need for a historical awareness of the origins and development of feminism and women's studies are continued in a more specific vein by Frederick Wegener, who concentrates in his essay on the recurrent figure of a woman physician as savior in Gilman's fiction. Gilman's high esteem for women doctors becomes obvious as Wegener cites the large number of references to them in her nonfictional writings, but it is particularly interesting to see how often she uses this figure as an example of the independent and fulfilled life to which women in general could aspire. Wegener alerts us to how significant both the fact and the idea of women medics were to Gilman and the wider society and shows how much the specific battles fought with the medical profession by these pioneering women reflected and affected the advances toward equality. This study clearly demonstrates Gilman's habit of using her fiction as a reformist tool by presenting examples of the attitudes she found around her and recorded in her diaries. As we remark how many of these attitudes, or vestiges of them, remain with us, we may see that part of Gilman's legacy is of resistance and awareness of social constraints and a constant need for the reassertion of female potential and independence.

When it comes to Gilman's conviction about the importance of being self-supporting in general we are perhaps on more familiar ground, especially when such convictions are put in terms of the choice between work and marriage. However, Gilman scholarship has tended to overlook one of the most direct fictional engagements with this topic: Gilman's play *Three Women*. Katharine Cockin and Marie Farr redress this oversight in their essays. Cockin places the piece in its right context – the parlor dramas of the Pioneer Players – pointing out that such dramas were themselves an integral part of the suffrage movement which presented "women talking to each other as a means of transformation and resistance." The very form of the action is therefore significant in that it centers on one woman receiving advice from two other women, rather than being guided by a well-meaning man. These older women thus function in much the same way as the women doctors examined by Wegener: they are presented as being repositories of good advice as well as being role models. In contrast to Wegener, who presents such relationships between women as wholly positive, Cockin points out that *Three Women* acknowledges the possibilities of conflicting views which may result in divisiveness. Gilman's protagonist resolves the situation by coming to her own conclusions rather than blindly heeding the advice of either of her woman mentors. In a manner reminiscent of Gilman's own wordplay, Cockin makes use of a simple typing error which converts *Aline* to *Alien* to advance discussion of this text in its published and prompt-copy forms. Aline, the woman who rejects the assumption that a woman must choose between family and career, is indeed regarded as misplaced, an alien in the context of the play. The methods she uses to convince, or seduce, her fiancé so that he yields the argument may also seem somewhat alien to our late-twentieth-century sensibilities and present another instance where this mother of feminism makes uncomfortable reading.

Farr extends the sphere of reference to include consideration of the story version of *Three Women* and looks at the story and play in the light of Gilman's general opinions and use of literature, remarking on her love of the theatrical and dramatic. In this closer study of the play text itself Farr illustrates how Gilman wove her personal experiences into the plot detail of a text which is clearly a vehicle for her views on social reform. Farr ends by drawing a parallel between Gilman's eventual experience of being "listened to politely," but not heeded, and our current danger of agreeing with the value of many of Gilman's proposals, but not actually acting upon them.

One pragmatic reformist suggestion for which Gilman is still well known, but which is rarely put into practice, is that of the kitchenless house. This concept is at the center of Yvonne Gaudelius's discussion of Gilman's ideas on architectural reform. The issues of the use and definitions of private space are still at the heart of much feminist debate on the advantages and disadvantages of the divide between public and private spheres. Gaudelius proposes considering Gilman a "materialist feminist" and goes on to assess her work and writings on reform in the light of this nomination. Positing that spatial relations exist because of social processes and that hence spaces themselves are carriers of gender ideology and economic thought, Gaudelius presents the concept of "home" as deserving consideration, especially in a feminist context, and also asserts the importance of paying attention to the physical space of the "house." This is one area of life where the least change has occurred over the sixty years since Gilman's death. The experiments of communities and communal living which followed her suggestions have largely petered out, leaving houses still with kitchens and often sold on the strength of their size and the standards of their fittings. We might link to this the remarkable success of figures such as Martha Stewart and Delia Smith, who help perpetuate the concept of the perfect domestic woman who finds fulfillment in imaginative and successful creation of dishes and decor as an ideal.[7] While these are perhaps extreme examples, the interrelated nature of social and private spheres which Gilman acknowledged and sought to combat persists in many forms today.

Gilman was well aware of how this apparent obsession with homemaking affects not only women's self-perception, but also their relation to the wider social economy and through that to the general relation between the sexes. The full title of her study of this area makes this clear: *Women and Economics: A Study of the Economic Relation between Men and Women as a Factor in Social Evolution*; it is worth recalling that it was this volume, published in 1898, which established her reputation as a social reformer. Naomi Zauderer focuses on this aspect of Gilman's thought in her essay, in which she considers Gilman as a social economist. She regards Gilman as providing a forcible contrast to Karl Marx by centering her economic theory on women – a group almost wholly disregarded in Marx's analyses. Zauderer reminds us that Gilman's tradition is the American one of the utopian socialism of Edward Bellamy and Lester Ward and presents a critique of Gilman and the habit of seeing things through a broadly Marxist filter, which provides new insights into how people perceive Gilman and her world.[8] Zauderer uses Gilman as a way to critique Marx and in so doing touches on the concept of alienation as part of economic theory, a reference which, following Cockin's comments on the misspelling of the character's name, raises possibilities for reading Alena in *Three Women* as a figure of the larger economic force.

Gilman's assertion of the importance of motherhood and marriage to society, which led to her placing them at the center of her economic theory and her reformist efforts, is something which Sandra Gilbert and Susan Gubar feel late-twentieth-century feminism overlooks to its detriment. Concerned about some current trends against the maternal role, they here offer a reassessment of Gilman's views which is not an unthinking paean of praise but an informed questioning of what we have chosen to inherit from her. They reveal that Gilman, the vociferous proponent of idealized motherhood and essentialist feminism, is also (paradoxically) a mother of the antimaternal and nonphysical stance and urge caution against a binary simplification of ideas which could result in motherhood being regarded as antifeminist.

Interestingly, Gilman's views on motherhood are ones that can most fruitfully be regarded in this bifocal manner. Having attracted opprobrium in her own time for sending her daughter to live with Walter Stetson and his second wife, Grace Channing (Gilman's close and lasting childhood friend), and despite the apparent arguments against the institution of marriage in her plays and short stories as well as her own severe misgivings prior to both of her own weddings, Gilman nevertheless advocated marriage in the majority of her writing and came close to deifying motherhood in her utopian novel, *Herland*. Gilbert and Gubar tackle this aspect of Gilman's views and thereby add to the current debate in feminism concerning motherhood.

The antiessentialist elements of Gilman's thought are reflected in her views on education as presented here by Deborah De Simone, who reasserts Gilman's right to be regarded as an educational theorist. Beginning with the observation that criticism of the educational system is an established fact of American life, De Simone points out that education was not inimical to motherhood and is still regarded as a major means of social improvement. Neither De Simone nor Gilman restricts the definition of education to institutionalized schooling, as both recognize that attitudes toward education and expectations of what it should achieve are bound up with attitudes toward the family. De Simone offers a comparison between Gilman and Amy Gutmann, showing how the criticisms of American education expressed by Gilman in the 1890s remain relevant to the views expressed in the 1980s. It is interesting to note that in both Gilman and Gutmann there is a definite agenda: educating children not only in intellectual and moral terms but also to be good democrats.

Our readings of Gilman in both sociological and literary terms are again broadened by Karen Stevenson's lively essay on hair reform. This was one debate in which Gilman advocated both change in outlook and direct action, which she herself does not seem to have adopted to the extent of cutting her own hair. Stevenson's essay is a story of the reinscription of women, as those who braved ridicule and cut their hair soon became victims of swiftly changing fashions in cut or style. She also shows how successes in thwarting imposed ideas of signs of femininity in terms of long hair and intricate coiffure were promptly undermined by adopting other signals, such as styling or dress, to reassert the aura of femininity. This is an entertaining and informative analysis writ small of the kind of swing in attitudes described by Gilbert and Gubar and also frequently held up for ridicule by Gilman herself.

Continuing the assessment of Gilman's role in the general development of feminist debate, Judith Allen points out that, in common with many feminists, Gilman couched her views on women and marriage in terms of a dualism between marriage and prostitution. Following a discussion of Gilman's views on the sexual contract, Allen goes on to suggest that the aspects of Gilman's theories which are now regarded as inappropriate or even redundant for feminist and reformist debate may be a result of those same theories having been highly pertinent then. Feminism, Allen posits, is perhaps more forceful as an argument of the moment: as society alters the subjects under scrutiny, the central issues of feminist debate change likewise. It is not in what was *said* that the foremothers of feminism are most useful, but in the courage and force of the saying and the way feminist analyses were integrated into contemporary concerns. It is in this context of *how* things are said that Catherine Golden reads Gilman's published poetry. As with the majority of her published writings, Gilman sought to use poetry as a political force and to this end made use of styles which had an established popular appeal. The influence of ballads in particular may be heard in many of her poems, designed to strike an immediate chord and be memorable, rather than be of high literary value. The threads of reformist zeal and sharp social observation (which are leitmotifs in several essays of this volume) are thus shown to be drawn together in her verse. Not all Gilman's poetry was for public consumption, however, and in the final essay Denise Knight offers an insight into the more hidden Gilman as revealed by her private poetry. Knight describes the handwritten verse (much of the rest of Gilman's work is in typescript) as "bold, impassioned, and often remarkably poignant"; while we may be familiar with the persona of a woman who would deserve the first two adjectives, it is the last which may surprise us. The fierce passions and desire to be loved which have been highlighted in many essays on Gilman, including several of the ones in this volume, are here the focus of attention and add greatly to our understanding of this remarkable woman.

NOTES

1. *The Diaries of Charlotte Perkins Gilman*, ed. D. Knight, 428.

2. "Similar Cases" was first published in the April 1890 *Nationalist* and later in Gilman's volume of poetry *In This Our World* (1893).

3. Gilman's fictional work is readily available in a variety of collections and readers, including Ann J. Lane's *The Charlotte Perkins Gilman Reader*, Barbara Solomon's *Herland and Selected Stories by Charlotte Perkins Gilman*, and Denise Knight's *"The Yellow Wall-Paper" and Selected Stories of Charlotte Perkins Gilman*. *The Yellow Wallpaper and Other Writings by Charlotte Perkins Gilman*, with an introduction by L. S. Schwartz, contains extracts from *Women and Economics* and *The Man-Made World* in addition to seven short stories, selections from *Herland*, and a complete text of *The Yellow Wallpaper*. There are many critical studies and collections of essays on Gilman's fiction and on *The Yellow Wallpaper* in particular; examples include *The Captive Imagination: A Casebook on "The Yellow Wallpaper,"* edited by Catherine Golden; *The Yellow Wallpaper*, edited by Thomas L. Erskine and Connie L. Richards; and Carol Farley Kessler's *Charlotte Perkins Gilman: Her Progress toward Utopia with Selected Writings*. It is worth noting that Ann J. Lane's biography of Gilman is entitled *To Herland and Beyond*. In contrast there remains only one collection devoted entirely to her nonfiction work, namely Larry Ceplair's *Charlotte Perkins Gilman: A Nonfiction Reader*.

4. Recent years have seen the publication of editions of Gilman's letters to Houghton Gilman, her diaries, and her poetry as well as publication of the letters of Walter Stetson, her first husband. There are also two biogra-

phies of Gilman and several readers. All of this is a testament to the power of personality which makes Gilman a figure in feminism as much for how she lived her life as for the views she propounded.

5. See *Simone de Beauvoir Today: Conversations with Alice Schwartzer 1972–1982* (London: Chatto, 1984), 317.

6. These readers remain the most accessible way to make a first acquaintance with the breadth of Gilman's oeuvre. The fact that Lane has been supplemented over the years by additional collections and new publications of Gilman's short stories, poems, and novels, whereas Ceplair remains the only collection devoted solely to her nonfiction, also reflects fairly accurately the mid- and late-twentieth-century preference for fiction over prose.

7. In her plenary talk at the second international Gilman conference, held at Skidmore College in June 1997, Shelley Fisher Fishkin wittily illustrated how many of the expectations and aspirations which Gilman regarded as most detrimental to attempts to improve women's lot were epitomized by the picture of domestic fulfillment and capability presented in the public personae of women who appear in the media with ideas and demonstrations of how to prepare and present a version of the ideal home. Martha Stewart seems to be the zenith of this industry, not only in appearing talented in every form of craft, but also in being an embodiment of a standard of living which is tantamount to fantasy for the majority of her audience. Whether we ourselves regard this zenith as a nadir or not would likewise reflect our own views on the lifestyle and aspirations being promoted.

8. Readers interested in Gilman's utopianism are directed to *A Very Different Story: Studies on the Fiction of Charlotte Perkins Gilman*, ed. V. Gough and J. Rudd.

Gilman and Feminism

ANN J. LANE

Charlotte Perkins Gilman and the Rights of Women
Her Legacy for the 1990s

When I finished the biography of the woman I came to think of as "my Charlotte" — a phrase that opens my text — I thought I was finished forever with her. But I had not anticipated two reactions: first, how hard it would be for me to give her up, and, second, how much extraordinary interest in her work would be generated in the years ahead, enough to merit a Charlotte Perkins Gilman Society and a *Charlotte Perkins Gilman Newsletter*, which reports on many activities around the nation from a variety of fields, and how many papers would be given regularly on both sides of the Atlantic. In the last week two new contributions crossed my desk, a book by a professor of English on Gilman and the meaning of her utopian writings and an essay by a professor of economics on the centrality to the field of economics, although not recognized, of *Women and Economics*. What a pity Gilman could not be around to observe her success; she would so have loved the seriousness with which so many feminists read her words. How sad it is that her grandchildren, both of whom are alive, will probably not feel the pleasure and satisfaction in her stead, because they probably do not.

Her daughter, Katharine, ended her life with unresolved ambivalent feelings about a mother she felt abandoned her, for whose pain she understandably had little sympathy. "My mother went to pieces when I was born," wrote Katharine in her maturity, "and it wasn't even a difficult birth," making clear her unwillingness to recognize her mother's mental illness. Gilman's grandchildren, Dorothy and Walter Chamberlain, saw their grandmother through their mother's eyes — as a woman who abandoned her maternal responsibilities and as an ideologue whose ideas and reputation embarrassed them.

The only member of the Gilman family who loved and revered Charlotte was a nephew's wife, who once enticed her husband into a woman's bookstore in Pasadena, California, to announce his famous relative. He was so distressed at the enthusiastic response by owners and patrons in the bookstore (an enthusiasm he did not share) that he never again publicly broke the silence about his distinguished aunt. Yet the reputation remains and makes it difficult to write on Gilman's legacy for the 1990s, not because her trenchant observations and analyses and the themes she stressed in her books, articles, speeches, essays, and poems are passé, but because her ideas and analyses apply as well today, alas, as they did when she wrote about them.

No one would deny that the world has changed in regard to issues of women and gender in the last sixty to one hundred years, yet when we look at what Gilman said about her world and realize how many of those observations apply to ours, we put in perspective the reality and significance of those changes. It is something that we should do more often; that is, look at what Mary Ritter Beard (1876–1958) called Women in Long History and think in terms of immense periods of time and space in order to understand fully the impact of the shifts and setbacks, and forward moves, we observe in our own time.[1] We who explore American culture, living on a relatively small canvas, tend too often to exaggerate our findings, or they turn out to be distorted because we live in such small batches of time and space.

I would like now to use my distance from Gilman as an asset, rather than the disadvantage I felt it was when I approached this topic and, in a very Gilman-like way, turn my drawback into an advantage by offering some general observations about her legacy for us in the nineties in this troubled world.

Feminist scholars, as we all know, have accomplished much in the last several decades. They have demonstrated that women have been an active force in the creation of history and culture. In the fields of social history, anthropology, literature, politics, religion, and philosophy, feminist scholars have made it increasingly clear that women have filled vital roles throughout all time. But the intellectual work women in the past have done is not fully utilized or credited, except as retrieved voices, as historic legacies, as expressions of our foremothers. And so we assign to our students, and ourselves read, what our predecessors wrote, or what others have said about what they wrote, and we pay homage to Aphra Behn, Mary Astell, Mary Wollstonecraft, Margaret Fuller, Olive Schreiner, and Mary Beard, among the many others who are compiled in Dale Spender's splendid collection *Feminist Theorists*. Ordinarily, however, we do not use their ideas for our own work and so we do not build on those ideas.

We do not have a sense of a developed intellectual history and we do not yet know our intellectual heritage as an integrated body of knowledge upon which we continue to build. I am not sure why. It has partly to do with the way feminist scholarship has evolved in the last twenty-five years. We have learned to read across disciplines, but we do not much read back in them. The major work in feminist theory has not been done by historians, with very few exceptions, so the important theoretical work by contemporary feminist scholars is generally not historically rooted.

We also (we being feminist scholars) do not, perhaps cannot, fully understand how severely we have been damaged by having been denied access to learning about ourselves. I also wonder if we do not know our intellectual heritage as a systematic body of knowledge because perhaps we do not truly have such a developed heritage. It, like us, has been damaged. Indeed, it is largely because of its damage that we are damaged. We cannot build on a heritage that has been denied us and in some cases been obliterated.

In the past that withholding of knowledge has caused each generation to begin anew as if there were no predecessors because to those denied that knowledge there indeed were no predecessors. Now that we know for the first time in history in a substantial way something of what we were not allowed to know until these last few years, we must move beyond retrieval of that history to incorporating and using that new knowledge, not just paying obeisance to its existence.

I would like to assess Gilman's legacy for us in the years ahead in three ways. First, a look at the weaknesses in her work to see how they stand today. Second, a general overview of her major notions as they still speak to us today. And finally, I would like to highlight a few specific ideas of hers that intrigue me and may make us uncomfortable and are, probably for that reason, rarely pursued.

Gilman's major flaws are easy to identify and even easy to explain and to understand, if not to justify. She held a simple, linear view of evolutionary progress, an uncritical belief in progress which was somewhat dimmed by her view of the twentieth century, as reflected in her only detective story, *Unpunished*.[2] She seriously neglected issues of class, race, and ethnicity and their complex interaction with gender. She believed in laws of racial development, which today are read, usually correctly, as racist and ethnocentric. She never questioned the superiority of the heterosexual, monogamous nuclear family structure as the natural result of evolutionary progress and highest form of human organization.

Gilman's reading of history and sociology that would identify her today as a racist is what it is and cannot be defended, only understood. But we must also recognize the neglect of race, leading to charges of racism by our feminist colleagues of color, directed against white feminist scholars, especially in the early days of feminist research twenty years ago. I like to think that those charges, true when initially made, are less true or little true now, because I do think that white feminist scholars have listened and learned.

On a personal level, in her private existence, Gilman was also a racist and anti-Semite, as private letters and journal entries indicate.[3] What that should tell us is that it is harder to free ourselves of cultural biases than we acknowledge. It may instruct us to look more carefully at our own thinking for signs of similar kinds of backwardness that is so pervasive that we too are unable to identify those lapses. By understanding how Gilman's categories were themselves contaminated by the reflections and replications of the very concepts she was criticizing, we can better appreciate how unable we probably are as well to free ourselves as much as we think we have from our own cultural limitations, even when we are certain we are doing so.

Given her ability to break so many other conventions having to do with domesticity, home, and child-rearing, Gilman's unfailing and relentless defense of heterosexual, monogamous nuclear families indicates how deeply embedded in her psyche was her belief in these things. Still, we should credit her with a very radical restructuring of her own family life, heretical in her time, even if she could not move beyond the heterosexual nuclear family. Since she had several intense, deep, and long-lasting relationships with women throughout her life (her longest, most intense relationships in fact were with women, although she married twice, the second time a long and happy marriage) I think it is fair to suggest — and I do this kind of thing rarely and cautiously — that her rigid upholding of that convention covers her own fears and terrors, her own attraction to women that she would not acknowledge, probably to herself, certainly to the world.

If Gilman's flaws are easy to acknowledge, so, I believe, are her strengths, and there are more of them. She sought to create a general theory of men and women in history from the perspective of gender. She advanced social thought immeasurably by making gender the center of her analysis, by making the *idea* of gender and subordination based on gender a central tenet in a way nobody did before she did. She took the disadvantages of her life — her poverty, her mental illness, her unsuccessful mothering, her sense of alienation and marginalization — and turned them into arenas to investigate. She wanted to know about *her* roots, *her* evolution, *her* history, but history, science, and sociology were not written about her, and so she wrote about them herself: the nature of sexual identity and how it is formed; the evolution of male/female roles and the origin of female subordination; the nature of work in society; the significance of child-rearing; the relationship between private and public spheres; limitations imposed by institutions of domesticity — that is, home, family, and motherhood; the use of technology in bringing about change. She wrote about all such questions, which were designed to make her audience, all of us, understand how society came to be and therefore how to change it to create a humane, just, and equitable society built upon principles of collectivity and community.

Gilman well understood that for most women a loving partnership and motherhood remain overriding goals, and so much of her work addresses the issue of how to resolve the tension between love and work, between intimacy and autonomy. She took the ordinary matters of everyday living for most women and men and put them in a large social context, making them appropriate and essential subjects for intellectual inquiry and social analysis.

By making gender the center of her analysis as *no one* had done before, she made the invisibility of gender oppression visible. To deny that centrality meant denying the entire body of her work, and so it came to be that her work was rendered invisible, in the same way that the subordination of women was made so pervasive and so seemingly natural as to be unnoticed and invisible.

Gilman was internationally known in her own era, disappeared for a long time, and is now back again. But I believe that the scope and range of her work – what she was really trying to accomplish, the hugeness of it – has yet to be appreciated adequately. She was best known for *Women and Economics* in her lifetime, and she is best known for her fictional pieces "The Yellow Wallpaper" and *Herland* in ours. Not in her own lifetime but only now does she have an audience to assess the full body of her work, without which we have not heard what she has to say to us.

In her first book, *Women and Economics* (1898), she examined the economic relationship between men and women and asserted that the economic dependence of women on men was the key to understanding the subordination of women. She then built on that central thesis in her next two books (*Concerning Children*, 1900; *The Home: Its Work and Influence*, 1903) by examining the way the home was the source of that oppression and the rearing of children replicated the social system. In Victorian America she stripped the sentimentality from marriage and motherhood and exposed what the sentimentality masked: the power relations that imprison women and children, although she did not lump them together. The home is an institution like any other, she said to a world that revered and idealized it, it is an institution owned by man, in which wife and children are forcibly held, by virtue of their economic dependence and his ideological power. In her study of children, she argued that children should not be treated as part of a family, but as vulnerable individuals who are citizens of the larger world. The "personal view of children constitutes the greatest unfairness in the way we raise them," she said. No private person, no parent, should be permitted to administer justice in secret and alone; it is reprehensible to place the child in the power of the parents, without a defense and without witnesses.

When she insisted that personal relationships (mother-child/husband-wife) are really social relationships, the reality of which is obscured because it is located in the privacy of the home, she was, although she probably did not know it, building upon Mary

Wollstonecraft's earlier effort to apply the same standards of citizenship to the domestic sphere as we do to the public sphere.[4]

Gilman then moved on to a sociological analysis of work, arguing that it is through the work we do that we receive a social definition of ourselves. The implication of that idea for women is that, whatever else we do, we are socially defined primarily as wives and mothers, for that is persistently regarded as our main work. So that work defines us in fact by our gender, whereas men's work does not define them primarily by their gender. Moving on again from this at the end of her life, Gilman addressed the question of ideology and its role in perpetuating what she believed was the primary inequity: gender subordination through the examination of religion.

Let me now look briefly at a few of Gilman's ideas that especially interest me.

First, Gilman's notion of collectivism, Bellamy nationalism, or socialism pervades all of her thinking. She argued that individualism, especially in its extreme version in the United States, was a severe liability in progressive change. In an interesting way she was really taking on the revered notion of American exceptionalism, but she saw it as a negative exceptionalism that was retarding change. It was a negative promise of American life, and it led to our backwardness among industrial nations in terms of social policy issues concerning family leave, child care, infant mortality, and health care, all of which are rooted in our outmoded notion of individualism. At a time when the United States was seen as the most advanced nation in the world, Gilman described it as socially backward among industrial nations. She said this seventy-five years ago, and we are in worse shape today than we were then, less progressive than we were then, and farther behind other industrial nations.

Her notion of collectivism, of the priority of the community over the individual, of the flowering of the individual within a context of community, had humanist roots, not in a liberal or individualist tradition of the Enlightenment but in a collectivism located in a reestablished genuine gender egalitarianism.

The key to our collectivity is in the work we do. Our collective social relationships shape our economic life; it is the key to production, but the reality that we work collectively is not reflected in the individualistic way we think about the social and economic order. We continue to hang onto what might be called the original animal theory of individualism. We live in a world dominated by interdependent social processes, but we are hampered by an ideology of individualism.

Gilman's words were accurate when she wrote them and they are, unfortunately, more compelling today. These are words and ideas and beliefs that we need especially to hear today, when the defense of community and family values is in the wrong hands and our allies, at least the public figures we thought were our allies, are resurrecting an outmoded and reactionary claim to individualism.

Gilman took the notion of alienated work – a concept critical to Marx's theoretical system – and gendered it in a most interesting way. To Marx, alienation is rooted in the way that man is separated from his work, that is, separated from the product of his work and separated from his fellow man by a class exploitative system that renders social cooperation impossible under capitalism.

Gilman gendered Marx's concept of alienation by approaching it from the perspective of the mother. The social relations of motherhood make it impossible for a mother to see the child as a whole person, as part of a larger community to which both mother and child belong. What she also suggested, but did not spell out, is that woman is alienated from herself as a whole person in a culture that values her in parts: as mother, wife, sexual being, but not as a fully formed autonomous person.

Gilman irritated and provoked. She poked fun at pieties and repudiated the most sacred institutions of her time and ours: marriage, motherhood, home, religion. But some of our glee fades as she challenges some of *our* pieties. Then our teeth begin to clench. And then we do to her what her mainstream critics have done: ignore that which makes us uncomfortable.

For example: she did not think much of what today we call female culture. Her eye was sharply focused on the oppression to which women were subject and the negative effect of that oppression. The unhappy result of subjugation through the ages, she suggested, was an inferior product. This is an idea with which feminists of her time had some trouble, as we do today. For Gilman, oppression had consequences. It made us less than we could be. It left us damaged.

Gilman and Feminism

Gilman had no doubt about what women were capable of achieving. She wrote three utopian novels to demonstrate her confidence in women's potential. She believed that women were once equal to men; she believed that in the future women would again be equal to, if not better than, men. She allowed for many exceptions, herself surely among them, and she placed great hope in the rising of the women's movement of the nineteenth century. Another fifty years (she wrote more than fifty years ago) will show more advance than the last five hundred. But throughout our androcentric history men have had power, which meant they had access to learning, to possibilities for growth and development, to the ability to pass on their knowledge to each other through the written record. They used that power to deny to women the resources *they* enjoyed. Women did the best they could with what they were given, and that effort must be acknowledged and applauded. But we should be careful not to take what women were forced to become and glorify and idealize their creative responses by describing those responses to a difficult situation as genuine choice.

Even the job we are assigned to do – mothering – we don't do especially well, she asserted. How could we? As inferior beings we cannot excel at society's most important task, educating and molding the next generation. What most mothers do is replicate defective notions of obedience, conformity to authority, and long-outdated individualism. In *Herland* she describes the proper way for a society to rear its young. We need to remember that although the concept of motherhood was central to Gilman's analysis, she did not assume that "mother" is necessarily synonymous with "good."

Gilman understood how male power has corrupted men in important ways. We need both male and female qualities to be fully human, she argued, but throughout most of time women have been denied opportunities – and it matters and it shows. It is not a comfortable idea for us to accept. We tend to avoid confronting our intellectual and personal handicaps, sometimes turning them into virtues. But Gilman did not write her books in order to make anyone, critics or supporters, comfortable.

The result of being placed in a subordinate position is that men's work is in general more important than women's work. The terms in which we judge a civilization – trade, crafts, arts, manufactures, inventions, political institutions, technology – are almost exclusively masculine since women are largely prevented from participation. If men were removed from a community it would more seriously paralyze that society than if women suddenly disappeared. "Women's work" can more easily be performed by men than "men's work" can be done by women. Men can easily learn to cook, clean, sew, even care for children, but the making and managing of the great engines of modern industry, threading the earth and sea, running major institutions, cannot so easily be undertaken by women.

Gilman believed there were few great women artists (expressing little respect for or knowledge of folk art) because women are permitted only to be consumers, not producers. Women carry decorations on their bodies, but man is the decorator. Men control literature as well. Only slowly are women being allowed into the realms of literary production, as readers or as creators. It is only a short time, she reminds us, since Harriet Martineau concealed her writing beneath her sewing when visitors came.

The feminist community has for thirty years stressed the positive creations of women, as we should, but Gilman is there to remind us how recent changes are and how limited. She also reminds us that we are so busy appropriating "feminine qualities as good," which many are, that we forget "masculine" qualities, some of which are also good: rational thought, pleasure in authority, hard work, discipline.

A separate brain can build a hut, but not a theatre – that requires a community. The brain of humanity is mainly on paper, in the written record. "Those who make books make the race mind," she said, "and through history that record has been controlled by men," and, in a rare reference to class, "men who bear the distinction of class interests."

Male energy tends to destroy and scatter, woman's to gather and nurture. She is patient, submissive labor. He is competitive and aggressive. But with all its faults "unbridled male energy," Gilman said, has advanced the world. As she usually did, she overstated her case, but the case is interesting nevertheless and one we should not easily forget. It helps to explain a great deal of behavior.

In *Herland* she had another angle: the superiority of human connectedness and the strength of a communal, socialized society. But of course these were women of tomorrow not of today. Great as some exceptional women are today, she remarked, we still have a long way to go to undo the legacy of weak and little women "with the aspirations of an affectionate guinea pig."

If Gilman underestimated the significance of women's culture, her words are important reminders that we must not forget the larger patriarchal world and the negative impact it has had, and continues to have, on us. She was not happy to see what new freedom meant to women in the early years of the twentieth century. But, she acknowledged, that is to be expected from a "subject class, suddenly released."

Gilman's last book, except for the autobiography, ended the intellectual journey begun with *Women and Economics*. It was published in 1923, was never reprinted, and is little known, but is an essential work to know if we are to understand her intellectual legacy. It is called *His Religion and Hers: A Study of the Faith of Our Fathers and the Work of Our Mothers*.

In her first book, *Women and Economics*, Gilman turned Aunt Catherine Beecher on her head by locating the home as the place of women's oppression. In this last work she repudiated the entire Beecher clan and their religion. She asserted that religion has done more disservice to humanity than any other institution or ideology. How? By its stress on blind obedience and self-sacrifice, by its focus on death rather than birth, and by its concern with the individual's life in the hereafter rather than the community's life in subsequent generations.

Gilman was not without a spiritual sense, as any reading of her work makes clear. But her faith is not in what we would today describe as "women's way of knowing." For that notion she had little respect. She had a deep, passionate belief in reason and deep suspicion of relying on "intuition." Relying on emotion is a way women have been kept enslaved because emotions, feelings, are no less learned than any of our other socialized learning. We "fall in love" with the kind of person we are socialized to believe is the kind of person we should love — and we are often wrong.

Women need to learn from men to value and use reasoned thinking, for only in that way can we free ourselves from the beliefs that we accept as given but that are, in reality, learned: religious acceptance of obedience and self-sacrifice; belief in blind, transcending love; belief in the existence of maternal instinct.

Gilman believed in what she called the female principle of nurturance and cooperation, but she just as firmly believed that this was a principle embedded in rational thinking. Passion and emotion can be, often are, dangerous to women, who need cool, reasoned thought to undo the socializing that teaches us to rely on our emotions, as if our emotions are not culturally created.

Despite an obvious debt to eighteenth- and nineteenth-century economists and materialists of a variety of sorts, she ultimately looked to the power of ideas as a primary tool to change thinking and therefore to change behavior. False ideas have shaped us throughout most of human history. The most pernicious are incorporated into religious ideology, she warns. If we see ourselves as wicked, as containing evil, as religion tells us, we will behave so and become so. False ideas have enormous power, she acknowledges, but there is a reality, a real world that ultimately modifies our ideas. The first person who asserted that the earth was round "had the opinion of all mankind against him but he had the earth on his side."

The body of work Gilman left behind is extraordinarily rich and there is still much to explore. Thinking and reading for this piece, I learned again how her fresh look at our fundamental assumptions causes us to look again at the assumptions of others and of ourselves.

Carolyn Heilbrun describes feminist scholarship as a struggle to make universities not "merely museums for the display of culture," but "theatres for its ongoing creation and re-creation." [5] It is just this goal that inspires feminist scholarship. Fred Astaire said the skill was in making it look easy. For us, the skill is in not making it look simple.

NOTES

1. Chapter 12 of Mary Ritter Beard's book *Women as a Force in History* is entitled "Women as a Force in Long History." In it she provides an overview of a variety of ways of defining "history" and in particular "long history," such as taking Herodotus as the beginning of what we now regard as history or widening the definition to include myth and legend. Her main argument is that regardless of one's definition of history and long history in particular, women are evident as a force but rarely accorded due recognition.

2. Excerpts from *Unpunished* appear in *The Charlotte Perkins Gilman*

Gilman and Feminism

Reader; however, since I wrote this essay the full text of the novel has become available, edited by Denise Knight and Catherine Golden.

3. For evidence of Gilman's racism, see, for example, her diary entries for 27 April 1881, 20 August 1883, 29 October 1886, 20 November 1886, and also her passing comment, "I was told that insanity had increased greatly among the Negroes since they were freed, probably owing to the strain of having to look out for themselves in a civilization far beyond them" (*Living*, 245). Her anti-Semitism is perhaps most pronounced in "With Her in Ourland"; see particularly chapter 6, "The Diagnosis," in which Ellador offers a solution to "the Jewish problem," namely that they should "leave off being Jews." Gilman's essay "Is America Too Hospitable?" likewise reveals racist and anti-Semitic views. For further consideration of these aspects of Gilman's opinions, readers are referred to Lisa Ganobcsik-Williams's essay in this volume.

4. A succinct outline of Mary Wollstonecraft's aims in writing *Vindication of the Rights of Women* (1792) may be found in her letter of dedication addressed to M. Talleyrand-Périgord, which forms part of the preamble to her volume. In this she states that "contending for the rights of woman, my main argument is built on this simple principle, that if she be not prepared by education to become the companion of man, she will stop the progress of knowledge and virtue; for truth must be common to all, or it will be inefficacious with respect to its influence on general practice."

5. See Carolyn Heilbrun, "The Politics of Mind: Women, Tradition and the University," *Papers on Language and Literature* 24:3 (1988): 231–244.

LISA GANOBCSIK-WILLIAMS

The Intellectualism of
Charlotte Perkins Gilman
Evolutionary Perspectives on Race,
Ethnicity, and Class

As a social theorist Charlotte Perkins Gilman placed the issue of
women's economic oppression at the center of her arguments for
social reform. Scholarship on Gilman has not been abundant, but
over the last forty years – and especially since the 1970s – critics
have drawn attention to the influence of her gender-rooted economic theories both on the American feminist movement and on
reformist social policy. As a feminist, I am inspired by this valuable scholarship. I have noticed, however, that while heralding
Gilman's merits as a role model for feminists/social activists, critics (such as Degler, Doyle, Scharnhorst, Lane, and Ceplair) tend
to mention – but not to deal in depth with – ideas in Gilman's
work which can be perceived as racist, classist, and nativist.[1] For
instance, in a 1981 collection of her fiction, *The Charlotte Perkins
Gilman Reader*, editor Ann J. Lane chose not to include some passages "that are racist, chauvinist, and anti-Semitic" (xxx).

I follow Lane's reasoning that "such sentiments dominated the
intellectual circles of the country, and . . . Gilman represents the
least outlandish wing in those circles" and I understand that Lane
was trying to emphasize the appeal of Gilman's long out-of-print
fiction by stressing that her "valuable ideas better deserve remembering and repeating" than do her prejudices (200–201, xxx).
However, I believe that leaving unexamined Gilman's thoughts
on race, class, and ethnicity blocks a fuller understanding of her
place within intellectual history in general – and within late nine-
teenth- and early twentieth-century social reform discourses in
particular. According to Larry Ceplair, editor of *Charlotte Perkins*

Gilman: A Nonfiction Reader (1991), relatively few Gilman scholars have responded to Carl N. Degler's 1956 call to explore Gilman's role within the history of ideas ("Charlotte Perkins Gilman," ix, 3). Ceplair contended that although she "is receiving her due from women's studies, the broader fields of cultural and intellectual history have still failed to alter their categories and concepts to include the thinking of Charlotte and the dozens of other worthy pre–World War I women social theorists" (4).

In this essay, I hope to contribute to a critical understanding of the reasons behind Gilman's elitism. Like other critics, I do not wish to excuse her naiveté and ignorance concerning the hardships encountered by people of color in the United States and the repercussions of condescending attitudes toward non–Northern European immigrants (Ceplair, *Nonfiction*, 7). On the other hand, I think that Gilman's biases were more complex than simple bigotry and that a major motivation for her judgments of nonwhites and immigrants, as well as of the poor, stemmed from her total commitment to the idea of human progress through social evolution.

From the 1890s until her death in 1935, Gilman propounded her ideas of social evolution through a myriad of genres, including short stories, reviews, lectures, letters, plays, poems, articles, novels, and sociological texts. Recurring themes throughout this body of work explain her conception of human progress. She believed, for instance, that people should work toward creating and maintaining social unity, as exemplified through "an intelligent conscious society" which would think and act in terms of community ("Socialist Psychology," 307; "With Her in Ourland," 184–185). Components of such a society would include pleasant, efficient, and clean living standards for all people; monogamous companionate marriages; childhood education stressing thinking, reasoning, and social responsibility; socialized transportation and other public services; personal and community safety; the adoption of comfortable, functional clothing; and economic independence for women.

Gilman maintained that social changes were occurring constantly, "even without our knowledge and against our violent opposition" (*Women and Economics*, vii). For example, at the time that she was theorizing, industrialization – causing a decline in home production and an exodus toward urban centers – propelled women into the workforce, against traditionalist opposition.[2] Although arguing that "the laws of social evolution do not wait for our recognition or acceptance: they go straight on," Gilman did not regard evolutionary forces in society as deterministic (146). Instead, she attempted to demonstrate "how some of the worst evils under which we suffer, evils long supposed to be inherent and ineradicable in our natures, are but the result of certain arbitrary conditions of our own adoption, and how, by removing those conditions, we may remove the evils resultant" (vii).[3] Gilman insisted that "evolution is a process of growth, to be helped and promoted" by humans, and noted "how irresistibly the social forces of to-day are compelling us further . . . an advance which may be greatly quickened by our recognition and assistance" ("Feminism and Social Progress," 142; *Women and Economics*, vii). Her belief in society's ability and duty to help itself dovetailed with her feeling that the time had come for "the thinking women of today" to work actively toward "improving" society (*Women and Economics*, vii). As a woman, intellectual, and writer/orator with a social vision, Gilman seemed to have a sense of herself as being in the vanguard of social evolution – an attitude which empowered her to urge others to understand and act upon her ideas for attaining social progress.

In the first three decades after the Civil War and at the beginning of the twentieth century, the American public – perhaps reeling with the task of trying to reorganize racial, ethnic, and class strata following the dismantling of slavery and the coming of Eastern European waves of immigration – "gave a handsome reception to philosophies and political theories built in part upon Darwinism or associated with it" (Hofstadter, *Social Darwinism*, 5). Gilman embraced and extended to the realm of human society the evolutionary biological theories that Charles Darwin and Alfred Wallace had made public in the 1850s. These theories stated that evolution by natural selection occurs when nature arbitrarily produces mutations in organisms and that organisms containing structures most adaptable to a given environment survive and reproduce. What I find most important about her decision to limit her scope to evolution is that, by doing so, she circumscribed her views on the "progress" of various races and ethnicities, but opened up possibilities for equalizing economic classes. This essay examines ways in which Gilman, by basing her concept of history and progress on evolution, became caught within what might be

Gilman and Feminism

categorized as an elitism of race and nationality, as well as within discourses and ideologies which many critics have considered to be classist.

In his 1991 *Reader*, editor Larry Ceplair discussed the subject of racism in Gilman's work.[4] Perhaps because he was dealing with serious, nonfictional writing, Ceplair felt a responsibility to view Gilman's words as reflecting her own attitudes and not those of some fictional character in a story. He devoted two paragraphs in his general introduction to the subject of Gilman's racism and periodically returned to the topic when introducing various speeches, books, and articles included in the reader. Ceplair suggested that, in part, Gilman's attitudes reflected those of the fin-de-siècle era in the United States and of most progressive reformers, who were oblivious to problems of racial segregation (7, 85). He concluded, however, that "the epithets she casually used in her articles and the attitudes informing her 1908 article on blacks cannot be explained away or rationalized. Nor can her failure to address any of the issues pertinent to the economic and social conditions of black women, or the racist policies of the largest women's organizations" (7). Although I agree with Ceplair that most of Gilman's references to race are not what one would hope for in a social reformer, I believe that this aspect of her work is worth attending to, because much of it illustrates the basic premises of her theory of social evolution.

"A Suggestion on the Negro Problem," for instance, was a 1908 article based on evolutionary discourse. Gilman wrote that Americans were experiencing different stages of evolution, with whites having reached a higher stage than blacks. She reasoned that a political democracy (which American whites had attained at least in name) and a socialized democracy based on principles of community welfare (which she believed many white Americans, such as herself, were working to attain) were marks of evolutionary social progress. Gilman explained that because African Americans were abducted from a more "primitive" tribal type of society and had, through slavery, been held under laws and living conditions calculated to suppress the spirit and skills of democracy, the black race had not been allowed to evolve socially: "On the field of economic competition into which the negro was so suddenly thrown he does not, as a whole, in fifty years, show equality with us — which is not remarkable . . . an alien race, in a foreign land; under social, economic, political, and religious conditions to which he was by *heredity* a stranger" (Ceplair, *Nonfiction*, 177; emphasis added).[5] Gilman saw this gulf between blacks and whites as wasteful, because it prevented them from joining in a united effort for social progress. Although she hoped for racial unity, she assumed that it would be on white terms, that blacks naturally would and should want to "progress" to white ways of living. Turn-of-the-century racial antagonism distressed her because potentially it could lead to larger conflict which would hinder or even reverse American progress toward social democracy. Therefore, she regarded as an element of hope and security the sign "that so many negroes, in this brief time, [since slavery] have made such great progress" (177).[6]

Gilman maintained that the worst blow to American democracy was the adoption of the slavery system, and her motivation for writing "A Suggestion on the Negro Problem" was to lobby for the uplift of the African-American race ("Ourland," 154−156). Nevertheless, by contemporary standards, her approach to the topic in this article was extremely callous and naive. Although she could have pitched her ideas to blacks as well as whites, Gilman's pronoun usage and the way she framed her "solutions" demonstrate that she was addressing a white audience. For instance, oblivious to black perceptions, she commented, "as slaves' inferiority was the very condition of our advantage, making possible their exploitation, *no complaint was then made of it*" (Ceplair, *Nonfiction*, 177; emphasis added). Our realization that this condescending attitude was probably unconscious perhaps only reinforces our perceptions of Gilman's callousness and ignorance in dealing with racial issues.

In laying a basis for her main argument in the article, Gilman drew upon a eugenics-style categorization of race characteristics to create a series of cause-effect statements explaining the "logic" of racial evolution in the United States:

> Given: in the same country, Race A, progressed in social evolution, say, to Status 10; and Race B, progressed in social evolution, say, to Status 4. Given: That Race B was forcibly imported by Race A, and cannot be deported. Given: That Race B, in its present condition, does not develop fast enough to suit Race A. Question: How can Race A best and most quickly promote the

development of Race B? . . . It is true that Race B in many ways retards the progress of Race A, and grievously offends against it; but it is also true that Race A was the original offender, and has a list of injuries to Race B, greatly outnumbering the counter list. It is also true that both races have served each other in many ways. (Ceplair, *Nonfiction*, 177–178)[7]

Gilman's opinion, therefore, was that since whites forcibly brought blacks to the United States, they had a responsibility to help them – and thus society – to "improve." She believed that the fact that so many African Americans had become self-supporting, valuable members of the body politic was evidence "that social evolution works more rapidly than the previous process of natural selection. The African race, with the advantage of contact with our more advanced stage of evolution, has made more progress in a few generations than any other race" (178).

One of Gilman's major worries concerning the black race was that the dismantling of slavery was costly and reconstruction was being handled inefficiently – thus detracting from social evolution. The solution she proposed was for state governments to "stop the lowering process" by requiring "not enslavement, but enlistment" of blacks in a "new army" ("compulsory at the bottom, perfectly free at the top") designed to produce community labor while teaching blacks to think, act, work, and function in society like white Americans (179–183). Gilman's descriptions and defenses of this "new army" in many respects read like a white slaveowner's fantasy: "This organization provides the machinery best to elicit and apply the working force of this great mass of people: and would do so at no loss whatsoever. If any man, privately, were allowed to govern the labor of, say, a thousand negroes, to his own advantage, he would not be asking 'who pays for it?'" (181). Meanwhile, her use of terms such as social "value" (historically grounded in the value-price of slaves) potentially takes on meanings that she probably did not intend: "the applied labor would result in improvements to the country of endless value, and the improvement in the negroes themselves would add steadily to their value as constituents of the body politic" (181). Gilman also couched in evolutionary terms her explanation for why her army plan would not become corrupted, by arguing that if it did then white Americans had not "advanced" nearly as much as they boasted they had and would be due for "some scheme of race betterment ourselves" (182).

Gilman's unfeeling, unrealistic, and patronizing perceptions of American blacks as a race which needed help to become "civilized" can, to a large extent, be attributed to the social climate of the Progressive Era. After all, "A Suggestion on the Negro Problem" was selected for publication, printed, and circulated in the *American Journal of Sociology*, which published two articles and four comments by Gilman between March 1907 and March 1909 (Ceplair, *Nonfiction*, 176). The sparsity of Gilman's work on (and references to) race also demonstrates her lack of interest in and/ or ignorance about the topic. "A Suggestion on the Negro Problem" was an attempt to explain, justify, and optimistically alter (through questionable means) the position of blacks in American society. A discussion of Gilman's philosophical approach to ethnicity should illuminate further her vision of racial status as natural and evolving.

Immigrants and immigration preoccupied Gilman to an even greater extent than did race. As various pieces of her published material, particularly that written during and after World War I, demonstrate, Gilman felt increasingly threatened by immigrants. In her 1990 biography of Gilman, *To Herland and Beyond*, Ann Lane states that the explanation for Gilman's "racist, anti-Semitic, and ethnocentric ideas . . . must reside primarily in the psychological realm, because the racist and nativist views that she held *did not fit with the vision she espoused of radical social and political transformation*" (255; emphasis added). In contrast, I believe that Gilman built a theoretical rationale about nationhood, which was based upon principles of social evolution, in order to justify and explain her fear and mistrust of foreigners settling in the United States.

In this essay I analyze Gilman's rationalizations about immigrants primarily in her 1916 text "With Her in Ourland." This sequel to her 1915 utopian novel *Herland* originally was serialized in Gilman's monthly magazine, the *Forerunner*, and until recently had never been republished – probably for the same reason that Ann Lane hesitated to reprint certain passages from it in *The Charlotte Perkins Gilman Reader*: "It is not the style alone that makes reading *Ourland* difficult today. . . . In some of her published writing, in *Ourland* in particular . . . she expresses beliefs that are Anti-Semitic, chauvinist, and racist . . . her ideas are dreadful and they seriously mar her contribution as a social analyst and theorist" (200–201). I supplement my reading of immigrant themes in "Ourland" with references to Gilman's autobiography, *The Living of Charlotte Perkins Gilman* (primarily written in 1926 and published in 1935), *Herland*, and three articles that she wrote between 1916 and 1923. Although race and ethnicity are closely bound in Gilman's work, this essay focuses on ethnicity and on race mainly in terms of nationhood. Her social evolutionary rationales for criticizing immigrants and "open" immigration policies were related to, and serve to illuminate, her evolutionary thoughts on the more straightforwardly racial issues which I have discussed.

Gilman believed that Americans descended mainly from the English, "mingled with the closely allied Teutonic and Scandinavian strains, of which the English are compounded" ("Is America Too Hospitable?" 293). Conveniently, because of her own racial/ ethnic background, this belief allowed her to accept and not feel threatened by popular speculations concerning the superiority and inferiority of various races and nationalities. As noted in *Herland*, Gilman felt that it was important to know one's "exact line of descent," and her own bloodlines were reassuringly traceable to America's white Puritan founders (75). On her father's side, she descended from the prominent Beecher clan of orators, social activists, and writers, whose first ancestor set foot in Boston in 1637, only seventeen years after the arrival of the *Mayflower*. Gilman's mother's family history dated back to Stukely Westcott, who assisted Roger Williams in founding the Providence Plantation of colonial America (*To Herland and Beyond*, 21, 35). Secure with this heritage, Gilman drew upon notions of racial/ethnic elitism to support her own philosophy of order and social control. This is demonstrated in terms of race in "A Suggestion on the Negro Problem," where Gilman did not hesitate to propose putting "them" in a compulsory army. When it came to ethnicity, Gilman's "founding fathers" ancestry afforded her the ability to endorse nativism: the policy or attitude of favoring native inhabitants of a country over immigrants.[8] She framed her brand of nativist elitism in terms of social evolution.

On one level, Gilman argued against an innate hierarchy of races/nations: "Almost any race is superior to others in some particular," she admitted ("Is America Too Hospitable?" 294). On a deeper plane, however, she rationalized her underlying ethnic and racial elitism into an evolutionary story through which white Americans had progressed to the highest standard – or, at least, possessed the best potential for reaching this standard. For instance, she did not consider the United States to be the world's finest nation unconditionally. Instead, she thought that Americans, led by (white) descendants of the founding fathers, had the best chance to develop democracy to its highest point because of their country's superior natural resources and because they had acquired, through evolution, the basic democratic ideals of their forefathers. "This youngest land . . . is the top of the tree . . . the last young nation, beginning over again in a new world . . . this should be the crown of the world," pleads Ellador in "Ourland" (125–126).[9]

Perhaps in Gilman's view the "perfect" world in which to establish a socialized democracy would have been one in which separate races/nations did not exist. She fantasized about such a society in *Herland* and in "Ourland" extended her commentary on the benefits of Herland life.[10] However, in "Ourland" and other writings, Gilman also addressed questions of racial/ethnic evolution. In "Is America Too Hospitable?" she argued that social evolution occurs unevenly in different races/ethnicities: it is "a mistake to suppose that social evolution requires the even march of all races to the same goal" (291). This idea justified, for Gilman, advocating social reform policies which were – for the most part – orchestrated by white Americans.[11] This idea of temporary race stratification ties in with Gilman's view that "because the human race is in different stages of development . . . only some of the races (nationalities) – or *some individuals* in a given race – have reached the democratic stage" ("Ourland," 155; emphasis added). "The well-ordered World Federation" of the future does not require becoming one nation politically or combining/intermixing races and ethnicities, Gilman added (291). By the time she wrote her autobiography, she had narrowed her view on the evolutionary potential of racial and ethnic groups. She claimed that World War I had strengthened her conviction of a "deep, wide, lasting vital difference" between races/cultures and the "relative degree of advancement" of each, which called for "varying treatment according to race and nation" (329).

Gilman dealt with the category "native" by admitting that

those she considered to be the first Americans "were not new people, just mixed Europeans" who came together at a certain place and time to establish a new country ("Ourland," 152). She explained her version of United States social evolutionary history most fully in "Ourland," through the mouthpiece of Ellador, an onlooker from another world:

> The current of social evolution burst forth over here like a subterranean river finding an outlet. Things that the stratified crust of Asia could not let through, and the heavy shell of European culture could not either, just burst forth over here and swept you along. Democracy had been – accumulating, through all the centuries. The other nations forced it back, held it down. It boiled over in France, but the lid was clapped on again for awhile. Here it could pour forward – and it poured. Then all the people of the same period of social development wanted to come too, and did, – lots of them. . . . All that "America" means in this sense is a new phase of social development, and anyone can be an American who belongs to it. (152)

Here and in other places Gilman emphasized that these "original" Americans arrived with the intention of building a nation and possessed understanding of how to do it ("Is America Too Hospitable?" 293).

Gilman contrasted those who "come with the intention of being Americans" ("Among Our Foreign Residents," 146) to participate in a democracy with "our swarming immigrants" who were flooding into this established nation in search of asylum and/or natural resources. Personifying the latter as "sneering stranger(s)," she accused them of wanting only to enjoy the benefits of a "great rich country" (289). In this way, Gilman made a case for "legitimate" immigrants, while arguing against "illegitimates" and open-door federal immigration policies. She viewed most immigrants as undesirable and criticized Americans who imagined "that 'the poor and oppressed' were good stock to build up the country." She continued, "The more competent, skillful, and daring were able to get on at home. The poor and oppressed were the underdogs, necessarily" ("Is America Too Hospitable?" 289).[12] In "Ourland," Ellador called such people victims of sociologically misguided governmental immigration policies that promised them better lives in the United States (154).

Though Gilman admired America's founders, she criticized (through Ellador) their lack of sociological foresight: "Here you were, a little band of really promising people, of different nations, yet of the same general stock, and *like-minded* — that was the main thing . . . it never occurred to you that the poor and oppressed were not necessarily good stuff for a democracy" (153–154). She firmly believed that for democracy to flourish, especially in a young country, a core community of intellect was necessary and citizens needed to be at the same stage of education and understanding.[13] Therefore, "the more kinds of races [nationalities] we have to reach, with all their differing cultures, ideas, tastes, and prejudices, the slower and harder is the task of developing democracy" (292). For this reason, Gilman adopted a stance against large-scale immigration, saying that in America it was too easy to expand the country because of land availability, and, rather than slowly developing a democratic community, immigration was causing the nation to swell in numbers "not by natural growth of our own stock but by crowding injections of alien blood" ("Ourland," 123).

Gilman's largest fear, therefore, was that "the highest social development," democracy, "is repeatedly destroyed by the crowding predatory lower forces with which it must struggle" ("Feminism and Social Progress," 142). "Evolution selects, and social evolution follows the same law. If you are trying to improve corn you do not wait to bring all the weeds in the garden to the corn level before going on," she insisted ("Is America Too Hospitable?" 291). Positioning herself against "present-day idealists" who called for unlimited immigration, Gilman offered a remedy to what she saw as potential American de-evolution: people should stay in their own countries and try to fix their governmental and social problems instead of fleeing to the United States (291). "Any people on earth who want a democracy and are able to carry it on," she said, "can have one at home. There is no power above them, which can prevent it. But if they do not want a democracy, or are unable to carry it on, they are a heavy drawback to us" (291–292).[14] Gilman argued that the government should not allow millions of immigrants to settle in the United States in hopes that the democratic way of life would allow them freedom and opportunity to develop knowledge and talents. Rather, she advised, they should stay at home and evolve specializations "in the privacy of each nation, so to speak," and then share them with the world (293).

In Gilman's eyes, population pressure was not an excuse for emigration, and a key way to hasten the evolution of democracy in crowded nations was to practice birth control, primarily by choosing celibacy: "An intelligent limitation of a population to the resources of a country is one of the most essential requirements" (*Living*, 330). The women of Herland, for instance, virulently opposed abortion, but voluntarily limited their reproduction to the number of people that their country's resources would support at a healthful, peaceful, comfortable, and unified standard of living (67–71). In her 1929 article "Feminism and Social Progress," Gilman advocated this practice of population control for all nations: "In crowded countries mothers will decline to produce those excess numbers whose pressure of population is the oldest and most permanent cause of war. There will be a distinct recognition of this main factor in reproduction, that too many people are by no means as valuable, or as happy, as improved stock. This calls for a high ambition, something to study and train for" (137). She emphasized that in order to practice voluntary population control like that modeled in *Herland*, society's concept of motherhood would have to change. A state of more highly evolved motherhood, said Gilman, would be termed "Social" or "Race" motherhood, because it would involve projecting a motherly sense of duty and responsibility onto society, rather than limiting these feelings to one man and one family (136).

Ironically, as Gilman espoused the unifying qualities of race/social motherhood, her own vision of a socialist democratic society narrowed. As her popularity and influence declined after World War I and women's success in the suffrage campaign, she grew increasingly protective of her country and of her regional New England heritage.[15] For Gilman, these concerns were closely tied. For instance, in "Ourland," written during the war, Ellador commented: "Your little old New England towns and your fresh young western ones, have more of 'America' in them than is possible – could ever be possible – in such a political menagerie as New York. . . . New York's an oligarchy; it's a plutocracy; it's a hierarchy; it reverts to the clan system with its Irishmen, and back of that, to the patriarchy, with its Jews" (157).[16]

Given her philosophy of social evolution, this comment can be interpreted as an example of how, according to Gilman, immigration that was unlimited in amount and nationality disrupted the

slow, natural growth processes of community unification and democracy. In contrast to her prewar progressivist-inspired optimism
about the successful "Americanization of all kinds of foreigners,"
in 1923 Gilman wrote that the immigrant influx was driving true
Americans to extinction and criticized Americans who were cheerfully willing to give the country over to foreigners ("A Suggestion on the Negro Problem," 178–179; "Is America Too Hospitable?" 289). "Our children will belong to a minority of dwindling
Americans, ruled over by a majority of conglomerate races quite
dissimilar," Gilman lamented in her autobiography (324). Her
concern over "the rapidly descending extinction of our nation" is
an important example of evolutionary discourse which fit with
her fears, statements, and explanations in "Ourland" about the
differences between those who came to the United States at the
same stage of democracy and the alien foreigners who surged in
later (324). Sounding doubtful, paranoid, and nearly defeated, Gilman suggested that perhaps Americans should give in to what she
was beginning to see as the inevitable evolution of American society into a new form of government led by the mix of races/
nationalities who were, in her eyes, taking over the nation. "Since
it is no new thing in history to have a given nation fail, give way
and disappear, while the progress of society continues in other
hands, we should perhaps contentedly admit our failure and wel-
come our superseders. Perhaps they will do better than we" (Living, 324).

Contrasting the Jews, Italians, Germans, and others living in
"exile" in New York City, with "my people" (New England farmers and fishers), Gilman described her 1922 retreat from the city
to her husband's "ancestral home" in "my native state" of Connecticut (316–317, 324): "Being a Connecticutter by birth, and my
husband's family well known and loved here, I have been welcomed" (325). In this section of her autobiography, Gilman said
more about the New England town and again expressed her fear
for its gradual extinction (326). She reiterated this sentiment later
in "Feminism and Social Progress": Americans are "leaving New
England to dwindle away and see its historic towns taken possession of by crowding aliens" (137).

Gilman, who had entertained a lifelong ambivalence about her
family, attached increasing importance to her heritage during her
later years. Although she had experienced an unhappy childhood

as an outsider and poor cousin, had survived her parent's divorce as well as her own, and had, to a degree, given up her child, almost every early newspaper and magazine review of her lectures and books highlighted her descent from "splendid stock" and her fine family connections.[17] Perhaps, as her popularity dimmed, Gilman sought the dignity and social status that her blood heritage/ancestry could provide. I suggest that her theories about immigration, emigration, and ethnicity reveal that much of Gilman's rationalizing originated from this personal base and that her evolutionary perspective on class similarly grew out of her own social and economic experiences.

An important study focusing on Gilman's relationship to class issues is contained in Dolores Hayden's *The Grand Domestic Revolution: A History of Feminist Designs for American Homes, Neighborhoods, and Cities* (1981). Although Hayden has laid the groundwork for a meaningful class-based discussion of Gilman, I find parts of her study to be contradictory, such as her claims that Gilman appealed "to a broad range of supporters," yet was really only interested in the welfare of professional married career women (203). I also believe certain of Hayden's pronouncements about Gilman's middle-class interests to be unfounded; according to Hayden, Gilman tried "to aim her arguments at middle-class married women and men" (202). After reading a broad spectrum of Gilman's writings, I have grown suspicious of statements such as these, for although she demonstrated ambivalence and/or lack of attention to class categories in her well-known works such as *Women and Economics*, "The Yellow Wallpaper," and *Herland*, she directly addressed class issues in now-forgotten works like "With Her in Ourland" and in writings such as "The Best for the Poorest" and "Socialist Psychology." My research has convinced me that it is too convenient for contemporary scholars to label Gilman as a middle-class (progressive) reformer who addressed middle-class audiences and/or promoted messages favoring middle-class interests (Ceplair, *Nonfiction*, 85). For instance, Jill Eichorn pegs *Herland* as "represent(ing) undeniably her white, middle-class background" by falling "into the white, middle-class, feminist trap of assuming that men are the only source of women's conflicts" ("Working Bodies," 170).[18] To me, such labeling indicates that scholars have presumed the transparency of a concept (class) which we instead should be trying to examine.

My purpose is not so much to address such scholarship specifically, but to emphasize that critical examination of class issues in Gilman's work has not been extensive and to suggest that as researchers we should tread cautiously on this terrain as we examine a wider body of Gilman's material. We should not limit the scope of our research on Gilman and class by assuming that since she was a well-known white, female figure at the turn of the century, she was representing and advocating some monolithic class perspective. As we look for treatment of class in her lesser-known public and personal writings, as well as in her more famous publications, we should not presuppose that her own class position must have been one so privileged that she had the luxury of not noticing class conflicts and inequities.

Much of Gilman's attitude toward class grew out of her own unresolvable class status and movement between a family pedigree on one hand and economic reality on the other – a situation which, for Gilman, threw the entire concept of class into question. By examining how she negotiated this situation, perhaps we can begin to dismantle class categories in order to understand their intersections and fluidity. I am not attempting to argue that Gilman occupied a fixed socioeconomic class location; instead, I wish to explore how her shifting position revealed to her the instability of class categorizations and how this realization contrasted with popular Social Darwinist and eugenicist arguments for the biological transmission of immutable "superior"/"inferior" social class traits. Most importantly, I speculate that Gilman applied evolutionary theory to class issues in order to explain her belief that all economic classes of Americans should and could reach the same living standard.

It is hard for me to imagine that Gilman would have been concerned primarily with the lives of middle-class women. She herself was not interested in attaining the markers of middle- and upper-middle-class female life of the time, which she saw as unnatural: the disassociation between women's and men's activities; the elaborate clothing; the "ultra-feminine" point of view; the petting and complacency ("Ourland," 97, 212–213). Gilman also critiqued the quintessential American middle-class values of private home and family. For example, as a contrast to such ideals, she pictured the women of Herland as living alone and eating food prepared in communal kitchens. In her own life, Gilman was a divorced woman who chose to live apart from her young daughter instead of creating a settled home. Besides rejecting middle-class female roles and values, her social reform vision opposed the self-serving laissez-faire capitalist determinism of Social Darwinist Herbert Spencer — whose philosophy was favored by the more comfortable classes of Americans during the latter half of the nineteenth century.[19]

Locating Gilman herself as middle-class is also problematic. She descended from what could probably be termed a middle-class heritage; Catherine Beecher and Harriet Beecher Stowe were her great-aunts. Yet Ann Lane and other biographers have chronicled how, despite her "blue-blood" family connections, she did not have access to the type of formal education which empowered some middle- and upper-middle-class women to establish friendships, develop skills, encounter role models, and form a supportive female community (*To Herland*, 68). Gilman grew up with little money, under the care of a single parent, and without a fixed home, as she and her mother and brother were shuttled from relative to relative (35–65). Throughout her lifetime, enduring what Lane calls "chronic poverty," she supported herself, her daughter, and later her grandchildren almost solely on the income generated by her writings and lectures (*Living*, xxii).

Contrary to some contemporary views of her as being hopelessly limited to middle-class interests, Gilman herself wrote enthusiastically in the 1890s that she was gaining "increasing acknowledgment as a writer and speaker of power . . . I am getting better known and better liked by more people constantly; especially 'the people' — which rejoices me. . . . The working men of these two cities know me and love me. That is well" (quoted in Ceplair, *Nonfiction*, 40).[20] Biographer Larry Ceplair, however, argues that for unexplained reasons Gilman left behind her working-class activity in 1896. He speculates:

The disintegration of the Nationalist Clubs, the Pullman strike, the presidential election — discouraged her. Perhaps she decided that the message of social consciousness she was in the process of developing and delivering could only be understood and implemented by the educated middle class. She may also have begun to wonder whether working-class people could rise above their terrible conditions and immediate needs and accept her long-term goals for social reconstruction. In any event, among the hundreds of articles she later wrote, fewer than one-half dozen focused on workers and working conditions, and most of those concerned middle-class working women. (43)

Ceplair also notes that Gilman wrote little about working-class women between 1898 and 1909, but that she occasionally lectured at working women's suffrage meetings and to Women's Trade Union audiences and contributed to the union's journal (86). Carrie Chapman Catt, probably referring to the early part of the century when Gilman followed *Women and Economics* (1898) with *Concerning Children* (1900), *The Home* (1903), and *Human Work* (1904), put Gilman first on her 1935 list of the twelve greatest American women "because there was a period in the woman's movement when she brought out first one book and then another . . . which were scientifically done and widely read by all classes of people. And I credit those books with utterly revolutionizing the attitude of mind in the entire country, indeed of other countries, as to woman's place" (quoted in Ceplair, *Nonfiction*, 2). My own reading of a variety of Gilman's work supports Ann Lane's summation of Gilman's philosophy:

Gilman was trying to carve from her unrepresentative life insights about how any woman might live in a world in which such an unrepresentative life as hers could become accessible to all women. Gilman understood that the locus of inequality was in the relationship between the home and the workplace. She did not speak for privileged women denied resources that their male counterparts enjoyed. She herself struggled for, and her work spoke to, a vision of a structurally equitable society in which ordinary women – and that meant unaffluent wives and mothers – could live and develop their gifts and interests. Gilman sought to take male forms – in literature and life – and redesign them to fit all humanity. (*Living*, xxi)

One area which demonstrated Gilman's attention to all classes and to social evolution was her thought on buildings for community living. "Just as Gilman believed that the human race was evolving in a more cooperative direction, so, too, she was sure that the physical form of human habitations was subject to evolutionary forces" (Hayden, *Grand Domestic Revolution*, 189). In *Women and Economics,* she introduced and justified her idea for kitchen-less apartment houses or the "family hotel" (242, 264–265). She explained the benefits of employing a skilled professional labor force to purchase and prepare food for residents and to perform housework and laundry tasks (241–247, 267). Gilman foresaw such dwelling places accommodating "professional women with families" (242). In *The Grand Domestic Revolution,* Hayden seems to interpret Gilman's use of the term "professional" in its usual sense, perhaps referring to medical, dental, secretarial, and other common professions (203). I believe, however, that Gilman was working to broaden society's notion of professional work to include skilled jobs such as cooking, laundering, and housekeeping.[21] Her evolutionary vision was that any and all women had the potential to train in a profession; or, at least, with the improvement of social conditions such as nutrition and education, most people should have been capable of training for some sort of professionalized employment ("Ourland," 240–241). "It isn't the difference between a bookkeeper and a housekeeper that must be considered; it is the difference between an organized business world that needs bookkeeping and an unorganized world of separate families with no higher work than to eat, sleep and keep alive" ("Ourland," 295).

Hayden argues that feminists like Gilman faced the problem of "how to escape from stereotypes about 'women's work' without exploiting women of a lower socio-economic class . . . the 'professional' domestic workers whom they planned to employ" (*Revolution,* 201). This is certainly a valid concern. However, Gilman's relatively unknown 1916 article "The Best for the Poorest" demonstrates her clear commitment to altering the plight of the urban poor by designing and erecting "model tenements" along the same lines as family hotels/kitchenless apartments. Such places would allow residents to return from their places of employment to households whose work had been done by "professionals."[22] The point of the article was that the urban poor should not be housed in terrible conditions and that building owners "should give, in return for their rent, a full measure of value in human living" ("The Best," 260). Gilman offered three recommendations to architects designing these apartment houses for human living: "first, to allow room for proper care of children; second, to allow room for amusement and association; third, to allow of such service as shall reduce living expenses and enable the woman to earn her share of the income . . . the last proviso means an arrangement for large food laboratories" to purchase, prepare, and make available meals for family dining (260). Furthermore, "space for amusement and association means that the builder of houses should recognize that these are human needs, that they must be met; and that they are better met when given to the families in the house, than when sought by individuals in the street" (260). To this end, she laid out floor plans for the model tenements, with one apartment per family, a kindergarten for babies and children, play areas for older children after school, dancing rooms, club rooms, dumb waiters, communal laundry and ironing facilities, drying rooms, and so on, and she estimated in detail building, operating, and staff employment costs. Gilman supported her proposal on apartment living for the poor by admitting: "Many suppose that the women of this class would not like it. Try them and see. Give them a chance to see what life would be like, with a day's work that was done at six o'clock – or five; and then a clean, quiet home with no work waiting there for them" (262).

Major concerns demonstrated in "The Best for the Poorest," as well as in, for example, the utopian works *Herland* and "Ourland," were the huge number of poor working women and men in the United States and the lack of nutrition and education ensuing from poverty. Gilman framed these problems in evolutionary discourse. "The idea of your *still not* being properly fed! – I can't get used to it," exclaimed Ellador the Herlander about the population of the United States, meaning that American society, with all of its natural and technological resources, should have long since "evolved" to being capable of figuring out how to distribute food equally to all ("Ourland," 296; emphasis added). This idea is an indictment against the nonpoor classes, because, in Gilman's judgment, those not hampered by the everyday drudgery of poverty should have taken time to think about how to promote the communal advancement of society to better living standards. In the same way, Gilman advocated education to kindle social evolution for the poor. In "Ourland," for instance, Ellador questioned Van, an American, about the function of comics in newspapers. When Van replied that "the lower classes" would not read the papers without the entertainment-lure of comics, Ellador countered: "And these 'lower classes,' so low that they take no interest in the news of the day and have to be given stuff suited to imbeciles . . . are they a large and permanent part of your democracy?" Eventually Van realized that Ellador was advocating the idea that "we ought to put out decent papers and see that people are *educated up* to them" (240; emphasis added).

In some ways, these examples of Gilman's approach to apartment hotels/model tenements and her thoughts on better nutrition, education, and wages for the working poor might reveal that on the topic of socioeconomic class she followed the stance of progressive reformers: "middle-class experts and professionals [who] would diagnose the ills of and prescribe the cures for the lower classes, thereby training them to behave as 'normal Americans' " (Ceplair, *Nonfiction*, 85). However, she was very much aware that "poor persons resent being treated as cases"; although her work does reflect a tendency to impose her ideas on others, it was the thinking of the middle class – not of the poor – that she was trying to change ("Ourland," 43). In writings such as *Herland*, "Ourland," and "The Best for the Poorest," Gilman questioned the reasoning behind "normal" middle-class American practices and beliefs, such as the sanctity of private home and family, the ideal of female exclusion from the workforce, the desire for elaborate "feminine" clothing, and Americans' right to practice laissez-faire capitalism. In addition, she blamed the situation of the poorly compensated underclass on complacent Americans who possessed enough leisure time to work toward changing the socioeconomic system, but who chose to ignore such issues. In contrast to such people, said Gilman, "What individual liberty has the working man? . . . What choice . . . has his ill-born, ill-fed, ill-clothed, ill-taught child?" ("Ourland," 241). Overall, her class vision seems to me to have been a broad one, for she hoped to secure – through the mechanism of social evolution – more equalizing physical conditions, so as to promote popular understanding and commitment to acting in terms of community unity and welfare.

Charlotte Perkins Gilman believed that she was exploring possibilities for social reform through the unbiased, natural laws of social evolution. I have demonstrated, however, how certain components of her evolutionary reform strategy were shaped by her own racial, ethnic, and class positions. Such components included her desire to prove that all classes of people had the ability to evolve, her aversion to non-northern European immigrants, and her conviction that such immigrants – as well as various ethnic groups – were evolving toward a (white) American way of life. Thus, I have argued that Gilman was dedicated to social evolutionary theory in part because it helped her to formulate workable underpinnings to rationalize her personal fears and biases. Most studies of Gilman's work have not revealed this aspect of her theoretical foundation fully, because in focusing on gender they have not examined in depth her relationship to race, ethnicity, and class.

Ann Lane, for instance, mentions as flaws Gilman's "simple, linear view of evolutionary progress" and "neglect of the role of class, race, and ethnicity and the way they intersect with gender" (*To Herland*, 294). Lane explains these "flaws" as being common among sociologists at the time. She also notes:

> Some thinkers of Gilman's era, such as Emile Durkheim, Max Weber, Sigmund Freud, and Thorstein Veblen, disavowed the prevailing belief that social sciences could be modeled on natural sciences. Their ideas were in most ways more compatible with Gilman's goals than the limiting natural-science model, but she was locked into nineteenth-century thinking because she had not the formal training and therefore the self-confidence to reject that which she had never studied systematically. (294)

As this essay indicates, attention to Gilman's political outlook on racial, immigration, and class policies can uncover other reasons why, as Larry Ceplair points out, she did not alter her basic evolutionary philosophy much throughout her lifetime (*Nonfiction*, 6–7).

To illustrate the effects of Gilman's evolutionary ideals on her interpretations of race, ethnicity, and class issues, I have drawn upon her utopian fictions, her autobiography, and nonfictional sociological pieces written between the 1890s and 1930s. This essay reflects an initial attempt to examine the important issue of the cultural elitism of Gilman's social evolutionary discourse.[23] Perhaps the social evolutionary model and its ties with Gilman's personal experience that I have explored here could also serve to illuminate her arguments on gender in new ways. I offer my interpretations as one starting point for scholarship examining Gilman's place in the potentially elitist discourses of turn-of-the-century democracy, intellectual history, and critical social reform.

NOTES

1. In her 1995 dissertation, "Working Bodies, Working Minds: The Domestic Politics of American Women in Labor 1896–1940," Jill Eichorn centers an examination of *Herland* on what she perceives as Gilman's racism and classism. To my knowledge, this is one of the first studies to approach Gilman's work with these considerations in mind. See also Dolores Hayden, *The Grand Domestic Revolution: A History of Feminist Designs for American Homes, Neighborhoods and Cities*; and Susan Strasser, "The Business of Housekeeping," *Insurgent Socialist* 8 (1978): 147–163.

2. Other signs of social evolution that Gilman identified were advances in public education and the abolition of slavery. Most prominent, she believed, was the "slow emergence of the long-subverted human female to full racial equality," as revealed in the women's suffrage campaign, through new roles for women in literature, and in style changes to more practical and less restrictive female clothing (*Women and Economics*, 146, 151–152). Gilman also argued that society was evolving beyond forms of social interaction which solely promoted family life and neglected individuals not involved in family relationships, such as single women, children in day nurseries, bachelors, and widows/widowers (298).

3. Gilman's conviction that evolution is not a predetermined selection process was in accordance with Charles Darwin's definition of natural selection in *On the Origin of Species by Natural Selection, or The Preservation of Favoured Races in the Struggle for Life*. Both Darwin's view of biological evolution and Gilman's view of social evolution diverge sharply from the eugenicist beliefs popular in the United States between the 1860s and 1940s. Gilman did not see evolution as a process through which only a genetically predetermined group could progress. She did, however, believe that humans could assist social evolution by adopting and discarding certain features of their lifestyles.

4. My references to race in this essay follow the popular contemporary definition of the term: human groups having a common origin and exhibiting a relatively constant set of physical traits, such as pigmentation, hair form, and facial and bodily proportions. In early work such as *Women and Economics*, Gilman spoke of race as the human race. In later pieces, like "A Suggestion on the Negro Problem," she used what I call our contemporary definition to distinguish between white and black races. She

also employed "race" in reference to nationality, as in "Ourland." At the time, there was no distinction made between ethnicity and race — concepts which have been regarded by scholars since the 1970s as being distinct.

5. Gilman subscribed to pre-Darwinian scientist Jean-Baptiste La-marck's (erroneous) idea that acquired traits are transmissible by heredity. She reasoned that once a person learned "civilized" behavior, these characteristics would be passed to his or her offspring. See Lane, *To Herland and Beyond* (254–257), for a discussion of this belief. Also see David Young, *The Discovery of Evolution*, for details on the place of Lamarck's concepts in relation to other biological theories of evolution.

6. A later (1916) example of Gilman's view of African Americans' problems as being socially constructed comes in chapter 10 of "Ourland," where Gilman pitted Herlander Ellador against a white sociologist from the American South. Ellador inquired: "If negroes cannot or will not work, why was one worth a thousand dollars? And how could the owners have accumulated wealth from their inefficiency? If they could not learn anything, why was it necessary to make laws forbidding their education . . . ?" (263).

7. As one of the basic premises of eugenics, founder Francis Galton created a "scientific" scale for judging and categorizing human types. Lowest on this scale were "Negroes" — in fact, they figured so low in Galton's estimation that he created a separate grading scale (Allen Chase, *The Legacy of Malthus*, 14, 102, 109).

8. Although Gilman's Puritan ancestors were immigrants, she considered herself to be a native of the United States for two reasons. First, as was typical of the dominant culture of her era, she ignored the existence and the rights of Native Americans. Second, she theorized that the building of American democracy was a "new phase of social development" ("Ourland," 152), whose "natives" were those who built it (people such as her ancestors).

9. Gilman argued, through Ellador, that the "Northern races" (northern Europeans and the British) were not inherently superior, but that civilizations set up by "Mediterranean and Oriental peoples held the world — were the world" for thousands of years and that only in the last few centuries had "Northern" societies progressed to needing a "higher" form of governance — democracy ("Ourland," 68–69). This illustrates a principle of social evolution that Gilman described in *Women and Economics*: "A thing may be right in one stage of evolution which becomes wrong in another" (209).

10. Herland was Gilman's model for a society in which gender, sexu-

ality, racial, ethnic, and class conflicts had evolved out of existence. As implied in *Herland* and stated more directly in "Ourland" and other writings like *Women and Economics*, the ultimate society for Gilman would have been one possessing Herland's socialized community qualities, where people of both genders could live on equal footing. Unlike contemporary utopias such as Marge Piercy's *Woman on the Edge of Time*, however, *Herland* ignored complications of ethnicity and race (by making Herland's population a single race and nationality).

11. White Americans were established in politics in part because they descended from immigrants like the English, who had been in the country for generations.

12. Gilman also dismantled the American metaphor for assimilation, the melting pot. She argued that the mix of foreigners had not been properly measured and was ruining the nation's democratic ideals: "You [the United States] have stuffed yourself with the most ill-assorted and unassimilable mass of human material" ("Ourland," 153). In "Is America Too Hospitable?" she explained that a melting pot is a crucible: "It has to be carefully made of special material and carefully filled with weighed and measured proportions of such ores as will combine to produce known results. If you put into a melting pot promiscuous shovelfuls of anything that comes to hand you do not get out of it anything of value, and you may break the pot" (290). In another analogy, she compared the melting pot with the unrestrained interbreeding of dogs, which does not produce "a super-dog," but tends "to revert to the 'yaller dog,' the jackal type so far behind them" (291).

13. An earlier solution that Gilman proposed was to educate immigrants before they would be permitted to enter the United States. See *Moving the Mountain*.

14. See page 154 of "Ourland" for a discussion of Gilman's position on the relationship of the poor and oppressed to monarchy and other governmental controls on society. Although she did gloss over factors (like lack of hope, illness, loyalty, and a sense of duty) which hold people back from rebelling against corrupt leadership, her views were not as naive as they sound here.

15. For an in-depth interpretation of Gilman's decline in popularity, see William T. Doyle, "Charlotte Gilman and the Cycle of Feminist Reform," v, 155, and 217–241.

16. Gilman couched her aversion to Jews and the Irish in evolutionary terms. For instance, she saw an American's loyalty to a previous home country other than the United States as evidence that he or she had not

evolved to a democratically minded state. "Even so long established residents as the Irish remain Irish — they are not Americans. They would willingly sacrifice the interests of this country, or of the world as a whole, for the sake of Ireland" ("Is America Too Hospitable?" 294).

Gilman discussed the Jews much more frequently than she did the Irish and developed an elaborate series of social evolutionary points to justify her feelings. A prime example of her views appears in chapter 10 of "Ourland," where she suggested that endogenous marriage practices revealed that Jews had not evolved out of a tribal stage, that primitive religious traditions and beliefs held Jews back from becoming civilized, and that due to these two problems Jews had developed "a peculiar intensity" of character: "their condensed spirit . . . becomes increasingly inimical to the diffused spirit of modern races" (267).

17. See, for example, folders 282–313, volumes 7° and 8°, and oversize folders 2 and 3, Gilman Papers.

18. Another example of what I perceive as recent derogatory and reactionary "convenience labeling" of Gilman occurred in a graduate literature seminar I attended in 1994. Many students dismissed "The Yellow Wallpaper" as uninteresting or limited in scope because it supposedly addresses a white, middle-class problem (Mitchell's rest cure) and was (seemingly) written by a middle-class white woman, who may have experienced — or would have had knowledge about — this problem.

19. Spencer believed that measures to assist the poor were self-defeating. He claimed that the sufferings and deaths of poor people were natural biological mechanisms for ensuring that the fittest — wealthy and therefore "superior" types — survived and propagated (Chase, *Legacy of Malthus*, 8, 517). His philosophy was a handy excuse for Americans to rationalize individualistic capitalistic struggles to attain financial success. By the turn of the century, it became "impossible to be active in any field of intellectual work without mastering Spencer" (33). His philosophy of "survival of the fittest" was adopted quickly by the wealthy, white, and privileged; some of his most dedicated admirers were American railroad tycoons and corporate businessmen. John D. Rockefeller invoked Spencerian principles to tell a Sunday school class: "the growth of a large business is merely a survival of the fittest . . . merely the working-out of a law of nature and a law of God" (quoted in Chase, *Legacy of Malthus*, 8). Gilman summed up her awareness of this view and drew attention to its results for the less fortunate through Van, the American sociologist in *Herland*: "I explained that the laws of nature require a struggle for existence, and that in the struggle the fittest survive, and the unfit perish. In our economic struggle, I continued,

Gilman and Feminism

there was always plenty of opportunity for the fittest to reach the top, which they did, in great numbers, particularly in our country; that where there was severe economic pressure the lowest classes of course felt it the worst" (63).

20. Despite her interest in the "working" class and socialism, Gilman avoided Marxist ideas about overthrowing capitalism to attain socialism through economic class warfare and the triumph of the proletariat. Primarily, she rejected the assumption that class violence would have to occur in order to create a new world order, and argued for socialized capitalism as a benevolently unifying force. She also believed that Marx's language and complex theories were inaccessible to most, that his deification of what he labeled "The Working Class" was ridiculous, and that he was naive to single out economic class because, in her view, social problems were rooted in gender relations. Gilman refuted Marxist socialism in "Where Are All the Pre-War Radicals?" (a short piece delivered at a 1926 symposium) and summarized her resistance to Marxist tenets in "Socialist Psychology," an unpublished article or lecture from 1933. Other works, such as "Ourland," *Herland*, "Feminism and Social Progress," and her autobiography, include explanations for her conflicts with Marxism.

21. It appears that Gilman's notion of professionalism closely followed Edward Bellamy's definition of the term. See pages 102, 124, and 138 of Bellamy's *Looking Backward: 2000–1887*, which, according to Larry Ceplair, Gilman read in the early 1890s (*Nonfiction*, 35).

22. The professional staff potentially – but not necessarily – could be made up of employees who themselves lived in such buildings.

23. In this essay, I have examined an array of Gilman's public writings – some of which, like *Women and Economics* and *Herland*, comprise her best-known work. However, as Ann Lane notes in *To Herland and Beyond*, Gilman's personal correspondence and journals betray another – perhaps fuller – sense of her thoughts on race, ethnicity, and class (255–256). In her newly published first volume of Gilman's diaries, editor Denise Knight also explains that in private Charlotte Perkins Gilman was a very different person from her public self and that she kept many of her most personal musings on odd scraps of paper in a folder called "Thoughts and Figgerings" (xix).

Women, Work, and the Home

FREDERICK WEGENER

"What a Comfort a Woman Doctor Is!"

Medical Women in the Life and Writing of Charlotte Perkins Gilman

By the last third of the nineteenth century, as more than one historian has noted, agitation in favor of opening the medical profession to women, both in the United States and in Great Britain,
had advanced to the forefront of the larger insurgency on behalf
of women's rights. According to Richard Shryrock, for example,
"Feminists at large saw in the admittance of women to medicine
a dramatic test case for their whole movement, and encouraged it
at every opportunity," so that, as a result, "the entrance of women
into medicine here was associated with a strong feminist movement."[1] Even more forcefully, Mary Roth Walsh asserts that
"a female physician could not have functioned autonomously in
nineteenth-century America" and that her "dependence on the
woman's movement was total."[2] Few cultural figures at the time
would have been better situated to observe this crucial interrela-
tionship between feminism and the women's medical movement,
or to grasp its importance, than Charlotte Perkins Gilman, whose
emergence coincides with the rise of American women as officially
accredited doctors and whose concerns and convictions would have
made her peculiarly responsive to such a phenomenon. Indeed, it
may be argued that women physicians came to play, in Gilman's
life and in her work, a role far more conspicuous and enabling
than we have yet appreciated and that the establishment of women
in a field like medicine uniquely dramatized the sort of progress
for which Gilman tirelessly campaigned.

It is surprising that such an important aspect of her career
should remain largely unexplored, for medical women accompanied Gilman at virtually every stage of her development, starting

at least as far back as her adolescence in Rhode Island in the mid-1870s, when "Dr. Studley, a woman physician," as she later recounted it, "gave a lecture to the school, on hygiene, which made an indelible impression on my earnest mind" (*Living*, 28). Just how ubiquitous the figure of the woman doctor became in her experience can now be determined, as never before (albeit with much independent sleuthing), from Gilman's recently published diaries.[3] Throughout her mid-twenties, for example, several entries document the friendship that developed with Dr. Elizabeth Keller (since 1875 one of the leaders of the pioneering New England Hospital for Women and Children) after Gilman heard a lecture that she delivered in Providence in February 1883 (*Diaries*, 173). Shortly after publishing one of her first significant articles, "Why Women Do Not Reform Their Dress" (1886), Gilman recorded the exchange of several social calls with the flamboyant, habitually cross-dressing Dr. Mary Edwards Walker, perhaps the most eccentric figure among American medical women of the day (*Diaries*, 355–356, 358). After her move to the West Coast in 1888, which "begins my professional 'living'" (*Living*, 107), as she later put it, Gilman's diaries amount almost to a roll-call of California's early women doctors, including such luminaries as Dr. Charlotte Blake Brown (founder of the Woman's and Children's Hospital in San Francisco), Dr. Elizabeth A. Follansbee, one of the leading women physicians in Los Angeles, the equally distinguished Dr. C. Annette Buckel, and a "Dr. Bullard" who is assuredly Rose Bullard, a respected Los Angeles surgeon who later became "the chairperson of public health for the Los Angeles district."[4]

Perhaps inevitably, the women doctors whom she met and befriended were apt to share Gilman's own beliefs and enthusiasms and to be involved along with her in many of the same activities. In Pasadena, early in 1890, Gilman attended meetings of the Social Purity Society with Dr. Kate Shepardson Black, a local physician and surgeon (*Diaries*, 416–426, passim); at the convention of the Pacific Coast Woman's Press Association (PCWPA) in San Francisco in the spring of 1891, Gilman became acquainted with various medical women, including Dr. Sarah I. Shuey, for whom she prepared a "paper . . . on equal rights in education for women" (*Diaries*, 451) and whom she would later come to know after her move to the Bay Area that fall.[5] Living first in Oakland, Gilman worked "to reorganize the Nationalist Club" (*Diaries*, 481) with Dr. L. J. Kellogg, a particularly close friend over the next three years.[6] Another friend, Dr. Myra Knox, hosted several meetings of the "Economics Section" of the Ebell Society, where Gilman read a "paper on 'Steps in Civilization'" and a "paper on Family & State" in February and May 1893 and where "Dr. Buckle [sic] & Shuey read paper on mammal training" at an earlier meeting, several weeks before they came "in the evening to hear my sex paper" (*Diaries*, 517, 530, 515, 530). With Dr. Julia F. Button, an Oakland physician, Gilman in April 1893 attended an "Ebell meeting to discuss motherhood" and collaborated on the formation of a "Parents Association" (*Diaries*, 527, 528, 531).

During her time in the Bay Area, she also became friendly with "Mrs. Dr. Kate Port Van Orden" (*Diaries*, 589), a physician and surgeon whose husband, like Dr. Kellogg's, would become Gilman's dentist for a time.[7] In March 1893 a mutual friend brought Dr. Amy Bowen, whom Gilman later invited to a "reception of the S.F. Council of Women" and recruited in her effort "to ask Board of Health to appoint a Woman Health inspector" in San Francisco (*Diaries*, 537, 549); Gilman approached the distinguished "Dr. [Emma Sutro] Merritt," head of the Department of Surgical Pediatrics at the San Francisco Children's Hospital, on the same matter and also "to see about [a] Woman's Alliance" (*Diaries*, 549, 526). In April 1894 she received no fewer than three calls from the visiting Dr. Frances Dickinson, described by Regina Morantz-Sanchez as a member of "a whole generation of prominent women physicians in Chicago" (*Sympathy*, 80), where Gilman would call on her a couple of years later; Dickinson was another figure to have a noticeable effect: "I take her in delightedly. We have splendid talk, and she stays over night" (*Diaries*, 611, 582–583).

Indeed, one finds scarcely a turning point, transitional phase, or important public event at which women doctors do not appear significantly in Gilman's life. Once she resumed compiling her diary in January 1890, after the long interruption that followed her breakdown in 1887, several entries immediately mention the friendship ("Like her very much. She talks to me") of Dr. Adele Amelia Gleason, who had recently established a sanitarium in Pasadena. Gilman would meet her again in Buffalo during her 1902 lecture tour, when she was "a shocking wreck. Poor woman! & she was so glorious" (*Diaries*, 409–412, 828). Preparing in June 1891 to seek a divorce from Walter Stetson, Gilman received both "advice" and a "letter of introduction to nice lawyer" from "Dr. [Dorothea] Lummis" (*Diaries*, 460), ex-wife of Charles Lummis (the journalist and editor who published some of Gilman's early poems and essays in his magazine, *Land of Sunshine*) and a PCWPA colleague later described by Gilman in the *Impress* as "one of our most brilliant members."[8] (In the same issue, Gilman's associate editor Helen Campbell, who described herself as "a medical student of that school," profiled a local homeopathic woman doctor. Campbell was a nationally known reformist with whom Gilman took over the *Impress* and whom she would come to refer to as her "Mother.")[9]

In March 1894, with divorce proceedings well in hand and as she prepared to take the difficult step of leaving her daughter Katharine with Grace Channing, Gilman acknowledged the generosity of another medical woman: "Dr. Knox called this morning and offered to lend me money to get out of here. Very friendly and enthusiastic" (*Diaries*, 578). Approached by Jane Addams (who had herself briefly studied medicine at one point), Gilman left California the following year and embarked upon her long period of living "at large," as she later called it, after accepting an invitation to visit Hull House, co-founded by, among others, the distinguished Dr. Alice Hamilton. She mentioned Hamilton in one of her letters to Houghton Gilman as "a fair frail little woman" with whom "I sat and talked, pleasantly and profitably," one evening in Addams's room (Hill, ed., *Journey*, 215). Her closest friends during this phase included a couple, "The McCrackens," who "were both physicians. Mrs. McCracken was a member of the Chicago Woman's Club, had often heard me speak; I had given parlor lectures in her house" (*Living*, 189). In Chicago around the same time, "Dr. Mary E. Green" called on Gilman a week or so after "Dr. [Julia Ross] Low" (*Diaries*, 611, 610), whom she later described to Houghton as "a great admirer of my work" (Hill, ed., *Journey*, 372). At a stop in Topeka in June 1896, during the first of her many lecture tours, Gilman was "met by Dr. [Eva] Harding" – a suffragist prominent in the kindergarten movement and the first woman from Kansas to be a candidate for the U.S. Congress – "and taken by her to her office" (*Diaries*, 623).

In New York City, where she moved in the winter of 1896, Gilman twice went "to see Dr. [Catherine D.] Burnette in Brooklyn" (*Diaries*, 651–652) and exchanged several visits with "Dr. Hussey," whom she accompanied to meetings of Christian Socialists and of the Unitarian Women's League ("She's a good soul"). This appears to be Dr. Mary Dudley Hussey, pioneer New Jersey suffragist (*Diaries*, 651–654, 661, 704, 819). Around the same time, in Jersey City, she "dine[d] at Dr. Florence De Hart's" (*Diaries*, 666), who was the first woman admitted to the Hudson County Medical Society and daughter of one of New Jersey's first women physicians. Revisiting Chicago early in 1897, Gilman met more than once with "Dr. [Leila G.] Bedell" and several other like-minded women to "talk on Man & Woman" and "on sex question," receiving social calls from Dr. Bedell on at least two other return visits to Chicago (*Diaries*, 659–660, 674, 752). After attending "our Suffrage meeting in the Legislative Chambers" in Harrisburg, Pennsylvania, during her lecture tour of April–August 1897, Gilman and some other delegates "all call[ed] on Dr. [Agnes] Kemp" (*Diaries*, 671), for many years a well-known local practitioner. One notes also a highlight of her lengthy stay in Boston in the fall of 1898 with Alice Stone Blackwell, who had practically launched Gilman's writing career a decade earlier by inviting her to provide a women's suffrage column for a Providence newspaper: "Two (women) doctors here to dinner. Dr. [Mary Alma] Smith & Dr. [Emma V.] Culbert[s]on. The latter extremely beautiful" (*Diaries*, 750). Also included "among my most honored friends" at this time, along with the other "brave progressive people" of "the Blackwell family," was her host's sister-in-law, "Elizabeth Blackwell, the first woman physician in England" (*Living*, 216). In both of her reports on the International Congress of Women in London in the summer of 1899, when she was also a fellow-guest with "two women doctors" (*Diaries*, 789) in Newcastle, Gilman mentions the attendance of "the first woman physician from Holland, Dr. Aletta Jacobs," her escort both then and at the next meeting of the congress (in Berlin in 1904), who also translated *Women and Economics* into Dutch at Gilman's request.[10] Once again on the lecture circuit out west from October through December 1899, Gilman stopped at Minneapolis, where she was met and hosted by "Dr. Eaton & Dr. Ripley" (*Diaries*, 801), referring to Cora Smith Eaton, physician and surgeon who was also president of the Minnesota Woman's Suffrage Association, and Martha Roberts Ripley, founder of the local Maternity Hospital, public-health advocate, and one of the most prominent medical women in Minnesota.[11]

There seem to have been few women doctors of any distinction whom Gilman did not meet in the many different parts of the country she visited throughout an extraordinarily itinerant decade, while medical women appear and reappear in her diaries, letters, and memoirs with a frequency that has escaped the biographical record on her life.[12] Perhaps the most memorable of these encounters, occurring on a visit to Philadelphia in June 1898, involved the redoubtable Dr. Hannah Longshore, "the first woman physician in the city. The old lady told me how when she began to practise the prejudice against women physicians was such that druggists refused to handle her prescriptions, or put them up incorrectly to bring discredit upon her. She was treating one sick woman, whose daughter was entertaining a suitor, and the young man told the girl that he would withdraw his suit if her mother employed a woman physician!" (*Living*, 246). The determination of such persevering women to establish themselves as doctors in the face of concerted and typically degrading antagonism came to epitomize, in Gilman's eyes, the larger struggle for professional acceptance and economic parity. Under her editorship, one issue of the *Impress* included in its feature "The Art of Living" a lengthy reference to the famous "Mrs. Garrett Anderson," an Englishwoman who "became a physician through much difficulty and tribulation on account of prejudice against women physicians. Since then, through her efforts, the path of the girl medical student has been made much more easy." A later issue excerpted an article in which the *Review of Reviews* reported the results of another such contest, wryly mentioning the decision to admit women to medical study in Scotland, after "an uphill fight for just twenty-five years."[13] Disputing an influential assumption about the supposedly desexualizing effects of medical education and training, Gilman hints at some of the more egregious behavior of those inhospitable to the prospect of women as doctors: "It is not being a doctor that makes a woman unwomanly, but the treatment which the first women medical students and physicians received was such as to make even men unmanly" (*Women and Economics*, 167).

The treatment that Gilman has in mind here is invoked repeatedly throughout her later writings. Tracing in one essay "the progress of women in any art, science, profession, trade or craft," she emphasizes "the struggles of women physicians . . . the injustice, the brutality, the wilful indecency with which they were shut out from lecture and clinic." [14] It is an experience on which Gilman elaborates at some length in *The Man-Made World*, graphically describing "the attitude of medical colleges toward women students" as "an unforgettable instance" of the obstacles facing those women who strove to enter the professions:

> The men, strong enough, one would think, in numbers, in knowledge, in established precedent, to be generous, opposed the newcomers first with absolute refusal; then when the patient, persistent applicants did get inside, both students and teachers met them not only with unkindness and unfairness, but with a weapon ingeniously well chosen, and most discreditable – namely, obscenity. Grave professors, in lecture and clinic, as well as grinning students, used offensive language, and played offensive tricks, to drive the women out – a most androcentric performance. (*Man-Made World*, 148)

Already familiar by that time from standard anecdotes of women's fortunes at American medical schools in the 1870s and 1880s, such incidents underlie Gilman's later reference to "the 'bitterness' and the 'unfairness' with which the medical profession – with press, pulpit, and public opinion backing it – strove to prevent women from studying medicine. The learned lecturer in the class-room, the many who would be called a 'gentleman and a scholar' outside of it, did not scruple to use offensive language, obscene stories, to drive the women students out." [15] Sardonically reminding her readers of "the contemptible tactics employed by our natural protectors to keep women out of the professions," Gilman cited the same examples yet again in her memoirs, after describing her conversation with Dr. Longshore: "In medicine, where one might have expected decency, those who taught in medical colleges deliberately employed obscenity in their lectures to deter women students. One of these records that she fairly starved herself that she 'might not have blood enough to blush with'" (*Living*, 246).

Even after they had bravely endured such indignities, these discouraging efforts persisted, as Gilman was well aware, long after graduation. As late as 1915 she insists that in the United States "we find women already able to enter the specialized professions, though by no means free from all handicaps; as for instance, where medical schools are open to them, but an equal chance in hospital practice is refused." Five years later, Gilman still has to underscore the shameful lack of "legislation to equalize opportunity for women workers, such as giving women medical graduates their fair share of appointments in hospitals."[16] For Gilman, this lingering hostility of an entrenched medical establishment to the notion of women as doctors remained symptomatic of the intolerance that greeted the wider prospect of emancipation for women. Regarding "education and democracy" as not only "the very greatest of our human gains" but also those "we have been the slowest to share with woman," Gilman introduces, in *The Home*, another recurring connection: "We have allowed them religion in a sense – as we have allowed them medicine – to take; not to give! They might have a priest as they might have a doctor, but on no account be one!"[17]

The ferocity of the opposition withstood by medical women, and the resoluteness with which they ultimately prevailed, thus made the woman doctor a singularly heroic figure in Gilman's work. *Women and Economics*, for example, mentions "Dr. Elizabeth Blackwell and her splendid sisterhood," alongside such leaders as Elizabeth Cady Stanton and Susan B. Anthony, in celebrating "the spirit . . . of all the women who have battled and suffered for half a century, forcing their way, with sacrifices never to be told, into the field of freedom so long denied them, – not for themselves alone, but for one another" (166–167). It is therefore not surprising that the organ for which Gilman agreed to write a weekly column throughout 1904, as contributing editor, should have been the *Woman's Journal*, "one of the most openly militant supporters of the woman physician," which "championed the cause of women doctors and challenged the right of society to erect barriers to stand in their way." It was published in Boston, which by the turn of the century "led the nation in the percentage of its physicians who were female" (Walsh, *"Doctors Wanted,"* 89, 185). Later, announcing in the *Forerunner*, a special issue of the *Medical Review of Reviews* "dedicated to the women physicians of America" (consisting entirely of "articles . . . from the pens of women physicians whose work has achieved national importance"), Gilman, as if participating in the occasion herself, reminds her readers that "medicine was practically the first profession open to women," declares that "in the laboratory, in the hospital, in institutions, at the bedside, and in public service, women physicians have performed a valuable function," and welcomes the forthcoming "Woman's Number" as "a tribute to their earnestness, enthusiasm, modesty, energy, perseverance, and scientific acumen." [18]

More broadly, one notices also how several of the leading themes of Gilman's work coalesce in her discussions of women doctors, who exemplified in her mind so many of her own most radical views and values regarding the welfare of women and of society as a whole.[19] Some of her firmest and most cherished allegiances, resulting in such important early projects as her sponsorship of a women's gymnasium in Providence,[20] stemmed directly from the impact of the lessons that she received on hygiene as she listened with her schoolmates to "Dr. Studley" in the 1870s: "Forthwith I took to 'dress reform,' fresh air, cold baths, every kind of attainable physical exercise. To that one lecture is to be attributed the beginning of a life-long interest in physical culture" (*Living*, 28–29). As an adult, she would applaud the lecturer for providing even more crucial guidance, declaring in the *Impress* that "books like 'What Our Girls Ought to Know,' by Dr. Mary Studley . . . , stand for the first uncertain and timid steps in the new path" toward "teaching children the truth concerning the most important functions of life" and toward "full and perfect instruction in matters which concern the happiness of life so closely." [21] Her remarks occur in an expansive and favorable review of *Child Confidence Rewarded*, "By Mary Wood Allen, M.D.," a prolific writer of such guides and "a well-known social-purity lecturer" and "defender of scientific motherhood" (Morantz-Sanchez, *Sympathy*, 218) already known to Gilman, who had attended a meeting of the "Woman's Club" in San Francisco two years earlier to "hear Dr. Mary Wood Allen on the teaching of girls. Very good" (*Diaries*, 491). Elsewhere in the *Impress*, Gilman's overview of a recent *Popular Science Monthly* issue extols one article in which another medical woman addressed related matters: "Mary Taylor Bissell, M.D., writes of 'Athletics for City Girls' in a way that ought to rouse a thrill of splendid womanly ambition in every flat-chested or roly poly school girl among us." [22] Maintaining that "it is no longer a question of whether we shall teach sex physiology and hygiene in our schools, but of how we shall teach them," Gilman observed in 1911 that "to meet the needs of those who wish to teach their children along these lines, and yet feel utterly unequipped to approach the subject, numerous books are now appearing," many of them by women physicians; she mentions, for example, a pair of such works by Dr. Edith B. Lowry and praises "a more extensive and far-reaching work . . . by Dr. Elizabeth Hamilton-Muncie."[23]

Her own volume on the subject, *Concerning Children*, poses at one point an extended hypothetical scenario in which Gilman portrays as "the ideal" in professionally trained "nurse-maids" an imaginary sister named Jessie, who "always did love children, and knew how to manage them from the time she was a little girl" (223). Jessie is now "studying all the science of it and practising in the kindergarten" (223), and her plan to bring some of her charges to "the Summer School of Child-study" (231) meets with the author's approval for one reason in particular: "It will be a regular picnic for the children. . . . And one of Jessie's friends is a doctor, and in a children's hospital, too. She ought to see that everything is right for their health" (231). Indeed, however unfortunate the comparison through which she elsewhere asserts the superiority of such a figure in this respect, the appearance of women in medicine seemed to Gilman almost guaranteed to enhance what she called the "standard of human motherhood" itself (*Women and Economics*, 184), confirming her notion that "the family will not be less loved because it has a skilled worker to love it." Among her "five mothers, equally loving" ("Hottentot," "Eskimo," "Hindoo," "German peasant woman"), one is "an American and a successful physician. . . . All might compete on even terms if 'love is enough,' as poets have claimed; but *which could best provide for her children?*" (*The Home*, 102).

Nor are these the only areas of human service in which Gilman found that medical women uniquely excelled. According to one issue of the *Impress*, a work that "deserves to be studied by every woman who would understand either home or public sanitation" is "a little book entitled 'Women, Plumbers and Doctors,'" in which "a wise woman . . . demonstrated the need of a triple alliance between them" with the help of "her medical studies." A charming article in 1915 cites the "special skill in the preserving of strawberries" on the part of "a physician and surgeon" who "was also a radical woman, a reformer and lover of reformers"; although "this woman's work as a physician was her real world service," she also demonstrated for Gilman, through such culinary abilities, the value of "the woman who helps develop the profession of preparing food, standard food, healthful, appetizing, dainty, and cheap food, to be conscientiously and artistically prepared and served to the hungry whenever they wish to have it."[24] Her effectiveness in so many different roles seems to have made the medical woman, in Gilman's eyes, an embodiment of uncompromising autonomy. Arguing in an early piece that "the woman who does human work, the teacher, writer, artist, doctor – anyone who is useful to her fellows as an individual – such a woman needs a name of her own, has one, and in the very nature of things keeps it," Gilman focuses, for illustrative purposes, on one such humanly useful worker: "The physician in good practice, some Dr. Douglas, of wide reputation, may marry John Smith or Jacob Wigstraw – Dr. Douglas she will remain to all who know her." (Only a few years later, when many "are learning by continued contact with established facts . . . that the essential activities of organized society are Human – and neither male nor female," she could observe, more pointedly, " 'Doctor' Smith no longer conveys instant assurance of masculinity.")[25]

Finally, even outside the public realm, women doctors constituted a model for Gilman in managing to harmonize their medical pursuits successfully with a thriving private life:

> One of the happiest marriages I know is where the husband and wife are both professionals in kindred branches. She is a doctor. They have a large family of beautiful, healthy children. "And what did the woman doctor do while the babies were growing?" is demanded. She did the most natural and reasonable thing, – restricted herself to office practice.[26]

Elsewhere referring to one of them affectionately as "the wife-and-mother-doctor" (*Living*, 190), Gilman might have had in mind here the McCrackens in Chicago, although other married physicians among her friends (the Kellogg-Lanes, the Van Ordens) would have provided additional evidence of a possibility that she obviously regarded as the professional woman's *summum bonum*. One is struck by the terms in which she recommends to "anyone who cares about child-training, either personally or socially," a booklet on "Home Training of the Prize Baby" by another husband-and-wife pair of physicians: "In the first place look at the authors – co-authors, co-doctors, co-parents – here is a Union. 'Doctors Clark & Clark' is on their letter-paper, a marriage that really is a partnership."[27]

Hygiene, dress reform, exercise, social service, the improvement of food preparation and child-rearing, access to full knowledge of one's body, the achievement of self-sufficiency, meaningful work, and professional distinction, and the retention of an individual identity in a marital union of equals – all of these ideals quickly became affiliated in Gilman's mind with the figure of the woman doctor, making her a prototype of that most provocative and iconoclastic new presence on the Anglo-American cultural landscape, the "New Woman," independently employed and usefully occupied.[28] Some idea of its value in her eyes may be gathered from the August 1882 entry in Gilman's diary, which mentions "a very pleasant talk" with her Providence friend Martha Lane involving the woman who would become one of the earliest of her medical friends: "Much of Dr. Keller of Boston. I am glad such women live" (*Diaries*, 136).

She had already responded at an even earlier age to the comprehensive appeal of "such women," informing her father at fifteen, "I am very much interested in Physiological aspirations to be an M.D." (Hill, *Making of a Radical Feminist*, 39); she would have derived some incentive from the abilities of her mother, who raised Gilman and her brother "with unusual intelligence and effectiveness, using much of the then new Kindergarten method, and so training herself with medical books that the doctor said he could do no better by us" (*Living*, 10). One senses in her later work a displacement of this youthful Aesculapian impulse onto the many other tasks that Gilman undertook in public life and that she obviously thought of in much the same terms. "The physician, the agitator for hygienic reform," as she remarked in 1898, "naturally sees disease and overlooks health, and the agitator for social reform must of course do likewise,"[29] in an analogy that clearly underlies the diagnostic language and clinical, often surgical images occurring throughout her prose or the way in which Gilman presents herself as a kind of social pathologist treating a badly diseased, even deformed, social organism or body politic. It is no accident that one of her essays, "The Home and the Hospital" (pairing two such spaces in a way that is itself revealing), should have occupied "The Family Doctor" column in a 1905 issue of *Good Housekeeping*. In perhaps her most overt exercise of this figuratively "medical" capacity, Gilman participated in 1920 in the first International Conference of Women Physicians, deliver-

Women, Work, and the Home

ing a lecture that was later published, along with a transcription of the lively debate that followed, in its proceedings.[30]

And yet there is, of course, even more tangible and immediate evidence of the extent to which she appreciated the notion of women as doctors: the variety of women doctors whom Gilman consulted herself and the number of times she depended on their services. From the "violent bruise and profusely bleeding cut" for which she received an "examination highly favorable" in 1882 from a "Dr. Tyney," who "says she would have sewed it if she had seen it Sat." (Diaries, 113–114), to more serious afflictions that later demanded the medical skills of the women mentioned in The Living and in her diaries and letters, Gilman resorted to women doctors with striking consistency throughout her life. During her troubled courtship with Stetson and again during the depression that followed the birth of her daughter, she recorded numerous appointments in Boston with "Dr. Keller, dear woman";[31] in Providence in March 1885, at a late stage in Gilman's pregnancy, "Dr. [Sophronia] Tomlinson calls, prescribes for cold, insomnia, and night sweats. I like her much" (Diaries, 199, 321). Following the move to Pasadena, and shortly after parting from Stetson for good, "I was driven to consult a physician, an excellent woman, Dr. Follansbee of Los Angeles" (Gilman's diary contains, in fact, over two dozen references to her from November 1890 through August 1891), "and found that there were now certain internal difficulties of a purely physical nature added to my mental ones with ensuing complications and need for prolonged treatment" (Living, 118). By the next year, in Oakland, "Good Dr. Kellog," with whom her ailing mother boarded for a time, also ministered to Gilman, whose memoirs quote three of the many diary entries between January 1892 and June 1894 in which she gratefully mentioned the doctor's counsel ("A wise physician") in the midst of her mother's final illness, during her turbulent involvement with Adeline Knapp, and afterward (Living, 137, 140).[32] On the possibility of conceiving a child with her cousin Houghton, Gilman was examined by "this good woman," Dr. Low, "a flourishing and capable physician . . . I am going to confide to her the open secret of my matrimonial intentions, and ask her to look over my machinery" (Hill, ed., Journey, 374, 372).

Although she also welcomed the advice of the male Dr. McCracken, Gilman's inclinations in such a matter would have poignantly corroborated one of the most common and compelling arguments at the time in favor of the medical education and training of women — the fact that so many women preferred to be treated by doctors of their own sex. Acceding to Dr. Low's diagnosis, Gilman informed Houghton that "she is the only one who has the 'inside facts.' I was going to have Dr. McCracken make the examination — but — since I have learned what love is I have learned some modesty too. I couldn't bear to have him. Come to think of it I never did have a man doctor — at that end! But I shouldn't have minded if I had. And now I do . . ." (Hill, ed., *Journey*, 374).[33] Finally, in an account that one historian has cited as "a fascinating first-hand description of one highly respected woman physician's empathic style" (Morantz-Sanchez, *Sympathy*, 213), Gilman describes at length the innovative treatment she underwent in New York, after a later recurrence of "the same old helpless gloom" and "the long continued misery and exhaustion" that had chronically bedeviled her adult life from "that remarkable woman, Dr. Mary Putnam Jacobi, one of our first to study medicine" and perhaps the preeminent American medical woman of her time (*Living*, 290–292; see also *Diaries*, 817, 819–823).

To be sure, such women were not the only doctors from whom Gilman sought medical attention for one malady or another throughout her life. Even so, the doctors of the opposite sex whom she did feel comfortable consulting — like the male Dr. McCracken, or her dentists, Dr. Lane and Dr. Van Orden — tended to be the husbands of physicians. One would have to look far indeed before coming upon a more detailed and moving record, compiled by an equally prominent figure during this period, of one woman's continuing reliance on women doctors.[34] And this pattern in her life becomes particularly significant in light of the one therapeutic experience at all widely known to her readers, Gilman's subjection to the infamous rest cure of S. Weir Mitchell, whose mode of treatment so notoriously typified conventional late Victorian doctoring of women. If anything, the stark contrast between the effects of the rest cure and her experiences with Mitchell's female counterparts illustrates just how urgent the availability of women physicians had become by the time Gilman began to write. Such a need, along with Mitchell's own strenuous and highly vocal opposition to the medical training of women,[35] adds a fresh dimension to our understanding even of a work as well known as "The Yellow Wallpaper," in which the tormented narrator's unresponsive husband, who threatens at one point to send her to Mitchell, is himself a doctor and readily differentiated as such from the many women doctors who appear elsewhere in Gilman's fiction. And it is in her imaginative work, even more than in her polemical or autobiographical writings, that one ultimately finds Gilman's richest and most substantial engagement with the ascendancy of the medical woman in turn-of-the-century America.

Just as she experienced at first hand the centrality of women doctors in the lives of women, so Gilman quickly became aware of the images of medical women widely circulating in Anglo-American culture throughout the last third of the nineteenth century and early in the twentieth. Demonstrating in a late essay the "general revolt or protest by women against their previous status," she draws from what she calls "that inexorable record of passing events, current literature," the following illuminating instance:

> The opening chapter of a popular novel, published within two or three years, describes a vigorous heroine who slips out early in the morning in her pajamas and some sort of wrapper, swims happily in a forest pool, and then climbs a beech tree to enjoy a marmalade sandwich which she had brought with her. As she returns to the house she is met by two grown children, who congratulate her on her forty-third birthday! The problem before this lively lady is how to take up again her study of medicine, in which she had made great advances before marrying. In this she does not succeed, but that she wishes to do it shows the change in women. Happy wifehood, proud motherhood and a comfortable income do not satisfy her; she has also the feelings proper to a human being, and wishes to function socially.[36]

Although she doesn't identify the novel in question, Gilman surely realized that many others would have served to make the same point, for the figure of the woman doctor (or "lady doctor" or "doctress") had already established itself long before as a new literary "type" throughout the English-speaking world and as one of the most popular and controversial representations of the New Woman.

Now seldom noticed by literary historians, the "lady-doctor" novel became a successful and quite common form of imaginative writing between 1865 and 1920; in one of the earliest examples,

My Wife and I (1871), Gilman's own great-aunt, Harriet Beecher Stowe, had portrayed two medically aspiring sisters. Also initially determined to achieve a medical education is the heroine of Bayard Taylor's *Hannah Thurston* (1863), which Gilman borrowed from the Providence Athenaeum in the fall of 1883 (*Diaries*, 235, 236). Nearly a year later, during a particularly traumatic phase of her early married life in Rhode Island, Gilman was avidly reading Elizabeth Stuart Phelps's *Doctor Zay* (1882), in its time one of the better-known novels of this sort (*Diaries*, 301, 306).[37] In September 1885 she began to follow with some displeasure the serialization of *The Bostonians* (*Diaries*, 332, 333), in which Henry James offers one of the period's more enigmatic and fascinating (and traditionally misunderstood) portrayals of a medical woman.[38] Another novel presumably familiar to Gilman, *Some Passages in the Practice of Dr. Martha Scarborough* (1893), by her "mother," Helen Campbell, involves a New England country doctor's young daughter whose own medical ambitions are strengthened by the arrival of a gifted woman physician from Philadelphia. Recalling her introduction to Dr. Mary Putnam Jacobi, Gilman remarks that "Charles Reade refers to her in his *Woman Hater*" (*Living*, 290), published in 1876 and yet another once-familiar work of this kind. Its medical heroine, Dr. Rhona Gale, is based on Sophia Jex-Blake, Jacobi's equally renowned English counterpart and leader of the famous Seven-against-Edinburgh campaign in the early 1870s (a great early *cause célèbre* of the women's medical movement).

Gilman was not only aware of this widespread literary and cultural vogue of the woman doctor, at a time when she herself increasingly gravitated to women doctors, but also did much to extend it, taking as one of the main purposes of her own imaginative writing the portrayal of medical women, who figure in more than half a dozen of her short stories and in no fewer than three of her four nonutopian works of longer fiction. Indeed, one of the few widely noted recurrences in her fiction – protagonists who are guided or influenced by an older, vastly more informed woman who tends also to be, coincidentally, a doctor – turns out to be even more pervasive than one had realized.[39] Two such mentors appear in *Benigna Machiavelli* alone, as the eponymous narrator, describing much the same pivotal educational experience from which Gilman later remembered benefiting at the same age in Providence, remarks that "when I was about fourteen I heard a woman doctor lecture on hygiene at our school" and "was tremendously impressed" by the lecture, which marked "the beginning of my training, physical training, I mean. I set up a Goal in my secret diary. 'I mean to be Strong,' I put down. 'As strong as I possibly can. And well, of course'" (55). Later moving to Chicago, where she is employed in social work reminiscent of Hull House, Benigna is even more impressed by the person she consults after being sexually accosted in a workshop: "There was a fine woman doctor I used to see at the Settlement and I went to her. 'Doctor,' I said, 'I am a young woman, working for my living. I find that some men are disagreeable and some dangerous. Will you give me some very clear advice, both as to the nature and the extent of the danger, and the best methods of self-protection.'" After observing, "You are certainly a very cool young woman," whereupon Benigna insists, "I want some straight, practical knowledge, anatomical and psychological," the doctor replies, "'You shall have it' . . . And she gave me books and pamphlets to read – quite a number of them." From these materials, as the narrator laconically but pointedly observes, "I learned a lot" (170–171).

A medical woman serves far less peripherally as the source of essential information, and of much else, in a more substantial work, *The Crux*, in which Vivian Lane's highly conservative New England parents ("Save me from these women doctors!" her mother exclaims at one point) object to her friendship with Dr. Jane Bellair, who espouses "out-door air" as "the best medicine for a cold" (45), implores Vivian's widowed aunt to pack up and return with her to Colorado to establish a boarding-house, and persuades Vivian herself to accompany them. When Morton, Vivian's undependable onetime admirer, suddenly appears in Colorado after years of wandering, Dr. Bellair, quickly discerning symptoms of the terrible malady that she herself contracted years earlier from a careless man, warns Vivian of the fact that he is suffering from at least one, and possibly two, sexually transmitted diseases that could prevent her from ever having children – the very effect that the infection has had in her case and the primary reason, as she informs Vivian, that she chose to study medicine in the first place. In Vivian and Dr. Bellair, Gilman offers her most complex account of a relationship that typifies much of her fiction about women doctors: "Vivian liked her, yet felt afraid, a slight, shivering hesitancy as before a too cold bath, a subtle sense that this breezy woman, strong, cheerful, full of new ideas, if not ideals, and radiating actual power, power used and enjoyed, might in some way change the movement of her life" (59). Change it Dr. Bellair certainly does, not only bringing Vivian out to Colorado and away from her stiflingly conventional northeastern home but also launching her as a kindergarten teacher, "ask[ing] her to undertake, as a special favor to her, the care of a class of rather delicate children and young girls, in physical culture" (271), and recruiting her to assist in the development of a girls' summer camp in the mountains – all in an effort to keep Vivian's mind occupied after the revelations regarding Morton. It would be hard, indeed, to think of a more commanding figure in the extensive literature of American or English women doctors during this period than Vivian's effective and conscientious protector in *The Crux*.

In purely recuperative terms, such a figure performs an even more immediate role elsewhere in Gilman's fiction, directing lost or despondent younger women back to health and enabling them to restore a self-esteem badly damaged by experience. Perhaps the most vivid illustration would be the eponymous protagonist of "Dr. Clair's Place," a tale in which Gilman may be said to have summed up much of her thinking on the mental and emotional well-being of women. Encountering on a train-ride a distraught and suicidal woman, the sympathetic narrator recommends a visit to a sanitarium in the Sierra Madres directed by "Dr. Willy Clair – she was Southern, and really named Willy,"[40] from whom the narrator herself has already received life-saving treatment after a nervous breakdown. In perhaps a too-obvious contrast to Mitchell's rest cure, or to the regimen inflicted upon the narrator of "The Yellow Wallpaper," Dr. Clair encourages the woman to keep a written record of her sensations and then sends it to the narrator, who referred the woman to Dr. Clair in the first place and who reproduces the woman's account in the narrative, allowing Dr. Clair's patient – as Dr. Clair did herself – to describe her condition in her own words. Clearly, "The Hills," as Dr. Clair has named her sanitarium, constitutes a paradise or ideal place, establishing an implicit continuity between this final story of a powerful woman doctor and Gilman's more programmatically utopian narratives.[41]

Yet this turns out to be far from the only role occupied by medical women in Gilman's imagination. In "Mr. Peebles' Heart," for example, it is not a young woman but a middle-aged man who is thus assisted, in this case by Dr. Joan Bascom, the protagonist's sister-in-law, who comes to live with him and his rather insensitive and imperceptive wife and whose advice (medically and domestically) works to the benefit of both. "Like the type of good medical doctor in the Gilman canon," Monika Elbert remarks, "Dr. Joan understands the psychology of those around her" and "prescribes the opposite of the rest cure" (see Knight, *Charlotte Perkins Gilman*, 191–192). Strikingly, however, this "type" is represented almost exclusively in Gilman by female, rather than male, physicians. Nor is the woman doctor's intervention always unambiguously positive in her fiction. What are we to make, for example, of a story like "A Coincidence," in which a self-absorbed woman with a serious eating disorder (uncorrected by the series of quack doctors whom she has a habit of consulting) "visits" the narrator's oldest friend one day and ends up staying five years rather than remain with her own sister's family? Convinced that her old friend desperately needs rest and a change of climate, and irritated at watching Mirabella (the freeloader) appropriate all of the candy that she brings as a gift for her friend each time she calls, the narrator enlists the assistance of a certain other friend: "I'd brought in my last protege that day, Dr. Lucy Barnes, a small quaint person, with more knowledge of her profession than her looks would indicate. . . . It was fine to see Dr. Lucy put her finger on Mirabella's weakness."[42] Mirabella is cured of that weakness when the narrator takes them both out for a long ride, bringing along "Dr. Lucy" and offering Mirabella a separate box of fudge; after eating a couple of pieces, Mirabella suddenly falls ill just as the carriage conveniently approaches her sister's gate. Immediately begging Dr. Lucy to help her, she agrees on the spot to return to the home of her sister (who exclaims, "I am so glad she has a real doctor!") and thus liberates the narrator's friend. The implication, clearly, is that Dr. Lucy, or the narrator in collusion with Dr. Lucy, has tainted the contents of one of the candy boxes, in a manipulative (and, to say the least, rather disquieting) exercise in what we are evidently meant to regard, without irony, as a kind of therapeutic food-poisoning.

Most of the time, however, the behavior of Gilman's fictitious medical women, although occasionally expedient, is not quite so irregular or questionable. Take, for example, the diverting, if implausibly didactic, one-act play *Something to Vote For*, in which Dr. Strong ("A woman doctor, from Colorado, interested in Woman Suffrage and pure milk") appears as the guest of honor at a meeting of an antisuffragist women's club, joined by a government milk inspector and by John Billings, head of the Milk Trust and an admirer of the club's president, a socialite named Mrs. May Carroll. In a rapidly devised series of stratagems, the resourceful and appropriately named Dr. Strong manages to enable the milk inspector to demonstrate the impurities of the milk trust's product, to expose Billings in a bribe attempt, to disabuse Mrs. Carroll of her romantic illusions regarding Billings (who is promptly dismissed), and to convert the entire membership of the club to the suffragist cause – thus neatly achieving, at one stroke, a fourfold resolution of the dramatic conflicts at work in the play and a good many of Gilman's own dearest social objectives to boot.

Even when appearing only momentarily, or remaining entirely offstage, women doctors throughout Gilman's fiction are instrumental in facilitating one redemptive outcome or another or become implicated indirectly or tacitly in another woman's gesture toward self-determination. Overwhelmed by the demands of family members, friends, boarders, and clubwomen thoughtlessly exploiting her solitude, the unmarried protagonist of "Encouraging Miss Miller" eventually adopts one of the suggestions advanced by her "doctor, who was a discerning woman," and is thereby freed to pursue "a profound interest in bacteriology" that leads her "to see her name associated, as a co-worker, with one of the most useful discoveries of her time."[43] In "The Widow's Might," Mrs. McPherson astonishes her three children by deciding to retain the property made over to her by her late husband: "I've made two thousand dollars a year – clear – off it so far, and now I've rented it for that to a doctor friend of mine – woman doctor" (Shulman, ed., *Yellow Wallpaper*, 145). Notice, also, the way in which Mrs. Gordins, in "Making a Change," explains to her son the conversion of their apartment into a thriving nursery that has rescued his suicidal wife from the trials of solitary, unvarying motherhood: "I rent the upper flat, you see – it is forty dollars a month, same as ours – and pay Celia five dollars a week, and pay Dr. Holbrook downstairs the same for looking over my little ones every day. She helped me to get them, too" (Shulman, ed., *Yellow Wallpaper*, 189). She helped, in other words, to line up clients, to locate children for the nursery – thus closely associating the presence of women doctors with another of Gilman's favorite innovative concepts – "baby-gardens" – and strengthening the connection that she discerned between the advent of women doctors and the kind of informed and professionalized methods of child care for which she persistently argued.

Perhaps nowhere in her writing, however, does Gilman convey more eloquently and succinctly the distinctive value of such a figure in her own time than in the story "Turned," as the protagonist, Mrs. Marroner, "who held a Ph.D." and "had been on the faculty of a college," discovers in her husband's absence that Gerta, their unmarried eighteen-year-old housemaid, is pregnant: "The thing to do now . . . is to see her through this safely. The child's life should not be hurt any more than is avoidable. I will ask Dr. Bleet about it – what a comfort a woman doctor is!" When he returns to find a deserted home, unaware that she has learned in the meantime that he is responsible for the pregnancy, her husband hires a few private investigators, who "made careful inquiries as to her 'past,' found where she had studied, where taught, and on what lines; that she had some little money of her own, that her doctor was Josephine L. Bleet, M.D., and many other bits of information" – clearly implying that her physician has assisted Mrs. Marroner in escaping her own husband and in forming an independent household with Gerta and the child (Shulman, *Yellow Wallpaper*, 174, 175, 180).

Probably the fullest and most elaborate example of the presence of medical women in Gilman's work occurs, however, in the novel that remains her most obscure, "Mag – Marjorie," a surprising work, in many respects the strongest and most substantial of Gilman's longer narratives and one that is particularly fascinating in the larger context of literary representations of medical women during this period. As in so many of her other stories, an unprotected, potentially "ruined" young woman comes profoundly under the rehabilitating influence of an older woman. Like Gerta in "Turned," Mag is seduced at sixteen by an older man (in this case, unpropitiously enough, a successful gynecologist) and is then rescued by Miss Yale, a financially independent woman in her forties who has made a career of sponsoring lost causes and who takes Mag to Europe, subsidizes her education, guides her through her pregnancy, and provisionally adopts her daughter. What is distinctive about "Mag – Marjorie," however, is that the young woman's mentor or patron is not a doctor, but encourages her protégée to become one herself: "I hope she'll choose the medical profession. We need women there. . . . 'You'll be useful, respected, beloved. You'll be able to save life – that is, if you choose medicine – to heal the sick; to help women and children – men, too.'"[44] Assuring Miss Yale, "You can trust me! I won't fail! I'll do just as you want me to. I'll be a doctor. I'll be a good one!" (100), Mag masters medicine, progressive thought, and fencing in Europe before returning to New England a decade later with an international reputation as a surgeon – the medical specialty perhaps least accessible to American women around the turn of the century.

Failing to recognize her after so many years, Dr. Armstrong, the gynecologist, finds himself powerfully attracted to Dr. Margaret Yale (as she is now called) and is determined at all costs to persuade her both to marry him and to surrender her profession, the notion of a woman doctor being anathema to him. In a rather bizarre effort on his part to subdue Margaret and to demonstrate his supremacy, Dr. Armstrong challenges her to a fencing match in which his greater physical strength would appear to give him an obvious advantage: "But ten years of youth and clean habits counts much in fencing, and while Margaret had no recent practise, she had had four seasons of it, under the best teachers in Europe. If he was hot, she was cold; that still, concentrated mastery which held her hand firm when another life trembled beneath it, held it now" (269). With her study of medicine and agility in fencing already linked much earlier in the narrative and her surgical skills thus indistinguishably merged with her athletic prowess (in a match clearly designed to stage the antagonism between the sexes), Mag's victory represents a triumph over her male opponent in another respect as well, as foretold by Miss Yale in encouraging her to study medicine in the first place: "I want you to Live, . . . and work – and succeed. You can study, take a profession, be a doctor, if you like, be a better one than he is! Get ahead of him in his own line, wouldn't you like that?" (47). Nonetheless, remarkably undeterred, Dr. Armstrong presses his suit (proposing marriage on the condition that Margaret relinquish her calling) and is firmly rejected, only to be followed promptly by his disapproving friend, Dr. Newcome, a respected pediatrician in Boston who has no problem with women doctors, has interacted with Margaret throughout on a basis of equality and mutual re-gard, and suggests to her not only that they combine medical prac-tices but also that they get married – thus achieving the kind of ideally full partnership embodied for Gilman by the McCrackens, the married doctors who befriended her in Chicago, or the "Doc-tors Clark & Clark" whose book on child care she would so enthu-siastically recommend to readers of the *Forerunner.*

This rather drastically abbreviated, foreshortened *Bildungs-roman*, far from "utterly banal,"[45] remains Gilman's major (al-though obviously far from her only) contribution to the volu-minous literature on women doctors between the Civil War and the First World War. While many of her contemporaries among American and English writers tried their hand at characterizing the medical woman, none to my knowledge tried so frequently or portrayed so many imaginary women doctors in so many different works. Part of what makes this series of portrayals so striking is that it occurs not only relatively late in Gilman's career but also near the end of the period that witnessed the initial rise of women in English and American medicine, shortly before the rate at which women entered the medical profession in England and the United States abruptly flattened, as it did by 1920, remaining stag-nant for decades to come. A reminder of the importance of women doctors even as they would soon begin dwindling in number, this aspect of Gilman's writing thus acquires a considerable historical poignancy, while the women doctors in her fiction help bring to an end the extraordinary wealth of imaginative representations of medical women in Anglo-American culture between 1860 and 1920. Within her own accomplishment, the comforting role that she ascribes to women doctors provides us with a timely occasion for reappraising not only Gilman's fiction, particularly her non-utopian novels (still underrepresented in critical scholarship and in editions or anthologies), but also many of the very concerns and preoccupations that lend her thought so much of its continuing power and authority today.

NOTES

1. Richard Harrison Shryrock, "Women in American Medicine," in *Medicine in America: Historical Essays*, 179, 198.

2. Mary Roth Walsh, *"Doctors Wanted: No Women Need Apply"*: *Sexual Barriers in the Medical Profession, 1835–1975*, 89.

3. *The Diaries of Charlotte Perkins Gilman*, ed. Denise D. Knight. Unfortunately, none of the many women doctors whom Gilman mentions (most of them only by surname) is identified in the notes to this edition, while few of them are even indexed (and then often incompletely). The identities of those figures insufficiently well known to be discussed in the historical scholarship have been established with the help of city directories of the period, obituaries in medical journals, or the resources of various local historical societies.

4. Regina Morantz-Sanchez, *Sympathy and Science: Women Physicians in American Medicine*, 286. For an earlier profile of these and other famous women physicians whom Gilman came to know during this phase of her life, see Adelaide Brown, M.D., "The History of the Development of Women in Medicine in California," *California and Western Medicine* 23 (May 1927): 579–582.

5. At a dinner hosted by the writer Kate Douglas Wiggin, Gilman met, among other guests, "a Dr. Salt[o]nstall, (lady)," likely to have been the successful surgeon Florence Saltonstall Ward, on whom Gilman would call at least once after moving to San Francisco (*Diaries*, 447, 590).

6. After her friend married Dr. Christopher S. Lane, a dentist and fellow Nationalist Club organizer, Gilman attended, at "Dr. Kellogg-Lane's" in September 1893, "a Populist conference" designed to "inaugurate social meetings to gather pop. forces" and later "a Social Populist meeting" as well (*Diaries*, 553, 555). Both Gilman and Dr. Kellogg-Lane also spoke, for example, at the annual California Woman's Congress of 1894.

7. Of her other miscellaneous encounters with medical women in San Francisco and Oakland, Gilman recorded several with "Dr. [Elizabeth J.] Corbett" in the summer of 1894 (*Diaries*, 584, 589, 592, 596), when she also attended "quite a class" in economics with several women, "Dr. Margaret Snell among them" (*Diaries*, 595), referring to an Oakland physician who taught at the Snell Academy, a girls' school directed by members of the Snell family.

8. "Pacific Coast Woman's Press Association," *Impress* (26 January 1895): 6. On the instabilities of the Lummises' marriage, cited as an illustration of "the emotional tightrope walked by women who wanted marriage *and* a career" (Morantz-Sanchez, *Sympathy*, 126), see Edwin R. Bingham, *Charles F. Lummis: Editor of the Southwest*, 6–7, 12, 14. Mary Austin, a mutual friend, briefly juxtaposes their marital situation with Gilman's as "another case on hand at the time which called for high partisanship" (*Earth Horizon: Autobiography* [Boston: Houghton Mifflin, 1932], 292).

Five years afterward, Gilman reencountered her now-remarried confidante in Chicago: "Dr. Dorothea [Lummis] Moore to dinner" (*Diaries*, 616).

9. Helen Campbell, "Modern Methods in Healing," *Impress* (26 January 1895): 11.

10. "The Woman's Congress of 1899," *Arena* 22 (September 1899): 343; "The International Congress of Women," *Ainslee's Magazine* 4 (September 1899): 151. The manuscript had been shown to "a scientific friend," "a woman – biological person – (doctor, I think)," who knew Gilman's work and whose criticisms were "all as to the errors in execution. . . . Of the matter she thoroughly approved – was impressed" (see *Journey*, 117–118). Moreover, in 1899 Gilman received "a most rational dignified letter, asking to translate my beloved book," only a year after its publication, "from Mdme. Schmall [*sic*] of Paris, an English born, medically educated, prominent 'feministe' of wide reputation" (Hill, ed., *Journey*, 300). Born in London, Jeanne Schmahl had come to Paris to study medicine, only to end up leading the arduous campaign that would result in 1907 in the passage of the Married Woman's Property Act (often called the Schmahl Law), granting Frenchwomen the right to control their own earnings. (Interestingly, Schmahl edited around the same time a periodical, *L'Avant-Courrière* [*Forerunner*], named after the organization that she had founded to demand such a law.) According to Gilman's later account, *Women and Economics* indeed "was translated into French – but alas! the translator couldn't find a publisher!" (*Living*, 270); it is not clear, however, if Schmahl was in fact responsible for the unpublished translation.

11. Nor were these her only such experiences on the road during this time. In Goldsboro, North Carolina, in May 1898, as the guest of her friend Clara Royall, Gilman attended a "concert by Inmates" of "a Negro Lunatic Asylum," where "Mrs. Royall's aunt is a physician" (*Diaries*, 726); the aunt is not mentioned in Gilman's notorious later recollection of this visit (*Living*, 245).

12. Of the many doctors named above, Mary Hill mentions only "Dr. Kellog Lane, staunch Nationalist co-worker, physician, and personal confidante" (*The Making of a Radical Feminist*, 188), while Ann J. Lane cites "the influence of Dr. Studley, a woman physician who taught hygiene," and refers to Gilman's friendship with "Dr. Gleason," the female Dr. Mc-Cracken, "Mrs. Van Orden, an old friend and physician," and "Dr. Low, a woman physician" (*To Herland and Beyond*, 59, 166, 187, 224, 226).

13. "The Art of Living," *Impress* (27 October 1894): 8; "Women in Public Activities," *Impress* (15 December 1894): 12.

14. "Things We Are Told," *Truth* 21 (June 1902?): 139.

15. "An Answer to a Letter," *Forerunner* 6 (1915): 146.

16. "Are We Pendulums?" *Forerunner* 6 (1915): 175; "A Woman's Party," *Suffragist* 8 (February 1920): 8. Still later, Gilman perhaps unnecessarily conceded: "Women in medicine would have shown more marked attainment but for the discrimination against them as internes in hospital practice" ("Woman's Achievements since the Franchise," *Current History* 27 [October 1927]: 14).

17. *The Home*, 214. Both roles are presented, in her last full-length study, as having originally belonged to women, before the establishment of more recent exclusions. Although "two of the oldest occupations of women, the world over, were that of helping other women to bring babies into the world and that of laying out the dead," according to Gilman, "so soon as the obstetrician found one large source of income in his highly specialized services, and the undertaker found another in his, these occupations became 'man's work'" and "a 'woman doctor' was shrunk from even by women" (*His Religion and Hers*, 72).

18. "Comment and Review," *Forerunner* 5 (1914): 110.

19. Except, it seems, for one issue, otherwise dear to her, on which a celebrated medical woman appeared perhaps too radical even for Gilman, as one can tell from the reference in November 1886 to her first meeting with Dr. Mary Edwards Walker, who favored men's clothing: "Like her; but am not converted. She has no feeling for beauty in costume; thinks it beneath intelligent beings" (*Diaries*, 355). (For her husband's more irreverent account of a later visit from Dr. Walker, see Hill, ed., *Endure*, 322–323.) On the question of reforming women's dress, no one was a more impassioned supporter than Gilman, who nonetheless invokes the same figure, long afterward, as proof of her contention "that the more narrowly specific is a proposed reform, the more narrowly intense become its advocates," citing "the limited ardor of Dr. Mary Walker, who became quite monomaniac on her one profound conviction – that women should wear trousers. She was a competent physician, I understand, and a brave, good woman, but no human intellect can maintain its balance on so small a topic as the redistribution of trousers" (*Living*, 219–220).

20. For an informative recent account of this episode, although without reference to the influence of women doctors, see Jane Lancaster, "'I could easily have been an acrobat': Charlotte Perkins Gilman and the Providence Ladies' Sanitary Gymnasium 1881–1884," *ATQ* 8 (March 1994): 33–52.

21. "Literature," *Impress* (24 November 1894): 10.

22. "Magazines of the Month," *Impress* (22 December 1894): 11.

23. "Comment and Review," *Forerunner* 2 (1911): 85.

24. "The Art of Living," *Impress* (1 December 1894): 8; "Why This Insistence?" *Forerunner* 6 (1915): 81, 82.

25. "The Woman of John Smith," *Kate Field's Washington* (2 November 1892): 277; "What Work Is," *Cosmopolitan* 27 (October 1899): 682.

26. "Should Wives Work?" *Success* 5 (September 1902): 502.

27. "Comment and Review," *Forerunner* 6 (1915): 27.

28. Her admiration, however, was not invariably reciprocated, nor her own iconoclasm always shared, as Gilman herself readily noted more than once in her memoirs. Explaining the failure of the *Impress*, "an excellent paper" that "was spoken of by a competent critic as the best ever published on the coast," she reported the results of "some inquiries as to the rather surprising lack of support, either in subscribers or advertisers," in California: "Said a prominent woman doctor, 'Yes, it is a brilliant paper, an interesting paper, but after what Mrs. Stetson printed in her first issue no self-respecting woman could have it on her table'" (*Living*, 173). Similarly, recalling a leaflet she had designed and "sent to all the names in my address-book," years later, in promoting the *Forerunner*, Gilman observed more cheerfully that "one name was evidently misplaced, for I received the following admirably expressed answer from a woman doctor in Boston: 'I am not interested in the work of Charlotte Perkins Gilman, in monthly or in any other form, nor do I know any one who is'" (*Living*, 308). Although such responses perhaps illustrate one historian's contention that "nineteenth-century women doctors never drifted too far out of the ideological mainstream" (Morantz-Sanchez, *Sympathy*, 61), they nonetheless remain exceptional in Gilman's otherwise remarkably affirmative contact with medical women.

29. "What Makes for Encouragement," *American Fabian* 4 (January 1898): 2.

30. "Community Conservation of Women's Strength," *Proceedings of the International Conference of Women Physicians* 1 (1920): 257–267.

31. After having a "good talk with her, personally and professionally," on one visit to Boston, as she noted afterward, "I am operated upon by Dr. [Helen L.] Betts," who appears to have shared a home with Dr. Keller, and, "who 'depilates' me & otherwise attends to my complexion" (*Diaries*, 199).

32. During this period, Dr. Kellogg-Lane also treated Katharine, whom Gilman took also "to oculist – Dr. [Elizabeth R. C.] Sargent" (*Diaries*, 555) in San Francisco, another of the many women doctors on whom she had called during her spring 1891 visit. On a stop in Denver during her 1899–

1900 lecture tour, Gilman accompanied Helen Campbell to a consultation with yet another medical woman: "Call on Dr. [Nettie H.] Boll[e]s – her doctor – osteopath, & get her view of the case etc." (*Diaries*, 802). (During a visit to Rochester, New York, according to one intriguing entry in her diary, Gilman took a "long walk with Miss [Mary] Anthony to see her doctor" [*Diaries*, 656], which would have been Dr. Marcena S. Ricker, beloved physician of Susan B. Anthony and her sister Mary during the last several years of their lives.)

33. For her first husband's expression of even more conventional sentiments along the same lines, over a decade earlier, see Hill, ed., *Endure*, 210–211, 268.

34. In other examples, at the National Congress of Mothers in Washington, D.C., in 1897, Gilman was tended by her fellow-delegate Dr. Cora Smith Eaton, the Minnesota physician who would later join Dr. Martha Ripley in welcoming her to Minneapolis, where "the two doctor ladies provide me with some 'Gelseminium,' for 'brain fag'" (*Living*, 187; *Diaries*, 802).

35. As expressed, for example, in his novel *Characteristics* (1891), published a year before "The Yellow Wallpaper," and in its sequel, *Dr. North and His Friends* (1900); see Catherine Golden, "'Overwriting' the Rest Cure: Charlotte Perkins Gilman's Literary Escape from S. Weir Mitchell's Fictionalization of Women," in Karpinski, ed., *Critical Essays*, 144–158.

36. "The New Generation of Women," in Ceplair, ed., *Nonfiction*, 278–279, 282–283.

37. In the heroine of *Doctor Zay*, according to Carol Farley Kessler, "exactly at the point when Gilman became unable any longer to focus upon keeping her diary, she encountered a model both for her own later life and for later utopian characters she would create" (*Charlotte Perkins Gilman: Her Progress toward Utopia*, 21–22). Yet it is clear from her extensive reading and from the cultural cachet of the "lady doctor" that many other such works would have provided Gilman with such a model; Phelps herself had portrayed a medical woman over a decade earlier in "Our Little Woman" (1872) and "Hannah Colby's Chance" (1873), short stories that were published in *Our Young Folks* at a time when that popular children's magazine would have been a fixture in the young Gilman's household.

38. For a reconsideration of his portrayal of Dr. Mary J. Prance, see my "'A Line of Her Own': Henry James's 'Sturdy Little Doctress' and the Medical Woman as Literary Type in Gilded-Age America," *Texas Studies in Literature and Language* 39 (Summer 1997): 139–180.

39. Well into her career, as Carol Ruth Berkin observes, Gilman "continued to write stories of wise, older women, strong and independent doctors . . . who appeared out of nowhere to guide some struggling girl to maturity" ("Private Woman, Public Woman: The Contradictions of Charlotte Perkins Gilman," in Karpinski, ed., *Critical Essays*, 151). Yet this essential pattern in her fiction has never been examined systematically. For brief but incisive remarks on the matter, see Lane, *To Herland and Beyond*, 59, 290; and Golden, "'Overwriting,'" 154–155.

40. "Dr. Clair's Place," in *The Yellow Wallpaper and Other Stories*, ed. Robert Shulman, 297.

41. Like, for example, *Moving the Mountain*, in which the male narrator, after vanishing in the Himalayas for thirty years, is rescued by his sister, who "studied medicine" and "practiced a while" and who "took excellent care of me up there on those dreary plains and hills" thanks to "all that medical skill of hers in the background" (*Moving the Mountain*, 15, 16–17).

42. "A Coincidence," in "*The Yellow Wallpaper*," ed. Denise Knight, 158.

43. "Encouraging Miss Miller," *Forerunner* 6 (1915): 311, 312, 313.

44. "Mag—Marjorie," *Forerunner* 3 (1912): 97, 98.

45. Gary Scharnhorst, *Charlotte Perkins Gilman*, 99.

KATHARINE COCKIN

Charlotte Perkins Gilman's *Three Women*
Work, Marriage, and the Old(er) Woman

The writings of Charlotte Perkins Gilman were familiar to the British women's suffrage movement, featured in recitations at events and reviewed in the movement's newspapers. This essay is concerned with a comparative analysis of the published text of Gilman's one-act play *Three Women* and the prompt copy of a production of the play in London in November 1912 for a women's suffrage organization.[1] As Marie Farr notes, there are several texts entitled *Three Women* by Gilman: her short story of 1908 was reworked into a play of the same title, published in 1911, and this published text was revised for the London production of 1912. The issues explored by the play were sufficiently controversial to bear such revisions: the imposition on (white, middle-class) women of a choice between work and marriage.[2] The play disrupts the assumption that such a choice is necessary, proposing instead that it is neither inevitable nor desirable by demonstrating that a woman may achieve both. However, *Three Women* is not only a play about the specific choices imposed on some women, but also one which explores the ways in which those choices are made. This is achieved in two ways: first, the apparently "natural" choice for a woman between marriage and work is deconstructed and revealed to be no real choice at all — a critique of gender ideology which was not unprecedented in drama (and in other genres) written by women in this period. Second, the play explores how choices can be made, specifically presenting a young woman asking advice from older women. The "three women" of the title represent an understated but distinctly alternative set of choices becoming available in women's suffrage discourse in Britain.

In November 1912 two performances of *Three Women* were given at Chelsea Town Hall, London, as part of a major event in the calendar of the Women's Freedom League (WFL). They were directed by Edith Craig (1869–1947), a woman who was attracting a nationwide reputation for directing plays for the women's suffrage movement.[3] The actors in Craig's production were members of a play-producing subscription society closely affiliated to the WFL, called the Pioneer Players.[4] This society was founded by Craig to produce plays for its membership at various London theatres which were hired for the occasion.[5] Many of the Pioneer Players' early productions were concerned with issues relating to women's suffrage or other political issues, such as the campaigns for food reform and against the censorship of the stage.[6]

Reading Edith Craig's production of *Three Women* in the context of her work with the Pioneer Players and other women's suffrage organizations reveals some of the difficulties which the play encounters in its critique of gender ideology. The changes made to the play in the prompt copy invite reflection on some of the complexities, if not difficulties, of Gilman's thinking. Craig's prompt copy emphasizes the ambiguities of the play, destabilizing the resolution in marriage and the representations of the female protagonist. Such changes were appropriate for a production associated with Craig at this time.

The Pioneer Players performed many plays before the First World War which were interested in women's independence in work and marriage. Some of these explicitly rejected marriage or represented women's relationship to a range of work, examining the tensions between class and gender conflicts through the roles of the prostitute and the sweated worker as well as the writer and actress. The representation of woman as worker in the Pioneer Players' productions was not limited to the nurturing role, but considered work for women as a source of self-development through a career and as a necessity, when women were the sole earners for dependents. Although *Three Women* was not one of the Pioneer Players' annual subscription productions and therefore was not acknowledged in the society's annual reports, and since it was not performed in a theatre, it eluded the main biblio-graphical work on London productions in this period.[7] Craig and members of the Pioneer Players would have been attracted to Gil-man's play for several reasons: both Craig and the Pioneer Players were associated with radical thinking, particularly feminist ideas developing from women's suffrage; the society's interest in inter-national culture was demonstrated by its productions of plays in translation (the first of these, Herman Heijermans's *The Good Hope*, was performed just over a week before the performance of Gilman's *Three Women*); the Pioneer Players produced plays by other American writers such as Florence Edgar Hobson, Marjorie Patterson, and Susan Glaspell;[8] members of the Pioneer Players were interested in the central issue of *Three Women* – the attempt to transform relationships between women and men. Moreover, as marriage was to be proscribed for teachers in Britain in the twen-ties, the proposition of *Three Women* was to become increasingly controversial.[9]

The society itself was not, as other critics have asserted, a "women's" company.[10] It was an organization in which women were always in a majority at all levels, but one which gave men equal access to membership. On some occasions men directed plays, and men were always members of the executive and fea-tured as a minority in other types of membership.[11] In this respect the Pioneer Players, like Gilman, were concerned to bring about change for both sexes by extending membership in humanity to women as well as to men. In addition, key members of the Pioneer Players' executive committee, Edith Craig, Christopher St. John, and Gabrielle Enthoven, had particular interests as lesbians in ex-ploring alternatives to marriage and the ideologies which that in-stitution maintains.[12]

Against this background, and in the context of Craig's work with the Pioneer Players, the deviations in the prompt copy from the published text become particularly interesting. *Three Women* is a one-act play which takes place over forty-five minutes and is set in the parlor of Mrs. Morrow, widowed mother of the protago-nist, Aline Morrow, a 25-year-old kindergarten teacher, who is faced with the dilemma of choosing between marriage to Dr. Gor-don Russell or maintaining her career in teaching. Aline's view of motherhood is unequivocal: "What are women for?" She dis-tinguishes between women as persons and women as women:

"as *persons* – [they are] for any kind of work they like. You always forget that women are persons. But as *women* – they are for children" (117). She seems to be claiming both a humanism for women and an essentialism; this not surprisingly baffles Gordon: "I can't see the difference. I see only the woman" (117). Gordon subscribes to the sexual double standard: he expects Aline to give up teaching after marriage since "the duties of the wife and mother come first in a woman's life" (117). He expects her to choose between marriage and career, while Aline demands the possibility/necessity of choosing both. While Aline's views are framed in the play as unconventional, they are limited in this respect; she refuses to choose between marriage and career, but she does not question marriage and motherhood as ideal or even desirable institutions for women. These issues were subjected to a more radical critique in plays directed by Craig for the Pioneer Players.

Another significantly conventional, rather than controversial, feature of Aline's argument at this point is the split between reason and desire; Aline avoids Gordon's distracting proximity, which she feels interferes with her concentration and ability to make a rational decision: "(*Takes both her hands . . . He slips his arm around her, draws her to him. . . . He tries to turn her face to his, but she breaks from him breathlessly.* No! No! Gordon – not yet! You – move me so – I find it hard to be wise (*He comes nearer*) Don't touch me – go and sit over there" (118). Gilman explores female sexual desire here. Aline's breathlessness and need to distance herself allude to sexual arousal; however, she perceives desire as disruptive and threatening to her powers of reasoning, which conforms to conventional discourse on sexuality.

The topic is further explored when, at Gordon's suggestion, Aline seeks advice from her mother and her unmarried aunt, Clara Upton. These two older women provide Aline with conflicting advice. Mrs. Morrow insists that marriage and career can be maintained together and insists forcefully, "DON'T GIVE UP YOUR PROFESSION FOR THE BEST MAN ON EARTH!" (119). This warning is given with such emotion that Mrs. Morrow is prompted to disclose her own sacrifice of career in exchange for marriage. She gave up the possibility of becoming a singer, exchanging "a Voice" for a husband. This metaphorical silencing is presented by Mrs. Morrow as "the loss of my life" (120). She is adamant that Aline should lose neither her Voice (career) nor her voice (right to choose). In her view Aline should follow her Aunt Clara's example, since she is happy and successful in her work as an artist.

However, Clara Upton's image is deceptive. She identifies two aspects of her unmarried life as causes of her unhappiness. One is not having a child; the other seems to be the sexual relationship with a man which marriage may imply. Clara's description of her yearning is incomplete; female sexual desire is signified through the unspeakable dashes: "It's not only the babies, Aline. It's the husband! Women are not supposed to care — They do — !" (121). Clara understands her mistake as choosing her career at the expense of motherhood and a sexual relationship.

Mrs. Morrow and Clara Upton discover that they have both been unhappy and regretted their past decisions, but disagree about the decision Aline should make. When Gordon returns, both women put their different arguments to him and, with conventionally feminine submission to man's better judgment, expect him to persuade Aline. However, although he abnegates responsibility to Aline, Gordon is convinced that sacrifice characterizes a woman's life: "After all, she must decide. . . . But a woman must choose between her career and marriage" (122), not both. Before the two older women make their final exit, Clara Upton, no longer vociferous but resigned, agrees with Gordon: "Well, Molly, he's right. You chose — I chose — now she must choose. Come. We must leave it to her. (*They go out much depressed.*)" (122).

Despite this, the inevitable sacrifice which this invites us to expect from Aline is not forthcoming. Instead Aline's new sense of self-determination is demonstrated by a change in her physical appearance and demeanor, which is ultimately (and unexpectedly) not motivated by seeking Gordon's approval. Gordon remarks, "I don't know you tonight, Aline. You are another woman, somehow" (123), while the stage directions describe her as "exquisitely dressed" and "mischievously" creeping up behind Gordon to startle him. The difference between Gordon and Aline is marked at the fundamental level of language: Gordon does not understand her; she talks in "riddles" and "sophistry." Even so, he reads her transformation as an erotic challenge: "You look about sixteen to-night! You are deliciously beautiful! And puzzling beyond words! You say you love me. I feel that you love me. You do, don't you dear? Yet you sit there talking like a judge. If I shut my eyes I seem to hear the New Woman laying down the law. If I open them – Lilith couldn't be lovlier [sic]" (123). Gordon's increased desire for Aline is articulated through infantilizing her. While her appearance and mannerisms have become more conventionally feminine and therefore attractive to Gordon, he categorizes her arguments as those of an inevitably unattractive New Woman. In contrast, Aline is now better able to control her desire for him: "*She lets him sit on the sofa beside her, and then faces him so calmly that he feels more remote than before*" (123).

Aline's response to Gordon's declaration is to claim that her love for him is unconditional. She recognizes that he is *both* a man and a doctor; she expects him to accept likewise that she is *both* a woman and a teacher. Her argument seems to be a demand for women to be included in a humanist framework. She summarizes the advice she has received thus: "I have advised with my family. I have seen the effects of this choice you require – the choice between living and loving. I have seen what it means to a woman to have love – and lose life. And what it means to have life – and lose love" (124). The terms in which the advice was given, and those in which Aline understands it, set "living" and "loving" as oppositional and mutually exclusive. In this scenario the prospective husband is placed in the role of love-giver but destroyer of life. Gordon's response is unapologetically framed in these terms: "It is the woman's problem, and must be faced. You have your Life. I offer you – Love. Which will you choose?" (123). This sustained ultimatum is met with Aline's sustained demand: "Both if you please." Only two speeches before the end of the play, quite incredibly, Gordon apparently changes his mind: "I thought I knew best about this Aline. But you may be right." He has the last lines: "We will try it together, Aline. Only love me!" The change is abrupt, and it is not clear what has caused it. Gordon seems to have been affected by Aline's emotional outburst rather than by her logical argument. When Aline "*sinks down on the cushions hides her face, sobs – or laughs,*" Gordon's attempts to comfort her are rejected: "*Then she turns her face and smiles up at him entrancingly, her head back on the velvet cushions, her two great roses lifted to her chin*" (124). The excess and ambiguity of this scene signify the metatheatricality of femininity as Aline's deliberate actions coalesce into a conventional pose.

Three Women seems to compare with many of Gilman's short

stories where a dilemma is overcome through the transformation of the individual and the plot is happily resolved.[13] The main actions in *Three Women* follow a fairly conventional dramatic syntax. An ultimatum is imposed. After advice is sought, a decision is taken to reframe the available choices; the either/or possibility is rejected in favor of both/and. The formulaic conventions of romance are sealed with the play's apparently happy ending: Aline Morrow succeeds in achieving marriage and work and transforms Dr. Gordon Russell's opinion to accommodate this. Yet the closure, with the promise of marriage dictated by the romantic mode of the play, is subtly undermined by the emphasis on the "three women" of the title and the prominence of the dialogue and transformation of the female characters. In this context, the closing embrace intimates an ironic perspective on the promise of happiness.[14] These ambiguities were emphasized in Edith Craig's production by manipulating significant features of the published play: the ending; the representation of "happiness"; and the process of making choices.

The ending of the play is provisional and in some respects open: the marriage agreement is uneasily and abruptly reached after considerable doubts; the future seems to offer some degree of struggle between the couple; Aline's emotional response is equivocal. This is stated clearly in the stage directions: it is not clear whether she is laughing or crying. The possibility of crying suggests Aline's sense of defeat or that she may have feigned tears together with her conventionally feminine dress in order to reinforce her logical argument, which seemed to be failing. The possibility of laughter is more disturbing, dependent on Aline's sufficient distance from Gordon to appreciate the ridiculous aspect of his ultimatum and to enjoy the empowerment which refusal (or reframing the terms of his argument) has brought her.

The extent to which the older women are happy is also questioned, as they are both revealed to be self-consciously acting out their happiness as a disguise.[15] However, it is significant that we do not see the older women as victims since they are neither objectified nor presented just from Aline's point of view. Instead, the older women are represented confronting their mistakes; they confess to their failures and are seen to undergo a change, albeit limited, marked by their "*depressed*" exit.

The play explores the process of making choices; the main, and extremely disruptive, choice in the play is imposed by Dr. Gordon Russell. Russell, like the male doctor in Gilman's other writings (e.g., *The Crux* and "The Yellow Wallpaper") is the carrier and enforcer of dominant ideology. He is therefore most in need of change. Mrs. Morrow deconstructs Gordon's assumption of masculinity by comparing the medical profession with the caring role in the family. She suggests that Gordon's argument could well be applied to his own abilities: if, as Gordon argues, Aline's work as a kindergarten teacher prepares her for her new role as mother, then his work as a doctor would equally qualify him as a babysitter. Gordon's insistence that Aline choose between her work and marriage registers as intransigent in contrast to the older women, who confront and reflect on their own decisions and provide a form of consultation for Aline. As sole representative of a monolithic, masculine perspective (there is no other male character in the play to offer advice to balance that of the older women) Gordon is thus subject to rigorous critique.

The dramatic shape of the play mentioned earlier foregrounds the relationship between Aline Morrow and Dr. Gordon Russell and the dilemma based on the choice to be made by a woman between marriage and career. The play is linear, chronological, and realist, presenting coherent, knowable characters whose actions seem to be resolved at the end. However, the title *Three Women* invites a different perspective, centering on the female characters. Marie Farr argues in her essay that the title signals a critique of the Hegelian model of thought. Gilman's play certainly seems to be about more than the dilemma of keeping the job and getting the man. The play foregrounds relationships between women and how these affect (even alter) relationships between women and men at a fundamental level. It defies stereotype, representing older women neither as victims nor as objects of ridicule. Rather it presents advice from older women as valued by the younger generation but significantly (and audaciously) presents this advice as both flawed and promoting change. In this respect the play refrains from idealizing the female agent of change, a temptation which was not resisted by all British writers supporting women's suffrage.

The representation of older women as capable of recognizing mistakes is comparable to the representation of the man in the play as capable of change. Change is brought about through rational argument, but that rational argument is based on an oppositional perspective. In the published play, this is unexpectedly highlighted by a typographical error. After Aline seeks "some sagacious advice on a very solemn question" from her aunt (120), the stage directions indicate the exit of "*Alien.*" Aline is very much an alien visiting the world of the older generation of women, gathering information on the way they think and live. She finds that she is unprepared to sacrifice herself; she wants it all and refuses to pay for it. This marks her difference. To Gordon her views are monstrous; she is the self-destructive and threatening new species of New Woman, a woman who is not a woman. The typographical error underwrites Aline's outsider status, foregrounding the difficulty of placing her unconventional ideas, if not the difficulty of realizing them.

Gilman's audacious exploration of unconventional ideas has been well documented by critics, particularly in her utopian fiction, which explicitly deals with the female as alien. In this play Gilman's outlook is optimistic in that she presents both women and men as capable of change. However, *Three Women* raises many questions and possibilities which it fails to answer or cannot explore further. In this respect it is typical of the "feminist play of ideas" produced by Edith Craig and the Pioneer Players for which they were castigated by such critics as Rebecca West and Virginia Woolf.[16] *Three Women*, like much of Gilman's shorter fiction (with the exception of "The Yellow Wallpaper"), appears to be formally closed and didactic, with, as Carol Farley Kessler notes, "cultural work" to do.[17] On closer examination, and particularly in the light of Craig's prompt copy, the ending of the play is unsettling in a manner which places it in the context of plays by other Pioneer Players dramatists (such as Cicely Hamilton, Jess Dorynne, Edith Lyttelton, and Florence Edgar Hobson) which strain against the realist form and its ideological frame. The prompt copy of *Three Women* makes cuts to the stage directions which prescribe the manner in which Aline's femininity is made apparent to Gordon, particularly the descriptions of the manipulative manner in which Aline looks at him. Of greater significance are the cuts to the ending of the play, specifically the episode in which Aline becomes emotionally upset and rejects Gordon's attempt to comfort her, and the final words of the play. Gordon's line "Only love me!" is cut, perhaps reflecting on the impact of this injunction as another ultimatum or condition set by Gordon, reappropriating his control of the situation even after Aline seems to have succeeded in changing his mind. The prompt copy therefore makes the ending of the play more ambiguous.

Craig and the Pioneer Players were involved in producing plays which parodied the concept of the New Woman,[18] which, as early as January 1894, had been identified as the site of a reverse discourse.[19] It seems significant, therefore, that it is Gordon in *Three Women* who terms Aline a "New Woman" at the moment when he is articulating his increased desire for her. Gilman may be suggesting that Aline's power, signified by the autonomy of the New Woman, threatens Gordon. His changed opinion is therefore motivated by a desire to control Aline in marriage. The romantic plot instigated by Gordon's ultimatum fails, even though the marriage appears to be ensured. Conflict seems to be read by Gordon as titillation, a prelude to inevitable conciliation, which Craig's cutting of "Only love me!" undermines.

In an ideal world, drama and desire would, for Gilman, be deployed differently, as indicated by the male narrator's response in *Herland* (99): "The drama of the country was — to our taste — rather flat. You see, they lacked the sex motive and, with it, jealousy. They had no interplay of warring nations, no aristocracy and its ambitions, no wealth and poverty opposition."

Since loving has already been opposed to living, loving Gordon on his terms could prove deadly for Aline. Perhaps the ending of Gilman's play indicates the extent to which even Aline's unconventional arguments and her determination to be independent within marriage risked being appropriated by Gordon as another attractive feature, a challenge which must be subjugated. The published text's final words "Only love me!" therefore form an injunction, a final demand, reinscribing Gordon's power. Gordon's designation of the New Woman role for Aline has already indicated his position and his inclination to disempower her.

Rosemary Hennessy has argued that the construction of the New Woman was determined by a conjunction of international capitalist, imperialist, and patriarchal discourses (*Materialist Feminism*, 105). The New Woman signified an attempted commodification of the potentially subversive threat of feminism posed by women's demands for education, enfranchisement, and equality in employment and under the law. The deployment of the image of the

New Woman was symptomatic of the instability of the bourgeois family, subject to pressures exerted by the increased education of women and their admission to professions. Nevertheless, women who had been castigated as New Women faced the dilemma of rejecting the views and values of older, conventionally feminine women, often including their mothers. The conventionally feminine or "Womanly Woman" was the object of trenchant critique by suffragists, while "New Woman" was a term of abuse constructed by masculine discourse to disarm an emerging feminism by "appropriating and rewriting the signifiers of an oppositional discourse" (107). This is one problematic feature of the ending of *Three Women* which Craig's prompt copy seems to be addressing by minimizing both Gordon's reappropriation of the situation and the implication of Aline's recourse to a manipulative femininity. By contrast, the effect of Gilman's ending to the play is to express the risk Aline takes in entering into marriage with Gordon, risking reinscribing the hegemony of patriarchy.

As Martha Vicinus has argued, the women's suffrage movement in particular made possible the forging of relationships between women which were ordinarily discouraged.[20] Even so, Gilman's play, like other women's writing in this period treating the New Woman phenomenom, presents relationships between women (those between older and younger women particularly) as sources of anxiety as well as sources of radical knowledge. Relationships with older women (distantly related but rarely their mothers) promise transformation for the younger generation of women. *Three Women* marks a generational difference between women, a mourning by the older woman for lost or unattainable opportunities and an unease of the younger woman, who must make a break from femininity. If femininity is frequently represented by the mother, the alternative is signified by the other (older) woman who is supportive, either in terms of advice or in terms of financial assistance. This scenario is also found in Gilman's short stories,[21] and is most clearly staged in Bessie Hatton's women's suffrage play, *Before Sunrise*, where the break from femininity is articulated by the older-other woman in metaphorical terms of a liberation from restrictive clothing: "Our minds are enveloped in moral stays, just as our bodies are pinched and tortured to take on an unnatural and ugly shape."[22] It is an underdeveloped and destabilizing feature of *Three Women* that the empowering agency of the other

woman is absent and that a triad of women is given such a prominent aspect but peremptory function.

If *Three Women* is a play which ostensibly explores the difficulties in changing relationships between women and men, it
implicitly urges the reassessment of relationships between women
(signified by both the title of the play and the function of the older
women characters). While Aline has been designated a "New
Woman" by Gordon (and inadvertently as "Alien" by the typeset-
ter) her relationship with the two older women, Mrs. Morrow and
Clara Upton, is less clearly defined. Aline seeks, but then rejects,
the advice of both her mother and her aunt. This is not presented
as confrontational and is therefore different from the father/son
conflict which characterizes male-authored Edwardian literature.[23]
The play nevertheless recognizes the differences between the
younger and the older generation of women, a phenomenon which
concerned cultural commentators involved in British women's
suffrage. Cicely Hamilton, for instance, argued for new ways of
thinking for women, but she was as aware as Gilman of the power
of dominant ideologies to prevent such oppositional perspectives
from taking effect. In her speech "The Spirit of the Movement"
given to the Central London Branch of the WFL, Hamilton argued that "behind the Suffrage movement is the new consciousness in woman that she is free to think for herself. . . . Think of
the years, of the generations, that women have been told they must
not think! . . . We see things with a view which is entirely different from that which our brothers had; they saw them as their fathers saw them, but we see things very differently from the way
our mothers saw them" (*Vote* [14 January 1911]: 140).

Hamilton's sense of a gendered perspective and a generational
rift between women is relevant to the argument posed by *Three
Women*. The break in a matrilineal tradition is signified in the
play by the depressed exit of the mother and aunt, which suggests
that the difference between women across generations is painful,
but it is invariably resolved through reconciliations between
women in relationships other than the mother/daughter dyad.
Both Hamilton and Gilman seem to agree on the value of addressing, rather than suppressing, differences between women. As
Hamilton argued: "We have got to allow for the difference of
opinion, and to encourage it."[24]

Some plays produced by the Pioneer Players before November

1912 had espoused rejection of marriage as a legitimate response to the legal subjection of women. These included Jess Dorynne's *The Surprise of His Life*, in which the female protagonist refuses to marry the father of her illegitimate child. He has been pressured by her father, concerned to preserve his business reputation under the guise of preserving the family honor. After learning that her aunt had faced a similar experience and had regretted her submission to an unwanted marriage, the younger woman decides that a marriage of convenience, or of any kind, must be rejected. The play ends with the prospect of setting up house with her aunt and with the promise of support from local suffragists. Like *Three Women*, this play represents women talking to each other as a means of transformation and resistance to oppression. Women's discussions about their experiences of marriage also occupy much of Margaret Wynne Nevinson's *In the Workhouse*,[25] and in Herman Heijermans's *The Good Hope* women talk about their experiences in a fishing community dependent on the daily risk of working on unseaworthy vessels because shipowners value profit above the sailors' lives. So while Gilman's representation of women talking is dramatically effective, as Marie Farr suggests, it was also a common dramatic feature of drama performed in support of women's suffrage in Britain.

Gilman was a familiar figure to readers of the WFL newspaper, *Vote*. In the months leading up to the production of *Three Women* in 1912, *Vote* had reviewed two of Gilman's books (*The Man-Made World* on 13 January and *What Diantha Did* on 17 February) and reported that her writings had been used in lectures and as recitations at suffrage events.[26] Gilman was therefore well-known to suffragists in Britain and to members of the WFL in particular, which covered international developments in women's enfranchisement, reporting on developments in the United States and elsewhere. Edith Craig's production of *Three Women* was one of several plays and entertainments which formed part of a three-day International Suffrage Fair organized by the WFL in November 1912. The fair, held at a time of political controversy, coincided with a march of women from Edinburgh to London to present a petition to the prime minister, which led to the founding of the Qui Vive Corps. In the same month Lansbury resigned his seat and forced a bye-election over the issue of women's suffrage and the so-called white slave (Criminal Law Amendment) bill was proceeding through Parliament.[27] The numerous events staged at the fair and the high profile of the march meant that *Vote* gave minimal coverage of Craig's production of *Three Women*. However, shortly before the fair, Craig's production of "a suffrage play" had been announced. The review remarked briefly that "this sprightly Suffrage play was much enjoyed."[28]

Gilman's play may have been chosen for production by Craig because it was a work of an American woman and could be said to enact the theme of the fair: "unity in diversity." Some writing by women in this period tends to be locked into a dualistic dynamic, merely reversing gender roles and failing to challenge underlying structures of oppression. There are, however, significant incidences of cultural engagement with differences and dissent between women as a means of promoting change, a means by which women can work together. These representations are radical in their intimations of a thoroughgoing "unity in diversity." This redefinition of femininity and desire goes beyond the formulation of the New, or even the Old Woman and beyond the dyad and the binary opposition of difference which characterizes the institution of marriage. *Three Women* addresses the phenomenon of attempts to reappropriate power from radical women; it entertains the idea that relationships between women involve acknowledging disagreements, that being divided on issues may not necessarily be divisive. More than exploring the implications of including women in such a democracy and the effect this may have on intimate relationships, Gilman's play touches on some issues which encompass the libidinal economy on which marriage is based as well as the social limitations which it imposes.

Gilman's *Three Women* exposes the painful exchange into which women are compelled to trade themselves (and their potential children) for marriage and economic security.[29] This process is denaturalized and scrutinized by Gilman's play, and new social relationships are explored. The instability in the treatment of the maternal-feminine in its guise of career-carer is confirmed in Craig's alterations to the play for her production. The proprietorial male gaze which can only see Aline as either New Woman or eroticized child is framed by the exchanges between the three women which envisage other possibilities. Aline's alien status is achieved when she refuses sacrifice and discusses the economy of child-rearing. While Aline's work as kindergarten teacher is seen to predispose her to the role of child-rearing, the corresponding exploration of Gordon's work as a doctor is more controversial. Even though Aline is cited as a "world mother," her insistence on sustaining her career as a kindergarten teacher, paid work as a career-carer, threatens the idea of the natural-maternal and the necessary and unpaid sacrifice which it entails.

For women challenging conventional femininity in the early twentieth century, the older woman (sometimes an aunt or friend of the family) offers a means of negotiating the difficult relationship between the radical daughter and the feminine mother. The triad or community of women emerges as a significant phenomenon, in some cases representing a challenge to the institutions of marriage, family, and heterosexuality.[30] In Gilman's *Three Women* the triad of women must be displaced by the impending marriage: she proposes merely a revision of the institution of marriage.[31] The radical opposition to all three institutions was already a reality for Edith Craig, the woman who directed Gilman's play in London as part of the WFL's political campaign for enfranchisement.

NOTES

1. The prompt copy, floor plan, props list, and play program fragments of Charlotte Perkins Gilman's *Three Women* are held in the National Trust's Edith Craig Archive, Ellen Terry Memorial Museum, Tenterden, Kent (hereafter ETMM); permission to quote from this material is gratefully acknowledged. The prompt copy consists of an annotated copy of the published play from the *Forerunner* (with the same page numbering) and relates to Edith Craig's production of the play at the Chelsea Town Hall on Wednesday and Friday, 13 and 15 November 1912, as part of the Women's Freedom League's (WFL) International Fair, which had been postponed from February 1912. This is the text which is cited below.

2. The short story preceded the play (*Success*, 1908) and featured an ending different from both published play and prompt copy.

3. Edith Craig (1869–1947) directed many plays in support of women's suffrage, including nationwide productions of *A Pageant of Great Women*, which she devised with Cicely Hamilton. Craig is cited in a national newspaper as one of the "stars" who is to contribute to the WFL's International Fair organized by Mrs. Kate Harvey of Brackenhill, Bromley, Kent (*Daily Herald*, 7 November 1912: 2). See my *Edith Craig: Dramatic Lives.*

4. The actors were all members of the Pioneer Players at the time of performance. Olive Terry (designated "Teevey" in the review and play programs) was an acting member from 1911 to 1912 and a member of the executive from 1911 to 1920. The other actors (Charles King, Ruth Parrott, Jane Comfort, and Elaine Limouzin) were all acting members of the society during the period 1911–1915. See Pioneer Players' Annual Reports (ETMM).

5. The Pioneer Players developed from Craig's involvement in producing plays both independently and through the Actresses' Franchise League (AFL) for various women's suffrage organizations. The AFL was involved in the International Suffrage Fair in the production of Evelyn Glover's *A Chat with Mrs. Chicky*, directed by Inez Bensusan, but the responsibility for Gilman's play is attributed to Edith Craig personally.

6. Craig's production of Laurence Housman's *Pains and Penalties* on 26 November 1911 at the Savoy Theatre incurred the wrath of the Lord Chamberlain's office, which was empowered to grant or withold licenses for publicly performed plays. *Pains and Penalties* concerned the treatment of Queen Caroline by her husband, King George IV, and his refusal to admit her to the coronation ceremony. Florence Edgar Hobson's play advocating vegetarianism, *A Modern Crusader*, was produced by Craig to raise money for the National Food Reform Association.

7. The Pioneer Players' constitution allowed the society to perform plays to raise funds for other organizations. Many of these plays were not recorded in the annual reports. It is likely that *Three Women* was one of these unofficial productions. For recorded productions see J. P. Wearing, *The London Stage, 1910–1919: A Calendar of Plays and Players* and Pioneer Players' Annual Reports.

8. Herman Heijermans, *The Good Hope*, translated by Christopher St. John, was produced on 3 November 1912 at the King's Hall. Florence Edgar Hobson's *A Modern Crusader* was produced on 30 April 1912 at the King's Hall. In it the older woman regrets her conformist life but is satisfied that she is able to financially endow the younger generation, who are able to put into practice some socially radical ideas. Marjorie Patterson's *Pan in Ambush* was produced on 6 February 1916 at the Court Theatre. This play features an invisible and mischievous Faun to whom marriage is a curse. Susan Glaspell (1882–1948) was the author of *Trifles*, produced on 9 February 1919 at the King's Hall, and *The Verge*, produced on 29 March 1925 at the Regent Theatre.

9. See Alison Oram, "Serving Two Masters? The Introduction of a Marriage Bar in Teaching in the 1920s," in *The Sexual Dynamics of History*, ed. London Feminist History Group, 134–148.

10. See Julie Holledge, *Innocent Flowers: Women in Edwardian Theatre*; Christine Dymkowski, "Entertaining Ideas: Edy Craig and the Pioneer Players," in *The New Woman and Her Sisters: Feminism and Theatre 1850–1914*, ed. Viv Gardner and Susan Rutherford, 221–233.

11. For detail of membership and activities of the Pioneer Players, see Cockin's unpublished Ph.D. thesis, "The Pioneer Players (1911–1925): A Cultural History," (forthcoming Macmillan).

12. Christopher St. John (Christabel Marshall, d. 1960), writer, lived with Edith Craig for most of their lives (from 1899). Tony (Clare) Atwood (1866–1962), artist and member of the New English Art Club, joined them in 1916, forming a *ménage à trois* which was sustained even after the backlash against lesbianism in 1928 with the trial for obscenity of Radclyffe Hall's novel *The Well of Loneliness*. St. John, Craig, and Atwood socialized with Hall and Una, Lady Troubridge, who lived nearby in Kent. Gabrielle Enthoven (1868–1950), whose unique theatre collection was donated to the Victoria and Albert Museum and now forms part of the Theatre Museum's collection, became first president of the Society for Theatre Research in 1948. Enthoven was a friend to St. John, Craig, and Atwood, but seems to have been less courageous in her response to the vilification of Hall. See Michael Baker, *Our Three Selves: A Life of Radclyffe Hall*.

13. Ann J. Lane, "The Fictional World of Charlotte Perkins Gilman," in *The Charlotte Perkins Gilman Reader*, xv.

14. A similarly destabilizing effect has been identified by Sheila Stowell in the drama of Cicely Hamilton, whose play *Jack and Jill and a Friend* (which she directed for the Pioneer Players in May 1911) closes with an embrace between the hitherto antagonistic couple. This uneasy, yet "happy" ending reminds a modern audience of the sinister closure of Harold Pinter's *The Homecoming*.

15. Joan Riviere ("Womanliness as a Masquerade," *International Journal of Psychoanalysis* 10 [1929]: 303–313) has influenced recent feminist critics interested in femininity as a denaturalized performance (see also Judith Butler, *Gender Trouble: Feminism and the Subversion of Identity*).

16. Rebecca West, "A Modern Crusader," *Freewoman* 2.27 (May 1912): 8–10. Virginia Woolf, "A Higher Court," *New Statesman* (17 April 1920), reprinted in *Essays of Virginia Woolf*, ed. Andrew McNeillie, 207–210.

17. Jane Tompkins, quoted in Carol Farley Kessler, "Consider Her Ways: The Cultural Work of Charlotte Perkins Gilman's Pragmatopian Stories 1908–1913," in *Utopian and Science Fiction by Women: Worlds of Difference*, ed. Jane L. Donawerth and Carol A. Kolmarten, 126.

18. In *The Conference* by Delphine Gray (Lady Margaret Sackville),

produced on 6 February 1916 at the Court Theatre, the "New Woman" phenomenon is the object of ridicule as an outmoded concept. The plays produced by the Pioneer Players before Craig produced *Three Women* employ the term "pioneer" rather than "New Woman" to signify feminist, conforming to common practice in the WFL newspaper.

19. "As New Woman is she known. / Tis her enemies have baptized her, / But she gladly claims the name; / Her's [sic] it is to make a glory, / What was meant should be a shame" (D. B. M., "The New Woman," *Shafts* [January 1894], reprinted in *The New Woman*, ed. Juliet Gardiner, 15).

20. Martha Vicinus, *Independent Women: Work and Community for Single Women 1850–1920*.

21. See Lane, "The Fictional World of Charlotte Perkins Gilman," xv.

22. Bessie Hatton, "Before Sunrise," in *Sketches from the Actresses' Franchise League*, ed. Viv Gardner, 16.

23. See Anthea Trodd, *A Reader's Guide to Edwardian Literature*.

24. "The Spirit of the Movement," *Vote* (14 January 1911): 140. To counteract this disturbing rift, women's history played an important part in identifying a female tradition for the women's suffrage movement. This was dramatized in Cicely Hamilton's play *A Pageant of Great Women* (1910), which she devised with Edith Craig, and in Christopher St. John's *The First Actress* (1911), both of which were produced by Craig for the Pioneer Players.

25. One suffragist reviewer remarked: "How the women in the end stick by each other and refuse the honour of any alliance with the man is well worked out" (*Common Cause* [25 April 1912]: 44–45). Margaret Wynne Nevinson's *In the Workhouse* was produced on 8 May 1911 at the Kingsway Theatre.

26. Janette Steer (ordinary member 1912–1913, acting member 1911–1912 & 1913–1915, of Pioneer Players) recited Charlotte Perkins Gilman's "An Obstacle" at Charlotte Despard's birthday party held at Caxton Hall, London (*Vote* [13 July 1912]: 204). Miss Munro was reported as having quoted two of Gilman's poems to illustrate her lecture, followed by a recital of a Gilman poem by Miss Mary Pearson at a meeting of the Croydon Branch of the WFL (*Vote* [3 February 1912]: 178).

27. *Daily Herald* [20 November 1912]: 2; *Daily Herald* [12 November 1912]: 5; *Daily Herald* [2 November 1912]: 5. The Honorable George Lansbury (1859–1940), Labour MP for Bow and Bromley, resigned in support of women's suffrage.

28. *Vote* [23 November 1912]: 59. The author of the play is designated incorrectly in this review as "Mrs. Charlotte Gilmans Perkin."

29. See Luce Irigaray, "Women, the Sacred and Money," in *Psychoanalytic Criticism*, ed. Sue Vice, 182–193. Irigaray argues that child-rearing is the natural sacrifice expected from women in patriarchy; to challenge the structure of this economy would involve estimating its costs. During the period in which Gilman's play was produced by Craig, Cicely Hamilton had taken on just such a challenge in *Marriage as a Trade*.

30. See Christopher St. John's play *Macrena*, produced by Edith Craig for the Pioneer Players on 21 April 1912 at King's Hall; and Gertrude Colmore's short story "The Nun," *Vote* [29 June 1912]: 175.

31. The proposition of an egalitarian marriage is realized in Gilman's short story "Making a Change" (1911), in *The Charlotte Perkins Gilman Reader*, ed. Ann J. Lane, 66–74. In Gertrude Jennings, "A Woman's Influence" (in *Sketches from the Actresses's Franchise League*, ed. Viv Gardner, 67–74), as in Gilman's *Three Women*, the apparently insurmountable differences between a couple make a prospective egalitarian union seem extremely difficult if not implausible.

Home Is Where the Heart Is – Or Is It?

Three Women *and Charlotte Perkins Gilman's Theory of the Home*

Contemporary scholars of Charlotte Perkins Gilman's work examine her fiction – especially the short story "The Yellow Wallpaper" – occasionally her poetry, but rarely, and then only glancingly, her drama. Yet some of her most radical ideas are embodied in her plays. Scholars, as Joanne B. Karpinski points out, have also been interested in her "relationships to other major thinkers of her era" as well as "her life and thought in the context of social issues" (*Critical Essays*, 9). A central issue for Gilman was the replacement of the sentimentalized idea of home with practical measures of reform, an idea she developed through the first decades of the twentieth century in her fiction, prose, and especially drama.

Theatre was dear to Gilman's heart: she loved attending performances and even acted in a troupe in Pasadena. As early as 1888 and as late as 1921 she was collaborating with Grace Ellery Channing in playwriting, though few of these plays apparently reached publication. Gary Scharnhorst's bibliography lists two one-act plays published in Gilman's journal the *Forerunner*, and Ann Lane's biography describes a third, presumably unpublished.

Gilman's interest in the theatre, however, developed at a time when parlor theatricals, evolved from the charade, became acceptable to the middle class and when both feminists and antifeminists began to use them to spread their messages for and against woman suffrage.[1] Gilman was not slow to see the possibilities of parlor theatricals for delivering her messages on social reform. Although she claimed that "the basic need of economic independence seemed to me of far more importance than the ballot," she

nevertheless worked for what she termed this "belated and legitimate claim," most specifically by writing the pro-suffrage play
Something to Vote For in 1911 and publishing it in the *Forerunner*
one month after *Three Women* (*Living*, 131; Friedl, *On to Victory*, 24–25). In the next month's issue she advertised performance rights to either play for $5.00 or a subscription to her jour-
nal, offering "Suffrage organizations or Clubs" the opportunity to
receive commissions for selling *Forerunner* subscriptions at these
performances ("About Dramatic Rights," 179).

Evidently, then, Gilman was aware of the efficacy of using dramatic form to embody her ideas for social improvement. A number of critics, of course, have commented on her use of fiction in
this way. Polly Wynn Allen, for example, says that Gilman knew
of stories' "educational potential. She recognized the capacity of
strong fiction to move people, confiding to her diary in 1893, 'If I
can learn to write good stories it will be a powerful addition to
my armory'" (*Building Domestic Liberty*, 145). Indeed, she used
both fiction and drama to embody her ideas, first, about women's
economic and social subordination to men, elaborated theoretically in *Women and Economics* and *The Man-Made World*, and,
second, about the retardation of human progress caused by the
restriction of women to the domestic sphere, an idea summed up
in *The Home*, which she called "the most heretical – and the most
amusing – of anything I've done" (*Living*, 286). And her ideas
were heretical, for they called for the emancipation of woman
from the home, not as a matter of equality but, due to the home's
wastefulness and inefficiency, as a matter of logic.

Her "heretical" ideas about the home may have begun coalesc-
ing as early as 1895, when she participated in the second convention of the Woman's Congress Association of the Pacific Coast,
which had as its theme "The Home" (Lane, *To Herland and Beyond*, 164). Not only does restricting women to the home keep
them from developing *their* potential, she believed, but also that
of the child and husband. The outdated concept of home itself
"hinders, by keeping woman a social idiot, by keeping the modern
child under the tutelage of the primeval mother, by keeping the
social conscience of the man crippled and stultified in the clinging
grip of the domestic conscience of the woman. It hinders by its
enormous expense; making the physical details of daily life a
heavy burden to mankind; whereas, in our stage of civilisation,

they should have been long since reduced to a minor incident" (315). These "primitive industries" of cooking, cleaning, and child care, Gilman insisted, must be modernized and made efficient by combining the needs of many households and employing professionals for each task instead of housewives, who, because of the variety of their burdens, remain inefficient and sometimes ineffectual amateurs. Yet as late as 1906 Gilman still saw women's options as miserably restricted: "we have so arranged life . . . that a woman must 'choose'; must either live alone, unloved, uncompanied, uncared for, homeless, childless, with her work in the world for sole consolation; or give up all world-service for the joys of love, motherhood, and domestic service" ("Passing of Matrimony," 496). Since reasoned discourse, as outlined in *The Home* and other works of social theory, did not necessarily move people to accept her revolutionary ideas, she turned to literature.

Revising the age-old androcentric love plot (which she termed "Adventures of Him in Pursuit of Her"), she found a "distinctly fresh field of fiction": the "position of the young woman who is called upon to give up her 'career' – her humanness – for marriage, and who objects to it" (*The Man-Made World*, 96, 105). *Three Women: A One-Act Play* dramatizes precisely that conflict and Gilman's proposed solution.

"Feminist scholarship of the last twenty years," says Ann Romines, "has begun to provide the tools we need to read women's writings about housekeeping not as safely minor diversions but as central, powerful, and potentially explosive documents of women's culture. . . . About the time of the Civil War . . . American women began to write about housekeeping in a new way, not as the unarticulated denouement of every female story but as subject and ongoing substance, in itself" (introduction, in *The Home Plot*, 9). By the end of the nineteenth century Gilman, too, became focused on the effect of housekeeping as "central, powerful, and potentially explosive," though, unlike the novelists Romines examines, she never assigned much value to women's culture, insisting that "social progress . . . [is] attained wholly by the male" outside the home (*Home*, 312). It is attained through the freedom to concentrate on one job: "Men, specialised, give to their families all that we know of modern comforts, of scientific appliances, of works of art, of the complex necessities and conveniences of modern life. Women, unspecialised, refuse to benefit their families in like proportion; but offer to them only the grade of service which was proper enough in the Stone Age, but is a historic disgrace today" (100). She argues, therefore, for the necessity of women's access to that specialization, so that they may also contribute to social progress.

Three Women presents Gilman's fictionalized solution – a prenuptial agreement acknowledging the woman's right to work – to middle-class women's economic (and therefore sexual) dependence on men in marriage. In December 1911, seven months after the play appeared in the *Forerunner*, she also published a story called "Making a Change," which uses essentially the same situation – a woman who wants to work and a husband who does not approve – but locates it *after* the wedding, thereby demonstrating her communal solutions to housekeeping and child care as practical and reasonable.

The short story "Three Women" was first published in *Success Magazine* in August 1908. After making some significant changes, Gilman then published it as a play in the May 1911 issue of her own journal, the *Forerunner* – directly under the motto beneath the masthead: "If a moral distinction between men and women is necessary, men may be blamed for the sins of commission – women for the sins of omission." The play reflects that motto, since the older women, Aline's mother and aunt, have settled for the omission of half of their potential lives, and Aline's dead father was the one exacting that sacrifice from his wife. But as with most of Gilman's creative works, the play's ending reflects her essential belief in social progress, for the young woman determines to avoid the older generation's mistakes.

In the similarly titled story and play,[2] the setting and plot are identical. The setting is the Morrow home, that average middle-class American home Gilman calls "the least evolved of all institutions," where she wickedly describes "keeping house" as "the running of the commissary and dormitory departments of life, with elaborate lavatory processes" (*Home*, 30, 69). The plot is simple: an attractive young kindergarten teacher, Aline Morrow, receives a proposal of marriage from a handsome and ambitious young physician, Dr. Gordon Russell. Like most men of his time, however, after marriage he expects her to give up her profession. Aline, however, intends to keep her career, insisting that she can arrange for the housekeeping and child care as well as teach. Seeking advice from her mother, who gave up a singing career for husband and children, and from her aunt, who refused love and marriage in order to continue her successful painting career, Aline finds that, ironically, the advice of each is to do the *opposite* of what she had done: her mother tells her not to "GIVE UP YOUR PROFESSION FOR THE BEST MAN ON EARTH!" and her aunt "*fiercely*" demands, "Forswear [your career]; forget it – and thank God for a good man's love" (119, 121). Neither is happy with her life's choice.

Despite Gilman's many years as a successful unmarried career woman (after her first marriage failed, she remained single until age forty), despite her firm commitment in fiction as well as in her personal life to women's relationships, and despite her ambiguity toward marriage demonstrated in "The Yellow Wallpaper," in *Three Women* she elevates marriage over single life. In fact, she sounds like Virginia Woolf's matchmaking Mrs. Ramsey in asserting, "People must marry. People ought to marry" (*Home*, 109). Because she remains a firm believer in the necessity of both work *and* marriage for a fully realized humanity, she makes Aline decide she will have both. And that will be possible only if Aline's lover revises the sentimentalized identification of home with women in which he (and most turn-of-the-century society) believes.

In the play Dr. Russell considers Aline's desire impractical, but Aline proposes solutions to the problem Gilman had targeted earlier in *The Home* – too many duties to allow the housewife to do any single one well. Aline says, "You know how we live here – you know how good the food is – and how cheap – and how little service is required, or management. If we had a house this way – with meals and service from outside – I could be as free as I am now" (118). Thus housekeeping and cooking are turned over to professionals who can raise standards by bringing education and experience to their work.

Aline's suggestion also answers Gilman's objection to the private home as expensive, wasteful, and inefficient – expensive because buying is done privately and not in bulk, wasteful because individual kitchens are needed, and inefficient because private cooks take the same amount of time to feed six as to feed thirty. After marrying Houghton Gilman, her second husband, Charlotte took her own advice and for six years arranged for them to get "table-board" from a commercial kitchen (*Living*, 283; Allen, *Building*, 59).

Avoiding an attack on Aline's plan, Gordon responds with a sentimental appeal to motherhood: "The best use of all your kindergartening will be to help you when your own little ones demand your care. Can you not foresee?" (118). Aline's indignant reply reflects Gilman's assumption that motherhood is the goal of all women: "Can I not foresee? You, a man, ask me, a woman, if I cannot foresee motherhood! I have foreseen it since I was a child" (118). When he assumes that "the Teacher would give way to the Mother," she pleads with him not to misunderstand her: "I should still be a teacher – and a better mother because of it" (118).

Gilman makes a similar assertion in *The Home*: a child "wants a strong, serene, lovely mother for a comfort, a resource, an ideal; but he [*sic*] also wants the care of a trained highly qualified teacher, and the amateur mama cannot give it to him. Motherhood is a common possession of every female creature; a joy, a pride, a nobly useful function. Teacherhood is a profession, a specialised social function" (328).

The mothers and motherhood which permeate the play reflect a central and troubling issue in Gilman's life, both because she had given up her daughter to the more stable home life of her first husband, who had remarried, and because her own mother was either unable or unwilling to demonstrate her affection. Mrs. Morrow may be the mother Gilman wished she could have been, but it is equally possible that she is the mother Gilman wished she could have had: in this interpretation, her mother, withdrawn and distant in life, is dramatically recast as the loving and devoted mother of Aline. Like Aline's mother, Charlotte's mother was musical and had developed "unusual talent" but had to sell her piano – giving up her music, not for a determined husband as in the play, but, since Frederick Beecher Perkins had deserted his family, simply "to pay the butcher's bill" (*Living*, 9).

Motherhood, always on Gilman's mind after she relinquished her child and suffered vilification as a "bad mother," is symbolically associated with all the women characters. Not only does Aline teach kindergartners who "*worship* her" – definitely a nurturing profession – but one pupil's mother calls Aline "a world-mother" who has "genius" (115). Her aunt, Miss Upton, longs for what she has denied herself; a "great critic" compliments her as an artist who "not only painted mothers and children" but "motherhood" itself (116). And Aline's mother finds her only consolation for giving up her career in her daughter.

Both older women use language such as "empty" and "spoiled" to describe their lives, and predict that Aline will be "hungry for love" but "starve" without work (120–121). Thus food and love are linked. Both the infantile food deprivation imagery and the asserted necessity of connectedness (the latter reminiscent of psychologist Carol Gilligan's 1980s research) suggest that Gilman saw women primarily in essentialist terms.[3] In fact, she has Aline promise Gordon to take care of the housework and family because that "is plainly the woman's duty" (123). Carol Ruth Berkin claims that "Gilman, like many of her contemporary feminists, could not ultimately envision woman liberated from the task of nurturance itself, could not imagine woman pursuing work for her own personal satisfaction or solely for its challenge to her mind and ambitions" ("Private Woman," 32).

Despite Gilman's linkage between women and nurturing work, I suggest that in this play, at least, she does seem to have her protagonist squarely facing the issue of personal satisfaction and demanding that it be part of the marital bargain. Polly Wynn Allen implies a similar conclusion about Gilman's "realistic" fiction: she claims that "except for the recurrent figure of Mrs. MacAvelly, no character is portrayed mothering other people endlessly without looking after her own needs" (Building, 162). After all, in The Home Gilman had shown she stoutly believed in an exchange of work: "Human progress rests upon the interchange of labour; upon work done humanly for each other, not, like the efforts of the savage or the brute, done only for one's own" (101–102).

Some of that interchange, according to Gilman, should be in shared child care. In Three Women Mrs. Morrow suggests that the couple could have the house, with Gordon's office on the first floor and living quarters above, so that he could be available to the children when Aline was out teaching. She offers to supervise Aline's children until they are old enough for the kindergarten and continues ironically: "And if those children were in mortal peril I guess a grandmother and a doctor-father – with a trained nurse –

could keep 'em alive until you were telephoned for" (119). In *The Home* Gilman had baldly stated that "the care and education of children are legitimately shared by the father" (288). She sees wife and husband as partners, though she admits that men "at present" do not do their share of this essential labor.

It seems significant that Gilman assigns both mother and aunt artistic talent, something she respected in her first husband, the painter Walter Stetson, but refused to claim for herself, saying, "I was never a careful writer" (*Living*, 241). And it is true that she wrote so quickly and voluminously that she rarely had time for revision. Yet her work in transforming the story "Three Women" into a play shows her awareness of dramatic conventions — probably from her acting experience in Pasadena after the separation from Walter (Lane, *To Herland*, 143) — and a definite talent for dramatic presentation. For example, in the play she adds a highly effective scene in which the sisters, mother and aunt, who have envied each other for years, reveal for the first time the buried secrets of their true unhappiness with what they have missed in their lives. Despite discovering that the other does not have the perfect life she envisioned, each maintains that her advice to Aline was right. Nevertheless, both agree that Aline must choose between love and work, just as they did (122).

Gilman refuses to make Aline choose and also refuses to collaborate in portraying women stereotypically. This surfaces when Dr. Russell (his professional title in the stage directions highlights society's emphasis on professionals as male), returning for the answer to his proposal, enters into a dialogue with Aline; as she argues rationally and her fiancé tries to persuade her emotionally, attempting to kiss, embrace, and caress her as she speaks, the stereotypes are reversed. Gilman may have "feared emotionalism in women," as Ann Lane concludes, because it has allowed them to be manipulated (305); if so, in this play she deliberately forecloses that possibility. In a speech from the play (which is similar in the story), Aline insists, with highly effective rhetoric:

Listen now. Let me say all I have to say, and then *you* may decide, if you please, whether to abide by *your* choice or not. You asked me to marry you — then made conditions. I am willing to marry you. *I* make no conditions. I do not say, "You must give up smoking," or "You must be a total abstainer," or "You must choose between me and something else you love." I love you, Gordon, unconditionally. (*He tries to embrace her, but she checks him.*) I love a man who is a doctor, a splendid doctor. I would marry the man and be proud of the doctor. You love a woman who is a teacher, a devoted one. You would marry the woman; she would be your wife. You wouldn't marry the teacher. She would go on teaching. (123)

But Dr. Russell easily dismisses her arguments as "sophistry" and responds with puzzlement to the disparity between her rational discourse and her appearance: "If I shut my eyes I seem to hear the New Woman laying down the law. If I open them – Lilith couldn't be lovlier [*sic*]" (123). His opposing the (supposedly un-attractive, even masculine) New Woman to the seductive first wife of Adam tells us which he desires.

That her critique of this type of gendered thinking was not new to Gilman is reflected in the crux of a play written more than twenty years before *Three Women*. Entitled *A Pretty Idiot*, this play was written by Gilman and her close friend Grace Ellery Channing during the summer of 1888 (Lane, *To Herland*, 139). In it, the heroine describes her ideal woman as someone "with both intellect and muscle, having a career of her own," while her suitor, who values only her "fresh and innocent youth" and her "exqui-site beauty," thereby proves himself unworthy of her (quoted in Lane, *To Herland*, 139). She finds her true lover in a man who values her in her entirety and does not dismiss her "masculine" ambitions – just as Aline is finally able to get Gordon to agree to a wife who is also a teacher.

But such positive endings, while *de rigueur* for drawing room comedies, in a sense reflect Gilman's wish-fulfillment. In actu-ality, the exchange just quoted between Aline and Gordon reflects Gilman's own experience with her first husband, Walter Stetson. Like Aline, Gilman told her suitor emphatically that her life's work was essential to her. At that time, in 1882, when she was but twenty-two years old and he twenty-four, she saw her choice as between a career and marriage, because "I like to be *able* and *free* to help any and every one, as I never could be if my time and thoughts were taken up by that extended self – a family" ("An Anchor to Windward," 866; see also *Living*, 83). Therefore she rejected his initial proposal. Two years later, however, she said "yes" to the proposal with the understanding she could have both, but found, according to Ann Lane, that her husband "heard the words, he understood their meaning, but he seems not to have comprehended the seriousness with which Charlotte held these opinions and their importance to her" (*To Herland*, 85). In a letter to Grace before the wedding Gilman emphasizes, not her marriage plans, but her "plans for teaching and writing and studying for *living* and helping," concluding, "Well, he knows what to expect" (in Lane, *To Herland*, 92). Like Gordon Russell, Walter Stetson did not know; in his journal Stetson revealed his view of Charlotte to be stereotypically Victorian: "She was innocent, beautiful, frank. . . . I loved all that I saw pure in her" (in Lane, *To Herland*, 82). And so, according to Lane, "They talked at each other, presenting arguments and counterarguments," but "his overriding goal was to win" (93).

The question of Gilman supporting herself after marrying was answered negatively by Walter – although he did make an exception for writing (Lane, *To Herland*, 93) – and this experience undoubtedly contributed to her emphatic judgment that it is wrong to consider such ambition "unwomanly" (*Home*, 280). In the short story "Three Women," Aline tells her mother, "I believe he'd rather wait [to marry], hard as it is, than to have my earning money make it easier for him. It's not reason – it's feeling. You can't reason against feeling" (522). Gilman recognized that unreasoning (and unreasonable) feeling of a threat to masculinity as psychologically powerful: man "considers any effort of the woman to support herself as a reflection on him. He has arrogated to himself as a masculine function the power of producing wealth; and considers it 'unfeminine' for a woman to do it; and as indicating a lack of manliness in him" (*Home*, 290).

That fear, unfortunately, is still very much with Americans, according to contemporary feminist critic Susan Faludi in *Backlash: The Undeclared War against American Women*. She cites "a little-noted finding by the Yankelovich Monitor survey, a large nationwide poll that has tracked attitudes for the last two decades," which reveals that during the past twenty years women as well as men (32 percent versus 37 percent in 1989) have consistently defined masculinity in the same way – not, as one might expect, as "being a leader, athlete, lothario, decision maker, or even just being 'born male.' . . . [but] rather, being a 'good provider for his family'" (65, 482). On this basis, a woman earning her own living attacks her partner's masculine self-image.

Although Gilman explored the inequities of gender issues all of her life, sexuality held great ambiguity for her. From her parents she learned that sexuality could mean death through childbirth or even desertion (Lane, *To Herland*, 38). From the women she loved as intensely as she loved men, she learned to separate love from sex. And despite her apparent bisexuality, in her creative work she focused primarily on heterosexual relationships. According to Ann Lane, in her theoretical works she insisted that sex was only for reproduction and did not change her stance to include "the expression of mutual love" until she published *Social Ethics* in 1914, three years after *Three Women* (284). Again and again she condemned excessive sexuality, seeing it as the result of exaggerated "unnatural" sex distinction between men and women, inextricably linking it to what she termed the "sexuo-economic relation," by which she meant, "She gets her living by getting a husband. He gets his wife by getting a living. . . . The sex-functions to her have become economic functions. Economic functions to him have become sex-functions" (*Women and Economics*, 110). And so the effect is to create "an exaggerated sense of the importance of food and clothes and ornaments" (*Women and Economics*, 120), an idea she developed further both in *The Home* and in a later work, *The Dress of Women*. Like Mary Wollstonecraft, Gilman saw that by encouraging women to stress sexual allure in order to attract men society inevitably kept women dependent and unable to develop their full human potential.

Nevertheless, Gilman recognized the potency and persuasiveness of "sex appeal" and was not above using it in her creative work. So in the opening of *Three Women* Aline, a rational being much like the public image of Gilman herself, pays little attention to her appearance and does not understand why her aunt, a "*vivacious, handsome, richly dressed, successful and popular*" woman of forty, wishes her to change her dress because her suitor is coming (115). But when he returns for her answer and Aline knows she must persuade Gordon to give up his traditional prejudice and accept her arguments, she appears "exquisitely dressed in a white, misty, clinging, shimmering gown with an elusive sparkle in it. Her hair is beautifully done, much more softly and richly than her usual method. A red and white rose are tucked in her hair, and she carries one of each in her hand" (123). Dr. Russell first is amazed and then spellbound: "I knew you were lovely, but I never knew you so enchanting" (123).

Whereas in appearance Aline fulfills Gordon's stereotypical expectations, by her actions she repudiates the submissive fairy-tale heroine, reminding us of Gilman's assessment that "Patient Griselda has gone out, or is going, faster and faster" (*Home*, 326). Aline's agreement to be his wife is offered "*very coldly and without interest*," while her refusal to give up her work is delivered "*gently, warmly, tenderly, with her heart in her eyes*" (123). In this "war of the roses" the flowers she wears symbolize love and life. When Gordon tries to make her choose between them, declaring, "It is the woman's problem, and must be faced," Aline uses all her feminine arts, including sobs and/or laughter – we are never sure which – to convince him she should have both (134). She "*smiles up at him entrancingly*" and says, "If I were a man – and a lover – and the woman I loved was willing to marry me, I don't *think* I'd let a thing like this stand between us."

At this point the play and story diverge. In the story Gilman makes it clearer that Gordon is so mesmerized by her beauty that he literally cannot think straight:

> "I thought I was right about this, Aline. I think so still – somewhere – but I can't bring it to mind. You – are so confoundedly beautiful! It isn't fair!"
>
> "I am not fair?" she asked, like a big-eyed child; and she was so fair that he gave a little cry and caught her to his heart.
>
> "I won't stand this any longer!" said he. "You have owned you love me – and I'm going to marry you! Do you hear?"
>
> "And I may do – what I think right? You'll let me?"
>
> She put up a hand against him, but her eyes, her mouth, her whole sweet presence, gave no denial.
>
> "I'll let you do anything you think right, Aline," he said solemnly. "Only love me!"
>
> And the roses were crushed and forgotten. (526)

This ending is psychologically more convincing than the ending of the play for two reasons. First, Aline's assumption of the child/woman role (eliminated in the play) as well as the role of enchantress provides motivation for Gordon's change of heart; second,

Gordon seems to retain mastery by "letting" Aline have what she wants.

The play, however, in emphasizing the force of logic, makes a stronger political statement. In this dramatic version, Gordon's capitulation comes more abruptly. When Aline tells him she wouldn't "let a thing like this stand between us," Dr. Russell simply says, "I *thought* I knew best about this, Aline. But you may be right." Her response – "My dear – you must take me as a teacher or not take me at all" – recalls her earlier refusal to deny herself either a working or a personal life and seems at the same time to deliver a gentle ultimatum. Gordon's acquiescence – and relinquishment of the mastery – is mirrored as much by his sitting down beside her on the sofa as by the final words of the play: "We will try it together, Aline. Only love me!" (134).

All of her life Gilman was concerned about systems of duality: masculinity/femininity, work/marriage, economic dependence/ economic independence. Ann Lane suggests that she "offered women" rationality "as a way of breaking down the dichotomy be- tween public/private, objective/subjective, active/passive, mind/ body, rational/emotional" and that after 1890 she was finally able to begin taking "the experiences that tormented her and chained her and project them onto a public screen, there to look at them, expose them, examine their sources and thereby put them to rest by understanding them" (305, 157). Thus it seems likely that Gil- man's personal attempts to refuse bipolarity – notable in her re- jection of the label "feminist" in favor of "humanist" and in her choices of both women and men as objects of love – contributed to her decision to have Aline refuse a choice between two paths, work and marriage, which are presented as opposites. The play's title, in fact, accurately depicts *three* women and three choices. The first two women make opposing choices – thesis and antithesis – while the third declines the false unity of a synthesis in which the two marital partners become one. Certainly Aline does wish to have both work and marriage, but while she envisions a "beautiful future together" she also wants "a beautiful future separately"; she does not intend to be swallowed up in the relationship (117). Therefore she makes clear that a distinction remains between the "wife" who marries and the independent self defined by her work. Gilman's concern is echoed by many contemporary feminists who find the system of dualistic thought prevalent in Western culture restrictive and identity-denying.

In one respect Gilman is like Susan Glaspell, who also published the same work as story ("A Jury of Her Peers") and play (*Trifles*). She focuses on marriage as silencing women like Aline's mother and Glaspell's Mrs. Wright, both of whom loved singing. But in this work Gilman seems to try to head off the situation she found in Henrik Ibsen's *A Doll House*, which she read in 1891 (*Diaries*, 2:442). So that Aline will not have to leave her husband's house, as Nora did in order to find herself, the author focuses on the young couple's having a clear understanding about their roles and expectations before they marry. This, according to Ann Lane, is what Charlotte attempted, consciously, in the hundreds of letters she wrote to Houghton Gilman before they married in 1900 (191). She did not want the same misunderstanding between them after marriage as after her marriage to Walter.

One reason for such misunderstandings, believes Gilman, is the hypocritical stance society takes toward the role young women are expected to play in romantic encounters. A speech by Mrs. Morrow found in the play but omitted in the story critiques such hypocrisy. When Aline suggests how difficult it is "to tell a man your views on post-matrimonial industry before he proposes," her mother responds, "Of course it's difficult! Whatever the girl does is difficult! She's supposed to be blankly innocent and unsuspecting, and to say 'This is so sudden!' else she's unwomanly. On the other hand, 'a true woman' always knows if a man loves her! If she does not foresee it all and stave him off in what they call 'a thousand delicate ways' – then she's accused of leading him on" (119). Perhaps inspired by Gilman's personal experience, these words describe a double-bind women still face nearly a century later.

Although by 1900 Gilman had resolved the work/marriage conflict in her own life with the marriage to Houghton, recognizing she could indeed have both, in the 1908 short story "Three Women" she seemed to tilt the balance toward marriage. But in the play written three years later she clarifies the priority of work. Whereas in the story she has Aline agree with Gordon that "the duties of the mother and of marriage come first" (491), in the play she repudiates that idea, saying, "No honestly – I don't agree with you. I think the first duty of anybody – man or woman – is to do their best work for the world" (117–118). Writing Houghton before their marriage Gilman says, "I would choose the work, if I died next day, just *because* it means so much" (quoted in Lane, *Herland*, 207). And she spelled out her belief more fully in the introduction to *The Home*: "We are here to perform our best service to society, and to find our best individual growth and expression; a right home is essential to both these uses" (4). What she predicted when women were no longer "narrowed by the home" (*The Home*, 277) was that, instead of supporting the entire family himself, a man would have "a vigorous helpmate, to honourably support herself, and do her share toward supporting her own children" (289).

By the 1930s when she was writing her autobiography she was able to evaluate the problems professional women were likely to have: "In our prehistoric status of 'domestic industry' there is some progress, but not much. The increasing cost and decreasing efficiency of domestic servants teaches most women nothing. They merely revert to the more ancient custom of 'doing their own work'" (*Living*, 320–321). She remained optimistic that this would change because the "double-pressure goes on; more and more professional women, who will marry and have families and will not be house-servants, for nothing; and less and less obtainable service, with the sacrifice of the wife and mother to that primal altar, the cook-stove. This pressure, which marks the passing of the period of domestic service and the beginning of professional service – cooked meals brought to the home, and labor by the hour – will gradually force that great economic change" (*Living*, 321). To date, that economic change, while bringing more women into the work force, has yet to provide more than Kentucky Fried Chicken or pizza deliveries. Domestic chores are still largely done by individual women – housewives – or not done at all. Only with child care has the communal idea caught on nationally, and its value is still being hotly debated.

Polly Wynn Allen suggests that the automobile, which moved people to suburbia and out of the urban settings where communal kitchens and child-care services were practicable, interfered with the development of Gilman's vision (*Building*, 167). She points to two 1920s projects influenced by Gilman's ideas: the Institute for the Coordination of Women's Interests in Northampton, Massachusetts, which from 1927 to 1932 "offered Northampton residents the opportunity to purchase inexpensive cooked food (delivered) from a community kitchen, house-cleaning services, and child care," and Yelping Hill, "a cooperatively owned summer colony in West Cornwall, Connecticut, [which] consisted of kitchenless cottages attached to common living and dining rooms, served by a child-care program" which operated until World War II (169). The post-World War II climate was not conducive to Gilman's ideas, because the government's propaganda machine was busily reidentifying women with babies and domestic life so that they would give up their jobs to returning soldiers (Evans, *Born for Liberty*, 229–241). However, in recent years the rise of feminism and ideas about social justice have spawned a number of communal projects worldwide. Allen points to Israel's kibbutzim, Sweden's "collective houses," and other "serviced residential projects" in Europe and the United States "as giving built expression to Gilman's communal ideal" (*Building*, 170).

One of these is being built today in North Carolina. In Carrboro, an Orange County town, a "cohousing" community appropriately named Arcadia will mingle private ownership of housing with shared services: residents will eat supper each evening in a "common house." Though Gilman would hardly have approved of rotating the cooking, which should be the work of a professional, she would approve the nationwide trend of about thirty cohousing sites "completed or under development" today, because they seem to mediate between utopian communal living and private households (Jackson, "Cooperative Community," A1, A14).

Despite these promising changes in social climate, reading *Three Women* raises issues as relevant to this end of the twentieth century as to its beginning. Students in my Women in Literature courses enjoy the play because it poses the problem of marriage/career so neatly. Although most are not convinced by Gilman's idealized ending ("We will try it together, Aline. Only love me"), reading Gordon as either lying or temporarily seduced, the women in the class, like Gilman herself before her marriage to Walter, firmly believe that they will have marriages with husbands who accept their careers as equal. But ideology about woman's place – in the home – has changed little in this century. Although American women today have greater access to education and employment outside the home than they did at the turn of the century, they are expected by society to care for the children; mothers, but not fathers, are blamed when "latch-key" children get into trouble. And they are still expected to "keep house." Yet "labor-saving" devices, research shows, do not provide women with more free time. As Ruth Schwartz Cowan concludes in *More Work for Mother*, "With all her appliances and amenities, the status of being a 'working mother' in the United States today is . . . virtually a guarantee of being overworked and perpetually exhausted" (213). Many of Cowan's historical conclusions echo those Gilman propounded in *The Home*.

A socialist who disclaimed Marx but built her philosophy on the economic basis of women's social status, Charlotte Perkins Gilman admired Elizabeth Cady Stanton and Susan B. Anthony as part of a period of "real heroism," but she never considered herself a pioneer. Rather, she said, "The pioneers of the Woman's Movement began with Mary Wollstonecraft, early in the last century, and ceased to be such when their message was listened to politely" (*Living*, 216). In large part, this is what happened to Gilman after the First World War: she was listened to politely. But today, with the Third Wave of Feminism overtaking us, women are listening to her intently once again. Her challenge to us is summed up in the question which serves as an epigraph to *The Home*: "*Shall the home be our world . . . or the world our home?*"

NOTES

1. I am indebted to my colleague Denise Sutton, now a Ph.D. student in women's studies at Clark University, for bringing this phenomenon to my attention through her unpublished paper "From the Parlor to the Proscenium: Women Take the Stage," 8 December 1992, where she points out, "The parlor play, performed in the domestic sphere of middle-class women, provided a medium which would enable the feminist movement to communicate on a large scale." See Karen Halttunen, *Confidence Men and Painted Women*, especially chapter 6, where she maintains that the "message of parlor theatricals was simply this: middle-class social life was itself a charade" (185).

2. Unless otherwise noted, all quotes from *Three Women* come from the published play text.

3. Carol Gilligan argues that "the psychology of women that has consistently been described as distinctive in its greater orientation toward relationships and interdependence implies a more contextual mode of judgment and a different moral understanding. Given the differences in women's conceptions of self and morality, women bring to the life cycle a

different point of view and order human experience in terms of different priorities" (*In a Different Voice*, 22). Joanne B. Karpinski concludes that Gilman "accepted the notion of essential as well as acculturated gender differences between men and women: the crux of her argument was that these differences were valuable enough to be fully expressed in every aspect of human interaction, rather than confined to a separate and unequal feminine sphere" (*Critical Essays*, 14).

YVONNE GAUDELIUS

Kitchenless Houses and Homes

Charlotte Perkins Gilman and the Reform
of Architectural Space

In the second half of the nineteenth century, many feminists devoted a great deal of attention to architecture, the divisions of space, and the intersections of space and gender. These feminists raised fundamental questions about what was called the private, or woman's, sphere and the relationship of the private sphere to the constructed architectural spaces that supported and helped create the private and public spheres. As Dolores Hayden writes, "They challenged two characteristics of industrial capitalism: the physical separation of household space from public space, and the economic separation of the domestic economy from the political economy."[1] As Polly Wynn Allen states, these feminists, both male and female, "became convinced that a collectively revised architecture would be crucial to the social empowerment of women."[2] They further believed that "the exploitation of women's domestic labor was central to the perpetuation of sexual inequality. They consistently proposed material solutions involving both economic and spatial change" (20). Of particular interest in these visions for architectural reform is the understanding that in calling for changes such as collective child care and collective housework, material feminists recognized the need to break down the isolation incurred through the gendered separation of public and private sphere. They sought to bring what were traditionally considered female activities into what was traditionally considered the male public sphere.

Among the many ways that Charlotte Perkins Gilman might be described, one is as a material feminist. In her writings she proposed a radical revision to our approaches to the architectural spaces of our daily lives as they both create and are created by ideologies of gender. Calling for collectives to provide services such as housecleaning, meals, and child care, Gilman suggested the design and creation of such spaces as the kitchenless house: a house in which neither women or men would be required to labor incessantly in order to produce a home. She argued that without such far-reaching changes the evolution of society would grind to a halt because women would forever be trapped in a space that forced them to remain without access to the public sphere and its attendant privileges.

Some of the earlier rethinkings of the domestic architectural spaces within the home established women more firmly in the private domestic sphere. For example, writers such as Catherine Beecher, Gilman's great-aunt, proposed a model for a home that was "above all a space for woman's domestic labor in the service of men and children."[3] The goal of projects such as Beecher's was to give women control over the private, domestic spaces of the home. Beecher believed that such control was necessary if women were to gain equal footing with the control that men had in the public sphere. While Beecher recognized that such a position did not give women access to the public sphere, she believed that women should follow this course of action for the good of society. While they might not gain power through such a strategy, they would gain their reward in heaven.

In marked contrast to this Gilman understood the need to liberate women from the confining domestic spaces of the home; it is her vision of women who are free from these constraints, and the implications that this carries for the evolution of society, that gives her work its compelling force as an analysis of architectural space. As Polly Wynn Allen states, "more than anything else, she wanted to liberate women from solitary, burdensome housework. To that end she urged women to pursue as many strategies as they could think of appropriate to the particular location and circumstances" (*Building*, 163). Gilman's strategies included a separation between women and the domestic sphere and, more completely, a removal of the duties traditionally associated with the domestic sphere from the house.

Women, Work, and the Home

It is obvious that the problem of architecture and its relationship to gender is not a new one. In their most optimistic accounts, authors such as Charlotte Perkins Gilman, Marie Howland, and Jane Addams predicted that by the end of the twentieth century the problems surrounding the inequities of architectural space and its dependent gender ideologies would very likely be solved.[4] However, in the writings of our own contemporary feminist architects and theorists we find many of the same issues that a number of earlier feminists were addressing. Just as nineteenth-century material feminists called for a close examination of how women's material conditions in the spaces in which they lived affected their lives, so writers such as Leslie Kanes Weisman in her book *Discrimination by Design* discuss how spaces and architectural designs manifest the restrictions placed on women by reinforcing patriarchal gender roles and definitions. For example, one of the more widely written about gendered spaces is the home, in which rooms such as the kitchen and the study can be classified in terms of gender, the kitchen being "female" and the study "male."

Architecture, in its broadest sense, can be considered the structure that we give to our environments. However, while potentially useful, this loose definition does not indicate the social, political, or economic values that are built and rebuilt into the literal and theoretical construction of this term. The gendered identity of architecture becomes neutralized through its supposed objectivity and through the institutional structures and discourses that give it definition. In this case, gender is assumed to be a prearchitectural given. As architectural theorist Mark Wigley ("Untitled") points out, this is due largely to the perpetuation of architectural canonical texts whose "laws" inscribe gender specification on space and form in architecture, while giving the illusion of being prearchitectural. In this case, gender in architectural space is protected from analysis by the very discourse that constructs it.

Factoring into the perpetuation of gender divisions are the dichotomies that are imbedded within architectural practice, theory, and discourse. A prime example of this type of dichotomy, generated by patriarchal systems of binary thought, includes the division of architectural spaces into those that are defined as art and those that position architecture as an everyday activity. As such, buildings that are based upon professional designs that contain sanctioned aesthetic decisions are presumed to be clearly different from buildings that do not involve such aesthetic decisions as a part of their design.

Architectural critic Diane Ghirado points out in her introduction to *Out of Site: A Social Criticism of Architecture* that there is a great deal of difference between Architecture with a capital *A* and architecture with a small *a*. Big *A* Architecture is Art (also with a capital *A*), whose existence and health rely upon a profession that cannot afford to have itself associated with the blue-collar activity of building. Ghirado states that "there is a tacit and often explicit professional agreement that nonarchitect-designed buildings cannot be considered Architecture" (11). That big *A* Architecture is kept separate from little *a* architecture is a matter of professional survival for architects.

Little *a* architecture, however, comprises approximately 80 percent of the structures that are built in the United States.[5] Just as literary canons are formed around the exclusion of, for example, the works of women writers, so too architectural canons are established. Not only do these canons exclude small *a* forms of architecture, but they also serve to keep in place the relationship between architecture and ideologies such as gender. Through the virtue of the power of art, big *A* Architecture legitimates what is built. A feminist analysis of architecture, by placing gender at the center of inquiry, necessitates a dialogue that unveils this paradigm. We need to move away from typical formal dialogue that establishes dualisms and dichotomies within architecture – for example, the distinctions between big *A* and little *a* architecture, public and private domains, interiors and exteriors, form and decoration, which are conditions in which one term, by necessity, becomes subordinate to the other. Inscribed in the language of the institutions (architecture, art, academia, etc.), these dualisms, represented as natural oppositions, make possible the gendering of space. As Wigley points out, "the feminine term in each case is produced as such in the very moment of its subordination by the other term which both depends upon it and upon a veiling of that dependence."[6]

Gilman clearly understood this mechanism of subordination and dependence and furthermore recognized that the economic structure of capitalism required it. She writes that "the labor of women in the house, certainly, enables men to produce more wealth than they otherwise could; and in this way women are economic factors in society."[7] In passages such as this Gilman shows that she recognized, while bemoaning the waste, that women's unrewarded labor in the home helped create the conditions that allowed capitalism to flourish. Material waste, as she documented in items such as her analysis of the costs of maintaining separate households, created the ideal conditions for an unregulated capitalist economy (Allen, *Building*, 77).

These material conditions also served to keep men and women separate. As long as women's unpaid labor in the home was necessary to allow men to earn more, women stood little chance of gaining access to work in the public sphere. At the same time, women's domestic labor was necessary to the ideology of the home, for it was women who created the domestic spaces which defined the home. Further, as Karen Franck states:

> Industrial capitalism depends on the home/work, reproduction/production, and women/men divisions for the large-scale consumption of goods generated by the needs of separate households in suburban locations and for the biological and psychological renewal of the wage labor force in the home setting. Industrial capitalism helped to create and continues to enforce the spatial separations that accompany these categories in contemporary communities in the United States.[8]

Without these separations, both spatial and ideological, between women and men, between households, and between communities, systems of collective labor would have been much easier to establish.

This understanding is, in part, what makes Gilman's calls for the reform of architectural spaces so radical. She understood that if these separations of space could be broken down then women would be able to benefit from the formation of collectives to care for domestic labor. Spatial separations produced waste, in terms of both consumption and labor.

Although the traditional division of labor is enforced by the dichotomy between private and public, we do not need to only lessen or eliminate the separation between the private and public in order to approach the problems inherent in the gendering of architectural spaces. To do so has the effect of removing the spaces themselves from analysis. Instead, we need to recognize that spatial arrangements between the sexes are socially created. In other words, as Daphne Spain indicates, "spatial relations exist only because social processes exist."[9] Such an analysis enables us to discuss rooms such as the kitchen in terms of the gendered division of labor. By examining the social processes that are in place in any given space we can move to an analysis of the ways in which specific spaces carry with them ideologies produced by social interaction.

In this sense spaces themselves become carriers of gender ideologies and "gendered spaces provide the concrete, everyday-life grounding for the production, reproduction, and transformation of status differences" (Spain, *Gendered Spaces*, 233). Further, as Spain writes, "'gendered spaces' separate women from knowledge used by men to produce and reproduce power and privilege" (3). In this manner, architectural spaces serve to maintain patriarchal hierarchies of power and privilege. In the nineteenth century, access to those spaces denied to women often meant access to power in the form of institutions such as the smoking rooms, schools, and corporate offices. As long as women could not enter these spaces, the knowledge held within them was sacrosanct. In this way gendered spaces function on both a physical and a metaphorical level.

Women were physically denied access to certain spaces; this alone limited their freedom of movement. As a result women often had to meet under the veil of domesticity. One example of this can be found in the importance of quilting bees to the suffrage movement of the nineteenth century. Safely concealed within domestic space as a site of women's congregation, quilting bees served as occasions within which women could discuss political matters such as suffrage. However, while gatherings such as quilting bees were important sites of women's resistance, we must recognize that women's opportunities to meet were nonetheless limited. Many public institutions were not accessible to women. This physical barrier reinforced the metaphoric exclusion of women from the production of knowledge. As long as women could not physically enter institutions such as universities, they would never be able to participate in the production of power, privilege, and knowledge taking place within.

Although it is important to analyze the ways in which spaces are gendered, we must bear in mind that these types of analyses are one-directional. That is, while these examinations seek to understand how design and space can be gendered, it is possible that they are simultaneously reproducing the very gender roles that they are seeking to undermine. For example, by discussing the kitchen in terms of gender we do not question the ways in which architectural spaces themselves create gender. In this sense spaces are forms of representation. This is not to say that no effect can be had by altering architectural spaces for, as Spain states, "while it would be simplistic to argue that spatial segregation causes gender stratification, it would be equally simplistic to ignore the possibility that spatial segregation reinforces gender stratification and thus that modifying spatial arrangements, by definition, alters social processes" (Spain, *Gendered Spaces*, 6–7). Changing spatial arrangements can effect a change in gender ideology, but this alone can also allow the construction of gender to remain unanalyzed and unquestioned as an element in the construction of architectural spaces.

As Mark Wigley points out, "place is not simply a mechanism for controlling sexuality. Rather, it is the control of sexuality by systems of representation that produces place" ("Untitled," 350). Wigley makes it clear that we must examine how architecture produces gender and how gender produces architecture. Without this type of two-directional analysis we grant gender the status of a prearchitectural given, ensuring its absence from analytical discourse. In this sense "it is fruitless to try to isolate space from social processes in order to say that one 'causes' the other. A more constructive approach is to acknowledge their interdependence," argues Spain (*Gendered Spaces*, 6). In other words while the spatial separation of architectural spaces may represent a social process that constructs gender, gender may equally well be a process that constructs architectural space.

If we do not recognize this dialectic then, as Wigley argues, gender becomes a concept that is "masked in the moment of its application to architecture, as an extra-, or rather, pre-architectural given. The question of sexuality and space here is the structure of this mask" ("Untitled," 330). He goes on to write that while the "definition of space is ostensibly the subject of architectural discourse, it cannot be simply interrogated by that discourse. On the contrary, it is protected from analysis by that very discourse. . . . Likewise, . . . the sense of a building's detachment from sexual politics is produced by that very politics" (331). If we accept this argument then we must acknowledge that it is not sufficient to analyze architectural spaces in terms of gender unless we also describe the ways in which architectural spaces construct gender. In other words we must analyze the ways in which ideologies of gender lead to the design of certain architectural spaces such as the kitchen and we must analyze the ways in which the architectural space of the kitchen produces a definition of gender.

Recognizing the need for this type of interactive analysis, Gilman made both the house and the home a subject of analysis. She understood that women not only had to contend with the spaces within the home, they were also confined by the spaces of the house. An ideology of gender leads to the construction of the "home," while the "house" can function as an architectural space which produces gender. In this sense it would not be enough for the use of domestic spaces to change. Instead, domestic spaces, such as kitchens, had to be analyzed and altered. Gilman did not propose that women merely left the private spaces of the home for the public sphere. While such a move might have proved sufficient to analyze the role of the spaces of the home in the oppression of women, it would have exempted the house from analysis. The dangers of this are, as Wigley argues, that "the boundaries that define the house are at once left behind as an 'illusion' and restored. Domestic space can only pose a danger inasmuch as the illusions that sustain it, like all enfranchised cultural images, are real" ("Untitled," 331). Gilman clearly understood this distinction between house and home, for she did not render her analysis of women's isolation in the home as being separate from the physical construction of the house. For example, in her call for kitchenless homes and houses, she clearly recognized the need for the very spaces of domesticity to be critically analyzed and reformed. It is not enough for women to move out of the private into the public if that move maintains the house as an inviolate third term. Not just the functions of the home must come into question, but also the construction of the spaces of the house as a means of creating and enforcing the construction and ideologies of gender.

In this sense, the house can be "understood as the intersection of a spatial system and a system of surveillance" (Wigley, "Untitled," 339). Spaces are designed and created just as systems of surveillance are. As Gilman determined, it is in the home that we find the intersections of these two systems as a controlling and confining structure of women's lives. As such, "place is not simply a mechanism for controlling sexuality. Rather, it is the control of sexuality by systems of representation that produces place" (350). For example, the kitchen, like all spaces, is not simply a neutral room which we can enter and leave at will. Instead, each time we enter the kitchen we (re)produce it. In this sense architectural space and gender both determine and are determined by each other, and each provides a space for the surveillance and maintenance of patriarchal gender relations.

The construction of gender by architectural spaces can be so complete that it comes to appear "natural." For example, as Nan Bauer Maglin writes:

> The notion that women are somehow born with kitchens as well as wombs, the insistence that "by nature" women are oriented to interior space is not natural but cultural. The development of this pervasive cultural image is tied up in the privatization of women's lives, the separation of work from the home during the complex events of industrialization, urbanization, and immigration in the United States after the Civil War. One part of this history is architectural – the selling of the ideal of the private, detached house with room for separate activities presided over by different family members.[10]

Gilman, in her call for kitchenless houses, was working against the selling of this construction of the "natural" through architectural spaces. By challenging the inclusion of certain spaces within the house, Gilman exposes these spaces as constructions and constructors of gender.

That Gilman understood this point is evident in her writings. She called for homes to be grouped as collectives with access to central services such as child care, laundries, and the provision of food. However, she did not stop at having these services provided outside the home; she removes from the home and the house those spaces constructed to serve these purposes. In this way the gendered ideology of both the house and the home can be broken. Gilman perceived that if these communal services existed, but there was still a space for them in the house, then they would remain part of the ideology which is perpetrated by the very construction, in the most absolute physical sense, of the house. The ideology of the home would never be far removed from a return to its constructed space within the house.

This understanding is also clearly evident in Gilman's fictional writing. In stories such as "The Yellow Wallpaper" the spaces of both the home and the house work against the narrator. She is confined to the nursery, a space which confines her in the dual senses of both home and house. In the home the architectural space of the nursery becomes defined by gender, while in the house the space of the nursery defines the construction of gender. In the first sense, the space of the home proves to be confining. Using a construction of gender that presents women as sickly, the architectural space of the nursery becomes the repository for the narrator's illness and eventual madness. The nursery, a room that might otherwise be seen as an attic, becomes women's domain within a very specific construction of woman.

Equally confining is the architectural space of the nursery in the house. In this space John, the narrator's husband, treats her as a child by confining her to the nursery. This relegates the narrator to the private sphere, interchanging her with her child. Indeed in some ways we can consider it to be the child who has some possibility of escaping the home, for the baby is not confined to the nursery that is located within the home. Instead he has exchanged places with his mother; the mother is now the resident of the private space within the home reserved for children. The architectural space of the nursery within the house constructs the gender identity and treatment of the narrator.

Simultaneously, the architectural space of the nursery also provides a system of surveillance. The narrator is trapped in the space of the nursery. The bars on the window and the locked door suggest that not only is she confined to this space, but she is also available for surveillance at any moment. She cannot physically leave the space of the attic and is constantly in a space where she can be found. At any moment John can climb the stairs and find her open to scrutiny. The element of surveillance suggests that gender constructions are closely guarded and maintained. There can be no escape from this construction of woman.

Despite this, the narrator is trying to escape from both the house and the home. For example, she asks to be moved to a different room, one that looks outside. This can be read as moving beyond both the house and the home. If she manages to move to a room that has access to the outside, she might gain access to the freedom of the spaces outside the home, spaces in which neither architecture or constructions of gender are so determined. However, as Judith Fetterly describes, John denies the narrator's request for a change of room:

> Yet he [John] denies her request for a room on the first floor with access to the air outside, and confines her instead to the attic where she can neither sleep nor rest. Later, when she asks to have the attic wallpaper changed, he "took me in his arms and called me a blessed little goose, and said he would go down to the cellar, if I wished, and have it whitewashed into the bargain." Yet while he may be willing to whitewash the cellar, he won't change the attic because "I don't care to renovate the house for a three months' rental."[11]

More significantly, I would argue, John will not change the narrator's room because he cannot permit the possibility of escape from the surveillance of gender afforded by the space of the nursery. It is necessary to preserve the ideological gendered spaces of the house and home.

By the end of the story the narrator is mad. Whether or not this madness is a legitimate form of escape, I would argue, as do Gilbert and Gubar, that "by the end of the story, moreover, the narrator has enabled this double [the woman behind the wallpaper] to escape from her textual/architectural confinement" (*Madwoman in the Attic*, 147). Her madness has also enabled her to escape from the house and the home as they define and are defined by gender.

The device of madness as a form of escape allows Jane to break out of both her gender role as mother and the architectural space of the nursery. However, implicit within Gilman's description of Jane's treatment at the hands of her husband is the way in which, within patriarchal conceptions of architectural space, women themselves are spaces available for colonization. Jane has no control over her treatment; through patriarchal institutions such as marriage and medicine her identity and her actions are controlled. In this way, she is an object of colonization for whom decisions are best made by an all-knowing patriarch in the form of John. By the end of the story Jane, in the form of her mad double, has been freed from this colonization. In this sense the escape from the wallpaper represents both an escape from the spatial confines of the room and an escape from the gender confines that comprise her identity as Jane.

While Gilman uses the device of madness in "The Yellow Wallpaper" to escape the ideology of the architectural spaces of the house and the home, the strategies that she suggested in her theoretical writings are those that have proved to be most fruitful for further exploration within the discipline of architecture. For example, when she discusses kitchenless houses Gilman presents us with an image which breaks away from the control over the construction of gender identities as it is accomplished and inscribed through the construction of architectural spaces. It is Gilman's vision of such radically reformed spaces that proved to be inspirational for women designers and architects who followed her.

Charlotte Perkins Gilman was not the only nineteenth-century writer who analyzed the relationship between gender inequities and the architectural spaces in which women and men lived their lives. The move toward some form of socialized housing was promoted by various thinkers such as Charles Fourier and Robert Owen. For example, Fourier "taught that the isolated household was an unacceptable impediment to the achievement of female equality" (Allen, *Building*, 20). In 1825 Owen, with the help of an architect, "developed a model for multifamily housing with community facilities that was both grand and provocative" (20). As a result of the work of writers such as these, a number of attempts to establish various forms of socialized housing sprang up around the country. Gilman visited some of these models and was, in some cases, strongly encouraged by what she saw. For example, she visited settlement houses such as Hull House and N. O. Nelson's model village of Leclaire, Missouri (85). In communities such as these Gilman saw the effectiveness of communal services such as cleaning, laundry, the provision of food. These visits served to reinforce her vision of a collective form of architecture that broke away from the confining spaces of the house and home.

What remains unique about Gilman's vision for socialized architecture is her statement that social evolution depended upon an architecture that freed women from the restricting confines of the home. As she stated, "we have seen what has been denied to woman by absence from the world; what do we find bestowed upon her by the ceaseless, enclosing presence of the house? How

does staying in one's own house all one's life affect the mind? . . .
The first result is a sort of mental myopia" (*The Home: Its Work
and Influence*, 215–216). Gilman effectively argued that unless
women escaped from this "ceaseless, enclosing presence" they
would never become full partners in society. As a result the evolution of the entire society, both male and female, would be
held up. Furthermore, once architectural space began to change,
women would be freed from the home and these same ceaseless,
enclosing presences would, by necessity, begin to change and, finally, no longer exist.

What emerged from the work of Gilman and this period of
material feminism was a sense of connection between the creation
of architectural spaces and the position of women. One of the most
positive outcomes was the creation of the Cambridge School of
Architecture and Landscape Architecture in 1915. Nearly five hundred women students studied at this school, open only to women,
before its closure in 1942. The school was begun on a very casual
basis when Henry Atherton Frost, a professor at Harvard, agreed
to teach a female student architectural drafting privately. This
number grew from one to five, and this informal and casual beginning eventually led to the formation of the Cambridge School.

During this 27-year period, the Cambridge School was staffed
by some of Harvard's best teachers, who took on work at the school
as a way of supplementing their incomes. According to Ellen Perry
Berkeley, its first teacher, Frost, "encouraged what he saw as the
special interest of the Cambridge student: 'in housing rather than
houses; in community centers for the masses rather than in neigh-
borhood clubs for the elect; in regional planning more than in
estate planning; in social aspects of her profession more than in
private commissions.' To Frost, 'her interest in her profession em-
braces its social and human implications.'"[12] The year before the
school closed, "Frost suggested an expanded M.Arch. of 'research
and design in the direction of (for want of a better term) socialized
architecture'" (207). Of course, we can question whether Frost saw
this as women's inclination because he felt that they were more
suited for this domestic type of architectural design – a type of
design that is typically not rewarded within the hierarchy of architectural spaces. In other words, he may well have thought that
it was fine for women to practice architecture as long as they designed small *a* buildings and did not aspire to produce Art, typi-

cally created for a wealthy elite or for corporations. However, in either case, schools such as the Cambridge School did lead to the involvement of more women in the field of architecture and systematically began to introduce ideas such as those of Gilman into the design and construction of architectural spaces.

The Cambridge School eventually closed in 1942 in large part due to the entry of the United States into World War II. As more men were being drafted, enrollments at Harvard's school of architecture declined and therefore women were accepted into the program in order to increase enrollment. Berkeley writes that "for the duration of the war, according to the agreement reached in 1942, the Cambridge School would 'cease' and Harvard would accept women students in its architecture program" (Berkeley, "Architecture," 208). After a struggle, Harvard did agree to accept women as candidates for degrees and to continue this policy after the war. This marked the end of the Cambridge School, for it never reopened, "even though Harvard's hospitality to women cooled in the postwar period" (208).

Nevertheless, by the 1920s women had begun to explore ideas of "socialized" architecture in the designs and spaces that they were creating; we can trace the influence of Gilman and the material feminists more directly beyond the evidence of the collective and socialist housing ideas that were prevalent among the women of the Cambridge School. For example, "feminist architects of the 1920s and 1930s (like Alice Austin and Ruth Adams) argued for kitchenless houses to spare women the drudgery of cooking. . . . Elisabeth Coit proposed in 1938 that the names of rooms be changed or eliminated to avoid potentially restrictive uses" (Spain, *Gendered Spaces*, 236). These kitchenless houses can be seen to come from the same impetus that fueled Gilman's earlier proposals to eliminate the kitchen from the house and home, replacing it with centralized services for the provision of meals. As Dolores Hayden writes, "for six decades these women, the material feminists, defined their movement with one powerful idea: that women must create new kinds of homes with socialized housework and child care before they could become truly equal members of society" (*Redesigning*, 29). Gilman was one of the primary feminists involved in this struggle.

Of course, while Gilman's ideas are inspiring, we do have to acknowledge the difficulties that arise in terms of her treatment of class and race. While a kitchenless home might prove to be a wonderful innovation for a middle-class white woman, she did not sufficiently analyze who would be doing the cooking and serving of meals and how these workers would be paid for this labor.

> All these attempts to define supportive residential communities for employed women and their families ran into two related economic difficulties. First, the economic value of housework was never adequately understood. Second, the economic value of the new services was unclear, in relation both to the old-fashioned system of hiring personal servants and the new commercial services and industrial products developed for ha-ven housewives. Such services, when produced by low-paid fe-male workers were cheaper, if less intimate and desirable, than community-generated alternatives. (Hayden, *Redesigning*, 91)

The kitchenless house did not automatically translate into a recognition of the value of women's labor. Instead, it transferred the burden of women's unpaid domestic labor to low-paid workers who were usually female and often nonwhite or immigrant. This is perhaps the most serious flaw in Gilman's revisioning of architectural space. By not accounting for the differences in the circumstances of women's lives, Gilman's solutions for the problems created by gendered architectural spaces proved not to be as liberating as they might otherwise have been.

Despite these flaws, visions of a reformed architecture such as Gilman's have led to changes within the practice of architectural design. For example, Daphne Spain states that "Hayden (1984) has proposed 'redesigning the American dream' to meet the needs of changing families; Werkle (1988) has documented the creation of housing cooperatives by and for female householders" (*Gendered Spaces*, 236). More designs are being produced that attempt to meet the needs of diverse populations of women. Architects are beginning to recognize that single mothers with young children have needs that differ from those of elderly women. Many contemporary architectural designs "stress the importance of multi-purpose rooms open to all members of a household, whether that household consists of a traditional nuclear family, an elderly person living alone, or a single parent with children" (236). While Gilman might not have recognized differences such as these in her writings, her analysis of the construction of gendered spaces can be seen as a part of a continuum of work that has led to an increased awareness of the ways in which architectural space plays a role in the construction of gender and the ways in which gender is responsible for the construction of certain types of architectural spaces.

In addition, architectural theorists have begun to question the ways in which gender and architectural space intersect in the formation of gendered identities and spaces. The vision that Gilman presented of spaces in which gender was neither predetermined by nor determined the use of space can provide strategies with which we might begin to construct architectural spaces that are not merely complicit in the construction of gender. Through her analysis of these interrelations Gilman firmly placed herself as one of the foremothers of architectural reform, a reform that might eventually lead to the possibility of spaces in which gender is not constrained and constructed by patriarchal definitions.

NOTES

1. Dolores Hayden, *The Grand Domestic Revolution*, 3.

2. Polly Wynn Allen, *Building Domestic Liberty*, 20.

3. Dolores Hayden, *Redesigning the American Dream*, 22.

4. For a complete discussion of these authors' various approaches see Hayden, *The Grand Domestic Reform*.

5. Kenneth Frampton, "Reflections on the Autonomy of Architecture: A Critique of Contemporary Production," in *Out of Site: A Social Criticism of Architecture*, ed. Diane Ghirado, 17.

6. Mark Wigley, "Untitled: The Housing of Gender," in *Sexuality and Space*, ed. Beatriz Colomina, 372.

7. Charlotte Perkins Gilman, *Women and Economics*, 13.

8. Karen A. Franck, "A Feminist Approach to Architecture: Acknowledging Women's Ways of Knowing," in *Architecture: A Place for Women*, ed. Ellen Perry Berkeley, and Matilda McQuaid, 204.

9. Daphne Spain, *Gendered Spaces*, 5.

10. Nan Bauer Maglin, "Kitchen Dramas," *Heresies* 3:3 (1981): 42.

11. Judith Fetterly, "Reading about Reading: 'A Jury of Her Peers', 'The Murders in the Rue Morgue,' and 'The Yellow Wallpaper,'" in *The Captive Imagination*, ed. Catherine Golden, 256.

12. Ellen Perry Berkeley, "Architecture: Toward a Feminist Critique," in *New Space for Women*, ed. Gerda R. Wekerle, Rebecca Peterson, and David Morley, 207.

DEBORAH M. DE SIMONE

Charlotte Perkins Gilman and Educational Reform

Within the last twenty-five years, a great deal of attention has been paid to the topic of gender discrepancy in education. From the psychological studies of Carol Gilligan to the philosophical writings of Nannerl Keohane, feminists and nonfeminists alike have been critical of the ways in which our young are taught.[1] As the works of Lawrence Cremin attest, Americans have always been critical of their institutions of education, so that gender issues seem merely the latest peeve in a long tradition of educational commentary – yet this is not so.[2] Two hundred years ago, Judith Sargent Murray, influenced by Mary Wollstonecraft, used the argument of "natural rights" to demand that female education in the new United States be grounded in reason, rather than in what was perceived as women's "natural characteristics." A century ago, Charlotte Perkins Gilman unleashed perhaps the most holistic and scathing critique of American education that focused specifically on issues of gender.

Gilman's interest in education stemmed from her feminist philosophy and her definition of the good society that combined religion with evolution, democracy with socialism, and motherhood with citizenship. As Jane Roland Martin demonstrated in *Reclaiming a Conversation*, Gilman's ideal of the educated woman was directly related to the earlier philosophical discussions of Plato, Jean-Jacques Rousseau, Wollstonecraft, and Catherine Beecher, her great-aunt. Each envisioned a different type of education for women, and therefore a different type of woman, yet all perceived women as an important fiber in the social fabric and a primary instrument in the transmission of democratic norms. Thus, Gilman's thoughts on the role, purpose, and goals of education fall within the realm of historical discussions of the good life and within the present controversy concerning moral or character education.

The title of the 1995 University of Liverpool Conference, "Charlotte Perkins Gilman: Optimist Reformer," suggested, first and foremost, that Gilman's ideas were and still are potent and inspiring. The title also suggested that Gilman offered the world an alternative and "optimistic" vision of life. I suggest that she not only offered the vision of a better and more gender-balanced society, but also presented education as the means to attain that goal. Although most studies thoughtfully present the roots and essence of her ideas on women, they do not sufficiently form the connection between her feminist thought and her ideas on education.[3] Consequently, the importance of education as the medium for the goal of feminism has been obscured, as has Gilman's full impact on American social thought. In this essay I examine the centrality of education to her feminist social philosophy and compare her ideas to present feminist commentaries on education and to the character education movement. The purpose of this exploration is not only to continue the conversation started by Jane Roland Martin regarding Gilman's educational ideas, but to suggest the influence of Gilman's thought within the modern feminist critique of education and to consider her contributions for the present character education debate.

From the integration of women writers into the curriculum to concern for the lack of exercise in adolescent girls, the range of research regarding gender issues in American education is extremely wide. While not all the news is bad — women now receive more doctorates than men — many of the results are disturbing: most elementary-school teachers continue to be female while most school principals and superintendents continue to be male; women still receive lower marks in math and science; and teachers, by and large, teach to their male students.[4] Feminist research in education tends to focus on issues of inclusion, efficacy, achievement, authority, and empowerment within the work culture, the curriculum, the methodologies used, and women's experiences. Few studies have discussed female education within a larger philosophical context of the relationship between education and society. It is from this larger perspective that both Gilman and Amy

Gutmann, in her book *Democratic Education*, consider women and education.

The most striking similarity between Gilman and Gutmann is their acceptance of the democratic tradition and their vision of education as the means both to reproduce society and to improve it. While neither Gutmann and Gilman's acceptance of democracy nor their view of education is particularly novel (one merely needs to consider Thomas Jefferson's dedication to both), it is important to recognize that the feminist critique of education is not advocating a revolution, but a reevaluation and transformation of the existing system. Joyce Antler and Sari Knopp Biklen in *Changing Education* remark that discussions of women and education have always been "integrally linked not only to social change in a general sense, but to feminism" (xvi).

The main question for both Gilman and Gutmann is what type of education is needed to create responsible democratic citizens — male and female. Both women view education broadly, recognizing that learning occurs within a multitude of institutions that work in some relation with the school. And though both view education as a political issue, Gutmann focuses on the question of "how authority over educational institutions should be allocated in a democratic society," while Gilman is more concerned with the question of access to education and to full citizenship within society (Gutmann, *Democratic Education*, 16).

Issues of influence and authority have always been at the crux of the feminist movement and will continue to be until parity is reached in the educational, social, political, domestic, economic, and artistic realms. In education, such issues can be approached from many perspectives, but Gilman and Gutmann consider them in terms of who shall have authority over education and what knowledge shall have the most influence within education.

Gutmann's interest in the first part of the equation leads her to explore the consequences of the educational philosophies of Plato, John Locke, and John Stuart Mill. She rejects all three theories on the grounds that Plato's "family state" constrains our choices "among ways of life and educational purposes in a way that is incompatible with our identity as parents and children" (28), Locke's "state of families" fails to recognize that children are members of both families and states so that "the educational authority of parents and of polities has to be partial to be justified" (30), and Mill's "state of individuals" holds individual freedom as its end, and "an education for freedom and for virtue part company in any society whose citizens are free not to act virtuously" (38). Gutmann's alternative "democratic state of education" recognizes that educational authority must be shared among parents, society, and professional educators, "though such sharing does not guarantee that power will be wedded to knowledge, that parents can successfully pass their prejudices on to their children, or that education will be neutral among competing conceptions of the good life" (42).

For Gutmann, society's disagreement over educational problems is a "democratic virtue," for without such differences of opinion, democratic deliberations over education could not occur, and authority could not then be shared. "The democratic virtue," she states, "is that we can publicly debate educational problems in a way more likely to increase our understanding of education and each other than if we were to leave the management of schools, as Kant suggests, 'to depend entirely upon the judgment of the most enlightened experts'" (11).

Gilman also believed that parents, the state, and professionals must share the responsibility for educating our youth. Like Gutmann, she recognized the reluctance of parents to view their children as members of society and as members of their families, and how this reluctance narrowed the scope of a child's education. With limited opportunity to compare the ideas of one's parents to those of others, Gilman warned that "constant association with one's nearest and dearest necessarily tends to a disproportionate estimate of their value" (*Home*, 173–174).

"Social evolution is mainly through the medium of voluntary action," Gilman wrote, "it is an educational process" ("Our Brains," 198). For Gilman, that process was directly linked to her definition of the good life. Strongly influenced by Edward Bellamy's Nationalist movement and by the emerging "culture of professionalism," Gilman's vision of society was firmly rooted in her belief that the "socialistic community is more highly organized than the individualistic one" and that collectivism nurtured and developed the individual by providing unity, equality of opportunity, and expert guidance ("Egoism," 1).[5] Like Gutmann, Gilman recognized that since "democracy rests on education, and the spread of ideals," popular government demanded rule by an informed and enlightened populace who had the responsibility to make informed decisions and to act upon their convictions.

While Gilman had great faith in the power of democratic deliberations to inform the public, she had greater faith than does Gutmann in the powers of experts to do the same. For Gilman, experts were specialists who managed a particular task for the public good. Child care, as Gilman demonstrated in her utopian novel *Herland*, was one such task that should be left to experts rather than to the biological mother:

> You told us about your dentists, she said, at length, "those quaintly specialized persons who spend their lives filling little holes in other persons' teeth – even in children's teeth sometimes."
>
> "Yes?" I said, not getting the drift.
>
> "Does mother-love urge mothers – with you – to fill their own children's teeth? Or to wish to?"
>
> "Why no – of course not," I protested. "But that is a highly specialized craft. Surely the care of babies is open to any woman – any mother!"
>
> "We don't think so," she gently replied. "Those of us who are the most highly competent fulfill that office; and a majority of our girls eagerly try for it – I assure you we have the very best." (83)

The culture of professionalism led Gilman to encourage mothers to approach child-rearing systematically and scientifically – to become experts in "how to make better people" rather than "how to make people better" ("Ideals," 93–101). As we shall see later, her interest in early childhood helped Gilman to envision the professionalization of the knowledge encapsulated within women's sphere and to call for institutions of learning that specialized in such knowledge, thus establishing women in new roles as experts.

Gutmann's *Democratic Education* paid much more attention to the issue of authority over education than it did to the issue of influence within education. Yet she does make it very clear that the concepts and methods of instruction must be nondiscriminatory, nonrepressive, and nonexclusive. Conversely, Gilman was particularly concerned with the question of what influenced the philosophy and pedagogy of education. Though she was sure education was the most effective and efficient medium to awaken people to the possibilities of the present and the future, she recognized that the content and methodologies within both the informal and the formal educative institutions could encumber the distribution and the pursuit of knowledge. Moreover, she charged education with thwarting the development of critical and imaginative thinking: two skills she believed crucial to citizens in a democracy.

According to Gilman, the school, the family, the church, and the community contributed to a natural state of "mental inertia" by emphasizing "Tradition and Authority" (*Human Work*, 32). Gilman strongly believed that the family was the most important educative institution, yet, as we have seen, she was concerned about the undue influence it might have on the education of a child. Familial instruction relied on parental authority and parents' awareness of the past: parental knowledge therefore became the "knowledge of all." While acknowledging that such instruction eliminated the need for children to repeat their parents' mistakes, she warned that parental authority imprisoned children by teaching blind acceptance rather than critical analysis of obsolete ideas. "To each child was given the thought-content of the parent mind, poked in like 'pigeon's milk,' before the child-mind was able to discriminate or criticize; and to the teaching of the parents was added the higher authority of the most aged" ("Our Brains," 105). Perhaps even more disturbing to Gilman and to Gutmann was how families further hampered the growth of children by teaching the "virtues" of obedience and submission while exposing them to the race, class, and gender biases and injustices inherent in the patriarchal construct (*Man-Made*, 26–43; Gutmann, *Democratic Education*, 28–33).

Religion had its historic place as an educational institution, yet where Gutmann feared that religious instruction could teach intolerance, Gilman held that religious instruction reinforced the unbalanced familial lessons while emphasizing the individual's unquestioned acceptance of and submission to dogma. Through morbid images, the religious methods of fear and guilt suppressed the powers of inquiry, doubt, and contemplation, thereby teaching submission to authority and championing blind trust of the written and spoken word.[6] "The major requisite in all religions," she remarked, was "a single mental facility – that of Belief. For almost the whole duration of religion Believing constituted at least seven-tenths of our piety" ("Our Brains," 189). Gilman criticized religion for impeding the thought processes essential to unfolding the truth, charging that in doing so religion corrupted its rightful calling — to assist the individual in the pursuit of knowledge and meaning.

Gilman's remarks on the educational system were based on her ideas of how learning should occur and on her limited experience of formal schooling. She was highly critical of the degree of competition in education and saw schools as institutions perpetuating the cultural dominance of desire and combat — what she considered to be male characteristics. "Desire, the base of the reward system, the incentive of self-interest" led to an unwillingness to learn when pleasure was not guaranteed, while "combat, the competitive system, which sets one against another," emphasized winning rather than the pleasure of learning or the exercising of the mind (*Man-Made*, 151). The real problem, for Gilman, was that self-interest, combat, and competition did not develop "thinkers" but a "weak, irrational mind, subservient to tradition, acceptance of wild theories and assertions, incapable . . . of mental exertion, feeding on the peppered froth of sensational journalism" ("Child Labor," 1137).

What distinguishes Gilman's critique from Gutmann's was her concern with the gender-specific nature of the curriculum and with knowledge in general. Insightfully, Gilman commented that the social and educational philosophy in the late nineteenth century was both determined by the androcentric nature of society and affected by the cult of domesticity. Acknowledging that "educational forces are many," she believed that women and men were educated by "social, political, and economic conditions" as well as "physical and psychic" factors. "All these conditions," she argued, "have been of androcentric character" (*Man-Made*, 145).

While the androcentric influences were pervasive, the varied educational forces had minor impact in the education of women because of women's prescribed domestic sphere: "Her restricted impressions, her confinement to the four walls of the home, have done great execution, of course, in limiting her ideas, her information, her thought-processes, and power of judgment" (*Women and Economics*, 65–66). Consequently, the "disproportionate prominence" women gave to what they did know further encouraged and sustained their subjugation, submission, dependency, naivete, and exaggerated femininity. As demonstrated in *Herland*, the characteristics of "true womanhood" were crafted only to satisfy the desires of men. Vandyck Jennings, one of three male explorers who discovered the female civilization of Herland, came "very promptly to the conviction" that "those 'feminine charms' we are so fond of are not feminine at all, but mere reflected masculinity – developed to please us because they had to please us, and in no way essential to the real fulfillment of their great process" (59).

The point where the androcentric culture most affected women was in the area of women's formal schooling since education remained masculine in its content and philosophy as well as in its methods and pedagogy. While recognizing the earlier efforts of Francis Wright and Catherine Beecher to establish alternative philosophies of instruction, Gilman maintained that the predominant educational philosophy was still too narrow since masculine traits were defined as *human* traits and female traits were defined as *other* (*Man-Made*, 146). Thus, women's emergence into secondary and higher education was but further immersion into institutions marked by the male characteristics of desire, combat, and self-expression. As such contemporary feminists as Nel Noddings and Margaret McKenna were to charge later, this imbalance in the nature of women's education resonated in the types of knowledge extended to women: the knowledge considered of most worth to women was the knowledge determined, accumulated, and organized by men; it was masculine knowledge presented within a masculine culture in a masculine way.[7]

Gilman openly criticized the inequalities in the established educational philosophy that glorified masculine knowledge while it neglected, devalued, and dehumanized the knowledge determined, accumulated, and organized by women; particularly in the realms of domestic industry and motherhood. In *The Home*, she denounced the continuation of housework as a set of "rudimentary trades" with no division of labor and no social advantage (90). In *Women and Economics* she exposed the educational omission of the domestic disciplines as deleterious to society and social progress. Noting the lack of education and professionalization in the area of "feeding humanity," Gilman remarked how each mother slowly acquired some knowledge of her trade by practicing it at the expense of the life and health of her family. Daughters began as ignorant as their mothers: "This 'rule of thumb' is not transmissible. It is not a genuine education . . . but a slow process of soaking up experience, – hopelessly ineffectual in protecting the health of society" (229).

Appalled that women were denied instruction in the biological and physiological aspects of pregnancy or the methods and problems of child-rearing, she criticized the system that simultaneously idealized the sentiments expressed in motherhood and degraded the knowledge required for motherhood. In "Our Place Today," a lecture given to a Los Angeles woman's club in 1891, Gilman noted how the knowledge central to motherhood was relegated to "the hoarded gossip of a hundred grandmothers, but no individual intelligence" ("Our Place"). She believed such individual intelligence should be scientifically determined and professionally administered. Describing the "senseless waste" of the present educational philosophy and practices, Gilman stated: "It is considered 'indelicate' to bring a young girl up with a knowledge and expectation of her coming duties. But if she is not trained when she is young – *when* is she to be trained? After marriage? After maternity? That is the way we learn. By experience . . . we learn by . . . practicing on our children – and by the time old women have learned their lessons half their children are dead!" ("Our Place").

Gilman's focus differs from Gutmann's in part because of the historical time in which she wrote. Where Gutmann writes at the end of the twentieth century, Gilman wrote at the end of the nineteenth, when the role of women in society and the educational opportunities available to them were fundamentally different. Yet the goals of education for Gilman and Gutmann are quite similar. Where the primary goal for Gutmann is to establish a racial- and gender-balanced educational system that involves all voices in the decision-making process, the primary goal for Gilman was to develop a gender-balanced educational system to foster a new definition of womanhood as well as new social norms to nurture and sustain that definition. In many ways, inclusion and equity are at the heart of both commentaries, and Gilman devised an educational tradition to give women an equal voice in the deliberations Gutmann recognizes as the virtue of democracy.

The need to improve society by redefining womanhood and the

role of women in society was the central focus of Gilman's work. Objecting to the modesty and naivete fostered by Victorian society's attitudes toward women, Gilman said such attitudes only created and perpetuated ignorance. In *Women and Economics* she criticized the portrayal of marriage to women as "the one road to fortune, to life" (86). Considering it a "cruel trick" that society barred women from actively pursuing men and marriage, their only means of "honorable livelihood and advancement," Gilman recognized the need for a wide range of alternatives for women and that these alternatives rested upon a greater diffusion of knowledge, regardless of its traditional spheres of influence (87). By exposing people to controversial ideas, by changing the social consciousness, and by educating the public to accept a new conception of womanhood, Gilman hoped that she could help create a more balanced society composed of intellectually, economically, socially, and politically autonomous women as well as men; in fact, Gilman hoped to create "the new woman."

Intellectual independence was the characteristic Gilman deemed most important to the new woman. As a child, she valued the supremacy of the intellect and the belief that ideas were "the important things of life" (*Living*, 27). Intellectual independence, she maintained, fostered individuality – for one must possess one's own thoughts in order to be one's own person. Since she viewed society as dependent upon the input and interaction of all individuals, the link between intellectual freedom and individuality was crucial. "The Yellow Wallpaper," a fictionalized account of her nervous breakdown, disturbingly portrayed a woman's descent into madness once her intellectual powers were denied her. The nameless author of the tale became incapable of constructively contributing to the society in which she lived once she lost her individuality and was refused her own thoughts. The story was written as a harsh criticism of a culture that undermined a woman's right to intellectual freedom and intellectual development, rights Gilman saw as instrumental to the well-being and progress of the individual and the society.

Another crucial element of Gilman's criticism of late Victorian society was the inability of women to pursue a career and to establish financial independence. Her thorough analysis of the overall development and effects of the economic repression of women in late nineteenth-century America resulted in her theory of the "sexuo-economic" dependence of women. Gilman argued that the individual was modified most powerfully by economic conditions and that humans were "the only animal species in which the sex-relation is also an economic condition" (*Women and Economics*, 5).

Gilman viewed women's inability to provide for themselves and establish economic independence as central to their subjugation within the home and their continued state of ignorance once placed there. Recognizing the various channels and options open to young men for achievement and growth, she strongly criticized the social prescriptions that limited a young woman's desires and experience "to a single channel and single choice. Wealth, power, social distinction, fame, – not only these but home and happiness, reputation, ease and pleasure, her bread and butter, – all must come to her through a small gold ring" (*Women and Economics*, 71).

Gilman believed that through intellectual and financial independence the new woman could attain social equality. Viewing the workplace as the door to society – where knowledge led to action and where communication led to socialization – she recognized how women's relegation to the home isolated them from other women, from men, from the larger life experiences of men, and from society at large. Exploring the harmful results for society of the doctrine of separate spheres, Gilman believed housebound women suffered from "mental myopia" and the monotony of "grinding work"; wealthy women suffered from idleness and boredom; and that all women suffered from loneliness and mental stagnation resulting from the lack of outside stimulation. Women had no place in a society she defined as "a masculine culture in excess" (*Man-Made*, 110).

While many women perceived suffrage as the key to the "woman question," Gilman, in the tradition of Elizabeth Cady Stanton, saw political equality as advantageous only insofar as women had attained intellectual, economic, and social equality. Utilizing the rhetoric and the sentiment of both the French and American revolutions, Gilman argued that as human beings and as members of society women were entitled to the same inalienable rights as men: the right to vote as well as the right to pursue knowledge, embrace a career, and own property.[8] Based on her belief in reform Darwinism and the linear progress of humanity, she maintained that for the continued progress of the human race, women must attain parity with men in order to end the subjugation that retarded human progress and to insure that humankind develops as a whole and not as two halves. In many ways, then, as Lois Magner indicates in "Women and the Scientific Idiom," Gilman used the laws of evolution and progressive change as a new argumentative base to move beyond the static, universal rights approach of her forerunners and to lay the foundation for equal education for women.

Since the days of Socrates, education has grappled with the question of whether its first obligation is to develop the human intellectual-academic sphere or the emotional-social sphere. Throughout most of history, the prevailing philosophy has aimed at developing both spheres, since, as Teddy Roosevelt quipped, "to educate a person in mind and not in morals is to educate a menace to society." However, moral education in the United States became problematic at the turn of the century and fell from grace in the 1960s and early 1970s. Now, in reaction to the paradoxes of American society – the increasing diversity of the population and the resurgence of bigotry on school campuses – and in the face of statistical evidence of higher rates in adolescent suicide, armed robbery, homicide, drug use, and pregnancy, character education is being resurrected as Americans perceive their society as morally rudderless and their children as ethically illiterate.

In his article "The Return of Character Education," Thomas Lickona suggests that moral education began to falter as logical positivism made radical distinctions between facts and values: the former were scientifically proven truths while the latter were not objective truths, but mere expressions of feeling. "As a result of positivism, morality was relativized and privatized – made to seem a matter of personal 'value judgment,' not a subject for public debate and transmission through the schools" (6). Further, the personalism of the 1960s, which emphasized individual rights and encouraged the criticism of social oppression and inequality, eroded moral authority and weakened social commitments, resulting in self-centeredness and civic irresponsibility. Moreover, America's pluralistic and secular nature became barriers to moral education in the public schools, as questions of constitutionality and tolerance were raised.

In many ways the resurgence of moral education is related directly to perceptions of the American family. Beginning with

Daniel Patrick Moynihan's 1965 report *The Negro Family: The Case for Action*, followed by Sylvia Hewlett's recent study *When the Bough Breaks: The Cost of Neglecting Our Children*, and combined with consistently high divorce rates, the American public is convinced that the family structure has crumbled. Where Gilman wrote of the family as having too much authority in the development of the child, Moynihan, Lickona, and many Americans charge that the family, particularly the single-parent family (which just so happens to be predominately female headed), has lost all authority and can no longer function as the child's primary moral instructor.

"Children are not born democrats," Mark Kann reminds us. "They must be educated for democracy" ("Character Education," 28). Since the family can no longer instill the values crucial to democratic citizenship, Americans once again have turned to the schools. The character education movement focuses on developing those shared ethical values that develop within individuals a strong sense of efficacy and agency. As the nagging question of "whose values" continues to be deliberated in the spirit Amy Gutmann would approve, the movement has identified a number of values common to all enlightened creeds and definitive of democratic citizenship. In focusing on responsibility, courage, perseverance, social respect, fairness, loyalty, justice, hope, critical thinking, and active participation, character education strives to develop autonomous and responsible individuals who cooperate with others in governing society. Clearly, the relationship between knowledge and action is central to the character education movement and to democratic citizenship.

It is on the issue of autonomy, and instructing individuals to be self-governing and responsible in the world, that Gilman had much to say and to contribute to the present character education movement. In focusing on gender discrepancies within education, she pointed out that the system, as is, cannot teach justice or tolerance or fairness, because of its inherently unequal treatment of the sexes. Character education, therefore, was inchoate until women became fully equal members of society and were allowed the autonomy and self-governance prized by all democrats.

Convinced that "the great social instinct, calling for full social exercise, exchange, and service" (*Women and Economics*, 302), existed within women as well as within men, Gilman called for an educational tradition that would prepare both sexes to participate actively and cooperatively in "the advance of civilization" (*Man-Made*, 155). She had a liberal notion of education, painting it in broad strokes, and declaring education's "real interests" as "the free exercise of natural faculties, the pursuit of knowledge for the love of it, the reverence for truth, the delight in feats of mental skill, and in all daily wonders of an unfolding world of fact and law" ("Child Labor," 1137).

Gilman maintained that women's intellectual powers should not be directed solely toward the home. Striving to establish women's role as an equal economic factor within society, she wanted women prepared for careers within the more diverse, traditionally male-dominated spheres of business, law, and medicine. In *Human Work*, Gilman demonstrated the need for women to be educated in, and to experience, the broader realms of knowledge and life since full social development, as well as "heath and usefulness, . . . requires a number of human beings with whom to feel, think, and act" (*Human Work*, 92).[9] In her attempt to organize and professionalize the knowledge encapsulated within women's sphere, Gilman hoped to provide women with larger life experiences that validated their personal ones. Thus, she envisioned professional instruction by women for women in the areas of marriage, motherhood, nutrition, child care, and domestic industry. Subsequently, women were to be taught to serve society through both the home and the workplace.

Specialization of knowledge within the traditional women's sphere would forge new channels for women's advancement. The specialization and professionalization of women's knowledge would also legitimize women's interests as relevant to the public good. According to Martin, in *Herland* "the interests of women, children, and the state become one, so that an education for citizenship is an education for mothers, just as an education for motherhood is an education for citizenship" (151). In comparing education for citizenship with education for motherhood, Gilman illuminated the imbalanced nature of the androcentric society and its disregard for the qualities of motherhood evident in citizenship. In accordance with her humanist definition of the good society, she advocated a restructuring of the androcentric culture toward a more holistic, balanced society. To achieve this balance, Gilman believed the male-dominated culture needed to be feminized:

through the reevaluation of the social values and attitudes toward women, through women's influence in the workplace and the associations formed with fellow workers, and, most important, through the feminization of education.

> To feminize education would be to make it motherly. The mother does not rear her children by a system of prizes to be longed for and pursued; nor does she set them to compete with one another, giving to the conquering child what he needs, and to the vanquished, blame and deprivation. That would be "unfeminine." Motherhood does all it knows to give each child what is most needed, to teach all to their fullest capacity, to affectionately and efficiently develop the whole of them. (*Man-Made*, 152)

If education was truly the most effective means to transform society, Gilman argued that "a conscientious and aroused society . . . cannot do too much to bring to [its members] all the social nourishment they can absorb, i.e. to provide the best educational environment" ("Our Brains," 333). The best educational conditions Gilman envisioned emphasized her belief that the "origin of education is maternal" and in the duties of the individual to society (*Man-Made*, 143.) Referring to education as "Social Motherhood," Gilman based her theory of education on those aspects of mothering that evolved as the extended period of human infancy demanded more care to prepare children for adulthood (Martin, *Reclaiming*, 162). Believing instruction to be the "last and noblest step in the life process," she defined education as "the application to the replenishment and development of the race of the same great force of ever-growing life which made the mother's milk" ("Small God," 2). The primary purpose of social motherhood was to "reproduce the race by reproducing the individual" and "to improve the race by improving the individual." Thus, the "complex social functions of education" were deemed "primarily a maternal process, and therefore individual" (*Women and Economics*, 178–179).

Though the origins of education were maternal, education was by no means the sole realm of women. In recognizing the importance of education for democracy and for the relationship between society and the individual, Gilman noted in *Women and Economics* that education "has long since become a racial rather than an individual function, and bears no relation to sex or other personal limitations. . . . Human functions are race-functions, social functions; and education is one of them" (179–180).

Through a variety of institutions, social motherhood was to teach the individual to "see clearly, to understand, to properly relate one idea to another, to refuse superstition and mere repetition of other people's opinion" ("Our Brains," 329). Like Lickona and the character education movement, Gilman strove to develop autonomous individuals; for rational behavior was possible only for self-governing people who could connect knowledge with action and could judge others' opinions in relation to their own. The powers of self-restraint, self-direction, and self-government enabled human beings "not to do as others do or as we are told, but as we ourselves see to be right" ("Ideals," 100–101). Thus, by teaching individuals to think logically, to envision multiple options, and to act rationally on their own decisions, public education insured that all human beings would "assume right functional relation to society" and avoid "that fatal facility in following other people's judgment and other people's will which tends to make us a helpless mob, mere sheep, instead of wise, free, strong individuals" (*Concerning Children*, 39).

Gilman's most cogent discussion of the concept of "social motherhood" appeared in *Herland*, a major work on issues of women and education. In this idyllic, all-female utopia, learning and child-rearing became a collective, social matter as child-bearing and birth remained an individual, personal matter. Rather than emphasizing the biological bond between a mother and her child, in *Herland* the maternal instincts are portrayed as evident within all women, making each woman a mother, whether biological or not. All individuals in society assume and share the responsibilities for the growth, development, and education of the next and future generation: the priority of both the individual and the community in *Herland* is to ensure social progress through the education of the young. As one citizen of Herland explains: "The children in this country are the center and focus of all our thoughts. Every step of our advance is always considered in its effect upon them – on the race. You see, we are *Mothers*" (66).

In her book *Caring: A Feminine Approach to Ethics and Moral Education*, Nel Noddings echoes Gilman in creating a theory of education based upon the maternal instincts of nurturing in an attempt to make "the voice of the mother heard in both ethics and education" (182). Her educational critique is based upon her analysis that caring and our "human relatedness" are the foundations of human morality and that our present system of education focuses more on reason and the intellect than on emotion and social norms. Like Gilman, Noddings sees the culture of the school and the methods therein as male dominated. Thus, she rejects "the excessive efforts at abstraction, objectivity, and detachment in our schools [as] a manifestation of the father's psychological need to take possession of the child" (182). The similarities in language as well as intent are clear; both discuss education in relation to motherhood, both view the predominant culture as devaluing motherhood and nurture, and both recognize the need to transform education so that the mother's voice could be heard. Nevertheless, since Gilman has not been seen as an educational theorist, it is not surprising that neither Nel Noddings nor Amy Gutmann cites her work or recognizes her influence.

While the relationship between knowledge and action is central to the character education movement, so is the tension between the individual and the community. In considering this tension, and the instructional goal to develop autonomous individuals, we are reminded that Gilman viewed democracy as an educational process contingent on an advanced state of social consciousness. Democracy was "an organization of public service" that would respond to the needs of the people only when "common rather than individual interests were acknowledged" ("Free Speech," 146). For Gilman, the needs of the individual were secondary to those of society, and self-worth could not be found outside the social relation. One of the main purposes of education, therefore, was to develop a sound moral character by teaching social service, not individual attainment.[10] Society was to develop two powers within individuals, "the two that seem . . . basically necessary for all noble life: a clear, far-reaching judgment, and a strong, well used will" (*Herland*, 66). These were the powers essential to forming wise, free, strong individuals. Judgment and will subsequently became the crucial ingredients of citizenship in fostering respect for others, in developing critical thinking skills, and in guarding against "the habit of acting without understanding, and also of understanding without acting" (*Concerning Children*, 51–52). These powers were to be developed via the "two main divisions in education . . . the things it is necessary to know and the things it is necessary to do" (*Herland*, 66).

Concurring with John Dewey, Gilman saw diversity and choice as the avenues where criticism and creativity, individuality, and love for learning formed. Efforts to stir the mind to criticism commenced through the use of art, photography, and film as well as through vocational education and the innovations of the elective systems in schools ("What Our Children," 706–711). For Gilman, criticism was based on experience and imagination; for one could not criticize something without some knowledge of it or without some vision of what it might be. Thus, education must emphasize imagination as well as truth and reason; self-discipline as well as self-restraint. Most importantly, education must combine all these skills to develop the faculties of reason so essential to rational and judicious-acting individuals. "To remember is useful and necessary," she remarked, "but to think ahead is the secret of conscious progress" ("What Our Children," 711).

The community was not only to educate individuals but was to produce responsive citizens. Autonomous men and women learned to recognize and value their connectedness with others and their interdependency with society. Gilman thought that these lasting bonds were formed by combining liberal education with vocational education. Instruction in "common knowledge" fostered a sense of belonging within a unified group, while lessons in "specialized knowledge" enabled individuals to work and "to take place in the vital processes of Society" (*Human Work*, 114). She saw education as an inalienable right, essential for "citizens of a democracy, members of a partially civilized society, [and] workers in a world where failure to work should be held contemptible" ("What Our Children," 708). All citizens were entitled to a "proper education" that offered a "broad general knowledge of the world . . . the development of life on earth . . . the appearances of the human race . . . the natural sciences . . . the main lines of industrial development" and of the social structures of city, state, and nation "with our duties and responsibilities therein" ("What Our Children," 708).

The development of socially conscious citizens and the expansion of specialized knowledge were to herald the establishment of a gender-balanced educational philosophy and system of education. Gilman proposed an educational system based on her belief in the existence of innate masculine, feminine, and human characteristics: masculine and feminine traits enabled racial continuation whereas human traits enabled racial improvement. In *The Man-Made World*, Gilman argued that masculine traits were desire, combat, and self-expression, and female traits were nurture, teaching, and industry (9–13, 28–30). Of the human traits she remarked: "Our humanness is seen most clearly in three main lines: it is mechanical, psychical and social" (15). Yet, more "prominent than these," wrote Gilman, "is the social nature of humanity" (15–16).

With education dispersing human qualities throughout society, Gilman believed that common attitudes and perceptions would be transformed. With a change in consciousness, education that disregarded sex-differentiation, sex-stereotyping, and gender-related traits would prosper. Learning would then become preparation for "human work" rather than woman's work. Since male and female characteristics referred to reproductive processes only, all other spheres of influence were considered common and accessible to both sexes. As social motherhood stressed the duty, responsibility, and relationship of society to the individual, education for human work emphasized the individual's duty, responsibility, and relationship to society. Social service and social consciousness were the crux of education, and particularly a gender-balanced education. Properly educated individuals were in "full touch with the whole great working world" and were able to support and recognize the value of their own work as integral to the larger whole (*Human Work*, 235).

The emphasis on social responsibility, specialized knowledge, and common characteristics in education created a system in which women could develop to their full potentials. In teaching women to dedicate their lives to the common good rather than the familial good, education liberated women from the "chamber and scullery work" of the home and helped them to recognize their connection, commitment, and contribution to the larger world. The emphasis on social responsibility enabled women to participate in "human work" and to become active members of the economy. Thus, education for social responsibility encouraged women to establish financial independence and become a "mother – with the great heart that enfoldeth the children of the Race" (*In This Our World*, 146).

In devising an educational system that deemphasized masculine and feminine character traits, Gilman enabled women to enter and to act as full and equal members of society. With women trained in similar manners, exposed to the same types of knowledge, encouraged toward parallel goals, Gilman's educational philosophy enabled them to assume a myriad of new roles and enter into various types of relationships with men. Through a gender-balanced education, women and men developed into socially active, intellectually stimulating, financially self-reliant, civically responsible, personally courageous human beings. Further, her teaching encouraged women to develop intellectual curiosity and a foundation of spiritual values fundamental to the stability and direction of democratic education.

"I am a teacher," Gilman declared in her autobiography (*Living*, 311). "I was not a reformer but a philosopher. I worked for various reforms, as Socrates went to war when Athens needed his services, but we do not remember him as a soldier. My business was to find out what ailed society, and how most easily and naturally to improve it" (*Living*, 182). The way she found "most easily and naturally" to address the problems of society was through education. She used her lectures and publications deliberately to educate present and future generations through the transmission of knowledge, values, and attitudes and by providing the information and sensibilities needed for humanity to direct the evolution of the race and the society. Her educational efforts were twofold: she wrote about education and she wrote to educate. Some of her writings commented on schooling, but, as we have seen, the focus of her attention rested upon society and her critique of the informal education rendered within the home and the community. Though written a century ago, Gilman's critique of womanhood and education remains potent as society continues to struggle with issues of gender and women continue to struggle for equality and independence. Her comments about education shed new light on our understanding of feminism and the character education movement, for we now see more clearly the connection between feminism and education at the turn of the century and today, as well as the limitations of character equation when the feminist critique of education is not considered.

NOTES

1. See Carol Gilligan, *In a Different Voice*; Carol Gilligan and Lyn Mikel Brown, *Meeting at the Crossroads*; Nannerl O. Keohane, "Educating Women Students for the Future," in *Changing Education*, ed. Joyce Antler and Sari Knopp Biklen.

2. See Lawrence A. Cremin, *Traditions of American Education*.

3. See Carl Degler, "Charlotte Perkins Gilman on the Theory and Practice of Feminism," *American Quarterly* 7 (1956): 21–39; Mary A. Hill, *Charlotte Perkins Gilman: The Making of a Radical Feminist, 1860–1896*; Ann J. Lane, *To Herland and Beyond*; Ann J. Lane, ed., *The Charlotte Perkins Gilman Reader*; Denise D. Knight, ed., *"The Yellow Wallpaper" and Selected Stories by Charlotte Perkins Gilman*.

4. See Herbert Grossman and Suzanne H. Grossman, *Gender Issues in Education*.

5. See Walter Metzger, "A Spectre Haunts American Scholars: The Spectre of 'Professionalism,'" *Educational Researcher* 16 (1987).

6. Gilman presented her views on religion, society, and education in the now relatively overlooked work *His Religion and Hers: A Study of the Faith of Our Fathers and the Work of Our Mothers*.

7. See Gilman, *His Religion and Hers*, 138–194; Nel Noddings, *Caring: A Feminine Approach to Ethical and Moral Education*, 182.

8. See Nancy F. Cott, *The Grounding of Modern Feminism*, 3–50.

9. See Gilman's fictional teachers in *The Crux* and "Making a Change," for whom teaching was as beneficial to them as it was to their students.

10. See Gilman, *Women and Economics*, 188; Amy Gutmann, *Democratic Education*, 35–49.

Motherhood and Reproduction

NAOMI B. ZAUDERER

Consumption, Production, and Reproduction in the Work of Charlotte Perkins Gilman

The cycle of consumption, production, and reproduction is rarely analyzed in its entirety. While both liberal economists and Marxists view production as a public activity that warrants critical scrutiny, they consider consumption and reproduction to be private activities that are largely determined by production. When defined in this way, consumption and reproduction fall outside the scope of conventional economic analysis. Charlotte Perkins Gilman, in contrast, gives consumption and reproduction the same careful attention ordinarily reserved for the production process alone. Her analysis reveals that Karl Marx and Frederick Engels's economic theory is divorced from the totality of human experience in that it neglects our prolonged period of dependency in childhood. In positing that the mode of production is the driving force in our lives, Marx and Engels failed to realize that we could also subject the family structure and the socialization of children to conscious human control. Gilman's theory, on the other hand, is premised on the belief that the organization of reproduction, like the organization of production, is a product of human artifice.

Gilman's economic theory also deserves attention because it complements Marx's analysis in two ways. First, by focusing on the experience of women, Gilman calls our attention to the pain of being excluded from social production. This is an issue that simply fell outside of Marx's range of vision. Second, by more fully examining the concept of ownership, Gilman's theory reveals some of the problems with conceptual categories employed by Marx, such as alienation and labor-power. Gilman's theory is both more and less radical than Marx's. It is more radical in that she calls into question the very notion of individual ownership of our labor-power, our product, and our children. It is less radical in that she did not see the abolition of private ownership of the means of production as the most critical element of socialist reform; in fact, she saw female-owned business enterprises as a step toward a more egalitarian society.

This essay also presents some of the limitations of Gilman's thought. For instance, Gilman paid insufficient attention to alienation in the process of social production, and this could be the downfall of the female-owned and operated enterprises that she advocated. In addition, she failed to take into account the reasons underlying our tenacious hold on the home and family as we know it. She perceived the modern family as merely an atavistic holdover from the past. In fact, the needs it fulfills under capitalism are different from those it fulfilled in previous historical epochs. The transformation of the family requires finding other venues for meeting these needs.

An adequate understanding of Gilman requires seeing her in the context of the American socialist tradition, a tradition that is not indebted to Marx. American socialism at the turn of the century, as represented by Edward Bellamy, Lester F. Ward, Thorstein Veblen, and Gilman herself, stemmed from the utopian socialist tradition, which had taken root in America in the mid-nineteenth century. The myriad utopian communities that were founded in the mid-nineteenth century under the inspiration of Robert Owen and Charles Fourier, among others, generally made the elimination of the family as an economic unit a central element of their project.[1] This pre-Marxian socialist tradition provides a stronger basis for socialist feminism than traditional Marxism does because it recognizes that social transformation need not begin with a change in the mode of production; the family can be acted on independently and simultaneously. In contrast, Marx and Engels viewed the family as part of the ideological superstructure, which could be permanently transformed only through a change in the ownership of the means of production.

While Marxism has never firmly taken root in this country, the American socialist tradition of which Gilman was a part has had a quiet, but substantial, effect on American society. In broad terms, American socialists differed from Marx in that they rejected class antagonism, considered the state to be a potentially benevolent force, and viewed the family as an independent influence in society. An adequate understanding of Gilman requires seeing her in the context of this American socialist tradition.

The terms "consumption," "production," and "reproduction" refer to different phases of our metabolism with nature, but these processes are extremely mutable. Our needs and the manner in which we produce and reproduce are the result of conscious human action. In other words, all three processes are subject to human control. Marx and Engels recognized the socially contingent nature of consumption and production, but the process of reproduction does not receive the same careful analysis in their work. It is as though, as Jean-Paul Sartre puts it, the Marxian individual is born ready to apply for his first job.[2]

According to Marx and Engels, "production is simultaneously consumption as well" (*German Ideology*, 130).[3] However, consumption in the proper sense is "the destructive antithesis of production" (131). We produce ourselves as we consume, and we consume vital resources, both internal and external, as we produce. In a more basic sense, we consume the product of our work in order to continue to produce. While consumption is, for Marx and Engels, an integral part of the production process, it also connotes destruction, the using up of resources. Thus, consumption is the opposite of production and reproduction, yet this destruction is a necessary part of creation. Production is the process by which we deplete our current reservoir of energy, while simultaneously using tools, which are the product of earlier collective efforts, to transform raw materials. We must destroy in order to create.

In the Marxian vision of production and consumption, we create ourselves in the process of production. The processes occur simultaneously. Marx and Engels fail to see that we are not born capable of participating in social production. In terms of the individual life span, there is a substantial period during which production and consumption are not simultaneous. As children, we consume resources for many years before we join the ranks of working men and women. By integrating reproduction into the cycle of production and consumption, Gilman's thought sheds light on some of the deficiencies in Marx and Engels's theory.

According to Gilman, we receive nourishment from society as a right from the moment we are born, so work should be viewed as a means of paying back the community for the support already received. In a prize essay read before the Alameda County Federation of Trades, Gilman states:

> For nine months the dawning life receives all and gives nothing. For twenty years, if conditions are right, the immature man is fed and clothed and loved and taught, with no commensurate return. After that, it is the business of the mature man to work, not for what he is to get, but BECAUSE OF WHAT HE HAS HAD. . . . Organized society owes to the individual every possible form of nutrition and education, precisely as the body owes nutrition to the cell. It is the right of the individual to be so cared for, because he is a constituent part of society. He, in return, owes to society all the labor which nutrition and education have made possible to him. ("The Labor Movement," written in 1892, republished in Ceplair, *Nonfiction*, 69)

In terms of the individual life-cycle, consumption is chronologically prior to production. We must be supported through our infancy and childhood in order to work as an adult. What we consume in infancy are the products of the previous generation's labor. This intergenerational exchange is part of reproduction.

Reproduction, for Marx, is a dual process involving the daily remaking of one's own life and the creation of other human beings. While Marx considers the creation of other human beings to be the first social relationship, he argues that the family relationship recedes into the background and becomes a "subordinate" one as the means of production develop (*German Ideology*, 49–50). Hence, when Marx speaks of reproduction, he is referring primarily to the daily remaking of our own lives through socialized production.[4] Since Marx argues that production is appropriation, it follows that workers appropriate their own labor-power through the production process. Thus, from Marx's perspective, the process of production is also a process of self-creation and self-appropriation. Of course, the worker also creates a product, which is appropriated by the capitalist. Since the worker is prevented from appropriating the product he has created, Marx concludes that the worker is the "owner of nothing but his labour-power" (*Capital*, 1:290, 1017).

For Marx, alienation stems from the fact that workers do not appropriate what they produce under capitalism:

The object that labour produces, its product, stands opposed to it as *something alien*, as a *power independent* of the producer. The product of labour is labour embodied and made material in an object, it is the *objectification* of labour. The realization of labour is its objectification. In the sphere of political economy this realization of labour appears as a *loss of reality* for the worker, objectification as *loss of and bondage to the object*, and appropriation as *estrangement*, as *alienation*. (*Economic and Philosophic Manuscripts*, 324; emphasis in original)[5]

The root of alienation is our inability to appropriate the embodiment of our labor. At bottom, the concept of alienation is premised on the idea of ownership – the notion of production as appropriation. The worker is alienated from her product because it is appropriated by the capitalist and alienated from herself because she must produce and sell her labor-power as a commodity in order to survive (Marx, *Manuscripts*, 324–326).

Marx's objection is not to the idea of the worker owning her capacity to labor; rather, he objects to a state of affairs in which the worker must sell her labor-power on the market. Thus, Marx does not call into question the idea of self-ownership. The problem with his conception of labor-power is that it only makes sense if we ignore the contribution that others have made to our development and sustenance before we were able to participate in social production.

In this analysis, Marx gives insufficient attention to the prolonged period of dependency in childhood during which we can take little credit for our own development. Indeed, it is almost as though Marx abhors the thought of the dependency of childhood. He wants to believe that human beings are entirely self-created:

A *being* sees himself as independent only when he stands on his own feet, and he only stands on his own feet when he owes his *existence* to himself. A man who lives by the grace of another regards himself as a dependent being. But I live completely by the grace of another if I owe him not only the maintenance of my life but also its *creation*, if he is the *source* of my life. My life is necessarily grounded outside itself if it is not my own creation. (*Manuscripts*, 356; emphasis in original)

While this passage is in the context of a criticism of religious belief, it reveals a deeper discomfort with the idea that we cannot take responsibility for the creation of our own lives. It is almost as though Marx views having a mother and childhood dependency as unfortunate features of the human condition that impair adult autonomy. To overcome this discomfort, he argues that we create ourselves and acquire ownership of our labor-power through the production process. He neglects the fact that our conception, birth, and childhood development are the product of other people's labor. (Of course, some parts of this process are more laborious than others.) While Marx recognizes that the concept of self-begetting "contradicts all the *palpable evidence* of practical life," he still feels compelled to cling to it, and this deficiency in his thinking is rooted in an underlying fear of acknowledging the weakness and dependency of childhood (*Manuscripts*, 356).

Gilman, on the other hand, recognizes that during the first approximately fifteen years of our life we have little control over our own development. We then have about a decade until we have children of our own to cultivate self-growth and repair any damage that occurred as a result of inept parenting (*Concerning Children*, 11). Indeed, at the age of sixteen, Gilman set out to mold her own character. She selected characteristics of fictional and historical figures to emulate, concluding her course of self-development with Socrates (*Living*, 48–60).

The foundation for Marx's concept of alienation is partially undermined by the acknowledgment that we owe our development to others. Once childhood dependency is taken into account, it is clear that we cannot entirely appropriate our own labor-power through producing it ourselves. According to Gilman, individuals do not own their labor: "Our labor is all collective and coordinate" (*Human Work*, 355). Her conception of "social energy" reflects this rejection of the notion of ownership of our labor-power. Social energy is the force stored in material products that "has been accumulating in humanity from its birth" (192). It flows from one individual to the next through objects and ideas. According to Gilman, "a noble and beautiful work ennobles and beautifies the beholder, listener, reader, occupant, – the user" (174). Since social energy is stored in all objects available for public use, each generation is exposed to more social energy than the last. For Gilman, impression creates the need for expression. Thus, each generation becomes more fully developed and more expressive than the previous one.

Social energy is a useful alternative to Marx's concept of labor-power. Like expended labor-power, social energy is stored in products. It differs from labor-power, however, in that it flows through the individual without ever being owned by him or her. Gilman avers that all impressions are merely incentives to expression: "We are transmitters of energy, not vats for storage" (*Human Work*, 304). Social energy is imbibed in the process of consumption and emitted through production. The desire to work is, for Gilman, a product of the need to expel social energy. It is not, as it is for Marx, an innate drive (see *Manuscripts*, 328–329).

According to Gilman, the retention of social energy is unnatural and painful, causing intense suffering (*Human Work*, 155, 284). This sheds light on Gilman's intentions in "The Yellow Wallpaper." Walter Michaels claims that the narrator must write herself into existence. For Michaels, the story is about a woman who is driven to produce, but she must first produce herself (*The Gold Standard*, 5, 28). The writing that takes place in "The Yellow Wallpaper" is a process of "self-generation." Michaels argues that the narrator is giving birth to herself: the creeping around the room is a return to infancy, and the rope connecting her to the bed is an umbilical cord. He concludes that the story reflects Gilman's belief that one must produce oneself in order to own oneself (6, 10, 12–13).

The earlier discussion of Gilman's awareness of childhood dependency and the difficulties that it poses for the idea of self-ownership reveals that Michaels's interpretation is inaccurate. Gilman certainly does not believe that self-generation is possible. Moreover, an understanding of *Human Work* makes it clear that the malady from which the narrator of "The Yellow Wallpaper" is suffering is the retention of social energy. The narrator is weak and nearly insane because her husband/doctor has prescribed a "rest cure" for her nervous condition, which requires that she stay in bed most of the time doing nothing but staring at the wallpaper. Needless to say, this cure makes her more emotionally unstable and miserable than she was before.[6] For Gilman, the woman whose life is devoted entirely to consumption and reproduction is analogous to a gland that is prevented from secreting (*Women and Economics*, 117). She is unable to perform her proper function in the social organism. That function varies from one woman to the next, just as it varies from one organ to the next.

Since, according to Gilman, the retention of social energy causes suffering, there is a biological imperative to expel social energy that complements the moral imperative to return to society what we have already received from it. Thus, from Gilman's perspective, consumption compels production, both morally and biologically. For Marx, human beings also feel compelled to produce, but this drive is unrelated to consumption. It is merely the expression of our species-being (*Manuscripts*, 329). In other words, Marx considers the drive to produce to be innate. Consumption is necessary to enable us to produce, but it does not create the drive to do so.

By and large, American socialists and political economists of the Progressive Era paid much more attention to consumption than Marx did. Indeed, this is a distinguishing characteristic of American socialist and progressive thought. American socialists and progressive reformers tended to believe that the capitalist system could be transformed at many different points in the cycle of consumption, production, and reproduction. They did not view collective ownership of the means of production as the primary imperative. From Thorstein Veblen's critique of "conspicuous consumption" to Florence Kelley's National Consumers' League, American radical thinkers advocated reining in capitalist greed by becoming well-informed, frugal, self-critical consumers.

Marx gave little attention to overconsumption outside of the capitalist class. When he distinguished between the process of consumption and the process of production, his chief concern was that, under capitalism, workers' productivity was increasing while their level of consumption was decreasing. He states that "the misery of the worker is in inverse proportion to the power and volume of his production" (*Manuscripts*, 322). The more workers produce, the less they have for themselves and the more they enrich the capitalists. "Labour," according to Marx, "produces marvels for the rich, but it produces privation for the worker" (325). Capitalism ultimately reduces the needs of the workers below the level of animals; fresh air, light, a clean habitation, and decent food become unnecessary luxuries (359).

Gilman also attributes insufficient consumption to the maldistribution inherent in capitalism. Just as the body circulates nourishment to all its organs, society, she contends, should distribute nourishment to all its members (*Human Work*, 183–184). Carrying on the metaphor, she further argues that the social organism "has safety, peace, shelter, warmth, enough to eat – and chronic indigestion!" (10). Our society, according to Gilman, is making "a steady diet of its own meat" (238). In other words, such a gross maldistribution of resources is a sort of social starvation. On this point, Marx and Gilman are in agreement: both attribute insufficient consumption to maldistribution, not scarcity.

While Marx's criticism of consumption under capitalism focuses largely on the tendency toward asceticism, Gilman, like Thorstein Veblen, focuses a great deal of attention on excessive consumption, even among those who are not wealthy capitalists.[7] This concern about overconsumption and waste is an aspect of American socialism that differs from traditional Marxism, and it stems from greater attention to the effects of consigning women to the home.[8] Gilman argues that women's absorption in meeting bodily needs causes each family member to develop "inordinate appetites" and "morbid tastes" (*Human Work*, 314, 353–355). As a result, the family becomes "a hotbed of personal indulgence" and "a little down-drawing whirlpool of antediluvian individualism" (315, 385). For Gilman, a life devoted to motherhood and consumption results in an obsession with the fulfillment of physical needs. In addition, she claims that the failure to professionalize and collectivize consumption and reproduction results in tremendous waste and inefficiency. The consignment of virtually all women to ministering to the needs of bodily maintenance is, according to Gilman, "a crude waste of half the world's force" (*The Home*, 316–317).

Similarly, Veblen's critique of "conspicuous consumption" in *The Theory of the Leisure Class* is largely based on its wastefulness and its tendency to prevent women from fulfilling "the instinct of workmanship" (232). By "wasteful," Veblen means that the activity "does not serve human life or human well-being on the whole" (78). He argues that servants and women are engaged in "vicarious leisure." Vicarious leisure can take the form of unnecessary household labor or idleness. In either case, it is the conspicuous waste of wives' or servants' time and effort to pay tribute to the wealth possessed by the male head of the household (55–56).

Gilman shares Veblen's disdain for conspicuous waste. She argues that the present organization of private life costs three times what is necessary to meet the same needs (*The Home*, 320–321). This waste has negative consequences for individual men and women as well as for the next generation. Far from enabling women to devote more time to mothering, conspicuous leisure "dries the very springs of motherhood," rendering well-off women completely idle. Thus, children do not benefit from having a mother who has no public responsibilities. Rather, her exclusion from production causes all her social and maternal instincts to shrivel up. Furthermore, the inefficiency of the isolated household forces men into occupations that are most remunerative, not most socially valuable or inherently rewarding (296–298).

According to Warren Susman, this abhorrence of waste and respect for efficiency is characteristic of the Progressive Era. Industrialism, or *Fordismus*, was a major component of American progressive thought. In *Culture as History*, Susman associates industrialism with "a belief in order, rationality, and science," "a respect for production [and] efficiency," and a recognition of the need for planning and state bureaucracy (83).

American socialism at the turn of the century was an outgrowth of this industrialist orientation. This, in and of itself, is entirely consistent with Marxism, but American socialism differed from traditional Marxism in that it was less antagonistic toward partial remedies, such as the establishment of state welfare programs, within the capitalist system. American socialists' respect for planning and efficiency translated into a faith in the powers of the state. Thus, many of them rejected the ruling class theory. They were more inclined to view the state as a benevolent force that could safely be entrusted with economic administration without first having to be captured by the proletariat.[9] The focus of American socialism was more on efficiency, redistribution, and protective legislation than on collective ownership of the means of production.

This rejection of waste and glorification of efficiency was not, however, a rejection of consumption. In discussing Veblen, Michaels claims that the "utopian" rejection of excessive consumption is a rejection of desire, pleasure, and life itself (*Gold Standard*, 48). This is a gross distortion of Gilman's and Veblen's thought. Michaels has taken Marx's criticism of utopian socialism and inappropriately applied it to radical American thinkers at the turn of the century.

Gilman and Veblen were not advocating asceticism; rather, they argued that we must not allow ourselves to be consumed by consumption. They, like Marx, envisioned a time when the conscious distribution of social resources in accordance with real human needs would put consumption in the proper perspective. Consumption, for these thinkers, is necessary to sustain life, but it is not the end of life. Utopianism, far from being the contraction of desire, is born of the belief that the fulfillment of everyone's basic needs is possible. The Progressive Era American socialist, as represented by Gilman and Veblen, believed that we have an abundance of social resources; we must simply redistribute them, so that everyone's consumptive needs can be met.

In addition to demanding redistribution, Gilman, like Veblen and Marx, argued that production must be oriented toward meeting *real* human needs. That is, all three theorists averred that we must consciously direct production toward the creation and fulfillment of needs that enhance the quality of life. One of their criticisms of capitalism was that it has a tendency to create artificial needs (i.e., the need to accumulate money or to make invidious comparisons to others), which, even if fulfilled, do nothing to make people happier (Gilman, *Human Work*, 323; Marx, *Manuscripts*, 358; Veblen, *Theory*, 78).

To say that production should be directed toward meeting real human needs is not to say that the fulfillment of material needs should be the reason for working. Gilman and Marx contend that production ceases to be human work if it is *compelled* by necessity. For Marx, what distinguishes human beings from animals is that we produce in the absence of immediate physical need (*Manuscripts*, 329). The gratification derived from production is far greater than that derived from consumption because work is the life-activity of our species (326). Our primary need, according to Marx, is to engage in free, conscious productive activity, and work is free only when it is not directed toward individual sustenance. For Marx, to produce in freedom from necessity is to follow the inner compulsion to produce without having the experience tainted by the need to earn one's bread.

Gilman also sees work performed in freedom from necessity as innately more gratifying than working to earn one's living. Both

Marx and Gilman reconcile working in freedom from necessity with working to meet real human needs by making the fulfillment of *collective* needs the purpose of our toil. When one's individual livelihood is secure, work becomes a conscious contribution to communal resources, rather than merely a means to sustain individual life. According to Gilman, only work that is performed as an expression of the "Social Passion" is free work. By "Social Passion," she means a natural evolutionary development that is manifested in "devotion to a 'cause' of any sort, a class, a club, a corps, [or] a union" (*Human Work*, 150). Work in a properly organized society is gratifying because it is a release of Social Passion. Gilman states: "The free and socially conscious human being works because he likes to, because he can't help it, because it is his honourable return in small degree for the immeasurable benefits he has received from infancy from his supporting society" (*Human Work*, 335–337).

Working to support oneself or one's family is, from Gilman's perspective, demeaning to the individual and indicates a false understanding of the economic process. It reflects a failure to realize that we reach adulthood indebted to society, and our primary responsibility is the repayment of that debt. According to Gilman, members of the working class abhor their lot, not only because they are overworked and underpaid, but because they are unaware that the labor they drearily perform has significance far beyond their own maintenance. They are blind to the importance of their work for the functioning of the social body (*Human Work*, 199, 354). Thus, for Gilman, the gratification derived from production is not innate. It is a product of social construction. In order to derive gratification from work, we must understand its true social significance. Under capitalism, people mistakenly believe that they work to support themselves, when, in fact, they are repaying their debt to society.

When work is correctly understood as social service, it becomes an uplifting activity. According to Gilman, "The solitary savage applies his personal energy to personal needs. The social group applies its collective energy to its collective needs. The savage works by himself, for himself; the civilized man works in elaborate interdependence with many, for many" (*The Home*, 84). The failure of individuals to recognize the significance of their work prevents them from experiencing the gratification to be derived from contributing to the common good. Thus, the wage system unnecessarily coerces people to work. For Gilman, the belief that the maintenance of the individual is the object of work is as absurd as the belief that the maintenance of teeth is the purpose of chewing (*Human Work*, 180).

If working to support oneself is demeaning, how can it be reconciled with Gilman's demand for economic independence? She has a very unconventional understanding of economic independence: "In a large sociological sense no civilized human being is 'self-supporting.' We are all interdependent; living not by virtue of our own exertions, but by virtue of the exertions of many other persons; those before us and those beside us, whose combined labors make up human life" ("Does a Man Support His Wife?" 9). However, she continues, "in an individual sense a man may be called 'self-supporting' who contributes to the world more in labor value than he takes out" (9). In other words, we are all interdependent in the grand scheme of things, but we don't make equal contributions to the collective. Gilman's understanding of economic independence is unconventional in that she requires the individual to contribute *more* than what is necessary for individual sustenance in order to be considered self-supporting. Despite the inefficiency of the isolated household, she claims that women do, in fact, produce enough to be considered "self-supporting" in the individual sense of the term, but she further contends that economic independence requires parity between what one contributes and what one receives. In the case of housewives, there is no direct relationship between their productivity and their standard of living ("Does a Man Support His Wife?" 10; *Women and Economics*, 11, 15). For instance, the wives of the richest men do the least work. It is in this sense that women, from Gilman's perspective, are not economically independent. What the housewife receives from society is contingent on that society's valuation of her husband's efforts.

For both Gilman and Marx, consumption is the beginning and the end of production. In addition to being a prerequisite of production, it is the collective purpose and end result of the production process. Both aver that production must be directed toward meeting human needs, but it rises to the level of human work only if it takes place in freedom from necessity. There is a tension, however, between producing to meet human needs and producing in freedom from necessity, which can be overcome only through socialized production. When we consciously work to meet collective rather than individual needs, we reconcile the need to labor with freedom.

According to Gilman, the paradigmatic example of toiling for the benefit of others is motherhood. Indeed, she argues that industry originated in the maternal impulse:[10] "Industry, at its base, is a feminine function. The surplus energy of the mother does not manifest itself in noise, or combat, or display, but in productive industry. Because of her mother-power she became the first inventor and laborer; being in truth the mother of all industry as well as all people. Man's entrance upon industry is late and reluctant" (*Man-Made World*, 36–37).

This vision of primitive society is significant in that it integrates production and reproduction. It explicitly undermines the notion that child care and production are mutually exclusive. In contrast, reproduction and production remained separated in traditional Marxian theory because reproduction was consigned to the private sphere. Aside from Engels's relatively brief reference to the need to bring women back into public industry in "The Origin of the Family, Private Property, and the State" (510; first published in 1884), Marx and his followers rarely discussed the process of reproduction. According to Marx and Engels: "Communism differs from all previous movements in that it overturns the basis of all earlier relations of production and intercourse, and for the first time consciously treats all natural premises as the creatures of hitherto existing men, strips them of their natural character and subjugates them to the power of united individuals" (*German Ideology*, 86). While Marx and Engels argue that all relations of production are the result of human action, they fail to apply the same argument to reproduction. Reproduction retains a strong natural component. Marx focused his attention on the alienation and exploitation experienced by the worker and neglected the experience of women excluded from social production. Gilman's theory, on the other hand, integrates production and reproduction and, in so doing, demonstrates the inadequacy of the notion of ownership of our product and consequently ownership of our children.

As discussed above, Gilman took issue with the idea that we own the product of our labor. She did not view production as appropriation. For Gilman, objects represent stored social energy, not the congealed labor of individuals. Again, she drew parallels between production and reproduction. She argued that our children, like other products of our labor, are social products and thus belong to society as a whole. Parents are merely the conduits of social resources. Gilman exhorts mothers to remember that they "*do not own these children* – that they are separate human beings with human rights" ("Who Owns the Children?" 28; emphasis in original). Similarly, we do not own the inanimate products of our labor. According to Gilman, the notion that an individual has a right to the product of her labor is a "sociological absurdity" (*Human Work*, 355). "All property," she argues, "is a social product, evolved in the course of social development, needed by society for the social service" (306). Neither the inanimate products of our labor nor our children can be considered our own.

In fairness to Marx, he believed that what is collectively produced should be collectively appropriated. The individual is alienated from the product when what is socially produced is appropriated by those who did not participate in the production process (*Manuscripts*, 330–331). Nevertheless, the concept of alienation lends itself too easily to misinterpretation. What Marx is really objecting to is a lack of control over the process of distribution. I think Gilman explains more clearly than Marx himself what he really meant. Alienation presupposes ownership. For Marx, overcoming "alienation" does not require that the product be restored to the individual worker or group of workers. It means that those who produce social resources should collectively determine how they are distributed. In rejecting the idea of ownership of our product, Gilman's theory makes the solution to maldistribution more obvious than Marx's theory does.

The concept of alienation is also problematic when it is applied to reproduction. In *The Politics of Reproduction*, Mary O'Brien, a Marxist feminist, avers that men, upon discovering paternity, developed patriarchy to overcome their alienation from their offspring, since they were prevented from overcoming their alienation in the same way that women do, that is, through reproductive labor (53). Unfortunately, the process by which the father appropriates the child results in the mother being alienated from the reproductive labor that she has invested in the child (57–58). There are several problems with this theory. First, it never calls into question the notion that children are property. Moreover, if this theory were true, the foundation of patriarchy could be destroyed through male participation in child care. If men engaged in reproductive labor, they would no longer be alienated from their children and thus would no longer need to subordinate women in order to lay claim to their offspring. Although more men are caring for their own children, male dominance is in no danger of collapsing. Clearly, something more is involved.

Gilman argued that the socialization of child care is necessary to enable women to become full participants in economic and political life. For her, the primary problem with our economic structure is not alienation, but the isolation of women in the private sphere. Working in isolation, women are prevented from developing the social consciousness that follows from working collectively (*Women and Economics*, 306; *Human Work*, 129, 132). Women's narrow range of interest and their inability to think about the common good then exert a negative influence on their husbands (*The Home*, 277). Thus, the isolation of women in the home hinders social progress. According to Gilman, "Only as we live, think, feel, and work outside the home, do we become humanly developed, civilized, socialized" (*Women and Economics*, 222). She agreed with the popular notion that the home should be a retreat from the world, but it will serve that function only when all domestic labor and child care are professionalized and socialized.

For Gilman, the socialization of child care will also produce more well-adjusted children and more fully developed adults in the next generation. The problem is overcoming our possessiveness of our children, not our alienation from them. If women were less possessive of their children, they could more easily accept the idea of entrusting their development to professional child-culturists. Most parents do not have the training, the skill, or the time necessary to foster their children's full development (*Women and Economics*, 293). Moreover, children require interaction with other children their own age and facilities designed for their use (*Concerning Children*, 42–44, 76–78).

Gilman does not advocate separating children completely from their parents. She envisions a society in which children will return to the home in the evening just as both of their parents do: "Direct, concentrated unvarying personal love is too hot an atmosphere for a young soul. Variations of loneliness, anger, and injustice, are not changes to be desired. A steady, diffused love, lighted with wisdom, based always on justice, and varied with rapturous draughts of our own mother's depth of devotion, would make us into a new people in a few generations" (*Women and Economics*, 292). According to Gilman, the socialization of child care enables us to have collectively what we could never have separately. Just as children in a class taught by a professional teacher have a richer educational experience than children taught by an untrained private tutor, children raised collectively benefit from the knowledge and experience that only professionals possess, while also learning from their interactions with one another.

Gilman emphasized the importance of professionalizing domestic work as much as she emphasized the need to socialize it. Domestic industry applies to a certain grade of work, not a special kind of work; it is "a stage of development through which all kinds pass" (*The Home*, 30–31). Since specialization and the division of labor have enabled the species to advance to this point, it only makes sense to extend the same principle to household industry. According to Gilman, no one would frequent a combined restaurant and laundry, or a kindergarten and carpet cleaning establishment, yet the ordinary household encompasses no less than six industries – cooking, laundering, cleaning, sewing, nursing, and teaching. Moreover, one woman must master all these trades ("Domestic Economy," 158).

Gilman views this state of affairs as atavistic and inordinately wasteful. Specialization, by its very nature, reduces the amount of work necessary to meet our needs. At the time of writing *Human Work* (1904), Gilman believed that, if we were to extend the principles of specialization and professionalization to the remaining domestic industries, the whole workday need not exceed four to six hours (234–235). It is, from her perspective, only social prejudices that have prevented us from doing so.

What Gilman failed to realize is that the modern home is not merely an atavistic holdover from the past. According to Eli Zaretsky, the home performs a different function in modern society than it did before production was socialized. In feudal times, identity was based on an individual's place in the division of labor. When production was taken out of the home, personal life became the basis for individual identity, and people came to view the home as the locus of personal life. Since personal differentiation is thought to occur in the home and women are considered to be essential to the maintenance of a true home, women's emergence into public life threatens our individuality (Zaretsky, "Socialism and Feminism III," 90−96).

This is at the root of the conservative resistance to fully integrating women into socialized production. The solution, of course, is for people to derive a sense of identity from their work and social activities. It is not clear, however, that people in Gilman's vision of the future would be able to individuate through their work.

Gilman viewed the specialization and collectivization of household industry as necessary to enable individual women to realize themselves: "Women need progressive organized industry as much as they need education or food or air − it is a condition of human existence and progression" ("The Ethics of Woman's Work," 17). She further contended that work is "the main line of organic relation" (*The Home*, 198). "The first duty of a human being," according to Gilman, is "to assume right functional relation to Society" (*Human Work*, 369). Women are prevented from fulfilling the human need and duty to relate to the world through specialized work when they are excluded from socialized production. In *Women and Economics*, she states: "Specialization and organization are the basis of human progress, the organic methods of social life. They have been forbidden to women almost absolutely" (67). For Gilman, a woman whose work is limited to ministering to the needs of her family is unmoored from society, buffeted about in a sea of her husband's and children's personal demands.

Gilman's insistence on the need to professionalize and socialize domestic industry has often been misunderstood as a demand for "market feminism." In other words, commentators have claimed that she is a liberal feminist in a radical's clothing. For instance, Michaels claims that Gilman's feminism is a "market phenomenon." According to him, Gilman wants to subject all facets of life to market exchange. In his interpretation of "The Yellow Wallpaper," production doesn't count unless it is for sale. To support this contention, he takes a passage in *Women and Economics* in which Gilman argues that farmers' wives go insane from working in isolation: he claims that they go crazy because they cannot sell their product on the market (*Women and Economics*, 267;

Michaels, *Gold Standard*, 17). Similarly, in *For Her Own Good*, Barbara Ehrenreich and Deirdre English claim that Gilman is "perhaps the most brilliant American proponent of the sexual rationalist position," which they define as a call for "assimilation" into the world of men with ancillary changes, such as day care (21).

In fact, Gilman is not applying market principles to every aspect of life, nor is she merely proposing that women assimilate into the world of men. She does propose that the professionalization and collectivization of domestic labor initially take the form of business enterprises, but this is not her final end. While this cannot be ascertained from *Women and Economics* (1898), a reading of her later writings, such as *Human Work* (1904), makes this clear.

Gilman is quite critical of wage slavery. She argues that the wage system, like slavery, unnecessarily coerces people to work (*Human Work*, 199–200, 218, 335). Like Marx, she views the wage-system as a stage we must pass through on the way to socialism: "The wage-system is as much a makeshift, temporary, and self-destructive system as was the feudal, the chattel-slavery, or any other of our progressive steps in economic adjustment, and is also as essential and natural a step as were any of these in their time" ("The Ethics of Wage-Earning"). Gilman sees women-owned businesses that provide cooked food or cleaning services as a necessary transitional step toward a society in which no one works for wages. In a lecture entitled "The Ethics of Woman's Work," she states: "Let me briefly consider and dismiss the money side of the question. So long as work is done for money and money is paid for work, women should do their work and receive their money as men do their lives long" (7). Her point is that women must be fully integrated into the wage-system before that system can be transcended.

Michaels's criticism of Gilman is based on the conflation of social production and the free market. What is most critical to Gilman is that everyone be able to participate in social production. Women, as active agents in the socialization of domestic labor, will transform their consciousness through working together and will simultaneously expand the public sphere. Her long-term goal is for women to participate on an equal basis in social production, not the free market.

The problem with the female-owned housekeeping enterprises

that Gilman advocates is that the work involved is not very challenging or intrinsically rewarding. Moreover, the workers in these enterprises are quite likely to feel some sense of alienation because they are not producing a lasting product at all. Gilman seems to think that the awareness that one is contributing to collective resources is all that is necessary to ensure that one's work will be gratifying. While contributing to the collective is a higher purpose than putting bread on the table, individuals also need to make a mark on the world. She recognizes this need at times, but she does not give it enough attention (*Women and Economics*, 116).[11]

One does not have to accept Gilman's contention that industry springs from the maternal impulse to agree that work that is viewed as a contribution to society is more inherently gratifying than work directed toward individual sustenance. Thus far, Gilman and Marx are in agreement. Marx, however, artificially separated production and reproduction, and we continue to do so today. While Marx recognized that production and consumption are simultaneous, he failed to see that reproduction is also simultaneously production. Ultimately, the only tenable distinction between production and reproduction is the degree of socialization. When domestic work is socialized, the distinction between productive and reproductive labor will virtually disappear.

Thus, Gilman's understanding of the cycle of consumption, production, and reproduction complements Marx's theory in several ways. First, it shows that childhood dependency is a part of the human life cycle that must be integrated into any coherent economic theory. Marx's neglect of this stage of human development leads him to focus too narrowly on the need to eliminate private ownership of the means of production in order to overcome alienation. In arguing that human beings create themselves through the process of production, he fails to see that, in terms of the individual life cycle, we owe our existence and our sustenance throughout childhood to others. Once this central fact is recognized, it becomes clear that we cannot meaningfully say that we own our labor-power or the product of our labor, whether that product is a child or an inanimate object. Since the concept of alienation is premised on such ownership, it is partially undermined by Gilman's analysis.

In addition, Gilman's focus on the experience of women enables her to see the pain of being excluded from social production and of spending one's life engaged in fulfilling the physical needs of family members in the isolated household. At bottom, Gilman and Marx are united in the belief that human gratification is derived from taking part in a socialized production process that is directed toward meeting collective needs; Gilman, however, offers a theory that encompasses a broader range of human experience and affords more means by which this social transformation can be effected.

NOTES

1. See John Humphrey Noyes's *History of American Socialisms*.

2. Sartre states: "Contemporary Marxists are concerned only about adults: to read them, one would think that we are born old enough to start our first jobs; they forget their own childhood and all that it entails; to read them, it is as if people experience alienation and self-objectification *first* through their own labor, rather than each living *first*, as a child, *through the labor of his or her parents*" (*Critique de la raison dialectique*, 47; my translation; emphasis in original).

3. While *The German Ideology* was completed in 1846, it was not published until 1932. Obviously, I cannot claim that Gilman was familiar with this text. For that matter, I have found no evidence that Gilman read any of Marx's other work. In fact, she wrote to Houghton Gilman, her future husband, "Can you read Marx? I can't now. Maybe never could" (quoted in Lane, *To Herland and Beyond*, 203). Nevertheless, Gilman had a general knowledge of Marxian principles, such as exploitation and class struggle. Her letters indicate, however, that her primary influences were American reform novelists, such as Edward Bellamy and Ignatius Donnelly, and Fabian socialists, such as George Bernard Shaw (203).

4. By socialized production, I mean work that has been subjected to the division of labor and is performed collectively. I do not use this term to indicate that the means of production have been nationalized.

5. *The Economic and Philosophic Manuscripts* were written in 1844, but were not first published until 1932.

6. Gilman underwent S. Weir Mitchell's infamous "rest cure" herself after the birth of her daughter (*Living*, 95).

7. Thorstein Veblen is one of the few social theorists whom Gilman cites in her work. She repeatedly makes reference to him in *The Home* and also mentions him in *The Man-Made World*. It is not surprising that she turned to him for inspiration. Like Gilman, Veblen defies easy categorization. Although he was trained as an economist, he also wrote from the

perspective of a philosopher, sociologist, and psychologist. While he was an incisive critic of American society, he was unable to detach himself completely from the values of the Progressive Era. Indeed, he represents that period of American history in his wholehearted commitment to efficiency (Mills, introduction, in *Theory of the Leisure Class*, x–xi).

8. The material feminists of the late nineteenth century, such as Melusina Fay Peirce and Marie Stevens Howland, are also part of this tradition. See Dolores Hayden's *The Grand Domestic Revolution.*

9. See Edward Bellamy's *Looking Backward* and Laurence Gronlund's *The Co-operative Commonwealth.*

10. It should be noted that Veblen also contends that primitive industry was performed by women, while men engaged in "war, hunting, sports, and devout observances" (22–23). Similarly, in *Pure Sociology* (1903) Lester Frank Ward claims that male activities in "primitive" society cannot be considered labor because labor is uneventful and repetitive work. According to Ward, only the work of women in "primitive" societies can properly be considered labor (270–271). Ward influenced Gilman to an even greater degree than Veblen did. She cites him in *Women and Economics* and, in her autobiography, she characterizes his Gynecocentric Theory as "the greatest single contribution to the world's thought since Evolution" (187).

11. Gilman also fails to address the class issue. While the middle-class woman who establishes one of these professional housekeeping services can point to some tangible product of her labor, that is, the enterprise itself, the workers in these enterprises have nothing to show for their toil except a paycheck. Housework, by its very nature, has no visible lasting effect. Of course, this criticism does not apply to the professional child-culturists who are also part of Gilman's schema. A cadre of child development experts would be able to see their labor crystallized in the emerging men and women of a new age.

JUDITH A. ALLEN

Reconfiguring Vice

Charlotte Perkins Gilman, Prostitution, and
Frontier Sexual Contracts

Gilman abhorred prostitution:

> Man . . . has insisted on maintaining another class of
> women, . . . subservient to his desires; a barren, mischievous
> unnatural relation, wholly aside from parental purposes, and
> absolutely injurious to society. . . . Many, under the old mis-
> taken notion of what used to be called "the social necessity" of
> prostitution, will protest the idea of its extinction. . . . An intel-
> ligent and powerful womanhood will put an end to this indul-
> gence of one sex at the expense of the other and to the injury
> of both. . . . One major cause of the decay of nations is "the
> social evil" – a thing wholly due to androcentric culture. (*Man-
> Made World*, 246–259)

Like many feminists of her period, the author of *Women and Economics* critically analyzed the interface between the two key sexual contracts: marriage and prostitution.[1] Arguably, her concerns
with prostitution – the depth and intensity of that concern – remain "underread" in existing work on Gilman, for reasons worth
exploring. The bulk of Gilman scholarship is literary in prove-
nance. Until recently, scholars have devoted most attention to
"The Yellow Wallpaper" and, to a lesser extent, *Herland.* Despite
important exceptions, existing work is textual and to a degree
biographical, rather than *contextual* in approach. With the period of twenty-three years separating these better-known Gilman
works, there has been insufficient attention to their place within
her larger oeuvre. She published at a prolific rate important and
critical nonfiction works in the 1892–1915 period. These include

Women and Economics, *The Home*, and *The Man-Made World*, as well as didactic novels such as *What Diantha Did* and *The Crux*. These indicative texts forge important links between the well-known 1892 and 1915 fictions.

The argument advanced here is that Gilman shared in a common, international, late nineteenth-century feminist critique of marriage and of other sexual economic contracts, most particularly, prostitution. Indeed, prostitution was a pervasive preoccupation throughout her theoretical writings of the 1898–1932 period. It was the centerpiece of one of her last nonfiction publications, "Parasitism and Civilized Vice" (1931).[2]

One of Gilman's most significant contributions to feminist theory of her period was her attempt to provide a sound biological basis for feminism through a reworking of evolutionary theory. The radical reconfiguration of the sexual contract of marriage, the eradication of the sexual contract of prostitution, and the confinement of the erotic contract to the reproductive were some outcomes that she hoped would result from feminism embarking on a biological and gynaecocentric trajectory.

A penultimate indicator of these beneficial outcomes would be the demise of the prostitute. Her position on prostitutes as *women* (as distinct from prostitution the institution) can disturb or offend current feminist sensibilities,[3] perhaps to an extent that compares with present criticisms of Gilman's notorious racism, ethnocentrism, anti-Semitism, class prejudice, and heterosexism.[4] Nonetheless, the reconfiguration of marriage and the demise of the prostitute as a significant sexual identity meant a corollary reconfiguration of "vice," which, in Gilman's schema, placed the more significant focus on men, upon male demand for prostitution. For she never accepted the view that prostitution was anything other than a trade, a living, for women, albeit an injurious and obnoxious one. For men, however, it was indulgence, recreation, pleasure, and a central, condoned form of male sexuality, with dangerous, ominous consequences for women, children, and "the race." Gilman sought to end prostitution because she saw it as the prerequisite for changing men's sexual behavior to more resemble women's. Certainly, the author of *Women and Economics* did not anticipate in 1898 that the apparent ending of women's widespread, visible dependence on prostitution for a living by the year of her death in 1935 might coincide with the development

Motherhood and Reproduction

of sexual behavior in women that increasingly resembled men's.[5] If she began her theoretical career analyzing the prostitution-economics-disease connection which spotlighted men, the unexpected challenge she faced at its end was the prostitution-sexuality continuum – for women.

The centrality of prostitution in Gilman's critique of marital economic dependence for women and our "Androcentric Culture" remains unacknowledged by biographers, scholars, and analysts of her texts.[6] It is not too much to say that, as for many other feminists of her period, worldwide, prostitution for Gilman epitomized the evils of women's situation.[7] Identifying it among "the three great evils most strictly due to our androcentric culture – war, intemperance, and prostitution," she noted that prostitution, because accompanied by "its train of diseases," had won for itself the distinct and grave title of "the Social Evil" ("The Oldest Profession in the World," 63). References to it haunted both *Women and Economics* and *The Man-Made World*. Indeed when explaining many key points of arguments, it is remarkable how frequently she drew on examples of prostitutes or prostitution.

Gilman represented individual prostitutes with some sympathy. The ex-madam of a brothel, Jeanne, for instance is a central character in *The Crux*, discussed below. Gilman showed a clear and realistic understanding of the systemic factors that led to women's recruitment into the trade. Nonetheless, she saw prostitutes as a group, a sexual-political entity, as the enemies of women's advancement. They weakened the bargaining position of all women. They helped sex-indulgent men deteriorate "the Race" (*Man-Made World*, 63). War was evil because sex-segregated men used prostitutes and, upon returning home, infected their sweethearts and wives, damaging generations to come (*Man-Made World*, 169). Prostitutes were the agents of all that was worst in men. They offered the most extreme example of the reversal of nature by which women exhibited sex-attraction plumage. In the frequent and needless changes called "fashion," prostitutes led the way, to please men's sex-indulgent demand for variety (175).

The protection of the institution of prostitution and men's prerogatives in it must be swept away as a precondition for progressive change for women. Gilman urged law reform. Practices presently not crimes, or only trivial offenses, would need to become seriously punished. Seducing girls into prostitution, living off the earnings and related extortion of prostitutes, and, above all, knowingly infecting a wife and "poisoning" an unborn child – all these practices must end (205).

Gilman's burning gaze at prostitution was as ferocious as that of her international contemporaries, such as Australia's Rose Scott and Vida Goldstein or Britain's Millicent Garrett Fawcett and Christabel Pankhurst, and it deserves a more substantial contextual reading by United States historians.[8] The tendency for histories of prostitution to be anchored within urban history, regional history, or the history of Progressivism and related reform has had one marked result: a relative underreading of the significance of prostitution for the history of sexual relations in the United States.[9] If anything, by contrast, Australian historians may have overread the counterpart significance of prostitution in colonial and postcolonial Australia.[10] A considerable amount of comparative historiographical unraveling would be required to explain divergent national approaches to prostitution. United States historians tend to "normalize" prostitution in history and to portray historical protagonists who are concerned about it adversely. This results in a body of work uncongenial to the understanding of Gilman's concerns in their historical context.[11] That task remains ahead.

Two novels, *What Diantha Did* and *The Crux*, several short stories, and selected Gilman articles centered upon women selling "sexualized" services.[12] She explored both utopian and critical views of the impact of sexual contracts upon women's lives, often locating her utopian explorations in a treasured topos – the West. Here she staged a fictional sexual contract collision in the prostitute-wife encounter.

Gilman's West embraced territory from Colorado to California. Her benign view of the West is understandable. It was the place of flight and refuge from her disastrous first marriage; it was the home of many of her most significant friends and associates; and it was the setting for beginning her career as a writer.[13] Gilman absorbed contemporary theories postulating "the frontier" as a zone of freedom, democracy, and innovation, first expounded in 1893 by Frederick Jackson Turner.[14] She represented women as holding a better sexual economic bargaining position in the demographically male-dominated West than in the female-dominated Northeast. This was a fascinating "Turnerian" outworking, though one with serious theoretical costs.

The ubiquity of prostitution and venereal diseases in western high masculinity zones was a stubborn fact Gilman faced. Indeed, she made it dramatically pivotal in *The Crux* and other writings. She believed that prostitution in the West was a coordinate of a strong marriage market for women. Anywhere that it was the major form of male sexuality was a place where men likely outnumbered women to a striking degree. Only through monogamous marriage could women undertake the best, most highly evolved, form of motherhood. For the good of the "race," reformed marriage was essential. So Gilman finally treated prostitution with a certain resignation, while also seeking its eventual eradication.

This contrasted with the stances of prominent feminist theorists in other white settler societies, upon whom Gilman's work was otherwise enormously influential. Australian feminists Louisa Lawson (1845–1920), Rose Scott (1847–1925), and Vida Goldstein (1869–1949) revered Gilman, while ex-patriot feminist Miles Franklin (1879–1954) befriended her in 1913, dubbing her "unquestionably the greatest American woman alive today."[15] Yet these Australian feminists, all with rural and "frontier" backgrounds, fiercely resisted the notion that women should sell "womanliness" or feminine attributes or skills, through *any* sexual contract, in arguments more utopian than Gilman's (Allen, *Rose Scott*, 118–124, 178–180). Finally, Gilman saw the sexual contract of marriage as inevitable for women's "race-function" as mothers and offered a consistently negative or at least deprived representation of spinsterhood and celibacy as "unnatural."[16] The task for feminism was to theorize and guide women toward making the best deal. This included renegotiation of the contents of the labor description of "wife" and "mother" and pursuit of combining these labors with other paid work and careers.

Gilman's concerns about prostitution should receive analysis in the framework of her evolutionary then gynaecocentric arguments for feminist economic and cultural transformation upon biological grounds.[17] Her exploration of the impact of venereal disease and its impact upon what she called "the Race" (meaning *Homo sapiens*) initially may seem to confound her recommendation that "unmated" northeastern women should go west to secure mates, for she was acutely conscious of the place of prostitution in segregated male communities (see *Man-Made World*). Arguably, she became increasingly convinced that women's ennoblement and advance could only proceed if, as a sex, they restored themselves to the position of being able to "choose" the fittest of men as partners and fathers of "the Race."[18]

Where could the project of restoring women's natural rights to select the best mates be even dreamed of or pursued? Only in places of skewed sex ratios, undersupplied with marriageable women, oversupplied with marriageable men, could the proper process of female-initiated sexual selection, fundamental to benign evolution, be reestablished. The consequences of prostitution, then, had to be faced by a pioneering group of "clean" women, to set the eugenic wrongs to right and to put the prostitute out of business. The opportunity for that confrontation existed in only one place at the turn of the century: the "woman-hungry" West.

Whatever may emerge from revisions in the international historiography of prostitution, it is clear that the place of prostitution in Gilman's account of androcentrism and of desired feminist transformation demands fuller analysis. Moreover, her creative use of new theories and paradigms, such as Turner's "frontier hypothesis," in a fascinating blend with her existing evolutionary adherence in *What Diantha Did* and *The Crux* bears scrutiny by historians not only of the United States, but also of other white, genocidal "settler societies," especially those of the British Commonwealth.

In *Women and Economics*, Gilman wrote:

> The personal profit of women bears but too close a relation to their power to win and hold the other sex. . . . When we confront this fact boldly and plainly in the open market of vice, we are sick with horror. When we see the same economic relation made permanent, established by law, sanctified by religion, covered with flowers and incense . . . we think it innocent, lovely and right. The transient trade we think evil. The bargain for life we think good. But the biological effect is the same. In both cases the female gets her food from the male by virtue of her sex relationship to him. (63)

This reiterates the long-standing feminist suggestion of an analogy between marriage and prostitution. Their semblance as sexual contracts troubled her both before her 1884 marriage to Charles Walter Stetson and after. Only a week after their wedding, the bride's diary records the couple's first fight on 9 May: "Get a nice little dinner. I suggest that he pay me for my services and he much dislikes the idea. I am grieved at offending him, mutual misery. Bed and cry" (*Diaries*, 280). She gave birth to a daughter, Katharine, nine months later. A complete mental breakdown followed. Her prenatal diaries conveyed a despairing and resentful account of the mindless drudgery of the dishwashing, cleaning, tidying, sewing, cooking, and marketing. These tasks were supposed to fill her hours and justify financial support as "wife." Her diary entries for 7, 15, and 16 August hint, too, at the problematic dimensions of the sexual side of the bargain. In response, she often failed to complete the assigned tasks.

Instead, long before anyone sent her to Dr. Silas Weir Mitchell's Philadelphia "rest cure," she had put herself into the pre—rest cure of the depressive – sleep. She would nap on and off most weekdays and, once pregnant, would be nauseous, sick, and always exhausted (see *Diary* entry for 21 September 1884). Gilman's "The Yellow Wallpaper" was her justly acclaimed fictional exploration of the horrors of the dependency of women on the marriage contract. This short story represented her construction of the case as a separated and soon to be divorced wife.

By the time Gilman published *Women and Economics* in 1898, her life and arguments about the marriage-prostitution relationship had evolved. She was engaged to her cousin, Houghton Gilman, and shortly to be married, to pursue her dream of a married life combined with a career that could keep her economically independent.[19] Though she held to the analogy between the two sexual contracts, as quoted above, her many references to prostitution centered on its condemnation, relative to monogamous love as the highest form of evolution in relations between the sexes. The ubiquity of prostitution in the late nineteenth century, a form of sexual relation she described as "morbid" and "unnatural," required explanation (*Women and Economics*, 72).

Much was at stake in explanations and interpretations of prostitution. Gilman wished to apply evolutionary theory to justify enhanced economic, political, and cultural options for women. If the utility of Social Darwinism for emancipating rather than enslaving women was to be established, the odious features of women's situation had to be rendered as a perversion of "nature" or an impediment to the correct biological basis of the progress of the human race (*Women and Economics*, 33). Rather than being "natural," institutions such as prostitution, and the economic dependence of women upon men generally, had to be shown to be a monstrous distortion of evolution and a positive threat to ongoing survival:

> Some hidden cause has operated continuously against the true course of natural evolution, to pervert the natural trend toward a higher and more advantageous sex-relation; and to maintain lower forms, and erratic phases, of a most disadvantageous character. . . . That peculiar sub-relations [*sic*] which has dragged along with us all the time that monogamous marriage has been growing to be the accepted form of sex union – prostitution – we have accepted, and called a "social necessity." We also call it "the social evil." We have tacitly admitted that this relation in the human race must be more or less uncomfortable and wrong, that it is part of our nature to have it so. (28–29)

So how did Gilman account for the prevalence of prostitution? The global framework for her explanation was that women, unlike the females of any other animal species, depended on men for food. Generally, women lacked access to independent survival in case they wished to resist this economic dependence. This meant that the attributes most economically essential to women to develop were those connected with securing men's economic support. A heightening of sex-distinctions between men and women, minimizing androgyny, was one evolutionary consequence of this culturally made female dependence, unauthorized by nature. Men called women "the sex," a chillingly accurate designation of female humanity's prescriptive raison d'être (*Women and Economics*, 49).

A corollary of this state of affairs was that men reduced economic competition for resources, by this exclusion of female humanity. Thus, depending on their area of economic specialization, men could bargain for decent livelihoods, across a wide range of trades, crafts, professions, businesses, and skills. By contrast, having half of humanity as its prescribed aspirants oversupplied marriage as a means of livelihood for women. As with all oversupplied trades, the results for its members were poor conditions and remuneration, little protection from occupational hazards, and, accompanying a weak bargaining position, being dispensable. Moreover, conditions of access to this oversupplied trade became more exacting, with wide scope to fall off the path of access or retention.[20]

Under these evolutionary circumstances, those women who failed to please men did not reproduce themselves. Women whose biological inheritances were most secure were those with maximum sex-distinction, the hyperfeminine, or "over feminized." In nature, Gilman observed, "the male carries ornament and the female is dark and plain." The males in fact compete to be most appealing to the females, who select the best, fittest mates. By contrast, with humans, "the females compete in ornament, and the males select" (*Women and Economics*, 53). This is a bizarre reversal of nature and true evolution, an artifact of culture. Here Gilman identified direct, literal eugenic consequences of this fostering of what she called "excessive sex-distinction." It engendered a demand – and one that was ever-increasing – for prostitution.

In the first place, the physically smallest, frailest, least vigorous of women became overrepresented in "the stock" of the human race (*Women and Economics*, 45). Extolled as the ideal of womanhood, their characteristics passed on to their sons, the fathers of the next generation, with the result of a general weakening of the species. This "breeding out" of more vigorous strains of womanhood led to a contraction in the genetic diversity of the females of the species. A gloomy survival prognosis followed (*Women and Economics*, 72).

Second, and most significant in the genesis of masculine demand for prostitution, was an artificially inflated level of demand for sexual indulgence through carnal relations. Observing the animal kingdom, she insisted that sexual desire was periodic and linked to the reproduction of the species. This increased desire was a product of the excessive sex-distinction that had emerged through forcing women to be economically dependent upon men. Men did not confine unchecked sexual indulgence to their wives, though its effects there were injurious enough upon the next generation and upon married women as a whole (*Women and Economics*, 42). Late-nineteenth-century feminists criticized women's and girls' vulnerability to sexual assault, seduction, pregnancies out of wedlock, and recruitment to prostitution. Gilman argued that a culture that enjoined single women to cooperate in excessive sex-distinction for a living made these hazards inevitable. The double standard of sexual morality ensured at least some supply of women for prostitution. That supply opened for all men the option of the purchase of sexual mastery, without requiring reciprocal desire:

> Where . . . man inherits the excess in sex-energy and is never blamed for exercising it, and where he develops also the age-old habit of taking what he wants from women . . . what should naturally follow? . . . We have produced a certain percentage of females with inordinate sex-tendencies and inordinate greed for material gain. We have produced a certain percentage of males with inordinate sex-tendencies and a cheerful willingness to pay for their gratification. And as the percentage of such men is greater than the percentage of such women, we have worked out the most evil methods of supplying the demand. (*Women and Economics*, 96)

Contemporary feminist theorists addressing prostitution seek to transcend repugnant moralism. Attentive to economic analyses, they argue that prostitution is work like any other. It is no better, no worse, than other jobs that the sex-division of paid labor in all known human cultures assigns to women.[21] Why did Gilman, with her distinctive focus on work and economics, decline this view? This could have left her critique of economic dependence of wives upon marriage intact. Was there not a fundamental difference between the prostitute and the wife, in that during her "currency" the prostitute earned the highest wages available to women?

Gilman's adherence to a particular version of evolutionary theory obstructed her embrace of a view of prostitutes as workers like any other. It retarded any sense of sisterhood or solidarity with them. For it was living through the artificial enhancement of sex-distinction, sex-attraction, and sex-indulgence which had exiled women from "race development." Prostitution was the most intense, extreme example of this tendency. Though men were far worse in their demand for excessive sex-indulgence, such indulgence did not retard them, because it was not, simultaneously, their occupation (*Women and Economics*, 44). Men developed, worked, invented, produced, mastered problems, and generally partook of a diversity of activities that developed them into higher forms of humanity – which she called race development. Women, cut off by their economic dependence on men, from "race" development, had only the option of putting their intelligence and energy and creativity into sex development (45–46). The results were catastrophic.

A connection between the economic dependency of the category "wife" and the prostitute could be drawn in a variety of ways. Gilman claimed that in rural and agricultural contexts a wife was a productive work partner in the enterprise. Therefore, men and women would marry young and exercise a sex-attraction that was "natural" and "normal" (93). In the industrialized cities, by contrast – and she clearly referred to the Northeast and mid-Atlantic cities – a wife was a consumer and nothing more. She lived off her husband. This caused men to delay marriage until they could provide fully for their own consumer. For the unfortunate fatherless adult son, with a mother and sisters to support, couples could delay marriage indefinitely, until husbands prepared to support his sisters were secured (93–94). This was the desperate plight of Ross, the fiancé of Diantha in Gilman's novel *What Diantha Did*.

The result of delayed marriage to an "unnatural" age inevitably meant an artificially heightened demand for prostitution. Sex ratios and marriage markets would be skewed, their "balance thrown out" as Gilman put it (*Women and Economics*, 94). Some desire for sex was "natural" in mature animals. She shared, at least partially, the pervasive cultural notion that "womanless" men met their erotic desires one way or another. It was a man's world. The condemnation of prostitution was proof that humanity regarded it as unnatural. Yet its tolerance was ensured because it served men's interests. So women, the prostitutes, received the blame (94–95). Police hounded them, but not their clients. Gilman in part condoned this. While the client indulged, admittedly to excess, a natural urge, the prostitute is "in most cases showing the falseness of the deed by doing it for hire – physical falsehood – a sin against nature" (95).

Gilman's definition of feminism placed a central focus on responsible motherhood of the race (*Homo sapiens*). Feminism postulated "a womanhood free, strong, clean and conscious of its power and duty. This means selective motherhood, the careful choosing of fit men for husbands. . . . This means a higher standard of chastity, both in marriage and out, for men as well as women. It means a recognition of the responsibility of socially organized mothers for the welfare of children" ("Feminism," 184–186). This focus intensified her concern about the ubiquity of prostitution. This evil institution not only potentially (if not actually) affected all women, but affected children, born and unborn, through inherited syphilis and gonorrhea. Her short story "The Vintage" explores the horrifying consequences of a man, Rodger Moore, marrying his beloved, Leslie. His doctor warned that he remained syphilitic from a past infection, contracted in a "brief black incident in his past . . . long since buried" (106). One frail, withered son, followed by stillborn and miscarriages, was the outcome of their union. Leslie never knew the reason:

> He had to watch it. He had to comfort her as he could . . . as her health weakened, her beauty fled from her, and the unmistakable ravages of the disease began to show, she did not know what was the matter with her, or with her children. She had never known that there was such a danger before "a decent woman," though aware of some dark horror connected with "sin," impossible to mention. . . . When she was taken away in the prime of her womanhood . . . Rodger was almost glad. . . . For a beautiful and vigorous young woman to see a slow, repulsive disease gradually overwhelm her is a misery the end of which deserves gratitude. (107–108)

Men clients and women prostitutes imperiled the vigorous motherhood she took to be at the heart of feminist objectives. Gilman exhorted mothers to take responsibility and blame for the perpetuation of prostitution. They should prevent prostitution by raising men with better values. In one of her more didactic short stories, entitled "His Mother," Gilman narrated the progress of Ellen, a New England woman who married an Italian, Mr. Martini. She bore one son and became maritally estranged, eventually widowed. By doting on her handsome son, Jack, she unintentionally raised a feckless rake. Mother and son parted over the youth's seduction and abandonment of a schoolgirl who was expecting his baby. She forwarded the occasional money he sent in the years thereafter to the abandoned girl, but learned that "the girl slipped out of sight altogether, left the town, and people judged by the silence of her family that they knew nothing of her, or knew no good" (75). Devoting her life to rescue work among fallen women, Ellen Martini eventually became a probation officer. She specialized in the detection and prosecution of men procurers of women for prostitution and the "white slave trade." This was her atonement for raising a son who caused such misery.

The culminating horror of the story unfolded. Ellen discovered that a procurer, responsible for the recruitment of several young women department store assistants whom she personally knew, was none other than her son Jack. He was one of those men who "lived on the earnings of fallen women, women whose fall they first bring about, and then carefully prevent their ever rising" (79). One night, her sources told her that he would return to his room to complete the ruin of his latest target. Sure enough, Jack brought the girl, after the theater and supper, "drugged and half-conscious," to his lodgings. There Ellen waited for him:

> he laid the helpless form down on his bed, standing a moment with a sneering smile. Then, turning as he threw off his coat, he met the gray eyes of his mother.
>
> "Just in time, I think, Jack," she said calmly. "This one can be saved anyhow. But I doubt if you can. . . . If you were a leper, Jack . . . I'd have to give you up. You are far more dangerous to society than that. I know your record now, for ten years back. . . . It's got to stop right here. As for this child — she's my girl now. I'll take care of her. . . . ." His mother, with black stone in her heart above the grave of her young love, spent a long life in trying to do good enough to make up for her own share in his evil. (79–80)

In both her fiction and nonfiction treatments of prostitution, Gilman faced squarely the demand for prostitution and the effects of men's sexual practices on prostitutes and all other women. Hating the evolutionary impact of the prostitute, she emphasized strategies to end prostitution. Unlike other reformers and authors of her period, she did not see prostitution in the eastern United States as an epiphenomenon, an outcome or symptom of mass European immigration or other causes.[22] Despite her later indulgence in nativism, anti-Semitism, and demands for the Americanization of immigrants, she would not allow prostitution, a fundamental institution of what she would later call "Androcentric Culture," to have its analysis displaced onto the dynamics of class, ethnicity, or race.[25] For her, it was always and finally about sex, about male dominance exceeding any distant natural boundaries to the detriment of evolution.

Gilman exhibited the optimism of other feminists of her era: namely that nothing was inherent or inevitable about existing sex relations.[24] Therefore, she sought to intervene on the question of prostitution and the eugenic consequences of male sex demand and female economic dependency. How did she propose ending women's economic dependency and eradicating prostitution? Two novels written a year apart provide some useful clues. Both were set in the West.

Gilman's *What Diantha Did* (1910) and *The Crux* (1911) both had as their central theme the reform of the marriage contract. In both novels, resolution resided in the woman/wife establishing a paid career just like her husband. This elimination of female economic dependence and servility and the development of the heroines' skills and experience took place in a context of western demography. Men outnumbered women three to one. If a man initially favored as husband and father proved unwilling to accept a working wife, then the heroine could find a man who would. Both novels asserted the justified restoration of "female-initiated" sex selection.

Also in 1911 Gilman published her most significant nonfiction work since *Women and Economics*: called *The Man-Made World, or Our Androcentric Culture*, it is usefully read in tandem with these two novels. The themes of restoring evolutionary balance through female economic independence and sex-selection and the demise of prostitution dominated this nonfiction text. Following sociologist Lester Ward's theories, she confidently posed "woman" as the race type, and man as simply the variant, evolved for the purposes of selection by the female (238). This provided "a biological base for Feminism" ("Feminism," 186). The reestablishment of the natural order in sex-selection would have momentous consequences, overcoming present evils, "The man, by violence or purchase, does the choosing – he selects the kind of woman that pleases him. Nature did not intend him to select; he is not good at it. Neither was the female intended to compete – she is not good at it" (30).

How could this change? Suasion was the task of nonfiction

Motherhood and Reproduction

texts. The *fiction* of this fertile period in Gilman's career explored how change might unfold. The stories of both novels warrant brief recounting.

Diantha Bell was the dutiful daughter of a failed breadwinner and his frail New England wife. Her father, the spoiled only son of an indulgent mother, had succeeded in being indisputable head of his household, which he had reluctantly moved to California in search of prosperity. The problem was that he had not succeeded in becoming "head of anything else" (*What Diantha Did*, 36). If he were on the way to bankruptcy, he would not hear of his female relatives making any contribution by developing profession skills. Diantha's romantic relationship echoed this problem. She and local grocer Ross Warden had agreed to marry six months before. Suddenly, she realized that she faced a long engagement. It might be "six years or sixteen" before Ross believed he could afford to marry. For custom decreed that he materially support his widowed mother and four unmarried and able-bodied sisters, two of whom were over twenty (19).

Against the wishes of both her own and her fiancé's family, Diantha moved to Orchardina, a male-dominated agricultural area. First, she worked as a housekeeper for a woman architect, who desperately tried to juggle motherhood, marriage, and career. She accumulated money and plans, studied business theory, and resisted pressure to return to dependency. With her savings, and the architect's backing, she opened a luncheon room for workers and a home-delivery dinner catering business. There she employed an army of young women, thereby liberated from "live-in" domestic service and all its hazards. Ross finally sold his store upon the marriages of his sisters and bought a ranch near Orchardina, expecting Diantha to give up her business to become his wife. She refused, sadly, but firmly. Only when she clearly had other admirers willing to accept her career did Ross relent, without being altogether happy about the arrangement. They married, had a child, and she continued back and forth between the ranch and her business. Ross only relinquished his ongoing tension about her independence when her business venture received favorable praise in international journals and inspired imitators. Ross admitted his mistake and prejudice and offered his wife wholehearted support in her venture. Naturally, they lived happily ever after.[25]

The Crux was a more complicated parable. It shared the theme of the reform of marriage with *What Diantha Did*, but was much more haunted by the other sexual contract of prostitution. Among Gilman's novels, it is her most trenchant and sustained critique of prostitution and its implications for men's and women's lives.

Vivian Lane, a 25-year-old spinster of Bainsville, Rhode Island, had been kissed nine years ago by Morton Elder, a local boy. Following his expulsion from his school for a drunken spree in New York City, he went West. Distracted, Morton "changed occupations oftener than he wrote letters" (*The Crux*, 41–42). At home, Vivian sat in the parlor reading Lester Ward, the Chicago sociologist, the critic of "Androcentric Culture," and the advocate of "Gynaecocentrism" (83). A local woman doctor, Dr. Jane Bellair, persuaded Vivian, Morton's sister Susie, and their spinster friend Orella to return to Colorado with her to run a boarding house in Denver. There, with a ratio of three men to one woman, all women who wanted to marry could do so. Vivian's 60-year-old grandmother joined them on the grand adventure.

The boarding house was a magnet for womanless men. The delighted New England women recalled the humiliation of waiting to be chosen by arrogant New England boys, who could have their pick: "Half a dozen boys to twenty girls, and when there was anything to go for the lordly way they'd pick and choose! And after all our efforts and machinations most of us had to dance with each other. And the quarrels we had!" By contrast, in Denver, "they stand around three deep asking for dances and they have to dance with each other, and they do the quarreling" (108).

Other characters in the drama included Dr. Hale, Dr. Bellair's partner, who was bitter toward all women except "fallen ones" (116), and Jeanne the cook, an enigmatic French woman, an ex-prostitute and madam with a retarded son, trying to give up "public life," while "private life won't have her" (98).

When Morton, now a traveling salesman, arrived, Vivian noted that his qualities had changed. "He danced well, but more actively than she admired, and during the rest of the [first] evening [after he arrived] devoted himself to the various ladies with an air of long usage" (130). Over the next few weeks, Vivian observed unhappily that he had "too free a manner, a coarsened complexion, a certain look about the eyes" (141).

On the night of Morton's return, Dr. Jane glanced out her window and noticed him cross the street to Dr. Hale's house. Something about his complexion in the lamp light made her uneasy (134). Then she found the laconic cook Jeanne at her door, demanding that Dr. Jane stop the romance from progressing further (Morton and Vivian had just announced their engagement) because, Jeanne declared, "He has lived the bad life." Dr. Jane replied, "Most young men are open to criticism." Jeanne would not relent: "He has had the sickness." Coralie, Anastasia, and Estelle, three young women in Jeanne's brothel, all became diseased after sexual intercourse with Morton. Eight years ago, Jeanne continued, "I have heard of him many times since in such company." Urgently Jeanne pleaded with the doctor, "You must save her . . . I was young once. I did not know as she does not. I married and *that* came to me! It made me a devil for a while. Tell her . . . about my boy" – meaning about the cause of her son's retardation (171–172).

Shocked, yet with her suspicions confirmed, Dr. Bellair confronted Dr. Hale, who refused to tell Vivian about his patient's condition (196). As a result, Jane told Vivian, complete with the medical facts of gonorrhea and syphilis as she knew them: "they are two of the most terrible diseases known to us; highly contagious, and in the case of syphilis, hereditary. Nearly three-quarters of the men have one or the other or both" (222). She warned Vivian of the consequences in stillbirth, miscarriage, birth defects, sterility, and early death from contracting the disease (225).

In a later conversation, Vivian's grandmother assured her that Dr. Jane was knowledgeable and concerned because her estranged husband had infected her, rendering her sterile. The desire to help other women and prevent the kind of suffering that she herself endured motivated Dr. Bellair's entry into medicine (243). Reeling from the horror of it all, Vivian asked if the statistics were true. "Our girls are mostly clean, and they save the race, I guess," replied the grandmother. "Remember that we've got a whole quarter of men to rely on. That's a good many in this country. . . . We're not so bad as Europe – not yet – in this line" (243–246).

Consequently, despite Morton's "indignant" arguments, Vivian broke her engagement to him and, opening the kindergarten she dreamed of, became an acclaimed teacher. Professionally established with numerous gentlemen admirers, she eventually allowed the love developing between herself and the previously misogynist

Dr. Hale to result in marriage. Again, this was with the understanding that the bride would maintain her economic independence by continuing with her school.

Gilman's West, in which all these progressive experiments in sexual contract renegotiation took place, recast prevailing stereotypes. Her own Californian experience and contact with colleagues of Frederick Jackson Turner at the University of Wisconsin confirmed her view of the fresh, democratic, and altogether modern possibilities for women of life in the West.[26] Vivian reflected in *The Crux* that the New England cast of mind of her family has "Out West" as "a large blank space on the map, and the blank space in the mind which matched it was but sparsely dotted with a few disconnected ideas such as 'cowboy,' 'blizzard,' 'house fires,' 'tornado,' 'border ruffian'" (93). Her relatives would be amazed to hear of "the broad beauty of the streets and the modern conveniences everywhere – electric cars, electric lights, telephones, soda fountains, where they had rather expected to find tents and wigwams" (101).

Dr. Jane Bellair, a proxy throughout the novel for Gilman's didactic voice, praised the West when trying to persuade the women to leave New England. Through her, Gilman expressed her demographic arguments for reestablishing female sex-selection. One woman, a schoolteacher, was hesitating about going. Her niece Orella countered:

> "I suppose you could teach school in Denver as well as here. And you could Vote! Oh, Auntie – to think of your voting!" "She's hesitating on your account," Dr. Bellair explained to the girl. "Wants to see you safely married! I tell her you'll have a thousandfold better opportunities in Colorado than ever you will here." . . . "If only women did their duty in that line there wouldn't be so much unhappiness in the world," she said. "All you New England girls sit here and cut one another's throats. You can't possibly marry, your boys go West, you overcrowd the market, lower wages, steadily drive the weakest sisters down till they – drop." (67)

The eugenic and the feminist projects interlink on Gilman's Western frontier. Vigorous women must find a skewed marriage market in which they can exercise the ancient and rightful female estate of sex selection. As importantly, they must carefully choose from the quarter of men uncontaminated by immorality, especially the diseases of syphilis and gonorrhea. This would be no easy task anywhere. In the West, lack of women meant also a relative lack of diversity of women. The proportion of prostitutes in the West may have been higher there than in the East or the South.

Gilman did not explicitly address this as a significant flaw in her schema. This was probably because, nonetheless, men lacked daily access to any women in much of the West. The prevalence of prostitution as the form of men's contact was in a sense the challenge facing vigorous womanhood. A prevalence for prostitution compared with marriage was an indicator of a good marriage market for women, one in which they could choose. With all those men needing, as Dr. Bellair said, "mothering and sistering – and good honest sweethearting and marrying, too" (75), Gilman proposed the elimination of prostitution. It was a key institution of our "Androcentric Culture." With the development of a human world, superseding androcentrism, all women and men would be partners in productive labor. Both the demand and the supply for prostitution would cease – and cease, she projected, within one generation.

Arguably, the analytic significance Gilman accorded to prostitution accelerated across her writing career, intensifying in the 1910–1916 period of wider international and wartime concern about "the red menace" of venereal diseases.[27] Her prostitution-disease focus also drew urgency from the local eruption of xenophobia and anti-Semitism as Eastern European Jewish immigration to Gilman's Manhattan suddenly soared to approach 2 million. Women and girls formed 43 percent of the Jewish Poles, Lithuanians, Russians, and Hungarians, many arriving without families or friends.[28] Moreover, her heightening interest in population issues, eugenics, matters of sex ratios, marriage markets, and "race progress" propelled her into a closer scrutiny of all factors deteriorating the American "stock." This ensured particular anxiety about birth defects and hereditary disabilities caused by venereal diseases.[29]

By the 1920s and 1930s, this concern widened her focus from prostitutes and the prostitution contract to the more generalized matter of modern, postsuffrage women's increased "sex indulgence" and "aping" the sexual mores of men and the "race" consequences. Ironically, this enlarged concern finally diluted the earlier specificity of Gilman's version of the prostitution problem, because its discussion was now surrounded by so much more general critique of the "sexolatry" of the modern age.[30] In these newly modern sex-relations, money was not exchanging hands, at least not directly. Here Gilman stood on the brink of what her peers called a new, recast analysis of sexuality. Embraced by many of her contemporaries, this view extolled sexual expression, experimentation, and the lifting of repressive and customary taboos. It claimed in particular to set women free, erotically speaking.[31] This view threatened the entire corpus of her theoretical legacy since the 1890s, however, in particular her blend of sexual economics and modified Social Darwinism. Insisting to the end on both the desirability and inevitability of the modern human return to the "natural" order of periodic sex-relations for reproduction, she ended her life declining to make the leap into that different and increasingly orthodox view of sexuality running entirely counter to her own.

Ironically, by time of Gilman's death in 1935, her dream that the prostitute might decline as a major figure in sexual culture might have seemed a reality, at least relative to the nineteenth-century prevalence, familiarity, and rhetorical currency of prostitution. Yet this "passing of the prostitute" coincided if anything with a heightening of Gilman's concerns about "sex and race progress." For that passing coincided with increased not reduced adherence to men's indulgence in sex on demand, a distortion of nature. Now all women, not just those set apart, experienced pressure to meet these demands and, in the solemn dictates of popularized Freudianism, received the brainwashing message that it was natural, good for them, and met their own real desires, no longer unhealthily repressed. Against her long predicted political unification of women as a sex against the common menace of prostitution and forced sexual service to men (see "The Oldest Profession in the World," 63), these developments posed a potent threat:

Another obstacle is that resurgence of phallic worship set before us in the solemn phraseology of psychoanalyses. This pitifully narrow and morbid philosophy presumes to discuss sex from observation of humanity only. It is confronted with our excessive development and assumes it to be normal. It ignores the

Motherhood and Reproduction

evidence of the entire living world below us, basing its conclusions on the behavior and desires of an animal which stands alone in nature for misery and disease in sex relation. ("Parasitism and Civilized Vice," 123)

Had Gilman lived through the 1930s and 1940s, we might speculate that she would have become a notable anti-Freudian crusader. A striking bridge would thus have been forged for other and later feminist theorists concerned with psychoanalysis, including Viola Klein, Simone de Beauvoir, Shulamith Firestone, and Nancy Chodorow. And for critics of feminist antipathy to psychoanalysis, a longer history of that resistance would be clearer and a more nuanced attention to its context reasonably could be required. That one of the earliest instances of feminist dissent from psychoanalysis came from the pen of a feminist up to that time so preoccupied with prostitution, venereal disease, and "sex relations" as Gilman was bears further reflection.

Gilman provides an important case study of the international "first wave" feminist analysis of prostitution. Her case demonstrates the wily and creative integration of feminist theory within then current discourses, and its intelligibility within wider public debates concerned, in this case, with science, evolution, the frontier, population patterns, disease, and public policy. As sharply, her case demonstrates the limited utility of certain contiguous discourses and new developments, leading to feminist dissent, resistance, and antipathy.

Prostitution began its place in Gilman's work as a subject of sexual economics and masculine distortion of nature in libidinous excess. She had not anticipated the proliferating analysis of masculine sexual excess in normative and positive terms, nor that equality for women might extend to erotic equality and a recasting of male sexuality as human, a paradigm for women as well. These discursive developments sidelined the earlier feminist analysis of prostitution as much in its categories and assumptions as in its substantive content. No one literally pretended that prostitution had been eradicated or that it no longer had significance for feminist analysis of the situation of groups of women relative to men. Changed understandings of sexuality, however, eclipsed prostitution's position as the emblematic institution of women's subordination. Continued appeals to it lost relevance and even intelligibility, even in the era of the Great Depression, as other preoccupations moved to the fore.

Notwithstanding the occasional flurry of clinical and journalistic interest thereafter, it was not until the 1970s that interrogation of Gilman's cardinal evil of androcentrism again received a recast *feminist* theoretical scrutiny. We should not be surprised at the suggestion that Gilman would have found little vindication in the work of late twentieth-century feminist successors on this longstanding matter of feminist concern. This is an important reminder of the historicity, the intensely context-specific character, of any feminist concerns for any place and period. An important corollary of this is that some of the most historically celebrated and significant feminist analysts, by definition, will not wear well. The more integrated they are into the discourses of their own period, and perhaps thereby the more intelligible to and effective with their own contemporaries, the less likely it is that they will withstand the application of presentist criteria often used by feminist historians appraising the history of feminism. Gilman on prostitution, then, may be an important cautionary tale in the all too common present critical pursuit of worthy foremothers, plausible predecessors, or at least past feminists of whom present ones can approve.

NOTES

1. See Gilman, *Women and Economics*, 63. For full discussion of the category "sexual contract" and of marriage and prostitution as specific and central sexual contracts in modern, "fraternal" democracies, see Carole Pateman, *The Sexual Contract*.

2. Gilman used prostitution-related analogies and direct examples drawn from prostitution in many texts. See, for instance, *The Home*, 97; *Human Work*, 253; *His Religion and Hers*, 41; "The Oldest Profession in the World," *Forerunner* 4 (March 1913): 63–64; and "Parasitism and Civilized Vice," in *Woman's Coming of Age*, ed. Samuel D. Schmalhausen and V. F. Calverton, 110–126.

3. Pateman argues that modern feminists carefully distinguish between condemnation of prostitution as an institution oppressive to women as a sexed group and condemnation of prostitutes as women, just as the Marxist opposes capitalism, not the worker. See *The Sexual Contract*, 209, and her "Defending Prostitution: Charges against Ericsson," *Ethics* 93 (1982): 557–562. Recently, this distinction has been criticized as "incoherent." See

Barbara Sullivan, "Rethinking Prostitution," in *Transitions: New Australian Feminism*, ed. Barbara Caine and Rosemary Pringle, 184–197.

4. See Susan S. Lanser, "Feminist Criticism, 'The Yellow Wallpaper,' and the Politics of Color in America," in *The Yellow Wallpaper*, ed. Thomas L. Erskine and Connie L. Richards, 225–256; and "Is America Too Hospitable?" *Forum* 70 (1923): 1983–1989; and "A Suggestion on the Negro Problem," *American Journal of Sociology* 14 (1908): 78–85. These latter positions and prejudices are pervasive throughout Gilman's journals, correspondence, and anecdotal examples in her major texts. The so-called Orientals of China receive most hostile representation in her work, fond as she was of claiming women were most oppressed and degraded in Asian societies. Middle Eastern cultures were another frequent target or illustration of the worst case of female dependence. As she aged, ever more shrill condemnation of Jewish cultural separatism and distinctiveness appeared in her personal and some published writings. Meanwhile, aboriginal populations of the world appear uniformly as barbaric peoples, doomed by evolution to extinction, including the "savage" Bushmen of Australia or the "squaw" laborer of the ancient Americas.

5. Gilman, "Toward Monogamy," in *Our Changing Morality: A Symposium*, ed. Freda Kirchwey, 59.

6. The analytical centrality of prostitution in Gilman's key texts receives little or no discussion in major biographical studies to date or in more minor essays and commentaries published during her lifetime and since her death.

7. Susan Kingsley Kent, *Sex and Suffrage in Britain, 1860–1914*, 33.

8. Ruth Rosen includes Gilman in a long list of eminent feminist activists and theorists who in various ways offered analysis of prostitution. Detailed comparison of this range of feminist interrogations of the origins, causes, maintenance, and strategies to address prostitution would be needed to provide the best evaluation of Gilman's contemporary influence and impact. See Ruth Rosen, *The Lost Sisterhood: Prostitution in America, 1900–1918*, 52, 58.

9. See, for instance, Timothy J. Gilfoyle, *City of Eros: New York City, Prostitution, and the Commercialization of Sex, 1790–1920* (New York: Norton and Company, 1992), and "The Urban Geography of Commercial Sex: Prostitution in New York City, 1790–1860," *Journal of Urban History* 13 (1987): 371–393; Joel Best, "Careers in Brothel Prostitution: St. Paul, 1865–1883," *Journal of Interdisciplinary History* (Spring 1982): 597–619; Neil Larry Shumsky, "Tacit Acceptance: Respectable Americans and Segregated Prostitution, 1870–1910," *Journal of Social History* 19 (1986):

665–679, and "San Francisco's Zone of Prostitution, 1880–1934," *Journal of Historical Geography* 7 (1981): 71–89; Ivan Light, "From Vice District to Tourist Attraction: The Moral Career of American Chinatowns, 1880–1940," *Pacific Historical Review* 43 (1974): 367–394; George M. Blackburn and Sherman L. Richards, "The Prostitutes and Gamblers of Virginia City, Nevada: 1879," *Pacific Historical Review* 48 (1979): 239–258; Carol Leonard and Isidor Wallimann, "Prostitution and Changing Morality in the Frontier Cattle Towns of Kansas," *Kansas History* 2 (1979): 34–53; David C. Humphrey, "Prostitution and Public Policy in Austin, Texas, 1870–1915," *Southwestern Historical Quarterly* 86 (1983): 473–516; Stanley Nash, "Prostitution and Charity: The Magdalen Hospital, A Case Study," *Journal of Social History* (1984): 617–628; Anne M. Butler, *Daughters of Joy, Sisters of Misery: Prostitutes in the American West, 1865–90* ; Jeremy Felt, "Vice Reform as a Political Technique: The Committee of Fifteen in New York, 1900–1901," *New York History* 54 (1973): 24–51; Marcia Carlisle, "Disorderly City, Disorderly Women: Prostitution in Ante-bellum Philadelphia," *Pennsylvania Magazine of History and Biography* 110 (1986): 549–568; Richard Tansey, "Prostitution and Politics in Antebellum New Orleans," *Southern Studies* 18 (1979): 449–479; John C. Burnham, "Medical Inspection of Prostitutes in America in the Nineteenth Century: The St. Louis Experiment and Its Sequel," *Bulletin of the History of Medicine* 45 (1971): 203–218; Roy Lubove, "The Progressives and the Prostitute," *Historian* 24 (1962): 308–330; Marian J. Morton, "Seduced and Abandoned in an American City: Cleveland and Its Fallen Women, 1869–1936," *Journal of Urban History* 11 (1985): 443–469; Christine Stansell, "Women, Children, and the Uses of the Streets: Class and Gender Conflict in New York City, 1850–1860," *Feminist Studies* 8 (1982): 309–335; Mary Murphy, "The Private Lives of Public Women: Prostitution in Butte, Montana, 1878–1917," in *The Women's West*, ed. Susan Armitage and Elizabeth Jameson, 193–206; and Marion S. Goldman, *Golddiggers and Silverminers: Prostitution and Society on the Comstock Lode*.

10. See, for instance, Anne Summers, *Damned Whores and God's Police: The Colonization of Women in Australia*; Miriam Dixson, *The Real Matilda: Women and Identity in Australia, 1788–1975*; Kay Daniels, "Prostitution in Tasmania from Penal Settlement to Civilized Society"; Judith A. Allen, "The Making of a Prostitute Proletariat in Early Twentieth Century New South Wales"; and Ann McGrath, "'Black Velvet': Aboriginal Women and Their Relations with White Men in the Northern Territory, 1910–40," in *So Much Hard Work: Women and Prostitution in Australian History*, ed. Kay Daniels, 15–86, 192–232, and 233–297.

11. See, for instance, Ellen C. Dubois and Linda Gordon, "Seeking Ecstasy on the Battlefield: Danger and Pleasure in Nineteenth Century Sexual Thought," *Feminist Studies* 9 (1983): 7–23.

12. See Gilman, *What Diantha Did*; *The Crux*; and "His Mother" and "The Vintage."

13. Gary Scharnhorst, "Making Her Fame: Charlotte Perkins Gilman in California," *California History* 64 (1985): 192–201.

14. Frederick Jackson Turner, "The Significance of the Frontier in American History," *American Historical Association, Annual Report*, 199–226.

15. Judith A. Allen, *Rose Scott: Vision and Revision in Feminism*, 126–127, 221–222; John Docker, *The Nervous Nineties*, 4–12; and Miles Franklin to Rose Scott, 19 June 1913, "Rose Scott Correspondence – Miscellaneous," Mitchell Library Manuscripts, State Library of New South Wales, Sydney, A2283, 828.

16. See, for instance, Gilman, "Feminism or Polygamy?" *Forerunner* 5 (1914): 260–261; and "The New Generation of Women," *Current History* 18 (1923): 734.

17. Gilman, "Feminism," reprinted in Ceplair, *Nonfictions*, 185.

18. An ambiguity in Gilman's use of the term "race" should be noted. Most frequently, in making her argument about the disastrous impact of women's economic dependence, not to say parasitism, under androcentric rule, she depicts women as blocked from race-developing activities in a species sense, contrasted with their overconcentration on sex-developing activities. That is to say, "race" means the human race. Yet, she does, at times, discuss "lesser," "lower," or unevolved "races" among humans. Her powerful nativism, reaching xenophobic proportions as she aged, had the result that she unself-consciously presented white America as the land of greatest hope for surpassing androcentrism and securing sex equality. As a corollary, the remaining cultures of the world tended to be hierarchically ranked. Susan S. Lanser was the first feminist critic to offer a detailed analysis of the systematic place of racism in Gilman's feminism, charging that Gilman saw patriarchy as a racial matter and devised feminism within a "racial cosmology." See Susan S. Lanser, "Feminist Criticism," 231–252. Moreover, this analysis is considerably deepened by the powerful essay on the racial ramifications of Gilman's key analyses of the rise of androcentrism and "the brute in man" by Gail Bederman – see her *Manliness and Civilization*.

19. For the most recent analysis of her courtship relationship with Houghton Gilman, see Mary A. Hill, ed., *A Journey from Within*.

20. Her arguments here make interesting comparison with those of acclaimed English suffragette Cicely Hamilton, author of *Marriage as a Trade* (1909).

21. See, for instance, Kate Millett, *The Prostitution Papers*; Lori Rottenberg, "The Wayward Worker: Toronto's Prostitute at the Turn of the Century," in *Women at Work — Ontario, 1850–1930*, ed. Janice Acton, Penny Goldsmith, and Bonnie Shepard; and Mariana Valverde, *The Age of Light and Soap and Water: Moral Reform in English Canada, 1880–1925*.

22. See, for instance, Ivan Light, "The Ethnic Vice Industry, 1880–1944," *American Sociological Review* 42 (1977): 464–479; and Egal Feldman, "The Prostitute, the Alien Woman, and the Progressive Imagination, 1910–1915," *American Quarterly* 30 (1967): 192–206.

23. One of her popular lectures on these subjects was "Americans and Non-Americans." For its listing see Gilman Papers, Folder 10.

24. Judith A. Allen, *Sex and Secrets*, 60–63, 80–82.

25. This novel was one of Gilman's earliest explorations of strategies for divesting human needs for nutrition, shelter, orderly surroundings, and other services generally provided without payment by wives, mothers, daughters, and other female relatives of their domestic associations, putting them instead upon a commercial footing.

26. Gilman's correspondence includes letters from a notable sociologist and colleague of Turner, Edward Alsworth Ross, concerning her participation in scholarly seminars on American social and economic themes at the University of Wisconsin, in which Turner was also a participant. She was undoubtedly aware of the currency of Turner's "frontier hypothesis" and seems to have concurred with it. See E. A. Ross to Gilman, 26 October 1907, Gilman Papers, Folder 139, the Arthur and Elizabeth Schlesinger Library on the History of American Women.

27. See, for instance, Allan Brandt, *No Magic Bullet: A History of Venereal Disease in the United States since 1880*.

28. Leonard Dinnerstein, *Uneasy at Home*, 15–18.

29. See, for instance, Gilman, "Prisons, Convicts, and Women Voters," "Humanness," "Sex and Race Progress," "Is America Too Hospitable?" "Progress through Birth Control," "Divorce and Birth Control," "Birth Control, Religion, and the Unfit," and "What May We Expect of Eugenics?"

30. See Gilman, "The New Generation of Women"; "Progress through Birth Control"; "Toward Monogamy"; and "Parasitism and Civilized Vice."

31. See, for instance, Samuel D. Schmalhausen, "The Sexual Revolution," and Smith Ely Jelliffe, "The Theory of the Libido," in *Sex in Civilization*, ed. V. F. Calverton and Samuel D. Schmalhausen, 349–436 and

456–471; G. V. Hamilton, "The Emotional Life of Modern Woman," and V. F. Calverton, "Are Women Monogamous?" in *Woman's Coming of Age*, ed. Samuel D. Schmalhausen and V. F. Calverton, 207–229 and 475–488; Floyd Dell, "Can Men and Women Be Friends?" and Beatrice M. Hinkle, "Women and the New Morality," in *Our Changing Morality*, ed. Freda Kirchwey, 235–249 and 183–196.

SANDRA M. GILBERT & SUSAN GUBAR

"Fecundate! Discriminate!"

Charlotte Perkins Gilman and the
Theologizing of Maternity

"Not all the long, loud struggle for 'women's rights,' not the varied
voices of the 'feminist movement,' and, most particularly, not the
behavior of 'emancipated women,' have given us any clear idea of
the power and purpose of the mother sex." So, somewhat surprisingly, mused Charlotte Perkins Gilman in the theological treatise
His Religion and Hers (1923) that she produced late in her career
as one of her generation's foremost speakers for just the feminist
movement from which she appeared to be distancing herself here.
Why would an emancipated woman who had spent a lifetime
struggling for women's rights and sex equality abjure her own
goals in favor of a quasi-Victorian celebration of maternity? In
particular, how could such a statement come from a woman who
had dramatically (and notoriously) relinquished her own maternal
role to the friend who became her former husband's second wife?
We argue here that although, with its uncharacteristic theological
focus, *His Religion and Hers* looks like a rather eccentric text in
the context of Gilman's overall career as lecturer on social issues,
polemicist, and fiction writer, its ambiguities reflect a curious rift
that runs through much of this writer's work and thought.

On the one hand, *His Religion and Hers* draws on the "gynecocentric" theories of Lester Ward, the "father of American sociology," to offer an ecstatic celebration of maternity as the primary
human model for loving kindness while also subversively glorify-
ing woman's evolutionary primacy in her role as mother. As Gilman sees the world in this work, woman was biologically as well
as morally the First, not the Second, Sex. On the other hand, the

theologizing rhetoric of *His Religion and Hers* frequently involves a notable misreading of Ward's ideas which itself camouflages beneath a sentimentalized vision of maternity a hostility to motherhood along with a view of mothering as a form of hostility. Indeed, the way in which Gilman conceives woman as the First Sex attributes a unique eugenic centrality to mothers that not only undermines the feminist movement's ideal of sex equality but even degenerates into precisely the racism that marks much Social Darwinist thinking about racial betterment. For all these reasons, a consideration of this book's ambivalent politics illuminates the contradictory strains of revolution and regression in the uses to which the concept of the maternal has been put by contemporary feminists as well as their precursors in Gilman's era.

"It was a man, so human as to be above sex-pride," enthused Gilman, "so great as to see the advantage of the world above the privileges of sex," who produced what was next "to the theory of evolution itself . . . the most important single precept in the history of thought" (57). She was commending Lester F. Ward, who himself recalled with considerable pleasure the occasion on which he first formulated his "Gynecocentric Theory" of the "Phylogenetic Forces" that shape all creatures. At the "Fourteenth Dinner" of Washington D.C.'s "Six O'Clock Club" on 26 April 1888, remembered Ward, he was asked to speak on sex equality to a group of feminist luminaries, including "Mrs. Elizabeth Cady Stanton . . . and a number of others equally well known" (297). Outlining his "view that the female sex is primary and the male secondary in the organic scheme, that originally and normally all things center, as it were, about the female," Ward claimed that "the theory, so far as I have ever heard, is wholly my own, no one else having proposed or even defended it, scarcely anyone accepting it, and no one certainly coveting it" (*Pure Sociology*, 296–297).

But of course the notion of female primacy was hardly original with Ward. Rooted in the Romantic movement's valorization of the organic and of nature's "wise passiveness," sanctifyings of the maternal had appeared in the writings of European thinkers from the German poet Johann Wolfgang von Goethe (who hymned the praises of "the Mothers") to the Swiss jurist J. J. Bachofen (who hypothesized the originatory power of a Matriarchate). Much closer to home, however, Ward would very likely have encountered the protofeminist eugenics asserted by Walt Whitman in what was entitled "Poem of Women" when it was first published in 1856 and later called "Unfolded Out of the Folds":

> Unfolded out of the folds of the woman man comes unfolded,
>   and is always to come unfolded,
> Unfolded only out of the superbest woman of the earth is to
>   come the superbest man of the earth . . .
> A man is a great thing upon the earth and through eternity,
>   but every jot of the greatness of man is unfolded out of
>   woman;
> First the man is shaped in the woman, he can then be shaped
>   in himself.

If Ward didn't associate his notions of "gynecocracy" with Whitman's vatic tribute to the originatory powers of women, Gilman herself might have. On extended lecture tours in the 1890s she carried only two books in her trunk: Olive Schreiner's *Dreams* and Whitman's *Leaves of Grass*, and as late as 1933 she declared that "Whitman and Ward are our two greatest Americans" (Scharnhorst, *Charlotte Perkins Gilman*, 41, 48). Certainly, when Gilman theologized the maternal in *His Religion and Hers*, she seemed to combine Ward's sociological conviction that, as far as evolution is concerned, "all things center . . . about the female" with the prophetic cadences of Whitman's assertion that "every jot of the greatness of man is unfolded out of the woman." In the process, she produced an analytic critique of patriarchal religions as well as a call for a female-centered spirituality that adumbrates the speculations of such contemporary feminists as Rosemary Radford Ruether and Mary Daly.

To begin with, in examining patriarchal religions, Gilman defined "His" traditional modes of faith – whether Jewish, Christian, Buddhist, or Moslem – as egotistical, elitist, misogynist, and most of all death-centered. Egotistical: for Gilman, the ideal of a personal afterlife or heaven reflects a materialistic, solipsistic, and short-sighted wish for individual gratification that should be supplanted by a desire to better not the existence of the individual but the future of the race. Elitist: according to Gilman, religious ideas of renunciation, providence, predestination, and obedience retard or inhibit intelligent inquiry while perpetuating unjust caste systems. Misogynist: in Gilman's view, orthodox injunctions about women's duty of submission to men as well as "blaming women for the sin and trouble of the world" (43) occur in all the major religions, which have "accepted and perpetuated man's original mistake in making a private servant of the mother of the race" (217).

But as this last formulation indicates, Gilman's most pointed contrast between "His" and "Her" forms of faith balances a charge that patriarchal religions are death-oriented with a summons for birth-directed maternal creeds. Man-the-hunter has stressed "the principle of struggle, conflict, competition," activities that merely generate problematic economic inequalities (271), whereas Woman-the-mother would promulgate "the principle of growth, of culture, of applying service and nourishment in order to produce improvement" (271). Agreeing with Ward that "the female is superior; she, more than the male, is the race type" (8), Gilman sounds like Whitman when she proclaims, "It is the mother who is rising, whose deep, sweet current of uplifting love is to pour forward into service" (277). If the characteristic male activities of hunting and fighting yielded religions based on a "strange death-complex" (35), women's role as nurturers would redirect spirituality onto life and growth:

> To the death-based religion the main question is, "What is going to happen to me after I am dead" — a posthumous egotism.
> To the birth-based religion the main question is, "What must be done for the child who is born?" — an immediate altruism. (46)

According to Gilman, the concept of divinity would itself undergo a transformation in a female-centered religion: "From [woman's] great function, birth, with its long period of prevision, its climactic expression in bringing forth the child, its years of unselfish service with rich results, she would have apprehended God in a widely different view from that of man — as a power promoting endless growth" (247). Banished would be the transcendent, patriarchal ruler of Jewish and Christian supplicants, and in his place would be an indwelling deity, whose imminence in human culture and whose political beneficence would strikingly resemble the attributes of the divine that are currently propounded by liberation theologists like Paul Tillich. For Gilman, then, "Seeing God as within us, to be expressed, instead of above us, to be worshipped, is enough to change heaven and earth in our minds, and gradually to bring heaven on earth by our actions" (292)

Like Elizabeth Cady Stanton in *The Woman's Bible* (1895) and Matilda Joslyn Gage in *Women, Church and State* (1893), Gilman protested against religions that had been used to lend God's sanction to the subjugation of women. Yet, simultaneously drawing upon Whitman and Ward, her theology of the maternal in *His Religion and Hers* also reflects a more general nineteenth- and early-twentieth-century reassessment of the feminine and in particular of the womb. Among male thinkers, of course, Whitman was the most powerful literary figure to reconceive the mother, but besides working in a tradition formulated by Bachofen (who noted in 1859 that "the phallic god" merely "stands as a son to feminine matter") he spoke for a range of other theorists, from Henry Adams (who somewhat nervously asserted that "the proper study of mankind is woman" because she represents "creative energy, the life force") to Robert Graves, who devoted an entire book and much poetry to musings on *The White Goddess*. Among contemporaries of Gilman, though, such ideas of maternal primacy were enunciated with special force not only by Lester Ward but also by the popular essayist (and perfect Whitmanite) Edward Carpenter and the sexologist Havelock Ellis.

At the same time, from Emily Dickinson to Mary Baker Eddy, Isadora Duncan, and H. D., Gilman's female precursors and descendants brooded on the sacred mysteries of female procreativity as modes of divine creation and models for human creativity. In "Sweet Mountains — Ye tell Me no lie" (1863), Dickinson lifted her eyes unto the Berkshires in a pantheistic and quasi-feminist celebration of earth goddesses, praying "My Strong Madonnas — Cherish still — / The Wayward Nun — beneath the Hill — / Whose service — is to You — ," while in "Demeter" (1921) H. D. assumed the voice of the maternal deity to proclaim to her worshippers that they should "keep me foremost, / keep me before you, after you, with you," and in a canceled passage from her prose work *The Gift* (composed 1941–1943) she insisted that "beneath every temple to Zeus . . . there was found on excavation . . . some primitive temple to the early Goddess . . . Maia, mama, Mutter, mut, mamalie, mimmie, Madre, Mary, *mother*." Similarly, in *Science and Health, with Key to the Scriptures* (1886) Eddy, who founded the Church

Motherhood and Reproduction

of Christ, Scientist, and whose acolytes were to devote a perpetual shrine entitled "Mother's Room" to her memory, preached the gospel of "*Our Father-Mother God, all-harmonious*" (16), and in *My Life* (1927) Duncan wondered whether "in all the universe there is but one Great Cry containing Sorrow, Joy, Ecstasy, Agony, the Mother Cry of Creation?"

As if fictionalizing Dickinson's, H. D.'s, Eddy's, and Duncan's paeans to procreativity, Gilman's utopian *Herland* elaborates on her statement in *Women and Economics*: "Maternal energy is the force through which have come into the world both love and industry" (126). Divorced from heterosexuality, the private family, and economic dependence, a fully liberated maternal feeling flows through the Amazonian society of Gilman's parthenogenic women, "out in a strong, wide current, unbroken through the generations . . . including every child in all the land" (95). Awestruck, the male explorers who come under the sway of this culture's serene "overmothers" are converted to what they call "loving up," a phrase that evokes the "stirring" within them of "some ancient dim prehistoric consciousness . . . like – coming home to mother" (142).

In *Herland*, too, an erotics of maternity complements the same reverential replacement of God the father with "Maternal Pantheism" that marks *His Religion and Hers*. Passion is not a prelude to motherhood but equal to motherhood, Gilman shows, explaining that "before a child comes, there is a period of utter exaltation [when] the whole being is uplifted and filled with a concentrated desire" (70). Similarly, the divine and all that is divine *is* "Mother Earth, bearing fruit. All that [the inhabitants of Herland] ate was fruit of motherhood, from seed or egg or their product. By motherhood they were born and by motherhood they lived – life was, to them, just the long cycle of motherhood" (59).

A number of Gilman's stories and sketches appear at least superficially to supplement *Herland*'s utopian vision of a liberated maternity, on the one hand, with a model of political activism based on a kind of surrogate or societal mothering totally in the control of women themselves and, on the other hand, with often satiric assaults on ways in which the sacred powers of maternity have been deformed by patriarchal structures. In celebrating maternity, for example, "When I Was a Witch" and "The Unnatural Mother" portray communal nurturance as the highest form of female heroism. Because she is maternally solicitous of others' nutritional well-being, for example, the central character of "When I Was a Witch" is angered by people responsible for bad food in the markets and hopes the "crowd that profit by this vicious business" will be gassed by their own awful products, while the protagonist of "The Unnatural Mother" is, ironically enough, castigated by her neighbors for putting other people's interests before concern for her own daughter and thereby saving an entire town from flooding: "She neglected her own to look after other folks' [children]" (65).

Focusing on what Julia Kristeva has called the "abjection" of the mother associated with the sexual division of labor enforced by a masculinist economy, "The Widow's Might," "Making a Change," and, most famously, "The Yellow Wallpaper" dramatize the sufferings endured by mothers whose helpless dependency on their husbands turns child-bearing or child-rearing into a living hell. In these works, the very processes of motherhood that Gilman elsewhere sees as potentially divine become infernal parodies of maternity that deplete, destroy, or infantilize women. The widow of the first tale, for example, is shown to have sacrificed thirty years of her life to a bad marriage and three ungrateful children, so she seems fully justified in her final decision to exchange the trivial "mite" her offspring want to give her for the might of an inheritance she has already earned by her own subversive labors. Scrutinizing the ill effects of maternal subjugation from a different perspective, "Making a Change" introduces a young mother whose renunciation of a musical career and confinement in the nursery cause her such misery that her child's crying leads her to attempt suicide: tellingly, she is saved by an understanding mother-in-law who professionalizes child care by opening a "Baby Garden" where, as in *Herland*, infants receive the specialized care and mothers the respite for self-development to which both are entitled. And finally, of course, "The Yellow Wallpaper" diagnoses the debilitating infantilization of its nameless protagonist as a symptom not only of the rest cure that destroyed Gilman's own first marriage and almost annihilated her sanity but also of the far more general social disease called patriarchy, an illness of the body politic that subordinates the sacred female principle to perverse family values promulgated by the male will to power.

Curiously, however, although all these texts register Gilman's revulsion against a maternity deformed by patriarchal imperatives, a more generalized horror of the maternal spills over to complicate this polemicist's overt didacticism. On closer examination, for instance, the five stories that we have just discussed yield less politically correct (albeit more inchoate) visions of mothers, motherhood, and maternity. Indeed, a most unmaternal hostility even to helpless creatures permeates several of these pieces. Operating out of what she herself confesses is "a state of simmering rage," the apparently benevolent social reformer who narrates "When I Was a Witch" (21) rescues cats and dogs from a miserable urban life by killing them all off and only practices successful magic when it is "black," that is, destructive. Tellingly, even when she seeks to deliver her fellow citizens from bad foodstuffs, she nauseates the wicked rather than nourishing the innocent. So, too, rather than expressing selfless love and grief, the heroine of "The Widow's Might" delights in denunciations of her family's exploitation and triumphs by secretly (and, as it might seem, selfishly) amassing her own wealth.

In a different but comparably confusing mode, several other sketches portray mothers who instinctively, almost viscerally, reject their children. The eponymous "Unnatural Mother," for one, certainly seems to show an antimaternal rather than a maternal reflex when she rapidly and automatically acts to save her town rather than her own child. As for the suicidal young musician of "Making a Change," Gilman's unusually vivid description of the auditory discomfort associated with infant care almost seems to justify this sensitive listener's impulse to self-destruction: "The grating wail [of the baby] fell like a lash – burned in like fire. . . . To any mother a child's cry is painful; to a musical mother it is torment" (66–67).

But if even such comparatively sprightly tales as "When I Was a Witch" and "Making a Change" incorporate unmotherly and antimaternal messages of hostility, the far more intense and classic "Yellow Wallpaper" encodes what, coming from the author of *Herland*, may well seem like a shocking fear and loathing of maternity in both its plot and (perhaps especially) its props. For the last few decades, to be sure, this text has been repeatedly interpreted by feminist critics in the light of its author's own assertion that she "wrote 'The Yellow Wallpaper,' with its embellishments and additions," to explain why she "cast the noted [Weir Mitchell's] advice to the winds" in order to go on to a healthy, productive life as wife, mother, writer, lecturer, and feminist. Yet if one reads the text unencumbered by presuppositions about Gilman's intentions, it becomes fairly clear almost at once that this story's premise has less to do with rest cures than with the physicality, the *materiality*, of maternity.

Indeed, if – as D. H. Lawrence once recommended – we trust the tale and not the teller, the work's hypothesis is that having a baby can drive a woman crazy, since, radically enough, the physical splitting of a woman into mother-and-baby might induce a virtual schizophrenic split in the female psyche. Equally horrifying, or so "The Yellow Wallpaper" suggests, child-bearing can breed just the animality, irrationally, and self-absorption exhibited by the tale's narrator rather than the spirituality, rationality, and benevolence commended in *Herland* as well as *His Religion and Hers*. Creeping by night like a cat ("most women don't creep by daylight"), gnawing her bedstead like a dog, the maddened speaker of this chilling work praises her already absent infant with remarkable disregard as merely a "dear baby" while apologizing that "I *cannot* be with him, it makes me so nervous" (*Reader*, 7). As for the infamous "nursery" in which the demented mother (who is Gilman's best-known fictional character) has been isolated and confined, it might be worth considering that this space – often seen as an ancestral attic for lunatics – *is* quite literally a *nursery* analogous to the nursing female body itself.

In *The Interpretation of Dreams*, first published a few years after Gilman penned "The Yellow Wallpaper," the founder of psychoanalysis expounded among other patterns of the "dream-work" a mode of "displacement" and reversal that might be said to mark the props and properties of the nursing body *qua* nursery in which the narrator of this story finds herself. Bed, chains, windows, walls, and especially wallpaper – all, here, through a process by which the body's inside becomes its outside and vice versa – might be said uncannily to represent just the fearfully repellent inferiority of which the pregnant–child-bearing–nursing woman becomes conscious as she comes to terms with the bodily signs of her own maternity. Thus, in Gilman's tale what is going on *inside* the maternal body is almost theatrically symbolized through what merely seems to be happening *outside* that body.

Clearly the yellow wallpaper itself is the narrative's most pertinent prop in this regard. Though this mysterious, skinlike stuff has often been interpreted as a projection of the narrator's rage (the phantom female figure behind it shakes bars to get out of patriarchal imprisonment) or as a sign of the woman's entrapment in archaic scripts (the puzzling design mocks all her efforts to understand its purpose and ultimately sentences her to madness), we would like to argue that the vexing paper can be understood in a number of different ways once we abandon Gilman's self-justifying rationalizations about the story along with some of our own political presuppositions. For example, if we read the tale as a fantasy about the literal sensations of fear and loathing that the experience of maternity induced in one woman, the ghastly *yellowness* of the paper, usually (and of course not wrongly) associated by contemporary theorists with patriarchal pollution, with the dire contamination of ancestral scripts, obviously expresses not just the central character's self-disgust, with its smell and color objectifying her horror at the physicality of her own body, but also the terrifyingly imminent and immanent walls of the womb itself, scarred with blood and biology. Scraping away at it, ripping it off, Gilman's protagonist might be thought to be tearing away at her own flesh in self-revulsion, almost as if trying to enact the miscarriage that would have saved her from her present fate.

Worse, it may well be that the baby who appears to play no part in the work's explicit plot finds his way into the weirdly physiological wallpaper that so repels the narrator. For after all, the pattern of the paper itself, with its "two bulbous eyes star[ing] at you upside down" (7), evokes something like a fetus, and "it turns a back somersault" (12) like the baby within the womb. Also, rather like an embryo, this "formless sort of figure that seems to skulk" evidently "sticketh closer than a brother" (8), "sticketh," indeed, as close as a child within a woman's body. Like the parts of an intrauterine or aborted fetus, "all those strangled heads and bulbous eyes" resemble "waddling fungus growths" (18). And at times the hideously repeated figure in the paper seems, unnervingly enough, to want to be born by breaking through some sort of birth canal: "many heads" try to "climb through" the pattern but "it strangles so . . . and turns them upside down, and makes their eyes white!" (15). Yet elsewhere, and at the same time, the ghastly thing vaguely suggests a demonic toddler: besides "waddling up and down" (9), it is "almost intact" and "makes [the narrator] tired to follow it" (10) because "it creeps so slowly" (11).

In this reading of "The Yellow Wallpaper," then, the mysterious rope with which the speaker eventually proposes to tie up what has been seen as her mad double becomes a severed umbilical cord that still, horrifyingly, shackles her to a diabolic infant, threatening to strangle not just mother and child but also the very concept of maternity in which both are enclosed. At the same time, however, through another one of the paradoxical and dreamlike reversals that mark Gilman's perpetually resonant tale, the rope also dissolves into an umbilical cord with which the narrator clamps *herself* into a womb-room out of which she refuses to be borne: "I am securely fastened now by my well-hidden rope," she gloats near the conclusion of the story, boasting, "you don't get *me* out in the road there!" Refusing entrance into the symbolic road, or birth-canal, where women (and babies) creep toward adult sexuality, she throws away the key that would allow her husband admission into this now immaculately intact womb/room where she may fear he would once again impregnate her in the "great" and "heavy bedstead."

Why did a feminist writer ostensibly dedicated to the sanctification of motherhood so demonize the processes of conception, child-bearing, nursing, and child-caring? What are the personal and cultural psychodynamics through which maternity is elevated to a paradisal ethical principle in *His Religion and Hers* while rejected as an infernal (even sulphurous) and degrading biological event in "The Yellow Wallpaper"? In meditating on these issues, it may be useful to begin by noting that, different as they are in their representations of motherhood, both "The Yellow Wallpaper" and *His Religion and Hers* (along with many of Gilman's other writings) obsessively return to this author's troubled experiences with both her own mother and her own motherhood.

As her mother's daughter, Charlotte Perkins believed throughout her life that her mother had inflicted great emotional harm by withholding physical affection. In order to prepare her child for a loveless world, Gilman recalled in her autobiography, Mary Perkins "would not let me caress her, and would not caress me, unless I was asleep." As her daughter's mother, Gilman was wracked with guilt by her own need to separate herself from the child, first through short intervals of travel and work but later (when Katharine was nine years old) by sending the girl across the country to live with her father and his second wife. In the harsh remembrances of Katharine Beecher Stetson Chamberlain herself, Charlotte Perkins was either "lying around in the hammock . . . enjoying nervous prostration" or "always scurrying," "too tired or too distracted" to provide proper care (Hill, ed., *Making of a Radical Feminist*, 233).

Interestingly, when we juxtapose "The Yellow Wallpaper" with *His Religion and Hers* so as to read the later text against the grain, as it were, it becomes plain that much of Gilman's maternal theology is compensatory. Perhaps because all the processes associated with conception, birth, and nursing were unusually disturbing to her, she was impelled to convert her own anxiety at maternity into a gospel of motherhood. Yet the vehemence of the theological rhetoric through which Gilman preached female superiority betrays a number of tensions that undermine a feminism otherwise usually sensible and rational.

Perhaps most obviously, Gilman's hymns to maternal nurturance are so excessive as to evoke the retrograde sexual ideologies associated with the Victorian Angel in the House: her encomium to woman's "great function, birth, with its long period of prevision, its climactic expression in bringing forth the child, its years of unselfish service with rich results" (247) recalls both Coventry Patmore's selfless heroine and Virginia Woolf's sardonic revision of that character. At the same time, her eugenic equation of maternity with racial improvement may explain her similarly Victorian-sounding claim that "self-expression is an essentially masculine attribute" (75). Indeed, her notion of female superiority as "the race type," compared to male inferiority as "the sex type" (62), leads Gilman to stereotype all men as "over-sexed males" (64) while likening human aesthetic self-expression to the courtship behavior and characteristics of lower species – for instance, the colorful plumage of male birds. Cautioning women that "normal sex, in the female, is a means to motherhood," this famous feminist seems to be saying, in a curious revision of Queen Victoria's notorious admonition, that on her wedding night every bride should close her eyes and think of the race. Certainly Gilman insists that although monogamy is in itself an insufficient antidote to the promiscuity natural to (all, inevitably oversexed) males, it should be practiced along with abstinence: "a natural monogamy does not imply continuous sex use" (84), she warned.

It is not surprising, then, that Gilman was puritanically scandalized by Sigmund Freud, whose "morbid philosophy," she fulminated, "assumes sex [i.e., the erotic] to be the mainspring of life," an idea she finds "so revolting to a healthy mind as to cause nausea" (165). Although she sardonically conceded that it might be "natural" if "the male, originated for sex use, should overestimate the importance of his raison d'être" (166), her vision of the human female as responsible for the elevation of the race through evolution meant, in her view, that women must angelically save men from their preoccupation with a sex urge that constitutes "a hindrance and a detriment to human progress" (167).

At the same time, such an emphasis on woman's destined role as Angel in the House of Evolution may help explain Gilman's otherwise mysterious efforts to distance herself from the very women's movement she herself had helped to launch and promote. Because this founding feminist came to feel that women's "essential purpose is to reproduce and to improve the race" (236), she found herself significantly alienated from — even repelled by — the New Woman of her age. In fact, her dislike of the female Flaming Youth she encountered in the early twenties takes a subtle homophobic turn in one passage that deserves to be quoted at some length:

> These poor little slouchy creatures, painting their cheeks and powdering their noses . . . adopting male vices, and so unutterably traitorous to the essential glory of their own sex as willingly to forego motherhood in order to share the barren pleasures of the other — are these the women from whose influence we are to expect a higher religion?
>
> Most certainly they are not. But these are not Women. These are really worthy of that absurd title with which men have tried to discredit the progressive women of our times — "the third sex." (236)

Slouchy and powdered, these "creatures" so shocking to Gilman are obviously flappers, whose blatant displays of "barren" sexuality appear at least as nauseating as the procreative female body depicted in "The Yellow Wallpaper." And her phrase "the third sex," probably meant to echo common caricatures of suffragists as insufficiently feminine manhaters or grotesquely masculinized battleaxes, may also derive from Edward Carpenter's investigations of what he called "the intermediate [or third] sex" in several books Gilman claimed to admire – *Love's Coming of Age* (1896) and *Intermediate Types among Primitive Folk* (1914). But while Carpenter praises such individuals as "remarkable" character types in whom there is a harmonious balance of feminine and masculine qualities, Gilman castigates them as "abnormal" and "ridiculous." At the same time, condemning the birth control movement as providing "a free ticket for selfish and fruitless indulgence" (285), she even goes so far as to defend the double standard, finding it "quite right" that "misbehavior is . . . more condemned in women" because "in all that affects the health and happiness of the race the mother is the most important factor" (285). The mother-centered social changes she envisions, she avers, are "deeper" and "more important, *than any mere feminist imagines*" (238; emphasis added).

But besides weakening her earlier commitment to the women's movement, Gilman's aversion to female physicality and her repudiation of the erotic actually led her to misread precisely the "gynecocentric" theories of Lester Ward that she claimed to be promulgating in *His Religion and Hers*. For Ward's contrast between the race-type female and the sex-type male shares little with Gilman's. In fact, arguing in *Pure Sociology* that "life begins as female" (313) and "the male is . . . a mere afterthought of nature" (314), Ward characterizes masculine "appetition" with delight rather than distaste:

> throughout all nature we find the male always active and eager seeking the female and exerting his utmost powers to infuse into her the new hereditary *Anlagen*. . . . This intense interest in his work is the *natura naturans*, the voice of nature speaking through him and commanding him, in season and out of season, always and under all circumstances, to do his duty, and never on any pretext to allow an opportunity to escape to infuse into the old hereditary trunk of his species the new life that is in him. (323)

Unlike Gilman, this author evidently revels in a voice of nature that tells the male to "fecundate!" by following his "appetitive interest" while admonishing the female to "discriminate!" by selecting the partner with the highest value for the race.

If Gilman's misreading of Ward's views on the masculine urge to "fecundate!" was disturbingly censorious, however, her skewed interpretation of his attitude toward the feminine responsibility to "discriminate!" was more problematic still. Though he has long been considered a leading exponent of Social Darwinism as well as eugenics, both of which tended to be politically conservative and racially retrograde, Ward dedicated his career to combating what he called the "gospel of inaction" he associated with William Graham Sumner's laissez-faire version of the doctrine of natural selection (Scott, *Ward*, 115). In addition, he vigorously critiqued ideologies of white superiority, claiming that "blacks under as favorable circumstances as whites would develop a civilization of as high an order as any in Europe" (121).

As if generalizing from Ward's Darwinian notion of genetic choice or discrimination to a species of political and social discrimination, however, Gilman essentialized and biologized race in *His Religion and Hers* and elsewhere, conflating physical evolution with moral improvement in often sinister or ludicrous ways. Her notion that "far-seeing Japanese women might determine to raise the standard of height, or patriotic French women determine to raise the standard of fertility, or wise American women unite with the slogan, 'No more morons!'" (86) certainly seems laughable. But the "negative eugenics" (69) of Herlanders aren't so funny. Here the "lowest types" of girls (including those with sexual drives) are "bred out" (82) of the species.

Even more distressing are the immodest proposals Gilman put forward in an essay entitled "A Suggestion on the Negro Problem" (1908), where this grand-niece of Harriet Beecher Stowe seriously suggested the establishment of a labor corps into which all "negroes . . . who are not self-supporting, who are degenerating into an increasing percentage of social burdens" (179), would be conscripted. Although she herself insisted that her "proposed organization is not enslavement, but enlistment," her enthusiasm for uniforms, titles, "construction trains," and "model farms" has an unnervingly protofascistic edge. And a comparably disquieting rhetoric marks a xenophobic article entitled "Is America Too Hospitable?" (1923). Here, cautioning against America's open door policy – "If you put into a melting pot promiscuous shovelfuls of anything that comes handy you . . . may break the pot" (290) –

Gilman concedes that "it is physically possible for all races to interbreed," but argues, chauvinistically, that "the wisest of both races prefer the pure stock" (291).

How might Gilman's misreading of, and misadventures with, the maternal illuminate the ambiguities that mark contemporary feminism's discourse on this mat(t)er so central to the very definition of femininity? Was the utopianist of *Herland* seduced and betrayed into uncharacteristic grandiosity, even arrogance, by deceptive myths of maternal power precisely because the abjection of motherhood to the species filled her with such dread that she could not bear to contemplate the materiality of its meaning? Might the nuances of her intellectual case history imply that when we in the current women's movement similarly idealize maternity we are doing so because we shudder to look upon what the poet Sharon Olds identifies as the process through which every mother has "lain down and sweated and shaken / and passed blood and feces and water and / slowly alone in the center of a circle [she has] passed the new person out"?

If we follow this line of thought, such diverse recent constructions of the maternal as those offered by Nancy Chodorow, Luce Irigaray, Carol Gilligan, and indeed Julia Kristeva can be read as redemptive fantasies that evade or repress the inexorable factuality of the flesh, the anxiety of maternity that still, inevitably, persists. Chodorow envisions a magical bond between mothers and daughters that bequeaths special sensitivities to women. Irigaray metaphorizes the mysteries of milk, nipples, tongue, and lips. Gilligan extols the nurturant and pacific skills women imbibe at the mother's breast. Despite meditations on the abjection of the mother, even Kristeva succumbs to the lure of maternal *jouissance.*

Like their famous "forerunner," all these thinkers struggle with the materiality of maternity through a spiritualizing rhetoric that echoes her paeans to what the Nigerian novelist Buchi Emechetta more wryly calls "the joys of motherhood." But the author of *The Home* and *Women and Economics* sought to be even more practical than many of our theorizing contemporaries about the material conditions of motherhood as a social institution. Indeed, Gilman's dream of "Baby Gardens" where infants bloom like tulips, tended by expert horticulturists and visited from time to time by happily independent biological mothers, pragmatically seeks to devise an institutional bridge between the horror that deforms "The Yellow Wallpaper" and the ecstasy that glamorizes *Herland*.

Yet, of course, the vocabulary of gardening – in particular the lexicon of uprooting, pruning, and cutting back that complements concepts of planting and blossoming in the allegory of the "baby garden" – has dark connotations which return us once again to the powers of horror. The American poet Linda Pastan's "Notes from the Delivery Room" makes this point perhaps most succinctly:

> Babies should grow in fields:
> common as beets or turnips
> they should be picked and held
> root end up, soil spilling
> from between their toes –
> and how much easier it would be later,
> returning them to earth.

Public and Private Faces

KAREN STEVENSON

Hair Today, Shorn Tomorrow?

Hair Symbolism, Gender, and the Agency of Self

While Charlotte Perkins Gilman is reasonably well known among sociologists for her biting criticisms of economic and political inequalities between the sexes, sociologists have paid less attention to her novels and lectures. However, her fictional work provides some of the most subtle and rounded parodies of conventional turn-of-the-century femininity and women's restricted and ultimately debilitating social role. While I do not intend to offer an appraisal or criticism of Gilman's fictional work, I draw on some of her lesser-known comments on the restrictions and limitations of a femininity constructed for men's pleasure, "mere reflected masculinity" (*Herland*, 59), as a starting point for a debate on a gendered identity increasingly seen as open to just the kinds of self-conscious reformulation Gilman had earlier proposed. With wit and sensitivity she allowed her readers to perceive the artificiality of the gender roles and, I suggest, to some extent she prefigured the poststructuralist view of gender as a fictional category, a performance of a specific identity designed to please, and so raised issues which remain relevant to feminists today.[1]

One such issue is the subject of this essay: hair. Gilman took to the lecture circuit in 1916 to promote short hair for women not only as healthier and more comfortable, but as a mark of women's political and ideological progress toward sexual equality. Hairstyling is certainly one arena in which acceptable hair for women and the portrayal of the female self have dramatically and fundamentally altered over this last century generally and within Gilman's lifetime particularly. Previous to the 1920s, long hair was the norm for more or less all Western women and had been for some centuries. As J. Herald states in *Fashions of a Decade: The Twenties*, by the end of the 1920s, despite male protest, public debates, and discrimination against shorn women, "Ninety-nine per cent of the American and Western European female population had their hair cut short" (29). I argue that the women who flouted hair conventions in the 1920s also invaded the previously male-dominated barbershops, transforming them into a sphere of female consumption. This was just the kind of action proposed by Gilman. First, women should please themselves in terms of style, developing more comfortable and more appropriate modes of dress and hairstyling for their modern lives. Second, women should participate fully in the public arena on the same terms and in the same numbers as men. These two issues are central to this discussion.

I begin by looking at the historical "hair" legacy that Gilman was determined to disrupt: the location of women's hairstyling in the private sphere and the established norms of hairdressing. I then consider Gilman's arguments in favor of short hair for women in an era when long hair was the norm and why, when the majority of women did eventually reject long hair and short hair became socially acceptable, she was so disappointed with the "progression" women had made in terms of the disruption of feminine ideals which did not serve women's interests. In her opinion women remained "as much the slaves of fashion as before" (*Living*, 318) and had failed to translate their political gains into a significant move toward full social equality. I argue that Gilman's disillusionment was related to the reinscription of gendered hair and style polarities. This was largely due to a continued assessment of short hair as *potentially* unfeminine; this created a need for heterosexual women to reassert their femininity by offsetting their short hair with other signifiers of heterosexual desirability. Feminine hair could be reachieved by, for example, using the services offered by the newly transformed barbershops, once a male-dominated social sphere, which became a female-dominated sphere of high consumption. However, in place of Gilman's disappointment, I argue that the style transgressions of women should be perceived more positively. The white European women who cut their hair in the 1920s in accordance with Gilman's wishes made a significant cultural statement about their role in society, rejecting the established tradition of long hair and bearing the social repercussions of this choice. Although specific forms of femininity were reachieved, women not only transformed the previously male-dominated barbershops into the largely female-oriented salons of today, but also disrupted the dominance of a monolithic feminine norm.

Hairdressing has a long history; ancient but sophisticated shaving sets have been found in Egypt dating from 2000 B.C. and street barbers were common in Egypt and ancient Greece. However, while hairdressing in the public arena has always been common for men, who would have their hair cut, curled, and styled and body hair shaved, trimmed, plucked, or removed, women (and upper-class men) have, until this century, been attended to privately. Throughout ancient Egypt, Greece, and Rome, slaves tended their mistresses' hair in the home, whereas men frequented often luxurious barbershops as part of their social round. The barbershop provided a space in which men could meet friends and travelers, exchange news, and discuss politics. In the Middle Ages in Europe, barbers in the Barber-Surgeon Guild also provided medical services such as minor surgery, bloodletting, and tooth-pulling (the origin of the red and white/blood and bandage barbers' pole). Here too, barber shops provided entertainment (the barbershop quartet) and gossip, and the local barber was usually seen as an intelligent friend and a man of some importance (see Cooper, *Hair: Sex, Society and Symbolism*, 153–158). While barbershops have been a male institution since classical times, there appears to be no female equivalent. Women have had their hair dressed within the private sphere, and this has been a largely female occupation or task from which men, apart from the few artist-stylists, were largely excluded. Indeed, the first ladies' hair salon, established in the 1600s, did not set a precedent but caused a moral furor, with church leaders publicly censuring male involvement in a female's private *toilette* as highly immoral.[2] Thus, the majority of women in the seventeenth, eighteenth, and nineteenth centuries continued to have their hair dressed privately, usually by friends or relatives or, for the wealthier, a female maid.

The only real forerunner of the feminized salons of the twentieth century was that belonging to Marcel Grateau, creator of the marcel wave. In 1872 Marcel ran a small hairdressing establishment in Montmartre catering to what R. Corson calls "the lowest class of women" (*Fashions in Hair: The First Five Thousand Years*,

492). He was unable to try out or develop his new waving technique until he offered to provide the service free of charge and, even then, there were few women who were interested in the *ondulations*. Over the years, though, as the new style gradually became better known and popularized by word-of-mouth recommendations, Marcel began to charge clients for it. It was still considered most unusual (and not quite ladylike) for a man to dress women's hair, especially in public, and only the poorer clients frequented Marcel's salon; the wealthier, paying for home visits, continued to have their hair dressed in private. However, when Marcel dressed the hair of popular actress Jane Hading in his own style, it was such a success that a new era in hairstyling was born. It became not only acceptable for the rich and famous to populate Marcel's salon (so acceptable that he began to take clients on the basis of competitive bidding), but *chic*. The style itself, which could be easily copied, became a less important item of consumption than the place in which one was styled: literally to have had a "marcel" wave. Again, however, despite Marcel's popularity among the Parisian elite, hairdressing remained for most women a private and time-consuming task. While Marcel and other professional "dressers" paved the way for women to be seen in public hair salons without foregoing their claim to respectability, these stylists merely *dressed* women's long hair in particular ways rather than fundamentally altering its overall style and length; cutting, or even trimming, women's hair was still unusual.

Thus, I suggest that Gilman's proposals for hair reform a decade before the bob began to be popular among women were certainly optimistic: she attempted to disrupt centuries of tradition in which long female hair had been accepted as routine.

Over the centuries, "dressed" long hair for women had been established as a social norm. Although hair lengths for men have fluctuated, women's hair, while being styled in innumerable ways, has remained long (in appearance if not in fact) and in almost every historical period women have worn their hair longer than men (see Corson, *Fashions in Hair*; and Synnott, *The Body Social: Symbolism, Self and Society*). From the artificial additions designed to lengthen the appearance of Norman women's plaits to the towering and often infested wigs of the seventeenth and eighteenth centuries, hairstyles have been of immense symbolic importance and have differed significantly between the sexes.[3] In many eras hair length in itself has been a sign of feminine beauty. Victorian ladies rarely cut their hair, which grew to great lengths; even now we have an annual "Long and Lovely" competition in which beauty is judged by hair alone.

However, the styling of women's long hair symbolized far more than gender. Hairstyles were more elaborate for wealthy women, who could afford to purchase the hair of others to make into elaborate wigs, toupees, and additions; poorer women may have had to sell their hair like Jo March in Louisa May Alcott's *Little Women*. Today, as L. Jones points out in *Bulletproof Diva: Tales of Race, Sex and Hair*, hair continues to be imported in vast quantities from poorer nations. Working-class women and those with sociopolitical or religious commitments wore their hair in simpler versions of the current style. In the years leading up to the Commonwealth (1649–1659), for example, political affiliations were symbolized by differences in hair and dress styles: Puritan women wore their hair in shorter, simple styles, whereas the Cavaliers of both sexes sported masses of ringlets and curls adorned with ribbons and jewels. Long hair was "put up" at a certain age to symbolize a girl's transition to adulthood, and later in life hair would be covered with caps to symbolize maturity and an end to the child-bearing years. A woman's long hair, pinned up neatly and covered, was seen as indicative of virtue, (literally) distinguishing her from loose (haired) women as well as from men. Witches have usually been depicted pictorially as having wild and unkempt hair.

Women's long hair has thus been treated in a dichotomous fashion. Unpinned, tumbling, or disheveled, hair is infused with sexual power. Indeed, the erotic appeal of long hair has been acknowledged by women with religious commitments. Catholic nuns traditionally shaved their heads on becoming "brides of Christ" and covered their heads with veils; similarly, orthodox Jewish and Muslim women cover their hair from the intrusive gaze of men. While this denial of the sexual power of hair was self-imposed, it has long been a form of retribution to forcibly shave the hair of despised or deviant women. Slave women were shaved regularly while in captivity. Collaborators with the British Army in Northern Ireland or with the German Army in France during the first and second world wars were shaved and paraded through the streets as punishment for their (usually sexual) sins (Cooper, *Hair*, 74). Hair color has also been of symbolic importance. As Susan Brownmiller points out in *Femininity*, the "Fairy Princesses" of our fictional heritage tend to be blue-eyed blondes or English Roses. Even Gilman makes assumptions about color. In *Herland* Alima is dark and swarthy, "a shade more alluring" than the other women and "several shades less able as a practical psychologist." She has a "far-descended atavistic trace of more marked femaleness" which, in part, leads to her eventual sexual betrayal (130). Further, coloring one's hair has historically been associated with the lower classes and the less virtuous: even today the "brassy blonde" invokes just such stereotypical connotations. Throughout history, ethnic and racial differences have also played a part.[4]

Although by the early years of this century it had been historically established that long hair could function as a signifier of intrinsic femininity, this ideal has flourished most successfully in white, European nations. This is largely related to ethnic differences in hair loss and balding patterns among men. Mediterranean, Asian, Indian, and African people lose their hair less frequently than do whites of northern European origin. In the East and in African countries where male balding is infrequent, the artificial polarity between long and short hair as indicative of femininity and masculinity is uncommon. For example, ornamented long hair remains a sign of masculinity among the Masai, long dreadlocks are an accepted aspect of male Rastafarianism, and long hair was traditionally treasured by Chinese and Japanese men until the pigtail of the Chinese workers became an object of racist scorn (Brownmiller, *Femininity*, 59).

It was arguments such as these that Gilman used to insist upon the artificial nature of gendered hair polarities. She argued that the vagaries of fashion suggested there was no "natural" reason for women to wear their hair longer than men and no reason why women's bodies should not be able to acquire the strength and purpose of those of men. Even if one were to refer uncritically to the sphere of the "natural," she pointed out that in "nature" long hair often "belongs" to the male and is not an obviously feminine attribute: "Why we should so admire 'a woman's crown of hair' and not admire a Chinaman's queue is hard to explain, except that we are so convinced that the long hair 'belongs' to a woman.

Whereas the 'mane' in horses is on both, and in lions, buffaloes, and such creatures only on the male" (*Herland*, 30).

Gilman's commitment to the women's health and hygiene movement led her constantly to dispute the dualistic convention which polarized masculinity and femininity as oppositional and incommensurable. Women, she suggested, were figuratively disembodied by the insistence on their frailty and otherness; she herself regularly exercised, desiring an unencumbered body, strong, and useful, "not a passive object she would wait for others to approve" (Hill, *Making*, 66). In this way Gilman stressed the goal of "humanity" for men and women, with each sex capable of combating its "miseducated sense of beauty and fitness." This re-education would acknowledge that "we have grown to consider most human attributes as masculine attributes, for the simple reason they were allowed to men and forbidden to women" (Hill, *Making*, 137, 82). In *Herland* Gilman shows through the gentle and childlike questioning of women unfamiliar with the gender norms of the larger world that "femininity" is an interpretive context that enables us to assign value to gestures, attitudes, and forms of bodily presentation that are of no intrinsic value in themselves. She touches on this again in "If I Were a Man," where she allows the reader to see the foolishness of women's "massed, fluffed hair" through the eyes of a comfortably cropped male (Lane, *Reader*, 34). All the women of *Herland* wear their hair short, "some a few inches at most"; although the male visitors are initially shocked by the women's "unfeminine" looks/locks, they soon become accustomed to short hair. Van notes how "light and clean and fresh-looking" it is compared to the artificiality of what the visitors have previously thought of as feminine. He points out that "those 'feminine charms' we are so fond of are not feminine at all, but mere reflected masculinity – developed to please us because they had to please us, and in no way essential to the real fulfillment of their great process" (59).

This fictional tactic has been successfully used by other writers claiming to offer a feminist critique (as Lane shows in her introduction to *Herland*). For example, in her feminist dystopia *The Handmaid's Tale* (1987), Margaret Atwood uses the same mechanisms that Gilman used in her earlier utopia to show the constructed and artificial nature of conventional femininity: both refer to the sexual properties of women's hair. While the inhabitants of "Gilead" have become accustomed to their comfortable but nunlike shifts and their covered heads, the occasional visitors do not comply with these dress codes:

> The women teeter on their spiked feet as if on stilts, but off balance; their backs arch at the waist, thrusting the buttocks out. Their heads are uncovered and their hair is . . . exposed, in all its darkness and sexuality.
>
> We are fascinated, but also repelled. They seem undressed. (38)

Gilman developed the points she made fictionally in *Herland* a year later on the lecture circuit (1916). She argued that long hair was not only more uncomfortable, time-consuming, and unhealthy (which it undoubtedly was – see Corson, *Fashions in Hair*), but, as a signifier of femininity, was clearly a social construct. A woman had "no more natural reason for wearing her hair long than a man" and would be a lot happier without it. Gilman was lecturing on hair and dress reform at a time when many women may have been more receptive to her arguments than earlier in her lecturing career. The onset of the First World War and the increasing participation of women in paid employment or war work made simplicity in dress and hair norms more important than previously. Wars and revolutions often have a profound effect on style, and the number of women now working in factories and on the land made long hair a nuisance. Styles became simpler: hair was tightly pinned around the head and occasionally cut shorter – although short hair was not generally adopted until the 1920s (see Asser, *Historic Hairdressing*). Clothing was also more practical and more suited to women's increasingly visible public presence.

However, although practical concerns were important, the symbolic function of the newer fashions was to stylistically align a woman with the twentieth rather than the nineteenth century. As short hair for women had previously been perceived as deviant, punitive, or a self-inflicted denial of sexuality, the women who did cut their hair, while opting for ease, were also making a significant cultural statement. They rejected the time-consuming burden of long hair, which for centuries had been a primary signifier of both sexual difference and gentility, in favor of short hair. Gilman argued that short hair was easy to look after, more comfortable, more practical, but was at the same time a rejection of cumbersome roles. The young woman who, for example, bought a cheap Gibson Girl blouse or bobbed her hair was choosing an ease and simplicity which fit better with her life but was, at the same time, buying the "look," the lifestyle. As E. Wilson suggests in *Adorned in Dreams: Fashion and Modernity*, "she bought a symbol of emancipation, glamour and success" (157). The purchase of the "look" here came to connote "individuality, self-expression, and a stylistic self-consciousness. One's body, clothes, speech, leisure pastimes, eating and drinking preferences, home, car, choice of holidays etc. are to be regarded as indicators of the individuality of taste and sense of style of the owner/consumer" (Featherstone, *Consumer Culture and Postmodernism*, 83).

In this way women aligned themselves firmly with the new century by the symbolism of their clothes and hair; bobbed hair, as emancipatory, was perceived as a challenge to the masculine-feminine polarity of the time. Short hair on women was met with invective and disdain by journalists, theologians, and conservative males who thought short hair and short frocks might undermine the established power differentials between the sexes. More surprisingly, short hair for women was also rejected as unfeminine by the barbers who stood to gain financially. Not until the long hair and beards of the hippies forty years later or the colored spikes of the punks in the seventies and eighties was such outrage expressed over hair. Debates raged well into the 1930s over the "hair issue," with magazines such as the *Ladies' Home Journal* regularly featuring articles on both sides of the hair question.[5]

Although the bob was advocated by fashionable icons such as dancer Irene Castle and actress Colleen Moore as well as by feminists such as Gilman, their arguments aroused fierce protest and enraged many. In a lecture to the Working Women's Protective Union (1916) Gilman's speech aroused particular contempt. Promoting short hair for women as indicative of their progression to a more equitable society, she argued:

> I am not asking you to go home and cut your hair, though I think we would all be much cleaner and happier and more comfortable with it short. You wouldn't do it anyway. But I do ask you if this isn't a joke: If a woman – who has no more natural reason for wearing her hair long than a man – goes and cuts

it off, people say, "Oh, shame: she wants to be a man!" But what do they say when the case is reversed? Whiskers are a man's natural prerogative, but now when he shaves off his whiskers and goes with a smooth face, why don't they say to him, "You want to look like a woman!" (Brownmiller, *Femininity*, 65–66)

Her arguments were bitterly condemned and were parodied by the *New York Times* on 16 March 1916 under the heading "Even barbers rebel at shearing women," where it was suggested that short hair for women sounded the end of "Romance, History, Literature and Poetry," that poets would talk no longer of fair tresses but of shaving, and that literature would "have to be rewritten" (13:3). Indeed, it is true that barbers were initially very resistant to the idea of short-haired women. The *Barbers' Journal*, for example, reported in 1923: "The close snip rage is raging worse than ever, and soon, if no indignant act of providence intervenes, masses of soft, lustrous feminine braids so much admired by man since the ape gave him his start, will be seen alone on elderly mothers and their surviving mamas" (Corson, *Fashions*, 610).

Even theologians condemned short hair, not only as unfeminine but as in direct contradiction to the word of God. They were wont to cite St. Paul's address to the Corinthians to argue that "it is a shame for women to be shorn or shaven. Doth not nature itself teach you, that if a man have long hair it is a shame unto him? But if a woman have long hair, it is a glory to her." One tract (*Bobbed Hair: Is It Well-Pleasing to the Lord?*) related women's short hair to their general insubordination: "The refusal to utter the word 'obey' in the marriage service, the wearing of men's apparel when cycling, the smoking of cigarettes, and the 'bobbing' of the hair are all indicative of one thing! God's order is everywhere flouted. Divine forbearance tolerates the growing evil for the present, but the hour of Divine intervention in judgement approaches fast" (Corson, *Fashions*, 615). Against these religious purists Gilman humorously insisted that "it was not the Lord who gave men short hair while women's is long. It was the scissors" (Brownmiller, *Femininity*, 65–66), again stressing the constructed nature of hair polarities – although with little success.

Gilman herself continued to be treated as an unnatural, "masculine" freak by the press. Moreover, despite the aims of Gilman and others, short-haired women throughout the 1920s not only continued to be met with disapproval and disdain but experienced prejudice from employers and husbands and were even threatened with dismissal by a number of businesses if they insisted on wearing their hair short. Marshall Field, for example, Chicago's largest department store, told one woman deemed "inelegant" that she was fired because she had failed to comply with their new hair regulations. These rules stated that bobbed hair was forbidden and that women who had already cut their hair should wear it slicked back and hidden under a net until it grew. Female employees had to endure regular hair inspections by superintendents, who would ascertain whether their hair was dignified enough for the store's image (*New York Times*, 10 August 1921: 13:1). The Chicago Railroad Offices also insisted that women must wear their hair long, despite the fact that their female employees were then forced to "spend half their spare time washing soot and cinders out of long hair" (*New York Times*, 13 August 1921: 8:4). Women, however, stuck to their guns: neither the threat of dismissal nor disapproval (nor, indeed, divine intervention) deterred women from cutting off their locks *en masse*; one estimate suggested that as many as two thousand American women were shorn every day during the late twenties. Apparently scores of women waited in line to be clipped by one well-known New York stylist, Signor Raspanti, or his staff: "3,500 are clipped there every week; hundreds are turned away" (Corson, *Fashions*, 611).

It began to seem as if Gilman had got what she wanted – to some extent at least. Women from all social backgrounds began to decidedly reject the time-consuming bother of long hair in favor of the historically unprecedented ease and simplicity of short and largely unadorned hair. And women had transformed feminine style norms in the face of considerable social pressure.

In an era of Social Darwinism, Gilman rejected biology in favor of culture,[6] emphasizing the plasticity of human nature and, largely through satire and humor, aimed to destabilize received notions of women's abilities and potential. However, her optimistic belief that human "nature" was capable of being revealed as a fundamentally cultural construct and that, once aware of this, women would be able to cognitively reject "femininity" in favor of "humanity" and personhood led to her eventual disappointment. By the time Gilman wrote her autobiography she believed that, despite liberal legislation and political gains, women had too often failed to reconstitute themselves as "people" – ungendered and free on the same terms as men – becoming merely a more modern "other," in thrall to new discourses of style, consumption, and sexuality. In this way, her proposed reforms were certainly "optimistic" in that she hoped that "femininity," once deconstructed, would be less resistant to its reconstruction in terms of a somewhat desexed androgyny than it turned out to be.

While the cut of men's and women's hair was similar in the twenties, the initial aim of feminists such as Gilman to undermine inequality was largely defeated by women's need to retain a form of femininity that was socially acceptable. Modern femininity could be signified by the daring move to short hair, but the trappings of stylishness (sticky setting lotions and sprays, sleeping in uncomfortable hair rollers, and so on) were retained in order to offset the perceived harshness of the look:

> The entrepreneur who opened a small neighborhood shop was responding directly and shrewdly to the mass appeal of short hair, for once a woman was free of the coil at the nape of her neck, it became her urgent mission to seek out new ways to feminize her head. To soften the look of a practical cut, she gave herself over to professional treatment: split curls and bangs dipped in gluey setting lotions, stiff marcel waves that were curled by hot irons, a permanent wave by electric machine, a monthly styling, a weekly set and comb-out, a shampoo and blow-dry, and as technology advanced, chemical straighteners and chemical frizzes, bleaches, lighteners, touch-ups, frostings, streakings, highlights and other permutations of color. (Brownmiller, *Femininity*, 75)

Even if Gilman had got what she wanted in terms of radical hair and dress reforms, this did not necessarily allow women to dispense with the trappings of a femininity designed to please men. On the one hand, short and unadorned hair was, as a fashion, short-lived; on the other hand, when women did wear their hair short most were determined to signify their femininity in other ways. While bobbed hair was, for a while, innovative, emancipatory, and stylish in itself, in later years, style was "all in the cut," the place of consumption, and the specific products or stylist used. Barbers increasingly claimed that it was only their artistry that could make a bob beautiful or feminize a shorn head. This led

Public and Private Faces

Gilman to complain in her autobiography, "I did expect better things of women than they have shown." While legislation meant there was "now nothing to prevent women from becoming as fully human in their social development as men," they often behaved "as foolishly as ever, if not more so," remaining the complaisant victims of fashion, "lifting their skirts, baring their backs, exhibiting their legs, powdering their noses" (*Living*, 318–319). Gilman had wanted androgyny rather than the reinscription of merely new forms of gendered dichotomies.

The artistry of stylists in "feminizing" our style choices has enabled hair salons to weather the vagaries of fashion. For, despite the bob's popularity and the ease and simplicity of caring for short, unadorned, and untreated hair, centuries of tradition are not so easily overturned. Longer hair lengths became more popular in the thirties and forties, and few icons of feminine beauty have had very short hair since. In the sixties the bob was still regarded by some as incredibly ugly, and in the eighties heterosexual feminists seemed to feel torn between the duty to be cropped and the desire for luxurious tresses.[7] Brownmiller admits that she would secretly like to wear her hair long, to be "irrefutably feminine" and "to stand on the safe side of femininity": "I know what some people think about short hair – they say short hair is mannish, dyky" (55). Even for Afro-Caribbean women, whose hair will not grow to great lengths and is tightly waved by nature, long, silky hair has been promoted as irrefutably feminine – again at great financial benefit to the hairstylists. Mrs. C. J. Walker, America's first black millionaire, made her fortune in Harlem by adapting the electrical perming device designed to curl white women's hair to straighten that of black women. As a fashion, the Afro was a short-lived and, with its more political overtones, less popular style option than Michael Jackson's curly-perm or Naomi Campbell's weave.[8] In *Chic*, a new magazine for "women who weren't born yesterday," older women reject the informal rule that they should cut their hair or hide it neatly away once they are over forty. Long, loose hair is argued to look glamorous and feminine on women of any age and is infused with sexual significance.

Thus, long hair continues to signify far more than gender alone. While Gilman knew that hair was able to signify identities beyond and within gender, her ideal was for an undifferentiated form of styling, one appropriate for both men and women – a form of androgyny which did not mark sex so obviously. For example, she argued that the same style of bathing suit was entirely appropriate for both men and women: "It is an exhilarating sight to see men and women, swimming together, walking or running on the beaches together, free, equal, not stressing sex in any way" (*Living*, 318). However, despite her commitment to androgyny, we can see that Gilman's arguments to some extent prefigured the view that in modern society the body is able to function as a manufactured object that can be read as a text, the displayed signs by which we/she perceive/d the character and status of another. Her disappointment lay in her belief that women had failed to transcend their sexual otherness by their largely voluntary immersion in the emerging consumer culture.

Yet despite her critique of the modern woman's shallow concerns (see *Living*, 318–319), Gilman remained optimistic about the future. In her opinion, the major battles had been won; all that remained was for women themselves to make use of new opportunities, to "advance in all manner of business and professional achievements . . . expect to work, to earn, to be independent." Thus, her view of humanity was fundamentally cognitive: now that there was "nothing to prevent women from becoming as fully human in their social development as men," women would only "overcome this backwash of primitive femininity" by a self-conscious and reflective act of will (*Living*, 319).[9]

Here Gilman seems to ignore the emotional and cultural aspects of consumption. Yet we should not focus exclusively on consumption as a purely cognitive or economic event, which derives straightforwardly from production. To account for women's continued attachment to the latest fashions and hairstyles, which may still be time-consuming and restricting, we need to acknowledge the emotional pleasures and desires which are celebrated in cultural imagery. Hair salons involve both production (of the image) and consumption (of the service) and can provide a form of narcissistic pleasure that cannot be reduced to the products consumed. Here it is not only the end product (if one can be said to exist) but the spaces in which consumption occurs and the manner in which services are delivered that are of fundamental importance to the experience of pleasure or displeasure. That is, consumption is indelibly social. The practical/economic and emotional/pleasurable spheres in which hair consumption is played out are reflected in the view that we should be individualistic, "ourselves," while also, at the same time, producing images of this self that are pleasing or satisfactory to others.

Historically, then, hair has always been an important signifier of a gendered self, but technological developments – such as those which allow for the permanent coloring or waving of hair – and the increasing importance that consumer items play in a creative reformulation of self have enabled hair to become one of our most versatile raw materials. While to some extent hair is "given" (its natural color, coarseness, curliness, and hair loss patterns largely determined by genetic heritage), it is on the cusp of nature and culture. Hair can be plucked, shaved, tinted, curled, straightened, colored, shaped, styled, and decorated. These different styles can signify complex identities and attitudes. Indeed, hair symbolism is a particularly powerful indication of identity, as this form of bodily signification is almost always voluntary rather than imposed.[10] Since the "bob" of the early twentieth century, the style choices we make have become an increasingly important signifier of self, infused with cultural significance. Consider, for example, the colored spikes of the punk, the shaved head of the skin, or the Rastafarian's dreadlocks. White, European women who cut their hair in the 1920s in accordance with Gilman's wishes made a similarly significant cultural statement about their role in society, rejecting the established tradition of long hair. Further, these women transformed the previously male-dominated barbershops into the largely female-oriented salons of today and disrupted the dominance of a monolithic feminine norm. This reflects the mass emergence of women into the public sphere over this century and indicates their growing consumer power as well as the greater stylistic effort, time, and expenditure that women are still expected to put into the regulation of their appearance than are men.

Modern feminists have developed, albeit indirectly, Gilman's concerns, suggesting that hairstyles, clothes, diets, fitness regimes, cosmetic surgery, wigs, hairdyes, and so on, can shape the malleable body, transforming it into a commodity, a "fictive" portrayal of self which may not serve women's interests. Since the 1960s second-wave feminists have increasingly focused on the artificiality of supposed femininity. In 1970, for example, Germaine Greer spoke out against the "masquerade" demanded by the constrictions of stereotypically feminine styles: "I'm sick of peering at the world through false eyelashes, so everything I see is mixed with a shadow of bought hairs; I'm sick of weighting my head with a dead mane, unable to move my neck freely, terrified of rain, of wind, of dancing too vigorously in case I sweat into my lacquered curls" (*The Female Eunuch*, 61). As well as generally having more hair than men, women continue to style and color their hair more often. Curling tongs, hair-dryers, rollers, gels, and sprays are more likely to be taken-for-granted female possessions. Hair can be curled, scrunched, or tied back for different looks, permanently or temporarily colored. Indeed it is a regular feature of hair magazines to show how many different looks can be achieved from one basic cut, whereas stability is the norm for men. Asser points out that men's hairstyles have changed relatively little compared to women's over the century — James Dean's hairstyle would be as acceptable now as in the fifties; men are not expected to wear their hair differently for dinner or a special occasion, nor do we expect men to use a "hint of a tint," appearing as a redhead one week and a brunette the next.

Similarly the norms for body hair are different. Women who sport hairy legs and underarms may still be viewed as "unfeminine." *Spare Rib* (1978:66) pointed out that "one aspect of our bodies has eluded a thorough public reassessment. Many of us still have to come to terms with our body hair. Why are we so sensitive about it?" While male body-builders, cyclists, or swimmers may shave or pluck their body hair for sporting reasons, men who shave these areas for pleasure or to enhance their beauty are most unusual. Even female pubic hair is to be trimmed and shaped to within the "bikini line" if women wish to wear modern swimwear rather than the shoulder-to-knee versions of Gilman's era.

The acceptability and style norms for facial hair also continue to be different for men and women. The most feminine eyebrows are plucked and penciled into a neat arch; eyelashes can be thickened and darkened by the application of mascara or lengthened with the use of false lashes. Although Brooke Shields is credited with the popularization of a more natural eyebrow line, few heterosexual women would sport Boris Becker lashes. However, hair elsewhere on the face is still most unusual for women, although it is acceptable for men. Facial hair can still be a cause of acute embarrassment for many women whether feminists or not; although it has become more acceptable to display leg or axillary hair, facial hair is unusual and has rarely been discussed as a potential and dramatic symbol of emancipation. A letter to *Spare Rib* pointed out that "underarm hair and light leg hair *are* OK now thank god, but believe me, bearded ladies with legs like gorillas are just never going to make it as an accepted minority" (November 1983: 136). In *Beauty Secrets: Women and the Politics of Appearance* W. Chapkis describes her debilitating fear of ridicule because of her visible facial hair. When she eventually surrenders to social pressure and electrolysis, guilt haunts her: "I have failed on both counts," as a woman, as a feminist (1–3).

What might be dubbed the final frontier in hair politics is again reminiscent of Gilman. While the women of *Herland* were allowed to wear their hair short, they had absolutely no facial hair, a fact that was interpreted as at least one sign of their femininity by their male visitors: "never before" had they "seen such complete absence of facial hair on women" (73). The women in Gilman's utopia are not faced with the dilemmas of women like Chapkis over whether or not the hair should be removed. They are "naturally" hairless, having no need of razors or electrolysis. Gilman here may reflect the view of prominent physiognomists such as Cesare Lombroso, who linked female hairiness with "less-developed" criminals and lower orders.[11] Certainly Gilman's perceptions of "less-developed" nations and peoples were much less liberal than her views on women, as Lane admits in her introduction to her edition of *Herland*.

While Chapkis is decreed by social norms to have "too much" hair, to be neither feminine nor masculine but an object of ridicule, having too little hair is distinctively unfeminine. Women who have been recipients of chemotherapy or who suffer from alopecia do not have the comforting myth of virility to fall back on as do balding men. Unless they are wealthy, women are expected in such situations to cover their "shame" with their freely provided, usually artificial-looking, acrylic wigs. Even women who can afford good quality wigs fear discovery: one cannot go out in the wind, play sports, go swimming. Those who reject the cover-up experience the same derision as the too hairy. One woman said of discarding her uncomfortable and ill-fitting wig: "Wherever I go I am laughed at . . . some people actually wind down their car windows for a better look" (*Spare Rib* [September 1982]: 122).

Despite all of these unofficial hair norms, which are unconsciously absorbed and embodied from early childhood (see Haug, *Female Sexualization*), both Synnott and Brownmiller describe the construction within second-wave feminism of a feminist rather than stereotypically feminine ideal. Second-wave feminists not only attacked the conventional norms for head hair but also criticized the fakery of the supposed hairlessness of adult women's bodies and the tyranny of a "beauty myth" that idealized a pre-pubescent smooth-bodied girl as a prototype for feminine desirability. For a while it appeared that feminists developed a new ideal: "medium to short hair lengths, easy to manage, without expensive styles and sets; no wigs, false eyelashes or curlers; no make-up; and axillary and leg hair not only unshaven, but even proudly displayed" (Synnott, *Body Social*, 120−121). As Chapkis says, "For years, I've displayed my hairy underarms and legs with defiant pride" (2). However, if such an ideal was ever accepted within feminism, it again was short-lived. As in the twenties, heterosexual women were aware of the conflict between the desire for simplicity and the politics of appearance. J. Radcliffe Richards summed up women's fears when she said that "some" feminists are "deliberately unpleasing to men" and "if women want men they must be willing to be pleasing to them" (*The Sceptical Feminist*, 187−188). After all, she pragmatically concludes, "there is nothing to be said for being deliberately unattractive" (193). So, after her initial exhilaration at being able to symbolize her feminist credentials, Chapkis continues, with more caution:

> But the hairy face is unusual and hence "unnatural" for a woman. And ugly. *God help me, I too think it ugly.* I too look askance at older women with their bristly chins.
>
> The rest of us, whose smoothly anonymous faces hide our secrets, look quickly away. We are reminded of what will happen if we are not ever vigilant. (2; emphasis added)

In our desire to be inconspicuous, to fit, there is also the hope of security and acceptance. Those areas where we differ from the norm are only experienced as individualistically original if they have been consciously chosen and fit with the expectations of our real and imagined communities. The fear of not fitting is a not unusual experience: "It was certainly a hairstyle, it could even be described as chic, but was it for me? I tried to imagine what 'the others' would say − I hoped they'd like it! . . : if I changed my image totally, then perhaps the others at school wouldn't be able to find a reason to tease me . . . I wanted so much to be able to belong for once" (Haug, *Female Sexualization*, 107)

Thus, while many heterosexual women want to disrupt the conventional standards of beauty and indeed have done so to some extent, many remain at odds with their looks – fearing they are "error" as well as "other." Brownmiller says, "I hated my martyrdom" (*Femininity*, 57); she admits that while she wants to fight against the double-standards of appearance, she also wants to look "youthful, dazzling, feminine." In order to "stand on the safe side of femininity," she knows that her "mannish" and graying hair must be offset and softened by adding other signifiers of femininity – makeup, colorants, earrings, and the like. *Hair* magazine (June/July 1995) still makes a distinction between "boyish" short cuts and "sensuous and soft face-framing layers." Although the model sports a "tomboy style," the use of gels and glazes and pastel makeup reconstitutes her as "Gamine": she is "*allowed* to flirt in all directions" (emphasis added). The dilemmas of modern feminism thus indicate the failure of Gilman's pursuit of androgyny. This aim, at least, is as optimistic today as it ever was. Theoretically and emotionally heterosexual women have rejected androgyny in favor of the pleasures of consumption. Even in periods when feminists were influenced by the case for androgyny, and during the proliferation of unisex stores and salons, difference and plurality have disrupted any attempt at coherence. What feminists might reject now is not long hair *per se* – for short hair is no longer a sign of transgression – but specific forms of consumption and construction.

Appearance continues to matter a great deal. The success of fitness studios, diet plans, cosmetic surgeons, fashion houses, and hair and beauty salons indicates the weight our culture places on physical presentation and the value of youth and beauty. Of course, this is not new: only the specific definitions of desirability change over time, not the fact that desirability can be defined. The stigma attached to those who fail to conform to the beauty myth whether through a perceived lack of control over their "unruly" appetites or by their age, color, or "deformity" is such that they are not only discriminated against (as Naomi Wolf has shown in *The Beauty Myth*) and distanced, sometimes physically as well as socially, from mainstream society but may also be attributed with negatively valued characteristics (see Finkelstein, *The Fashioned Self*). The weight of such social pressure means that many of Gilman's optimistic aims remain unrealized. While she accepted that appearance could be read as indicative of character and ideology, her optimism lay in believing that the deconstruction of oppressive forms of femininity would lay bare this artificiality to the extent that it would no longer prevail. Women continue to be more vulnerable to sociocultural definitions of desirability than do men, reflecting women's continued relative subordination.[12]

Thus, our self-conscious construction and reconstruction of identity transforms the self into sign, an object increasingly produced in order to signify our characters and status. While clothing can be played with, taken off, changed, used to say one thing one day and something else the next, hair, despite its plasticity, remains a more constant signifier of self. Identity is open to a supposedly self-conscious reformulation. Hairstyles, clothes, diets, fitness regimes, cosmetic surgery, wigs, hairdyes, and so on, can shape the malleable body, transforming it into a commodity, a "fictive" portrayal of self (Finkelstein, *Fashioned Self*, 4): "People *construct* and use their bodies, though they do not use them in conditions of their own choosing, and their constructions are overlaid with ideologies. But these ideologies are not fixed; as they are reproduced in body techniques and practices, so they are *modified*" (Frank, "For a Sociology of the Body," 47; emphasis added). This century has thus witnessed an explosion in discourses of expertise and consumption choice, a plethora of "knowledges" and lifestyle options fundamental to late modernity. As A. Giddens remarks in *Modernity and Self-Identity*, this emphasis on a chosen and modifiable lifestyle makes the "self" a "reflexive project" (75) for which each one of us is responsible. The availability of consumer items, in a reflexive society, enables us to *further* our self-development and can provide the support to discover a world of possibilities. As one creates the "self," so one creates the body: via expert advice bad habits (using too many heated hairstyling products) are replaced with good skills (deep conditioning cream and towel drying) in order to meet the predefined rational goal of healthy looking and beautiful hair – one gets what one wants.

This rejection of essentialism and the idea of a prefigured self stresses action, choice, and self-construction, denying a self absorbed from the external. Identity becomes, via consumption, largely a matter of personal choice; indeed, for Giddens, choice is obligatory in late modernity, for behaving in terms of convention is reconstituted as chosen behavior in the context of modernity's multiplicity of diverse options. It often seems, then, as if personality is an off-the-peg item, formulated via our discursive wardrobe: a "performance" of a fictive self whose symbolic significance is acted out for and can be interpreted via the scrutiny of others. Indeed this scrutiny is fundamental, for our performance must be comprehensible to the imagined community to whom we appeal — as, of course, *their* performance must be intelligible to us. Finkelstein notes: "They may be wearing a hair piece, using hair dye or displaying a sun-tan or have had plastic surgery or a hair transplant. We know that appearances are created and that dressing after a particular fashion is done in order to convey a certain impression" (*Fashioned Self*, 1). The increasing dominance of such "lifestyle enclaves" becomes possible in late modernity, where consumption has become disembedded from the conventions of the community. This process of individualization has enabled the proliferation of styles, which, while they cross-cut or destabilize fixed status groups, at the same time allow for the development of "imagined communities" with which we wish to identify. It is indeed ironic that, despite the increasing emphasis on the body as a manufactured object, influenced significantly by its historic and spatial locale, we have become increasingly obsessed with its textual significance. Can the body *really* represent the real?

> Sister Carol wears locks and wants a Black revolution
> She tours with African dancers around the country
> Sister Jenny has relaxed hair and wants a Black revolution
> She paints scenes of oppression for an art gallery
> Sister Sandra has an afro and wants a Black revolution
> She works at a women's collective in Brixton
> Sister Angela wears braids and wants a Black revolution
> She spreads love and harmony with her reggae song
> All my sisters who want a Black revolution don't care
> How they wear their hair. And they're all Beautiful.
> (Christabelle Peters, "The Politics of Hair," cited in
> Mercer, "Black Hair," 54)

Thus, the value accorded to a performance of gender invokes a spectrum of power which Gilman showed was significant only within a specific interpretive context. That men should so *desire* to perform in a way that would locate them within the power spectrum as masculine utterly confuses the women of *Herland*. This is one way in which Gilman delightfully and playfully shows that gender is a cultural phenomenon not only capable of polarizing the sexes and according value to behaviors valueless outside of the gendered interpretive lens, but capable of enshrining gendered relations as part of the "natural order." At a time in history when many accepted gender polarities as fundamental features deriving from one's sex, Gilman's androgynous vision was ahead of its time. Now, however, her vision has been superseded.

Gilman was unprepared for the fetishization of the body that was to come. Her view of the body as a producer of goods and commodities that would be freed from the constraints that hindered its free movement in the world has been superseded by the commodification of the body as product. She did not expect or hope for, and was disappointed by, the transformation of the body as an instrument of labor to a commodity itself. The performance of the body is, as Finkelstein notes, "a representation of the social order" (*Fashioned Self*, 52). While Gilman realized this and aimed to liberate women from an oppressive form of feminine embodiment, she underrated the power of the sexually divided social order and its mistrust of the willing freak.

NOTES

Sections of this chapter are expanded in "Hairy Business" in *Organising the Sexed Body*, ed. R. Holliday and J. Hassard (London: Sage, 1999).

1. Indeed, at the first international conference on Charlotte Perkins Gilman (Liverpool, 15–17 July 1995), Ann Lane, in her opening plenary session, pointed out that while Gilman is respected and admired by contemporary feminists, her ideas and arguments have rarely been acknowledged as relevant and useful for explaining issues of concern to modern feminism. This essay seeks to rectify this.

2. The first ladies' hair salon is believed to have been opened in the 1600s by "Champagne," a French peasant who, because of his accidentally discovered skill at dressing female hair, was taken to Paris by an unknown benefactor. His salon, however, did not set a precedent because of the church's condemnation. Champagne, despite this condemnation, continued to live well by visiting prosperous female clients and dressing their hair, privately, in the latest styles (see Cooper, *Hair*).

3. I am concentrating here on head hair and the long/short dichotomy. It is important to acknowledge other aspects of hair symbolism; coloring techniques, for example, are of equal importance. Further, the gendered ways in which facial hair, body hair, and axillary hair are dealt with are also capable of signifying the self.

4. Race was rarely, if ever, discussed by Gilman in relation to hair or dress reform (and was not always addressed sympathetically in relation to other issues). However, racial heritage has an important impact on the type of hair one has and what it is possible to do with it. For a fuller discussion, see Jones, *Bulletproof Diva*; and Mercer, "Black Hair/Style Politics."

5. It is difficult to do justice to the sheer amount of antagonism aroused by these "short-haired viragos." For a much fuller summary of this as well as the conservative reaction to women's use of hairdyes and makeup, see Corson, *Fashions in Hair*, 609–617.

6. Although Hill (*Making*) suggests that Gilman was not always consistent on this point, her views of immigrants, blacks, and Jews, for example, were sometimes offensive. However, Lane (introduction to *Herland*) believes that Gilman related "undeveloped" ideas or peoples to a lack of "proper" education: again stressing the cultural rather than biological nature of individual capacities.

7. See Haug, *Female Sexualization*; Brownmiller, *Femininity*; Mercer, "Black Hair/Style Politics," *New Formations* 3 (Winter 1987): 33–54.

8. In *Black Beauty and Hair* magazine (Winter 1994:57) D. Philips ("The Beauty of Natural Hair") points out that "we are being fed an alien concept of beauty which does not reflect our natural image." However, this is one page among many, all packed with wigs, perming tips, ads for "relaxers," and articles on weaves and hair extensions. Philips concludes: "We guiltily agreed as soon as that special occasion arrives, we all too often rush to straighten our hair, our natural hair not being deemed appropriate" (ibid.; see also Jones, *Diva*; cf. Mercer, "Black Hair").

9. Gilman thus appears to have moved away from her earlier acknowledgment of the emotional pleasures of glamorous narcissism. Letters to a close friend in 1881 show that in her youth she expressed a quite sensuous attachment to her "heavy masses of lustrous hair" and beautiful clothes "for my own delight": "Say, I feel ever so pretty. I have the loveliest new way of coiffuring . . . [it] is soft, clinging, mysterious, and extremely pretty" (cited in Hill, *Making*, 86).

10. That is, within certain constraints; either formal (for example, the armed forces demand short hair) or informal (managers are expected to have "serious" hair). This is particularly so for women, as the film *Working*

Girl highlights: as a secretary Melanie Griffith is allowed to wear long blonde hair; as a manager she knows she must cut her hair and change her image.

11. For further discussion of these views, see Finkelstein, *The Fashioned Self.*

12. In the last decade, the highly visible possibility of wealthy women taking lovers "for fun" rather than for financial and emotional support may turn the tables a little. Certainly with the advent of groups such as the "Chippendales" men appear to be expected to put more effort into their appearance than previously and may well be more often judged in terms of their physical attributes.

CATHERINE J. GOLDEN

"Written to Drive Nails With"
Recalling the Early Poetry of
Charlotte Perkins Gilman

Charlotte Perkins Gilman is best known as the writer of *Herland* and "The Yellow Wallpaper," not as a poet; nonetheless, she began her public career as a poet and wrote poetry throughout her life as a means of social criticism.[1] In its optimist vision, Gilman's poetry remains as incisive today as upon its original publication. This is especially true when examining her poetry in light of her feminist theories in *Women and Economics*, the treatise which established her reputation as a feminist social critic.[2] For Gilman, poetry was a literary vehicle – another genre in which to analyze the patriarchal construction of "woman." Her nearly five hundred poems expose problematic aspects of traditional domesticity in American culture and press for the reorganization of "house service," including child care. Although her first volume of poetry, *In This Our World*, uncritically assumes progress and reflects her class-privileged, Anglocentric orientation (as Ann J. Lane, Susan Lanser, Gary Scharnhorst, and others have acknowledged of much of her work), it is a daring critique of the gender dynamics which denied white, middle- and upper-class turn-of-the-century women participation in the new industrial world. Compact texts, the poems in the section entitled "Woman" effectively introduce Gilman's theories to students of modern feminism. In offering broad outlines for socializing housekeeping and child care, "Woman" anticipates her dominant social and theoretical agenda from *Women and Economics*: to take women's unpaid house service out of the home and professionalize and socialize it.[3]

Although Gilman writes in her autobiography, "Poetry was always a delight to me" (*Living*, 28), she tended to deny the artistry of her verse. Similarly, turn-of-the-century reviewers praised her "indignant passion" but pronounced her poetry "less lyric or dramatic than polemic and brilliant."[4] Horace Traubel, Walt Whitman's literary executor, even urged those who "do not think Mrs. Stetson a poet" to "Forgive yourself possible prejudices and hereafter talk less about rules of art and a little more about its substance."[5] Still, Gilman's satirical verse in *In This Our World* enjoyed a near cult following among socialists in the United States and England.[6] She earned the praise of contemporary luminaries including Upton Sinclair, George Bernard Shaw, Lester Ward, Woodrow Wilson, and William Dean Howells, who ranked Gilman's "Similar Cases" and her other "civic satire" with James R. Lowell's 1848 *Biglow Papers.* Influential editors like Howells were enthusiastic about her socialist/nationalist agenda, but Gilman did not achieve renown as a poet, as Howells predicted. As Gary Scharnhorst notes, "The chorus of praise for *In This Our World* is all the more surprising in light of Stetson's irregular scansion and informal style of verse" (*Charlotte Perkins Gilman*, 40). Gilman did not craft her work carefully, nor does her poetry follow any of the prevailing literary schools, making it hard to place it in the context of turn-of-the-century American women's poetry. Rather, her poetry responds to impulses from different literary schools: while *In This Our World* reflects some of the concerns of American realism in its attempt to depict elements of real life truthfully, in subtle ways Gilman's poetry also betrays the influence of Whitman, whom she considered America's greatest poet. However, as Scharnhorst and Denise Knight point out, her poetry is considerably more conservative and didactic than Whitman's, sacrificing imagery to promote her feminist perspective.[7]

Her own estimation of her first book of poems explains why Gilman has long been recognized as more powerful for her message than for her artistry. Emphasizing the didactic purpose of *In This Our World*, Gilman told an interviewer in 1896, "I don't call it a book of poems. I call it a tool box. It was written to drive nails with."[8] She recognized that a "tool box" could dismantle the prevailing exploitative assumptions of patriarchy as well as build new worlds. In poetry, fiction, and prose, Gilman crafted her own tools to present what she calls in her autobiography "important truths, needed yet unpopular. . . . All my principal topics were in direct contravention of established views, beliefs and emotions" (*Living*, 304).

Gilman saw no point in writing without a social purpose; she records: "If I can learn to write great stories, it will be a powerful addition to my armory."[9] The word "armory" forcefully conveys her recognition of the need to defend her radical views and her intent to make fiction a literary vehicle, driving her socialist and feminist ideologies. Poetry, like fiction, gave her the chance to reorganize her gendered world and expose the absurdity of a society that locked women into domestic roles for which many were unsuited. Gilman wrote passionately, as if no one had critically examined gender relations before. However, her short fiction and journalism, as Shelley Fisher Fishkin points out, conform to a highly subversive countertradition of women fiction writers and journalists who wrote on substantive rather than frivolous issues; these include Gilman's great-aunt Harriet Beecher Stowe, Margaret Fuller, and Anne Royall (with whose work she was familiar). Challenging overbearing "love-plots," Gilman turned to fiction, in particular, to resolve painful conflicts arising from the rigid gender conventions of human experience which defied ready solution. Many of her stories have joyful endings: shrewd, talented female protagonists do achieve success. Similarly, to extend Fishkin's argument, poetry was another genre that Gilman subverted in order to satirize gender relations. In both genres she tested alternative ways of reordering a world of women and men in an untiring effort to expand what Fishkin refers to as "the horizons of gender."[10]

Not foregrounded in *In This Our World*, the feminist poems in the forceful middle section, "Woman," are placed between more traditional themes in the first and third sections, respectively "The World" (containing "Similar Cases") and "Our Human Kind" (renamed "The March" in later editions).[11] Gilman's poems in "Woman" subvert patriarchal ideologies, challenge female subjugation, and argue for equal rights — issues with which we are still grappling today. In "Woman," grim depictions of women's lives and calls for women's empowerment denounce the sacrosanct construct of the "mother-woman," which leads Kate Chopin's Edna Pontellier to suicide in *The Awakening* and drives Gilman's own heroine to madness in "The Yellow Wallpaper." In "Woman," Gilman indicts economically dependent wives who serve the home and rear their children incompetently; she marshals efforts in the service of social change for women. My aim here is not only to retrieve *In This Our World* but also to elevate "Woman," giving it prominence alongside *Women and Economics* as an essential part of the daring agenda of a feminist who argued that "women are not underdeveloped men, but the feminine half of humanity is undeveloped human" (*Forerunner* 1 [December 1910]: 12).[12]

Women and Economics is more sophisticated than *In This Our World*, but the two have much in common. In 1897 Gilman was working on the expanded third edition of *In This Our World* while she revised the manuscript of *Women and Economics*. As publication history would suggest, the two works share socialist, humanist, and feminist ideologies, which Carl Degler points out in his introduction to the 1966 reissuing of *Women and Economics*. *In This Our World* and *Women and Economics* also illustrate Gilman's belief in Social Darwinism and her favorite trope of comparing gender dynamics between humans and animals, using animal behavior to lend universal validity to her arguments and their conformity with "nature."

Although both her poetry and prose are easy to read, *Women and Economics* is a reform tract written at times as a pseudo-scientific study. More detailed and thorough than her poetry, this feminist treatise gives way to redundancy, yet at its heart is the "sexuo-economic" relation, which Lane considers a "brilliant formulation" (251). Anticipating this construct, her poetry urges the reorganization of husband-wife relations and house service, including child care; my discussion reflects this threefold emphasis.[13]

In "Woman," Gilman confronts the subordination of woman, a central theme in much of her work. In the opening stanza of "To the Young Wife," she challenges the economic dependence of late-nineteenth-century women:

Are you content, you pretty three-years' wife?
Are you content and satisfied to live
On what your loving husband loves to give,
	And give to him your life?[14]

Her questions are obviously rhetorical, but the repetition is worth noting. The first query, "Are you content," reads like a general question to a newlywed; the anaphora makes the second statement read more like a challenge than a question: an economic pinch is added, and the tone is harsher, more incredulous. The end-rhyme pairing of "live" and "give" urges the reader to ask, as Gilman does: must life be made up of wholly giving over oneself? Irony suffuses the rhymed pair of "wife" and "life"; again, we hear Gilman questioning: may a wife have no life? Her consistent use of regular meter and end-rhyme in this and other poems could be seen as a strategic means to disarm, for it lends a singsong quality offsetting her bitter message against female subjugation in marriage.[15] The repetition of "give" emphasizes Gilman's astonishment that a wife freely gives up far more than her "loving husband" gives to her.

Gilman's contempt for economically dependent wives who submissively accept "what your loving husband loves to give" grows stronger in "Females" and "Wedded Bliss." "Females" recalls the tension between constraint and freedom in "To the Young Wife." However, in this poem Gilman turns to the animal kingdom to illustrate that, unlike the human sexes, the animal sexes have a full range of experience and status. She sets up the argument in simple terms in the stanza which both opens and ends the poem:

The female fox she is a fox;
The female whale a whale;
The female eagle holds her place
As representative of race
As truly as the male.

Comparing women to vibrant, independent animals, Gilman underscores the unrealized potential of half the human race and seeks to lend universality to her argument that women could be as fully capable as men. In breeds as diverse as eagles and whales, the female emerges equal to her partner. The startling differences between men and women, implied in the body of the poem, are not in conformity with "nature" but socially created. Although stanza two offers a less forceful domestic picture of hens and cows, each "fares as well her other half," and stanza three returns us to images of females in liberty and/or flight equal to the males'. The speaker changes to the wife in the fifth stanza, but this viewpoint — "I earn my living as a wife" — is glossed over through repetition, a major poetic device for Gilman. The repetition of the first and final stanza privileging the vital female fox, whale, and

eagle stubbornly silences the arguments of "those inferior females [who] wive" and hold "a parasitic place / Dependent on the
male." The circularity of the poem conveys Gilman's refusal to
endorse or even listen to the primitive viewpoint of the dependent
wife despite this speaker's exclamation: "ye slander me! No para-
site am I."

Gilman contends that the "sexuo-economic" relation sustains a
primitive individualism bolstered by the family as the basic social
unit; as a collectivist and a socialist, she argues that community
must become the basic social unit, so women's individuality need
not be submerged into the family system. Repeatedly in *Women
and Economics*, Gilman stresses that "We are the only animal species in which the female depends on the male for food, the only
species in which the sex-relation is also an economic relation"
(5).[16] Gilman's oversimplification of this issue in poetry and prose
speaks to her neglect of social class (as Lane also points out in
To Herland and Beyond, 295–296). While nineteenth-century
women of a small, privileged class were fed and cared for by men in
Gilman's industrial society, most women in the late nineteenth century, as well as throughout history, were not removed from the
process of production, although they were subordinated to men
economically and sexually. However, the "sexuo-economic" relation effectively locates the source of women's subordination in the
home, locking wives into passive, stultifying roles that, in turn, are
deemed "natural" for them.

Women are restricted to the home, kept dependent and "inferior," and denied the opportunity to be "representative[s] of race /
As truly as the male," all allegedly to care for children. Gilman
elaborates the exploitative ideology of patriarchy further through
animal analogy in *Women and Economics*, offering the dramatic
example of a wild cow and a domesticated "'milch cow,' such as
we have made" (47).[17] A wild cow, aside from her maternal capacity, is bovine, rather than feminine, and "fares as well as her other
half" because she is allowed to develop freely and naturally. For
economic reasons, we have exploited the milch cow's maternal
function, making her a milking machine bred only for that purpose. So, too, we have domesticated wives for child-bearing and
housekeeping, encouraging them to be feeble and weak.

With a twist of feminist irony, "Wedded Bliss" continues the
theme of the disparity between the sexes. Often considered a

feminist version of Walt Whitman's "The Dalliance of Eagles," "Wedded Bliss" replaces the beauty of an elaborate mating ritual of two eagles in flight with a series of facetious images of ill-suited animals mating.[18] Males and females take the form of three sets of different species, all equally unsuited to wed. The third and final stanza reads:

"O come and be my mate!" said the Salmon to the Clam;
  "You are not wise, but I am.
  I know sea and stream as well;
  You know nothing but your shell."
  Said the Clam, "I'm slow of motion,
  But my love is all devotion,
And I joy to have my mate traverse lake and stream and
    ocean!"
They wed, and cried, "Ah, this is Love, my own!"
And the Clam sucked, the Salmon swam, alone.

Like other poems puncturing men's notion of their superiority, "Wedded Bliss" deflates the fulfillment commonly expected in late-nineteenth-century marriage. The commanding eagle "soared," the patronizing lion "prowled," and the haughty salmon "swam." Each takes leave of his rooted mate, who simply "sat," "browsed," or "sucked." More than the first two stanzas, the third emphasizes the servile personality of the wife and the confinement of the home (likened to a clam's tight shell) and functions as a mocking testimony to male dominance. Continuing this theme with a happy resolution in her parable "Two Storks," Gilman allows the female stork to astonish her mate: this mother stork who has previously used her wings only for "brooding tender little ones!" is also master of the art of flying and soars alongside the astonished father stork. As this parable suggests, Gilman considered male dominance an accident of sex, not a result of leadership, and she argues in *Women and Economics* that men also suffer from their superabundance of power.

The reality of female subjugation clouded Gilman's tireless campaign for equal rights. In its attention to the immobility of "woman," "Wedded Bliss" anticipates *Women and Economics*: "The absolutely stationary female and the wide-ranging male are distinctly human institutions" (65). In her treatise, she describes how women, kept in a state of marital immobility, have developed a servile personality – faithfulness, submissiveness, self-sacrifice, and dependence.

Gilman believed women must evolve from compliant "clams" into self-assured, independent professionals, contributing to the work of the world. As Fishkin notes in her examination of Gilman's fiction and journalism, "Like Fanny Fern a generation before her, and like Tillie Olsen a generation after her, Gilman takes a clear, fresh look at what Olsen calls the 'hard, everyday essential work of maintaining human life'" ("'Making a Change,'" 237). Gilman's poems take a hard look at the exploitative ideology of a society that kept half its population in the kitchen. Her plan for socializing household industry was designed to liberate women from "house service," as she calls it in *Women and Economics* and *The Home*. In her provocatively titled journalism (e.g., "Kitchen-Mindedness," "Mind Cleaning," and "Teaching the Mothers"),[19] she daringly critiqued kitchens and housekeeping, the very topics which filled women's journals of her day. Her poetry, much like her *Forerunner* journalism, attacks traditional attitudes that keep women "kitchen-minded" and housework a gendered function.

A dark poem, "The Mother's Charge" grimly portrays a mother passing on the limitations of "what she herself has come to think ... a right condition" (*Women and Economics*, 72). Aware of the duties her daughter will assume once she becomes a wife and mother, the dying mother "Poured these instructions on the gasping child":

> "Begin at once – don't iron sitting down –
> Wash your potatoes when the fat is brown –
> Monday, unless it rains – it always pays
> To get fall sewing done on the right days –
> A carpet-sweeper and a little broom –
> Save dishes – wash the summer dining-room
> With soda – keep the children out of doors –
> The starch is out – beeswax on all the floors – "
>
> (9–16)

Directives intermingle with housekeeping tips; the dying mother even tells her daughter how to behave as she washes, sews, irons, gardens, and, ultimately, becomes a housewife, "smile, smile always, dear – / Be brave, keep on – I hope I've made it clear."

In this poem Gilman also preserves the tradition of a powerful concluding couplet:

She died, as all her mothers died before.
Her daughter died in turn, and made one more.

Serving as a dark epitaph, these two lines fix the pattern of unfulfilled mothers and daughters who repeat their mothers' lives and mistakes. Painfully aware of her own economic dependency, the mother keeps the daughter ignorant and innocent until her deathbed; thus she serves her daughter's economic advantage and prepares her for the marriage "market."

In *Women and Economics*, Gilman places this dying woman's daughter within a larger context of "isolated women, each beginning again where her mother began before her" (231). For example, the quality of food preparation is low because a young wife learns of cooking only by practicing upon her own family. Thus, she risks the "health of her family . . . and each daughter begins again as ignorant as her mother was before her" (229) – as ignorant as the daughter in "The Mother's Charge." Gilman criticizes the ignorance of wives buying in small amounts and at short intervals, lacking the knowledge to make nutritious meals. Just as a man no longer builds his own house, but relies upon an architect, so, Gilman logically concludes, every woman need not prepare food for her own family; she might rely upon a trained professional who can make cooking a science of "preventive medicine" and an art of "noble expression" (230).

Like the leading spokespersons of the emerging home economics movement at the turn of the century, Gilman advocated the adoption of industrial models of order and efficiency into the home.[20] Unlike most home economics professionals, she moved beyond a critique of the outmoded methods of housekeeping to challenge the traditional assumption that each individual woman is responsible for maintaining her private home for her husband and children.[21] She offered a more progressive vision of work within the home: a division of labor among housekeeping duties (e.g., cooking, cleaning, and managing a household), training, and specialization, elevating house service to a profession, an applied science (230). Gilman recognizes that "those women or those men who were adapted to this form of labor [housekeeping] could become cooks, as they would become composers or carpenters" (240). Those who might elect housework as a livelihood would be paid wages for their work; they would benefit from "the new and higher methods of execution" (246). Specialized industry with labor-saving devices would be a vast improvement on the existing "clumsy method of housekeeping," requiring the "beloved wife and revered mother . . . to do the chamber-work and scullery work of the world," and her daughter after her (245, 246).

Gilman idealistically foresees a future in which women are liberated from the drudgery of household service, but the tone of poems like "The Mother's Charge" is remarkably similar to such late-twentieth-century poems as Marge Piercy's "What's that smell in the kitchen?" where "All over America women are burning dinners" and "Burning dinners is not incompetence but war." However, Gilman did not anticipate the need for revolt; the women in her poems do not burn their food in defiance of patriarchy. Until their death, they serve what she mockingly calls the "Holy Stove."

In her poem "The Holy Stove," Gilman uses an elaborate, melodious rhyme scheme (*abccbdedde* in the first stanza, as was common in political ballads and songs) which bears an ironic relation to her sarcasm against female subjugation and conveys humor. Opening like a ballad, and boiling over with exclamation marks, this poem sings forth against the cook-stove that Gilman's plan for socializing household industry would quickly eliminate:

> O The soap vat is a common thing!
> > The pickle-tub is low!
> The loom and wheel have lost their grace
> In falling from the dwelling-place
> > To mills where all may go!
> The bread-tray needeth not your love;
> > The wash-tub wide doth roam;
> Even the oven free may rove;
> But bow ye down to the Holy Stove,
> > The Altar of the Home!
>
> > > (1–10)

However, in the three remaining stanzas of the poem, "The Altar of the Home" becomes the sacrificial altar to which women offer up "Art and Love, and Time and Truth . . . with Health and

Youth, / In daily sacrifice," as they daily "toil to keep the altar crowned" with no hope of "a fairer faith, / Of a lifetime free from pain" (16–22).

Recontextualizing marital relations within a religious framework, Gilman emphasizes women's painful servitude and men's insensitivity. She continues her mocking religious analogy until the end of an increasingly bitter poem: she consecrates the wife, "the priestess at the shrine"; blesses the Cook-Stove, "a sacred thing"; and hallows the Home, the institution forcibly held by man in which, she believed, women and children are held captive. However, in her powerful closing lines, Gilman sets sarcasm aside to speak directly to the imbalance of power in abiding gender relations: "The Holy Stove is the altar fine, / The wife is the priestess at the shrine – / Now who can be the god?"

Gilman conveys the same tone of entrapment in "Six Hours a Day":

> Six hours a day the woman spends on food!
> Six mortal hours a day. . . .
> With fire and water toiling, heat and cold; . . .
> Toiling for those she loves, the added strain
> Of tense emotion on her humble skill,
> The sensitiveness born of love and fear,
> Making it harder to do even work.
> Toiling without release, no hope ahead . . .
> While the slow finger of Heredity
> Writes on the forehead of each living man,
> Strive as he may, "His mother was a cook!"
>   (1–3, 7–11, 24–26)

Between its opening and closing exclamation marks, the poem seethes with discontent: cooking is "toiling without release, no hope ahead." Gilman typically used repetition to drive her messages, and here the threefold repetition of the word "toiling" intensifies her anger that women spend so much time preparing, serving, and disposing of food. Yet, by refusing to cook, a woman also puts at risk her status as wife and mother. Gilman pokes at the ties between women's roles of housekeeper, wife, and mother. Living under the traditional assumption that house service is a gendered function, women cannot escape the fate of cooking and scrubbing because, as she concludes the poem, "the slow finger of

Heredity / Writes on the forehead of each living man, / Strive as he may, 'His mother was a cook!'" The writing on the forehead "of each living man" imparts the stain of domestic work. Similarly, in "Kitchen-Mindedness," she laments: "Kitchen-bred men born of kitchen-bred mothers" maintain a "narrowness of vision" (11).

Despite its darkness, "Six Hours a Day" conveys the broad outlines of Gilman's larger agenda for socializing household industry refined in *Women and Economics*. Her description of the untrained housewife "Struggling with laws she does not understand / Of chemistry and physics, and the weight / Of poverty and ignorance besides" introduces the idea that cooking is a nutritive science requiring specialization and training. In her reference to the "allied labors of the stove and tub, / The pan, the dishcloth, and the scrubbing brush," we see the beginnings of her division of household labor. Her emphasis on time in "Six Hours a Day" — "Six mortal hours a day to handle food" — shows why she argued in *Women and Economics* (as well as her journalism and *The Home*) to take kitchens out of the home (families in an apartment house would take meals together, but the meals would be prepared by trained experts and taken in a common dining room; likewise, private homes would be kitchenless, and families in a group of adjacent suburban homes would eat together in a common eating-house).[22] The references to time in this poem also prepare us for the argument in *Women and Economics* that the division of household work into allied industries would require the service of fewer women for fewer hours of the day, increasing women's potential for productive industry in the world (245).

In the second stanza of "To the Young Wife" Gilman also focuses on a cook's intimate involvement with dirt in the private home:

Are you content with work, — to toil alone,
To clean things dirty and to soil things clean;
To be a kitchen-maid, be called a queen, —
　　Queen of a cook-stove throne?

　　　　　　　　(5–8)

Gilman, who mockingly crowns her young wife "Queen of a cook-stove throne," uses the rhetorical question here to urge women to challenge their lot. Her message largely stands in opposition to the cult of domesticity presented in countless advice books and popular magazines (e.g., *Godey's Lady's Book*) from the turn of the century. In the words of Dr. W. J. Truitt, author of the advice book *Know Thyself* (1911), "The queen who sits upon the throne of home, crowned and sceptered as none other can be, is — mother. Her enthronement is complete, her reign unrivaled" (35). Rather, in "To the Young Wife," Gilman implores women to remember the days of their "ardent girlhood" when they longed to be "wise" and "strong." "Seeing the world today," Gilman, in the sixth stanza, poses this challenge: "And are you quite convinced this is the way, / The only way a woman's duty lies — / Knowing all women so have shut their eyes?" Challenge turns to condemnation as the poem continues, and Gilman sentences the young wife in the tenth and final stanza to "slavish service hour by hour — / A life with no beyond!" Advancing her bitterness toward house service in *Women and Economics*, Gilman argues: "All that is basest and foulest she . . . must handle and remove. Grease, ashes, dust, foul linen, and sooty ironware, — among these her days must pass. As we socialize our functions, this passes from her hands into those of man" (246–247). She notes that the professional cleaner in a city, for example, is more and more frequently a male. Moreover, in Gilman's progressive vision of socialized household industry, homes would be easier to clean since the cook-stove would be removed.[23]

Household service, if socialized as industry, would no longer be gender specific. In Gilman's model, "a woman could choose her position, train for it, and become a most valuable functionary in her special branch, all the while living in her own home; that is, she would live in it as a man lives in his home, spending certain hours of the day at work and others at home" (*Women and Economics*, 245). Elevating the wife's status to her husband's, this model would even leave the woman working outside the home time for "other occupation" (245).

Although Gilman was aware that such plans alarmed her readers, she believed her model of reform offered a realistic assessment of the future. However, she does not suggest a realistic plan for its execution. In this respect, her landmark treatise is as naive as her poetry and some of her overly optimistic short fiction. She overlooks who, specifically, are the specialized workers who would train for "useful" and "honorable" household professions in her future collective society. Placing faith in Darwinian evolution, she believes in natural selection and the inevitability of an evolving cooperative society:

> It seems almost unnecessary to suggest that women as economic producers will naturally choose those professions which are compatible with motherhood. . . . If women did choose professions unsuitable to maternity, Nature would quietly extinguish them by her unvarying process. Those mothers who persisted in being acrobats, horse-breakers, or sailors before the mast, would probably not produce vigorous and numerous children. If they did, it would simply prove that such work did not hurt them. There is no fear to be wasted on the danger of women's choosing wrong professions, when they are free to choose. (245–246)

Just as Gilman neglects to explain with precision the socioeconomic classes from which women professionals would be drawn, she does not resolve who would assume the cost for the specialized training of household professions. However, she does elaborate on how the socialization of household industries will benefit not only women but the home, currently an economic entity "of arrested industrial development" (247).

Gilman also believed that turn-of-the-century child care was in an "arrested" state of development and feared for the home-kept baby.[24] Her poems depict mothers as foolish, inexperienced, and inadequate, preparing us for her advocacy of community child care – the most radical aspect of her agenda. "False Play" depicts one such "poor mama," trying hard to make her child love her:

> "Do you love me?" asked the mother of her child,
>   And the baby answered, "No!"
> Great Love listened and sadly smiled;
> He knew the love in the heart of the child –
>   That you could not wake it so.

"Foolishly" believing her baby does not love her, the mother grieves until the baby concedes to her tears and joins "in the lying play." The baby appears wiser and more powerful than his naive mother.

The fourth stanza of "To the Young Wife" uses rhetorical questions to suggest that young, inexperienced mothers should not raise their children:

> Are you content to rear your children so?
> Untaught yourself, untrained, perplexed, distressed,
> Are you so sure your way is always best?
> That you can always know?
>
> (13–16)

The "perplexed," "distressed" mother in "To the Young Wife" is a far cry from the trained education specialists Gilman thought could better tend young children. Children – often described as "wailing babies" (e.g., "Women of To-day") tended by "untaught," "untrained" mothers – would be happier and better served by child-care professionals in a "baby garden," her equivalent of a modern child-care center.

More than any other poem in "Woman," "Motherhood" provides the contours of Gilman's plan for collective child care, an essential part of what she calls the "new Motherhood":

> The motherhood of the fair new-made world –
> O glorious New Mother of New Men!
> Her child, with other children from its birth,
> In the unstinted freedom of warm air,
> Under the wisest eyes, the tenderest thought,
> Surrounded by all beauty and all peace,
> Led, playing, through the gardens of the world,
> With the crowned heads of science and great love
> Mapping safe paths for those small, rosy feet, –
>
> (75–83)

Like cooking, child care is elevated to a "science," supported by love and care. The "garden" metaphor accentuates the nurturing aspect of her child-care system, in which the trained professional would not replace but supplement the mother. The fourfold repetition of "Taught" introducing lines 84–87 contrasts with the "untaught" mother in "To the Young Wife." The repetition and placement of "Taught" emphasizes education, suggesting that child care would extend the kindergarten movement to infancy. Thus, it is not surprising that in *Women and Economics* and *Concerning Children*, Gilman's design for kitchenless apartment houses for professional women with families included in its blue-print a day nursery and kindergarten staffed with well-trained, professional nurses and teachers.

"Motherhood" also introduces Gilman's belief that child care would promote an awareness of collective rights and duties. In her poem she describes how each child will learn "to love all mankind and serve them fair / By seeing, from his birth, all children served / With the same righteous, all-embracing care" (87–89). Gilman was a socialist and a humanist, and the communal aspect of child care was critical to her social agenda. She builds upon her poetic introduction of "righteous, all-embracing care" in *Women and Economics*, where she describes how from birth all children would benefit from the companionship of children their own age hitherto available only to twins (288). Not smothered by maternal love, children raised in a large group will learn the virtues of modern life as well as comradeship and collective interest and action; the child will consider him/herself as one of many children, a part of humanity. Raised in a community child-care center, a child will become a member of a "civilized community," "a growing, self-realizing individual" (290), and not "be such people as we see about us" (284). Such will be possible, Gilman idealistically argues, with the creation of a "new Motherhood," giving rise to a "wiser, stronger, and nobler mother" (290) and child.

In *Women and Economics* as well as *Concerning Children* and *The Home*, Gilman argues for an "organized human motherhood" (294): women could develop their power and assume their maternal identity without losing their human identity. She maintains that the mother "will love her child as well, perhaps better, when she is not in hourly contact with it, when she goes from its life to her own life, and back from her own life to its life, with ever new delight and power" (290). She attests in *In This Our World* and later advances in her theoretical works that mothering is not genetic. Women can give birth to children – an animal function – but not know how to raise or educate them effectively (*Women and Economics*, 283). She concludes, "No mother knows more than her mother knew: no mother has ever learned her business; and our children pass under the well-meaning experiments of an endless succession of amateurs" (293). In "Women of To-day," she even blames the high infant mortality on "amateur" mothering:

And mothers? Pitying Heaven! Mark the cry
  From cradle death-beds! Mothers on their knees!
Why, half the children born — as children die!
    You don't keep these!

                        (17–20)

The multiple exclamation points in this stanza mark her scorn for mothers who raise their children at home. Further, Gilman believed that "some women there are, and some men, whose highest service to humanity is the care of children," not just their own children (*Women and Economics*, 283).[25] Child care had to be collective to ensure the best care for all children and to advance the human race.

With a socialized motherhood, a woman could become "a world-servant instead of a house-servant" (*Women and Economics*, 269) and a better role model for her children. Babies would be the "business" of professional child-care workers who would study infancy as a stage of human development and benefit babies and their mothers, in turn. Her radical call for community child care, commonly heard in our time, would permit women to seek full-time jobs outside the home. Today many women work out of necessity rather than to achieve their individual potential, as Gilman idealistically envisioned. In the progressive, collective society described in *Women and Economics*, some women would gain their economic independence as wage-earning cooks and household workers; others could achieve autonomy as successful musicians, able child caretakers, or social servants. In stories such as "A Garden of Babies" and "Making a Change" and her utopian novels, *Moving the Mountain* and *Herland*, Gilman's brand of socialized motherhood dramatically improves her fictional characters' lives. In *Moving the Mountain*, men and women live together, justly and happily, in a humanist, feminist, and socialist world which has bred out the male-dominated ways of mothering and educating children; trained specialists (outlined in *In This Our World* and described in her theoretical works) quickly raise a new generation in which virtually everyone lives together democratically and cooperatively. Gilman offers a more extreme version of a collective motherhood in *Herland*. In this utopia without families and men, children are raised by a genuine community of women.

Gilman also envisions an emancipated new woman in her poem "She Who Is To Come":

A WOMAN – in so far as she beholdeth
    Her one Beloved's face;
A mother – with a great heart that enfoldeth
    The children of the Race:
A body, free and strong, with that high beauty
    That comes of perfect use, is built thereof;
A mind where Reason ruleth over Duty,
    And Justice reigns with Love;
A self-poised, royal soul, brave, wise, and tender,
    No longer blind and dumb;
A Human Being, of an unknown splendor,
    Is she who is to come!

"She Who Is To Come" is a woman first, then a mother. Following the colon, the succession of line-opening nouns suggests that wife and mother equal body, mind, and self, a human being, in all its glory and potential. "No longer blind and dumb," the new woman emerges as a symbol of strength, reason, wisdom, and love. She is complete with a maternal identity and a human identity.

Within *In This Our World* Gilman aims to lift the restrictions imposed on women as wives and house servants and also to awaken them to the "right motherhood" (a term used in her essay "The New Motherhood" as well as *Women and Economics*), portrayed in her fiction, explicated in her nonfiction, and importantly foreseen in her poetry. "Girls of To-day" conveys her optimistic prediction that young women of today will achieve collective good for the human race:

    . . . You have work of your own!
    Maid and mother and wife,
    Look in the face of life!
    There are duties you owe the race!
    Outside of your dwelling-place
        There is work for you alone!
                    (30–35)

Her insistence that the time "now is here" reinforces her belief in the inevitability of what proved to be a very threatening domestic ideology. Traditional attitudes resisted change even as women entered the workplace, institutions of higher education, and public reform arenas, including women's suffrage. Gilman was a social evolutionist, an optimist reformer, who neither advocated class struggle nor confronted class relationships in the ways that she challenged the "sexuo-economic relationship" between husbands and wives. At the turn of the century, she predicted more advances for women in the next fifty years than in the past two hundred. She pinned her hopes for change on technology, not revolt, and in her optimism for the future she did not consider that old ways could be welded to technological innovations.

Given Gilman's daring critique of gender dynamics and her awareness of society's tendency to cling to the past, feminist readers today may find themselves wanting more from her than a vision of a progressive future society. But essentially that is what Gilman offers, first in her poetry, then in her prose. In her poetry as in her fiction, although not in her own life, solutions came readily and painlessly. Speaking reflectively of her literary imagination in her autobiography, Gilman notes, "I could make a world to suit me" (*Living*, 20). Although she probably realized that utopian ideals were limited motivators of social change, she aimed to "make a world" so appealing that men and women would recognize the need to revise the exploitative ideology of her day. Women still do not receive wages for housework or equal pay for equal work, but some of her most incisive ideas – housecleaning services and community child care – have become realities.

There are other limitations. In poetry and prose, Gilman analyzes and criticizes relations between the sexes to promote emancipation from the home and women's participation in the larger world of professional work. Although by the 1890s she was admittedly a socialist, hers was a humanitarian socialism, and she rejected the Marxist notions of class struggle and class violence. For Gilman, issues of gender took precedence over matters of class, so she separated herself from radical feminists within socialist circles. Her ideas and plans for change in *In This Our World* and *Women and Economics* are extremely provocative but also optimistic and oversimplified. Both her published and unpublished writings give insufficient attention to issues of social class, race, and ethnicity, weakening her agenda for liberating women, as Lane,

Lanser, Scharnhorst, and others have acknowledged.[26] Moreover, as Lanser so effectively argues in her critique of "The Yellow Wallpaper" as a "sacred feminist text," and as Scharnhorst advances, Gilman's work reflects racism and class privilege.[27] We cannot deny also that these biases, in part, reflect the "psychic geography" of Anglo-America at the turn of the twentieth century, evident in the work of other women writers of her time, such as Virginia Woolf. In her idealism, Gilman emerges insensitive to the plight of working-class women, racial minorities, and immigrant women. We can assume an intended middle- and upper-class audience for *In This Our World* and *Women and Economics*, given, for example, her references to a domestic servant problem (apart from "wife" as "house-servant"). Thus, when I speak of Gilman liberating women, it is a small, privileged class of women.

Nonetheless, Gilman's legacy is still valuable for its optimist vision. Although she underestimated the way some women found strength and power within a female community, she focused insightfully on the oppressive patriarchy that controlled women's lives as she attempted to elevate women to equal status with men. Her discussion of gender in *In This Our World* and *Women and Economics* still makes a startling contribution to feminism today.

NOTES

1. I direct the reader to an essay about *In This Our World* by Carol Farley Kessler, "Brittle Jars and Bitter Jangles: Light Verse by Charlotte Perkins Gilman," *Regionalism and the Female Imagination* 4:2 (1978): 35–43; reprinted in *Charlotte Perkins Gilman: The Woman and Her Work*, ed. Sheryl L. Meyering, 133–143. Because Gilman's verse is not well known, Kessler intentionally quotes greatly from it, although she does intersperse some interesting commentary between poems. Gary Scharnhorst offers insightful comments about the reception of *In This Our World* in his book *Charlotte Perkins Gilman*. See also Denise Knight's reading of Gilman's poetry in relation to Whitman's, "'With the First Grass-Blade': Whitman's Influence on the Poetry of Charlotte Perkins Gilman," *Walt Whitman Quarterly* (Summer 1993): 18–29.

In This Our World was written under the name of Charlotte Perkins Stetson, and only 168 of her poems were published in its various editions. Her later work appeared, for example, in *Life* and *Saturday Review of Literature*. For more discussion of Gilman's later poetry, see Scharnhorst's recent essay, "Reconstructing *Here Also*: On the Later Poetry of Charlotte Perkins Gilman," in *Critical Essays on Charlotte Perkins Gilman*, ed. Joanne Karpinski, 249–268.

2. Deemed an outstanding feminist in her own time (along with Olive Schreiner and Ellen Key), Gilman, ironically, repudiated the term "feminist" when it came into use in her later years. In *To Herland and Beyond* Ann J. Lane places Gilman "on the margin of the women's movement, where one might think she would find a home because of a shared belief that issues of gender take precedence over issues of class" (231).

3. In *The Home* and *Concerning Children*, Gilman elaborates and refines her ideas from *Women and Economics*. As Lane argues in *To Herland and Beyond*, "to know only *Women and Economics* is to be familiar with only part of her ideas. It is to settle for the ground floor and to neglect the enticing staircase that leads to more elaborate and intriguing rooms above" (254). Nonetheless, Gilman's later works, particularly *The Home*, are derived from *Women and Economics*.

4. See William Morton Payne, *Dial*, 1 September 1898, 134; Charles Lummis, *Land of Sunshine* 4 (September 1898): 201, quoted in Scharnhorst, *Charlotte Perkins Gilman*, 40.

5. See Horace Traubel, *Conservator* 9 (September 1898): 109, quoted in Scharnhorst, *Charlotte Perkins Gilman*, 42.

6. I recommend Gary Scharnhorst's thorough discussion of the publication history and reception of *In This Our World* in *Charlotte Perkins Gilman*, 38–44.

7. After 1890 Gilman often wrote free verse fashioned after Whitman, whom she called "America's greatest poet" (quoted in Scharnhorst, *Charlotte Perkins Gilman*, 41); before 1890 she usually wrote verse with regular meter and rhyme. See Knight's essay "'With the First Grass-Blade'"; and Scharnhorst's discussion of Gilman's *In This Our World* in *Charlotte Perkins Gilman* (1985).

8. Gilman, *Topeka State Journal* (15 June 1896), vol. 7, quoted in Scharnhorst, *Charlotte Perkins Gilman*, 40. Gilman elaborates this point in her autobiography: "I have never made any pretense of being literary. As far as I had any method in mind, it was to express the idea with clearness and vivacity, so that it might be apprehended with ease and pleasure" (*Living*, 284–285).

9. Undated, this quotation comes from a folder in the Charlotte Perkins Gilman papers marked "Thoughts & Figgerings."

10. I recommend Fishkin's essay, "'Making a Change': Strategies of Sub-

version in Gilman's Journalism and Short Fiction," in *Critical Essays on Charlotte Perkins Gilman*, ed. Karpinski, 234–248.

11. A few powerful feminist poems, such as "An Obstacle," are included in the first and longest section, "The World." However, "The World" is comprised mostly of nature poems and prayers, which one reviewer for the *Unity* commended to Unitarian ministers; this section includes some humorous verse considerably informed by Social Darwinist thinking and sarcastic verses about the nature of humanity, like "Similar Cases," which earned the deep praise of numerous critics including Floyd Dell and Howells. "Our Human Kind" largely contains political anthems on labor and Nationalist themes. Both sections convey Gilman's sociology, later developed in *Human Work*. A few of Gilman's poems from *In This Our World* have been reprinted in various anthologies. "She Walketh Veiled and Sleeping" and "The Anti-Suffragists" from "Woman" and "The Prophets" from "The World" are included, for example, in *The World Split Open: Four Centuries of Women Poets in England and America*, ed. Louise Bernikow (New York: Random/Vintage, 1976). Additional reprints include "The Anti-Suffragists" and "Six Hours a Day," in *On Common Ground: A Selection of Hartford Writers*, ed. Alice DeLana and Cynthia Reik (Hartford: Stowe-Day Foundation, 1975). The poems in "Woman" are not uniformly strong, so I have intentionally concentrated on those that are most powerful, provocative, and not easily available.

12. Although not much scholarship has been written on *Women and Economics*, several pieces make a major contribution. In his 1966 introduction, Degler makes a significant argument about the importance of the work in its own time and its relevance to women's issues today. Lane also offers extensive insightful comments about *Woman and Economics* and Gilman's other prose works in *To Herland and Beyond*. I also recommend Joanna Zangrando's paper "Work, Class, and Domestic Ideology: Charlotte Perkins Gilman and the Home Economists at the Turn-of-the-Century." Zangrando talks about Gilman's nonfiction works and raises important limitations involving class in Gilman's work on gender, points which Lane also makes. *Women and Economics* has subsequently been reprinted by Ayre in 1972 and, most recently, by Prometheus Books as part of the Great Minds Series (1994).

13. The themes in most of the twenty-nine poems in "Woman" fall easily into one of these three categories: wife (and marriage), housekeeper, and mother. The substance of some poems touches on more than one role, so I have listed them under each. The following poems concern Woman as Wife: "To Man," "Women of To-day," "To the Young Wife," "Reassur-

Public and Private Faces

ance," "Girls of To-day," "We, as Women," "Wedded Bliss," "The Modest Maid," "Unsexed," "Females," and "The Mother's Charge." These poems concern Woman as Housekeeper: "Six Hours a Day," "To the Young Wife," "Women of To-day," "The Holy Stove," "The Mother's Charge." The following pertain to Woman as Mother: "Women of To-day," "To the Young Wife," "False Play," "Motherhood," "Reassurance," "Mother to Child," "In Mother-Time," "Girls of To-day," "We, as Women," "If Mother Knew," "The Mother's Charge," "A Brood Mare," "A Mother's Soliloquy," and "Baby Love." The remaining poems, not easily grouped, deal with a range of different aspects: for example, the woman's condition, the future of women, and women's suffrage. These include "She Walketh Veiled and Sleeping," "An Old Proverb," "Services," "The Anti-Suffragists," "Women Do Not Want It," "Feminine Vanity," and "They Wandered Forth."

14. All quotations are from the 1899 Small, Maynard edition of *In This Our World*. Arno Press reprinted this edition in 1974.

15. Kessler also notes, in passing, that Gilman's choice of poetics may have made the reader more receptive to her radical ideas.

16. See *Women and Economics*, 22 (nearly exact wording), 95 (almost exact wording), and 210.

17. For a full discussion, see *Women and Economics*, 44–47.

18. Scharnhorst suggests that in "Wedded Bliss" Gilman rewrites Whitman's "The Dalliance of Eagles" from a feminist perspective. Other critics, such as Denise Knight, have suggested that Gilman's poetry often betrays the influence of her much admired Whitman. Knight, in "'With the First Grass-Blade,'" describes the similarities between specific poems, such as Gilman's opening celebratory poem "Birth" and "Song of Myself," and notes cases where she satirized Whitman's verses, such as "Wedded Bliss."

19. "Kitchen-Mindedness," *Forerunner* 1 (February 1910): 7–11; "Mind Cleaning," *Forerunner* 3 (January 1912): 5–6; "Teaching the Mothers," *Forerunner* 3 (March 1912): 73–75.

20. These include Ellen H. Richards, Isabel Bevier, Mary Davies Swartz Rose, Henrietta Goodrich, Florence Nesbitt, Caroline Hunt, and Alice P. Norton.

21. For more discussion of Gilman and the home economics movement, see Zangrando's "Work, Class, and Domestic Ideology."

22. Meals could be brought to the home or apartment house for those who preferred. In its plan for common eating houses and its system of collective child care, Gilman's reform resembles the kibbutz system in Israel today.

23. Gilman adds, however, that her model "will not prevent, either, the

woman who has a dilettante fondness for some branch of cookery, wherewith she loves to delight herself and her friends, from keeping a small cooking plant within reach, as she might a sewing-machine or a turninglathe" (*Women and Economics* 251).

24. Gilman wrote extensively on this topic in the *Forerunner*, *Woman's Journal*, and other magazines. I recommend to the reader, for example, "Teaching the Mothers," *Forerunner* 3 (March 1912): 73–75; "The New Motherhood," *Forerunner* 1 (December 1910): 17–18; and "The New Mothers of a New World," *Forerunner* 4 (June 1913): 145–149.

25. This comment seems to challenge the conventional notions of her generation. However, as Lane points out in *To Herland and Beyond*, Gilman did not contest the traditional view that the care of children belonged to women alone (262). See also *Concerning Children*.

26. For example, my colleague Joanna Zangrando specifically looked for allusions to class differences among women in the Gilman Papers, Schleslinger Library, Radcliffe College, but found Gilman unaware of such issues. However, Gilman's "adopted mother," Helen Campbell, wrote on issues of working-class women, and Gilman lived with Campbell in California in 1894–1895 while they edited the *Impress*. Moreover, Gilman earned a gold medal from the Trades and Labor Unions of Almeda County in 1893 for her essay "The Labor Movement" (1892; CPG Papers, Shelf 177, 3268). These suggest her knowledge of working-class women's experiences. Also, she was the only person who did not support a literacy requirement to vote, a common method to disenfranchise blacks. See also Lane's discussion of Gilman's limitations (*To Herland and Beyond*, particularly 251–254, 295–296) and Susan Lanser's article "Feminist Criticism, 'The Yellow Wallpaper,' and the Politics of Color in America," *Feminist Studies* 15:3 (1989): 415–441.

27. Lanser's and Scharnhorst's forceful critiques direct our attention to a side of Gilman evident in the *Forerunner* and other writings that I find discomfiting; in the journal which she single-handedly produced for seven years, Gilman chastises the "lazy old Orientals" who do not want to work, exhibits anti-Semitism, and, like other "nativist" intellectuals of her time, argues against the influx of "undesirables," favoring immigrants of a "better stock." In her defense, Gilman does note the injustice to the Jews; see *Women and Economics*, 9 and 78. In the *Forerunner* (1913), for example, she also speaks against the oppression and mistreatment of the Indian, African, and Mexican.

DENISE D. KNIGHT

"But O My Heart"

The Private Poetry of Charlotte Perkins Gilman

In 1894, a few months after Charlotte Perkins Stetson (Gilman) published her first volume of poetry, she received a congratulatory letter from William Dean Howells proclaiming her a "gifted prophetess." "[The poems] are the wittiest and wisest things that have been written this many a long day and year," Howells wrote. "You speak with a tongue like a two-edged sword. I rejoice in your gift . . . and wonder how much more you will do with it." [1] Howells didn't wonder for long. Second and third editions of the critically acclaimed volume quickly appeared, and over the course of her lifetime Gilman would publish nearly five hundred poems. Unapologetically didactic and designed to advance her social philosophies, Gilman's *public* poetry — much of which originally appeared in *In This Our World* and in her popular press magazine the *Forerunner* — is finally receiving scholarly attention. A second volume of verse, *The Later Poetry of Charlotte Perkins Gilman*, which she was preparing for publication in the weeks before her death, was finally published in 1996. [2] Many of the poems in that edition, like those in *In This Our World*, reflect the influence of reform movements such as Nationalism and Social Darwinism in shaping Gilman's ideology. Other common topics in her published poetry address issues affecting women: the prevalence of domestic subservience, economic disparity between the sexes, and a call for a social motherhood system that would enlist the skills of professional child-care workers. Like her earlier collection, *The Later Poetry* includes satirical works, philosophical poems, and occasional verses. Gilman's *private* poems, in contrast, while substantial in number, have been virtually ignored. Yet it is in the private verse that her most authentic poetic voice emerges. Bold, impassioned, and often remarkably poignant, the handwritten verses that remain among Gilman's personal papers are an invaluable source of information about a side of her that she preferred to keep concealed from nearly everyone outside her immediate circle.

Critic Cheryl Walker, in the introduction to *American Women Poets of the Nineteenth Century*, notes that "the typical nineteenth-century American woman poet was well educated and spiritually keen, showed unusual intellectual promise before she was out of her teens, either remained single or found married life frustrating, suffered intensely and relatively early from the deaths of loved ones, turned to writing to ease financial burdens or a troubled heart, and sought the support of an influential male."[3] Gilman conformed to most, but not all, of the tenets identified by Walker. She was spiritually keen, intellectual, and oppressed by her first marriage. Unlike the "typical" poet, however, Gilman was largely self-educated (she was enrolled briefly at the Rhode Island School of Design); while she did not suffer from the death of loved ones early in her life, the void that was left by her parents' marital separation triggered a profound sense of loss. It is also arguable as to whether or not she "sought the support of an influential male"; her professional relationship with American author and editor William Dean Howells has been well documented, but it was he who initiated the contact with Gilman through his now-legendary praise of her satirical verse "Similar Cases" in 1890.[4] Walker also notes that among the common subjects for the nineteenth-century woman poet was "the poem of secret sorrow, in which she reveals that her life has been blighted by experiences she hides from public scrutiny" (xxvi). That type of verse is, in fact, prominent among Gilman's private poetry.

The rich body of private verse, numbering over one hundred extant pieces, falls into four loose, and often overlapping, categories: occasional poems, conventional verse, spiritual meditations, and intimate verse.[5] The largest of these categories — the "intimate verse" — is comprised of a substantial body of poems that can be further divided. It is on one of these subcategories — specifically those poems written to or about members of Gilman's intimate circle: Martha Luther, Walter Stetson, Adeline Knapp, and Houghton Gilman — that this essay focuses.

Highly charged, provocative, and often sensual, the most private of the private verse requires both historical contextualization and perceptive study on the part of the reader. From this intimate poetry emerges a profile of the complex emotional webs in which Gilman often found herself entangled. While an assessment of the role of the private verse in her life is speculative, it seems, in part, to have served a therapeutic purpose: through the poems, Gilman could speak her deepest hurts, her highest ambitions, her darkest fears.

The conditions affecting Gilman's early childhood, which subsequently shaped her adult relationships, have been well documented by her biographers.[6] Her father abandoned the family during Gilman's early childhood, and he became "a stranger, distant and little known" (*Living*, 5). The impoverishment that resulted, both emotional and financial, was enormous: the family "was forced to move nineteen times in eighteen years" (*Living*, 8). Gilman's mother, Mary Westcott Perkins, "having suffered so deeply . . . and still suffering for lack of a husband's love," consciously denied her children "all expression of affection" so that they would neither desire it nor miss it (*Living*, 10). Although her mother's devotion to her children was "tireless" (*Living*, 23), the emotional neglect took its toll.

The elusiveness of love, stemming from her mother's practice of withholding affection, is a recurring theme both in Charlotte Gilman's life and in her private verse. The impact was profound: Gilman was wary of intimate relationships throughout her life (see *Living*, 10–11, 78).

Her early love of poetry may have been a way for Gilman to escape the anguish caused by the absence of familial affection. She not only committed "miles of it to memory" (*Living*, 28), but began composing her own fairy tales and verses at an early age. "No one had a richer, more glorious life than I had, inside," she wrote in her autobiography. "It speaks volumes for the lack of happiness in my own actual life that I should so industriously construct it in my imagination" (*Living*, 23). At the age of sixteen, Gilman "wrote the first bit of verse that seemed to [her] real poetry, a trifling thing about white violets." Proud of her accomplishment, she read it to her mother, who "listened with no apparent interest." The confidence of the "budding poetess" quickly eroded. "A trifling incident," Gilman reported in her memoirs, "but it hurt so that it was never forgotten, and I did not go to her so readily with later verses" (*Living*, 70).

Indeed, in some of the private poems, Gilman's metaphorical depiction of a helpless child needing to be cradled and comforted betrays not only hurt, but the emotional vulnerability and fear of abandonment that resulted. Yet in other poems she casts herself as a confident and independent woman who sacrifices her youthful dream of love for the pursuit of "larger truths." The private verse frequently focuses, however, on the theme of unattainable happiness, suggested metaphorically through Edenic or paradisiacal imagery, which seems to represent a place beyond the reach of the poet/speaker. In poem after poem Gilman laments the loss of idealized love and castigates those whom she holds accountable for contributing to her pain.

While once characterizing her public verse as more of a "tool box" than a book of poems, insisting that "it was written to drive nails with,"[7] Gilman might have said the same about her private verse. Never is this more true than in some of her poems to Martha Luther — the young woman with whom she shared a "romantic friendship" from 1879 until Luther's marriage in 1882.[8]

As Carroll Smith-Rosenberg, Lillian Faderman, and others have observed, romantic love between women was relatively common during the second half of the nineteenth century — in part because it was viewed as innocuous, as nonsexual, and as good practice for marriage.[9] The so-called schoolgirl crushes were considered harmless; the largely accepted view of such relationships was that they were nonsexual, since "real" sex required a penis. Effusive declarations of love between women were commonplace, particularly in a climate where premarital sex with men was condemned. While Gilman described her friendship with Martha Luther, whom she befriended at the age of eighteen, as involving "love, but not sex" (*Living*, 78), the degree of emotional intensity in their relationship is striking. Martha satisfied Gilman's craving for intimacy and affection, and Gilman, who had no intention of marrying, believed that her relationship with Martha would "make up to me for husband and children and all that I shall miss."[10]

On Valentine's Day, 1880, Gilman sent Martha a verse that begins with praise of her physical beauty: she comments on Martha's "large grey eyes," her "glossy hair," and her "willowy grace."[11] She then reaffirms her love for Martha, referring to herself in the third person and invoking metaphors from the natural world to describe their relationship: "Unto her thy heart dost still incline / Like to the oak tree and the clinging vine." An overt declaration of love follows:

> I love thee much! Thou hast in black and white
> A fond confession that I well could wish
> Had never met the garish light of day,
> That I had ne'er been tempted to exhume
> From the dark caverns of my deep hearts gloom.

The confession of love, once exhumed from "the dark caverns" of Gilman's heart, was repeated in her letters, poems, and diaries, in which she frequently declared her devotion to Martha. The two even exchanged a pair of matching bracelets that they vowed to wear as a symbol of their union.[12] With each passing month, Gilman's emotional investment in the relationship deepened; her letters openly declare her love: "I think it probable (ahem) that you love me however I squirm, love the steady care around which I so variously revolve, love me and will love me — why in the name of heaven have we so confounded love with passion that it sounds to our century-tutored ears either wicked or absurd to name it between women? It is no longer friendship between us, it is love."[13] Just two months later, however, when Martha Luther became engaged to Charles A. Lane of Hingham, Massachusetts, Gilman was devastated.

A poem written on 13 December 1881, shortly after Gilman learned of Martha's engagement, effectively illustrates her dictum that her verse — even that which was considered private — was "written to drive nails with." The poem metaphorically drives nails into Martha's very soul and reproaches her for betraying their love. At the same time, Gilman used the poem to mourn the loss of the love they had shared. She makes an impassioned appeal to Martha to consider the consequences of her impending marriage. The poem begins:

> Tender and small they rise in jostling crowds
> Each with a throng of memories at its back.

Tender and small are they, but O my heart!
Each little name and all the thoughts behind
Hath arrows poison tipped.

(*Diaries*, 862–863)

Intending at first simply to mail the poem to Martha, who lived nearby, Gilman ultimately changed her mind, and the poem was never sent. When Martha dropped by for a visit, however, a week after it had been composed, Gilman read the verse aloud (see *Diaries*, 95). Striking back produced the effect that Gilman had desired: Martha wept as Gilman read the poem; after her departure, Gilman's diary notes that she passed a pleasant day painting a "jolly little [picture]" and playing the card game whist. In a letter written to her Providence, Rhode Island, friend Sam Simmons, shortly before she composed the poem, Gilman compared the loss of Martha to an amputation: "Cautery has stopped the *danger*, but [I] feel the *loss of the limb* as sensibly as ever."[14] Reconnecting with Martha's emotions, then, seemed to be vitally important in terms of recovering at least part of her amputated spirit.

This particular poem both adheres to and departs from many of the intimate verses that are part of Gilman's private canon. Similar in theme, yet somewhat more intense than many of the poems, "Unsent," as she titled the verse, begins with a catalogue of the various terms of endearment she used to address Martha: "sweetheart," "dearest love," "darling," and "little girl." This poem, however, speaks to a relationship that apparently went beyond the same-sex romantic attachments that were sanctioned by conventional society.

In the first stanza, Gilman presents herself as the object of Martha's betrayal and as the victim of her brutality. Casting Martha as the villain who pierces her heart by shooting poison arrows, Gilman launches an impassioned appeal that both historicizes and romanticizes their former relationship. Over the course of the poem, she depicts her own torment and suffering and alternates reminiscences of their former passion with rebukes and accusations. Thus, this poem paradoxically serves both as a weapon to inflict pain on others and as a tool to rebuild her wounded psyche.

In the second stanza, Gilman's resistance to letting go of the relationship is underscored by her emphatic underlining of the possessive pronoun "my," by her image of clinging arms, and by her triple repetition of the phrase "my little girl." She writes:

"My little girl!" *My* little girl! No more,
Never again in all this weary world
Can I with clinging arms & kisses soft
Call you "my little girl!"

The finality of their breakup is reinforced by the use of the negatives "no more" and "never again," while the alliteration of "weary world" resonates with the subliminal intimation "we were," implicitly contrasting their former intimacy with their current distance.

The third stanza describes Gilman's anguish at the loss: the "pain," the "tears," the "sobs" that she must endure but "that will be heard." She is emphatic that Martha must acknowledge her pain:

"My darling!" O my darling! How my heart
Thrills at the words with sudden quivering pain,
Rises and beats against the doors of speech
And sends hot tears and sobs that will be heard.

By the fourth stanza, Gilman has begun to measure the very worth of her own life against the loss of Martha:

"Sweetheart!" You *were* my sweetheart. I am none,
To any man, and I had none but you.
O sweet! You filled my life; you gave me all
Of tenderness, consideration, trust,
Confiding love, respect, regard, reproof,
And all the thousand thousand little things
With which love glorifies the hardest life.

Writing primarily in the past tense, Gilman again contrasts her life then — at the height of her relationship with Martha — with her life now, at its apparently lowest point to date. Gilman had placed Martha at the center of her existence; now, having been abandoned and betrayed, she proclaims her "self" to have been effectively eradicated. "I am none," she writes. But there is also a qualifier. "I am none, / To any man." Not only has Martha abandoned her relationship with Gilman, but she has replaced her with a man, suggesting her compliance and complicity with the social code that ultimately favors what Adrienne Rich would later define as "compulsory heterosexuality," the patriarchally controlled political institution that sanctions conventional relationships between women and men.[15] This sense of being replaced, and the perception that Martha has somehow succumbed to the social pressures to conform, is significant, particularly when we remember that less than a month after composing this poem, Gilman would meet Walter Stetson and plunge into a complex and ultimately destructive relationship that would be characterized by her simultaneous and conflicting attempts to assert her independence, to replace Martha's love, and to resist a new relationship every step of the way.

In the fifth stanza of the poem, the lines between romantic love and lesbian sexuality, and between sensuality and eroticism, become blurred:

Think dearest, while you yet can feel the touch
Of hands that once could soothe your deepest pain;
Think of those days when we could hardly dare
Be seen abroad together lest our eyes
Should speak too loud. * * There is no danger now.

While the first two lines of the stanza are sensually evocative with their allusions to physical touch, the last three lines bespeak a love forbidden by the dictates of conventional society. Gilman affirms, and reaffirms at the beginning of the sixth stanza, that there is now no danger of discovery. In the sixth stanza, she recalls a day the year before when "you and I asked nothing of the world / but room, and one another." Here too, the desire for room – or space – would suggest a dimension to their relationship quite apart from that not only tolerated – but even encouraged – by late-nineteenth-century society.

Gilman's allusion to "that day a year ago," moreover, seems to commemorate a significant turning point in defining the terms of their relationship, a point, perhaps, at which they either crossed the line from socially condoned nonsexual behavior to an expression of their sexual love or came to an understanding of their mutual commitment. Either way, having broken her pledge, Martha has "life" ahead of her, while Gilman has nothing: no lover, no comfort, no hope, no Martha, whom she viewed as a veritable life-force. In stanza seven, she writes, "I held your heart / In that large empty space where mine was not." And then the bitter charge of abandonment and betrayal: "And you? You must have had mine in your hands / Keeping it warm until another came / To fill the place, and mine was given back." At this point, the spiritual amputation has been replaced by the metaphorical excision and subsequent rejection of a vital life-sustaining organ.

Wounded and weakened by Martha's rejection, Gilman next invokes a metaphor of herself as a newborn infant abandoned by its caretaker — left helpless, hungry, desolate, alone, and cold. Martha, who is depicted here as a cruel, calculating, and paradoxically nonmaternal mother figure, exercises full control over the sacrifice of the innocent. "You cannot wonder that the thing should cry," Gilman charges at the end of the stanza. As speaker of the poem, however, she regains control in the ninth stanza, conceding that "even now" she still believes that Martha trusts her word. "Believe me," she writes, "That if your happiness or smallest good / Depended on my silence, not a word / Would ever reach you." Gilman's insistence that she would remain silent if only she believed that Martha would be well served by her decision to marry Charles Lane is negated by her belief that Martha is making a costly mistake. Moreover, in stanza ten, she reaffirms her love and dismisses any chance that her feelings will change.

In the final stanza of this poem, there is a self-imposed conclusion to Gilman's diatribe. She suddenly withdraws, overcome by fatigue: "I am too tired now / To tell you all I could." Her "goodbye" at the end of the poem does not signal her final word on the breakup; rather, the physical, emotional, and spiritual exhaustion simply compels her sleep.

Just weeks after writing this poem, Gilman was introduced to Providence artist Charles Walter Stetson. Stetson quickly became enamored and proposed marriage two and a half weeks later. She promptly declined, citing among her reasons her desire for independence. She was also candid with Stetson about her love for Martha and how profoundly she had been affected by the loss. In a long poem titled "Answer to a Letter from Charles Walter Stetson," in which he had responded to the reasons stated by Gilman, then twenty-one, for wishing to remain single, she addresses her love for Martha (*Diaries*, 867–868). The poem is typical of many of her private verses in its treatment of recurring themes: the elusiveness of love, the abandonment of her hope for happiness, her drive for independence, the sacrifice of youthful dreams for the pursuit of larger truths. Chiding Stetson for his apparent misunderstanding of her reasons for preferring work to marriage, Gilman intentionally foregrounds the fallout from Martha's departure in several of the stanzas:

> Do you think it is nothing to lose a friend
> > More dear than words can tell;
> Whose tender love was the only light –
> The only radiance soft and bright
> > That on that pathway fell.

> Do you think it nothing to go straight on
> > When a love like that was dead?
> To shrink together with bitter pain
> And then plod steadily on again
> > With a heart within like lead.

In its entirety, the poem establishes Gilman's resolve to deprive herself of love (and marriage) in order to avoid inevitable pain and to instead devote herself to social service. Fear of intimacy plagued her for years after her relationship with Martha was terminated. The still-unresolved pain of her mother's lack of affection, coupled with her early loss of Martha, caused Gilman to believe for some time that depriving herself of intimate relationships was a way to avoid further pain. Again and again, through the fourteen-stanza poem, she expresses resentment toward Walter Stetson for thinking that those choices had been easily or arbitrarily made. Her somewhat contentious and repetitive interrogative "Do you think?" underscores her perception of Stetson's insensitivity. For his part, Stetson quietly complained in his journal about the didacticism that often characterized Gilman's verses: "I confess I wish she'd strive more for beauty in poetry than for didactics, for when she does let herself forget to preach she writes very very tender & lovely things" (Hill, ed., *Endure*, 291). Coincidentally, just one day after Gilman was introduced to Walter Stetson, she composed a poem titled "The Suicide's Burial," in which she wrote about both the stigma of suicide and the vilification of the victim by those who bury the body under the veil of darkness.[16]

After a turbulent two-year courtship, Charlotte Perkins married Walter Stetson. Many of the extant poems from their early years together contain an intimate conversation in verse characterized by a passion and intensity that departs markedly from Gilman's publicly articulated account of their relationship. Yet in several of the private poems, the tension and turbulence that also marked their relationship is pronounced. In her autobiography, in fact, Gilman concedes that "there are poems of this time which show deep affection, and high hopes, also doubt and uncertainty" (*Living*, 83).

As Gilman's wedding day approached, she frequently turned to poetry as a means through which to express her reservations about the impending marriage. One of these verses, "In Duty, Bound," depicts the "weary life," the "wasting power," and the death of "high ideals" that women experience when they sacrifice their individualism in marriage. Significantly, Gilman went public with the poem, despite its description of her private anguish, publishing it in the 12 January 1884 issue of *Woman's Journal*. The metaphors of bondage and isolation embedded in the poem are powerful; images of pain and despair are etched into every line.[17]

Around the same time, Gilman wrote another poem, this one unpublished, lamenting the sad condition of her relationship with Stetson, mourning the loss of her youthful dreams, and expressing a thinly veiled death wish. Thematically similar to "In Duty, Bound," the untitled poem, inserted into the back of her diary for 1883, reads as follows:

Alone am I, chillhearted still, and dreary;
Alone art thou, sadhearted, worn, and weary;
    Alone indeed are we.

Alone art thou, by wifely love's desertion;
Alone am I mid life-dreams wide dispersion,
    Watching youth's visions flee.

Alone art thou, I know not of thy sorrow.
Alone am I; and all life's long tomorrow
    Looks desolate and grey.

Alone art thou. No one to soothe thy sighing
Alone am I, my heart within me dying.
    O Life! Why dost thou stay!
               (*Diaries*, 889)

The theme of mutual loneliness, and a future destined to be governed by desolation and heartache, is reinforced by the juxtaposition and repetition of the words "Alone am I" and "Alone art thou." Clearly, Gilman's ambivalence about marriage was underscored by her desire to work. As she had informed him in a letter written shortly after their courtship began, her desire to work eclipsed all other ambitions: "As much as I love you I love *WORK* better, & I cannot make the two compatible. . . . It is no use, dear, no use. I am meant to be useful & strong, to help many and do my share in the world's work, but not to be loved" (*Endure*, 63). The repetition of "alone" also reinforces their divergent views on marriage. Stetson alone felt that marriage would help to settle his fiancée's restless spirit; she, on the other hand, feared that it would compromise her desire to help humanity.

Gilman's anxiety about her maternal competence is also evident in some of her private works. In one untitled verse dated 1 April 1883, she expresses her lack of preparedness for motherhood and appeals to God for guidance. Repeatedly, she asks rather dubiously, "Can I" be a good mother?; she declines to assert the opposite, "I Can." She seems to offer ample resistance to the notion of motherhood by presenting herself as a woman who is ill-prepared to assume the role. In two of the stanzas in particular, she alludes to the two opposing forces of her nature – the side that conforms, the other that questions:

Can I, who hardly know
    If I am truly seeing
The half-formed instincts fleeing
    Within me to and fro –
Can I, who've scarce begun to grow
    Bring others into being?

Can I, who suffer from wild unrest
    Of two strong natures claiming each its due,
    And can not tell the greater of the two;

Who have two spirits ruling in my breast
Alternately, and know not which is guest
    And which the owner true.

(Diaries, 882)

As fate would have it, Gilman became pregnant within a month after her 2 May 1884 marriage to Stetson. The theme of sacrifice continues to appear in the poems written during her pregnancy, as does her attempt to reconcile herself to performing the roles of wife and mother. In one poem written in her eighth month of pregnancy, she invokes the conventional metaphor of a flower to represent their unborn child:

Long strove I on the upward way, alone:
With ceaseless toil, and hardfought weary hours.
Till God, whose name is Love, brought thee, my Own;
And thou didst bring me flowers. . . .

And now — closehidden — warmth beneath my heart,
At all unreckoned cost of health and power —
O Love! Dear Love! Of my own life a part
I make for thee — A Flower!

(Diaries, 895)

Gilman's ambivalence about the "Flower," however, is still apparent. The pregnancy does not come without a price; rather, it has exacted an "unreckoned cost of health and power."

Gilman was also capable of writing poems in which she declared unconditional love for Stetson, as in a Christmas poem that accompanied her gift of violets, written sometime after their marriage:

Dear Heart of Love! Sweet Comforter! My Own!
Chief Treasure of my life!
These little violets alone
Speak for your loving wife.

Dear Heart of Love! Sweet Comforter! My Own!
No frankincense have I
Only these violets sweet and blue
To tell the love I have for you
The love that does not die.

(Diaries, 895)

Walter Stetson also wrote private verse; his poems, in fact, were often more expressive than Gilman's. An incurable romantic, Stetson poeticized everything from the most intimate details of their wedding night to his hope for a return of the intense sexual passion that they had shared early in the marriage. In one collection of poems, around which he painted tiny watercolor portraits of Adam and Eve in the Garden of Eden, Walter Stetson looked ahead several months to May 1887, from the vantage of a very troubled marriage, at which time he predicted, in verse, that their former intimacy would be renewed and their happiness restored (see *Diaries*, 896–898). In May 1887, however, rather than reveling in the ecstasy of a second honeymoon, Charlotte Stetson was undergoing the rest cure for neurasthenia at Dr. S. Weir Mitchell's sanitarium. Ironically, on Valentine's Day of that same year, Stetson had written a poem in which he accused Gilman of taking "comfort" in her illness and admonishing her to "hold fast to Love" rather than to "grieve and feel your Work undone" (*Diaries*, 898). This he wrote just two months before her departure to seek treatment for nervous prostration from Dr. Mitchell.

With her divorce from Walter Stetson pending some four years later, Gilman found comfort for a time in a relationship with Adeline ("Delle") Knapp, a woman with whom she lived in California for nearly two years in the early 1890s. In her autobiography, Gilman identified Knapp as the person with whom she had "sincerely hoped to live continually" (*Living*, 143). Her diaries describe Knapp as "my love," "my girl," and "my delight," reminiscent of her romantic friendship with Martha Luther, but with even greater intensity. Some years after their relationship ended, Gilman confessed in a letter to her future second husband, Houghton Gilman, that she had been deeply in love with Knapp. She revealed that she had felt "really passionate love . . . for her," that she had "loved her that way," but that she was neither "sorry . . . nor ashamed" (Hill, ed., *Journey*, 246). Moreover, in a poem written to Knapp around 1891, Gilman alluded to her earlier disappointments in love and expressed the belief that she had finally found the real thing. The first two verses read:

To me at last! When I had bowed my head
In patience to all pain – buried my dead—
　　Forgotten hope, accepted the long night

With only stars for guide – far, cold, and bright –
Content to work and love, uncomforted.

Then, in an hour, a brightness came and spread
And all the dark sky flushed with rose and red
And gold-lit flowers laughed out – so came the light
    To me at last!

(Diaries, 899)

The juxtaposition of images of long, cold, comfortless nights in
the first stanza with the sensual, and even sexual, warmth of the
second stanza reinforces the role that Adeline Knapp played in
providing Gilman with companionship and love. The metaphorical depiction of dawn, or enlightenment, in the second stanza,
coupled with the imagery of heightened sexual arousal, reinforces
her confession that she loved Knapp "that way."

Another poem, titled "To My Dear Sweet Heart," written to
Knapp around 1891, suggests that their relationship successfully
accommodated, at least temporarily, both Gilman's desire to work
and her need for love – a balance that she had not been able to
strike during her marriage to Walter Stetson:

I am so happy every day!
    Dear Heart! – Sweet Heart!
I'm sorry when you go away,
But I have work I love like play –
And by and by you come and stay –
    Dear heart! Sweet heart!
(Gilman Papers, Box XVI, folder 205)

The allusion to the shared bed in the second stanza ("Our
blessed bed so broad and white") and Gilman's playful reference
to "Delight" – her pet nickname for Delle Knapp – offer additional evidence that their relationship was probably sexual in nature. Despite Gilman's hope that their love would endure, it ended
during the summer of 1893.

It was, of course, Houghton Gilman with whom Charlotte Stetson finally found the enduring love and happiness that had for so
long eluded her. While a number of her letters to Houghton have
survived, there are only a handful of extant poems in which she
comments on their relationship. In one, titled simply, "When I
came to know Houghton," written in April 1897, shortly after

they were reacquainted as adults, the void in her life seems finally to be filled. The emotional intensity that characterized her earlier poems, however, is noticeably absent. After acknowledging the course that her life has taken, she alludes in a calm, more confident voice to the new, positive direction in which it seems to be going:

> Sudden, a little glade of level grass,
> Elm trees and robins, lilacs, and a swing –
> Old times – old faces – things I used to know,
> And things I knew not – lovers – friends – a home – .
> It's good to look at.
>
> (*Diaries*, 847)

In this poem, Gilman appears to be considerably more reticent – she is looking to the future, contemplating, assessing, evaluating, taking things slowly. She is much more in control than in her earlier relationships, as suggested by both the language and structure of her poem, in which she abandons formal poetic conventions in order to engage in one of her few experiments with free verse.

In another poem, titled "To Houghton: Thanksgiving 1902," Gilman emphasizes, among other things, her gratitude for his support of her work. The first stanza reads:

> I am so thankful, Heart of Mine!
> So thankful through and through
> For Life and Light and Comfort Sweet
> Enough to wear, enough to eat,
> And growing power to Do!
> I am thankful, Heart of Mine
> For peace and power and Work, divine,
> But most of all for you –
>   Most thankful, Sweet, for You!
> (Gilman Papers, Box XVI, folder 205)

In addition to enumerating Houghton Gilman's positive qualities – his tenderness, caring, and patience – the verse also confirms that Gilman has finally struck the balance between the impulse to work and the need for a loving relationship which she had been seeking for so long.

Gilman's private verse is an invaluable resource for readers examining the complex dichotomies between her public and private lives. Characteristically, the verse shows a woman struggling to preserve her "self" in relationships where she both craved and feared intimacy. Her private verses are at once both weapons and tools; they wounded with one hand and healed with the other. And, of course, they legitimized her most personal experiences. Most of all, however, the private poems provide a glimpse of the vulnerable side of Charlotte Perkins Gilman — a side that she sought valiantly to shield from public scrutiny.

NOTES

1. Letter from William Dean Howells to Charlotte Perkins Stetson, 11 July 1894, Folder 120, Charlotte Perkins Gilman Papers, Schlesinger Library, Radcliffe College, Cambridge, Massachusetts. Quoted by permission.

2. At the time of her death, Gilman left the collection of 167 poems, tentatively titled *Here Also*, with her longtime friend Amy Wellington for posthumous publication. Wellington, however, was unable to secure a publisher. That edition, which I edited, was published by the University of Delaware Press in 1996 under the title *The Later Poetry of Charlotte Perkins Gilman*.

3. See Cheryl Walker's *American Women Poets of the Nineteenth Century*, xxxii.

4. For an account of the professional relationship between Gilman and Howells, see Joanne B. Karpinski's essay "When the Marriage of True Minds Admits Impediments: Charlotte Perkins Gilman and William Dean Howells," in *Critical Essays on Charlotte Perkins Gilman*, ed. Joanne B. Karpinski, 202–221.

5. Gilman's private poems remain unpublished and in manuscript in the collection of Gilman Papers, Schlesinger Library, Radcliffe College. The occasional poems, primarily but not exclusively the product of her youth, are typically witty verses written to commemorate special events: Valentine's Day, birthdays, the acceptance of an invitation, the receipt or presentation of a gift. The conventional verse addresses common subjects and employs traditional poetic conventions and rhyme schemes; this body of verse comprises the smallest of the four categories and more closely resembles public verse in content and in form. The spiritual meditations generally center on the poet's appeal to God for guidance, direction, and strength; numerous examples of spiritual verses remain among her private papers.

6. See, in particular, Mary A. Hill's biography, *Charlotte Perkins Gil-*

man; Ann J. Lane's *To Herland and Beyond*; and Gary Scharnhorst's *Charlotte Perkins Gilman*.

7. Quoted in Scharnhorst, *Charlotte Perkins Gilman* (40). The term is from the *Topeka State Journal* (15 June 1896), vol. 7.

8. Gilman and Martha Luther Lane remained friends until Gilman's death in 1935. Gilman's autobiography states that the two became friends when Gilman was seventeen (48), but her diaries suggest that she was eighteen when they met.

9. See, for example, Lillian Faderman, *Surpassing the Love of Men*.

10. Letter from Gilman to Martha Luther, dated 24 July 1881, quoted in Hill's *Charlotte Perkins Gilman*, 77.

11. The poem, titled "To Martha Luther, 1880," is reprinted in appendix B of *The Diaries of Charlotte Perkins Gilman*, ed. Denise D. Knight.

12. Gilman reported in her diaries that "Martha & I get a pair of lovely little red bracelets with gold acorns dependent theron, to be worn by us as a badge, ornament, bond of union, etc. . . . Martha comes surreptitious over P. M., I let her in unseen, she prowls up to my room, and we spend the afternoon in tranquil bliss. . . . She returns as invisibly as she came, at which I am exalted" (*Diaries*, 14 May 1881, 58).

13. Letter from Gilman to Martha Luther, dated 15 August 1882, quoted in Hill's *Charlotte Perkins Gilman*, 83.

14. Letter to Sam Simmons, dated 14 November 1881, *Diaries*, 860–862.

15. See Adrienne Rich, "Compulsory Heterosexuality and Lesbian Existence," in *Adrienne Rich's Poetry and Prose*, 203–204.

16. *Diaries*, 865–866. "The Suicide's Burial" was likely inspired by Walter Stetson's painting *Burial of a Suicide*. The evening before she wrote the poem, Gilman attended Stetson's art lecture, at which the *Burial of a Suicide* was probably exhibited, since Stetson had been working on it in the weeks before the lecture.

17. The original manuscript version of "In Duty, Bound" is reprinted in the *Diaries*, appendix B, 890.

NOTES ON CONTRIBUTORS

Judith A. Allen is professor of history and gender studies at Indiana University, with research interests in feminism, Australia, and women and crime. She has published on Rose Scott and on prostitution.

Katharine Cockin is a lecturer in English at Hull University. She completed her Ph.D. dissertation on the Pioneer Players (1911–1925) at Leicester University in 1994 (forthcoming Macmillan) and is interested in Gilman's drama in the context of the women's suffrage movement in Britain. She has published a biography, *Edith Craig (1869–1947): Dramatic Lives*, and is indexing the Edith Craig archive.

Deborah M. De Simone is assistant professor of education and women's studies at the College of Staten Island, the City University of New York. Her research focuses on issues of gender within democratic educational traditions. Her publications have appeared in the journals *Willa* and *Social Education*. She is currently at work on the education of American children within the Japanese internment camps on Manila during World War II.

Marie T. Farr is associate professor of English at East Carolina University. She first came across Gilman's *Three Women* while teaching a Women in Literature course and that sparked her interest in Gilman's theatrical background. In reviewing Gilman's diaries for the *New England Quarterly*, she found evidence that Gilman's interest in theatre was lifelong. Farr has also served as the founding director of the Women's Studies Program at East Carolina.

Lisa Ganobcsik-Williams is a doctoral candidate in rhetoric and nineteenth-century American literature at Miami University in Oxford, Ohio, and teaches at the University of Warwick. Her doctoral dissertation, "Revisioning American Democracy Through Evolutionary Rhetoric: Charlotte Perkins Gilman in Dialogue With Social Reform Discourses," focuses on Gilman's position within turn-of-the-century American intellectual history.

Yvonne Gaudelius is assistant professor of art education and women's studies at the Pennsylvania State University. Her research interests include the areas of feminist art criticism and feminist aesthetics in relationship to art education. Her work on Gilman has focused upon the area of Gilman's revision and conceptualization of architectural space. Currently she is exploring Gilman's writings in relation to the idea of the surveillance of gender. Recent publications include "When Art Turns Violent: Images of Women, the Sexualization of Violence and the Implications for Art Education" and "Postmodernism, Feminism and Art Education: An Elementary Art Workshop Based on the Works of Nancy Spero and Mary Kelly."

Sandra M. Gilbert is professor of English at the University of California, Davis. Perhaps still best known for her collaborative book with Susan Gubar, *The Madwoman in the Attic*, she has published widely on feminism and women's writing, recently co-editing the second edition of *The Norton Anthology of Literature by Women*, again with Susan Gubar. She is also a poet, whose published volumes include *Emily's Bread* (1984), *Blood Pressure* (1989), and *Ghost Volcano* (1995).

Catherine J. Golden is associate professor of English at Skidmore College. She is the editor of *The Captive Imagination: A Casebook on "The Yellow Wallpaper"* (Feminist Press, 1992) and *Unpunished* (with Denise D. Knight). Her work on "The Yellow Wallpaper" and Gilman's other fiction and prose has appeared in *Studies in American Fiction, Critical Essays on Charlotte Perkins Gilman* (G. K. Hall, 1992), *Re-visioning Feminism around the World* (Feminist Press, 1995), and several books on American women writers. A founding member and now executive director of the Charlotte Perkins Gilman Society, she organized the Second International Gilman Conference (1997) with Judith Allen (Indiana University) and Joanna Zangrando (Skidmore College). She is also the author of many essays and reviews on Victorian book illustration published in *Victorian Poetry, Victorian Studies, Victorian Periodicals Review, Salmagundi*, the *CEA Critic, Profession 95*, and *Woman's Art Journal*.

Val Gough is a lecturer in English at the University of Liverpool. She has published on Virginia Woolf, Charlotte Perkins Gilman, and language and gender, and she is currently working on two books: *Hélène Cixous: Feminist Mystic* and *Looking at Language and Gender in Literature*. She co-organized the first international conference on Gilman at the University of Liverpool, July 1995.

Susan Gubar is Distinguished Professor of English at Indiana University. Perhaps still best known for her collaborative book with Sandra Gilbert, *The Madwoman in the Attic*, she has published widely on eighteenth-century literature, science fiction, and women's writing, recently co-editing the second edition of *The Norton Anthology of Literature by Women*, again with Sandra Gilbert.

Denise D. Knight, a recognized expert on Charlotte Perkins Gilman, is professor of English at the State University of New York at Cortland, where she specializes in nineteenth-century American literature. She is the author of *Charlotte Perkins Gilman: A Study of the Short Fiction* (Twayne Publishers, 1997), editor of *The Late Poetry of Charlotte Perkins Gilman* (University of Delaware Press, 1996), editor of *The Diaries of Charlotte Perkins Gilman* (University Press of Virginia, 1994), and editor of *"The Yellow Wall-Paper" and Selected Stories of Charlotte Perkins Gilman* (University of Delaware Press, 1994). She is co-editor with Catherine J. Golden of *Unpunished*, a detective novel by Charlotte Perkins Gilman (Feminist Press, 1997). Knight is also president of the Charlotte Perkins Gilman Society and editor of *Nineteenth-Century American Women Writers: A Bio-Bibliographical Critical Sourcebook* (Greenwood Press, 1997). Her work on Gilman has appeared in *Women's Studies, Walt Whitman Quarterly Review, American Journalism*, and *ANQ: A Quarterly Journal of Short Articles, Notes, and Reviews*, and several books on American literature.

Ann J. Lane is professor of history and director of studies in women and gender at the University of Virginia. Her publications on Gilman include *To 'Herland' and Beyond: The Life and Work of Charlotte Perkins Gilman* and *The Charlotte Perkins Gilman Reader*. She edited and introduced for the first time in book form *Herland*.

Jill Rudd is a lecturer in English at the University of Liverpool. She works on women's writing and also on late medieval English literature. She has published on *Piers Plowman* and on animals in Gilman's fables and poems. With Val Gough, she co-organized the first international conference on Gilman, held in July 1995 in Liverpool.

Karen Stevenson is a lecturer in sociology at Staffordshire University. Her areas of interest are the sociology of the body, cyberbodies, and sexuality.

Frederick Wegener is assistant professor of English at California State University, Long Beach. He is the editor of *Edith Wharton: The Uncollected Critical Writings*, and his essays have appeared in *New England Quarterly, Modern Language Studies*, and *Texas Studies in Literature and Language*. He is working on a study of imaginative representations of medical women in Anglo-American culture from 1860 to 1920.

Naomi B. Zauderer lives in New York and works as an organizer for the

National Writers Union/UAW Local 1981. The article in this volume is a chapter of her dissertation, which approaches Gilman's work from the perspective of political theory. Prior to moving to New York, she served as president of the Association of Graduate Student Employees at the University of California, Berkeley.

BIBLIOGRAPHY

CITED WORKS BY GILMAN

The majority of Gilman's published and unpublished papers may be
found in the collection held by the Schlesinger Library, Radcliffe
College, Cambridge, Massachusetts.

"About Dramatic Rights in 'Three Women' and 'Something to Vote For.'"
Forerunner 2 (1911): 179.

"Among Our Foreign Residents." *Forerunner* 7 (1916): 145–146.

"An Anchor to Windward." In *The Diaries of Charlotte Perkins Gilman*,
ed. Denise D. Knight, 866–867.

"Beginners." Folder 165. Charlotte Perkins Gilman Collection.
Schlesinger Library, Radcliffe College, Cambridge, Massachusetts.

Benigna Machiavelli. Forerunner 5 (1914). Rpt. New York: Bonanza, 1994.

"The Best for the Poorest." *Forerunner* 7 (1916): 260–262.

"Birth Control, Religion, and the Unfit." *Nation* 134 (1932): 108–109.

"Child Labor and the Schools." *Independent* 64 (1908): 1135–1139.

Concerning Children. Boston: Small, 1900. London: Watts, 1907.

The Crux. New York: Charlton, 1911.

"Divorce and Birth Control." *Outlook* 125 (1928): 130–151.

"Does a Man Support His Wife?" Pamphlet. (Rpt. from *Forerunner.*)
Folder 250. Charlotte Perkins Gilman Collection. Schlesinger Library,
Radcliffe College, Cambridge, Massachusetts.

"Domestic Economy." 1904. Rpt. in *Charlotte Perkins Gilman: A
Nonfiction Reader*, ed. Larry Ceplair, 157–168.

The Dress of Women. Serialized in *Forerunner* (1915).

"Egoism, Altruism and Socialism." *American Fabian* 4 (1898): 1–2.

"Encouraging Miss Miller." *Forerunner* 6 (1915).

"The Ethics of Wage Earning." Before 1900. Folder 254. Charlotte
Perkins Gilman Collection, Schlesinger Library, Radcliffe College,
Cambridge, Massachusetts.

"The Ethics of Woman's Work." Unpublished lecture dated 31 January
1894. Folder 171. Charlotte Perkins Gilman Collection, Schlesinger
Library, Radcliffe College, Cambridge, Massachusetts.

"Feminism and Social Progress." In *Problems of Civilization*, ed. Baker
Brownell, 29–32. New York: Van Nostrand, 1929.

"Feminism or Polygamy?" *Forerunner* 5 (1914): 260–261.

"Free Speech." *Forerunner* 5 (1914): 146.

"The Girl in the Pink Hat." 1916. Rpt. in *The Charlotte Perkins Gilman
Reader*, ed. Ann J. Lane, 39–46.

Herland. 1915. Introduction by Ann J. Lane. New York: Pantheon, 1979.
London: Women's Press, 1979.

"His Mother." 1916. Rpt. in *"The Yellow Wall-Paper" and Selected Stories
of Charlotte Perkins Gilman*, ed. Denise D. Knight, 73–80. Newark:
Delaware Press, 1994.

*His Religion and Hers: A Study of the Faith of Our Fathers and the Work
of Our Mothers*. New York: Century, 1923. Westport, Conn.:
Hyperion, 1976.

The Home: Its Work and Influence. 1903. New York: McClure, 1910. New
York: Source Book Press, 1970.

"Humanness." *Forerunner* (1913): 52–53.

Human Work. New York: McClure, Phillips and Company, 1904.

"Ideals of Child Culture: A Talk." In *Child Study for Mothers and
Teachers*, ed. Margaret Sanger, 93–101. Philadelphia: Booklovers
Library, 1901.

"If I Were a Man." 1914. Rpt. in *The Charlotte Perkins Gilman Reader*,
ed. Ann J. Lane, 32–38.

In This Our World. Oakland: McCombs and Vaughn, 1893. Rpt. Boston:
Small, Maynard and Company, 1899; also New York: Arno, 1974.

"Is America Too Hospitable?" *Forum* 70 (1923): 1983–1989. Rpt. in *Charlotte Perkins Gilman: A Nonfiction Reader*, ed. Larry Ceplair, 288–295.

"Kitchen-Mindedness." *Forerunner* 1 (1910): 7–11.

"The Labor Movement." 1892. Rpt. in *Charlotte Perkins Gilman: A
Nonfiction Reader*, ed. Larry Ceplair, 62–74.

The Living of Charlotte Perkins Gilman: An Autobiography. New York:
D. Appleton-Century, 1935. New York: Arno, 1972; Harper, 1975.
Madison: University of Wisconsin Press, 1990.

"Mag – Marjorie." Serialized in *Forerunner* 3 (1912).

"Making a Change." 1911. In *The Charlotte Perkins Gilman Reader*, ed.
Ann J. Lane, 66–74.

The Man-Made World, or Our Androcentric Culture. New York: Charlton,
1911. New York: Source Book Press, 1970.

"Mind Cleaning." *Forerunner* 3 (1912): 5–6.

Moving the Mountain. New York: Charlton, 1911.

"The New Generation of Women." *Current History* 18 (1923): 731–737.

"The New Motherhood." *Forerunner* 1 (1910): 17–18.

"The New Mothers of a New World." *Forerunner* 4 (1913): 145–149.

"The Oldest Profession in the World." *Forerunner* 4 (1913): 63–64.

"Our Brains and What Ails Them." *Forerunner* 3 (1912): 22–26, 49–54, 77–82, 104–109, 133–139, 161–167, 189–195, 215–221, 245–251, 273–279, 301–307, 328–334.

"Our Place Today." 1891. Unpublished lecture. Charlotte Perkins Gilman Collection. Schlesinger Library, Radcliffe College, Cambridge, Massachusetts.

"Parasitism and Civilized Vice." In *Woman's Coming of Age: A Symposium*, ed. Samuel D. Schmalhausen and V. F. Calverton, 110–126. New York: Liveright, 1931.

"The Passing of the Home in Great American Cities." *Heresies* 3:3 (1981): 53–55.

"Passing of Matrimony." *Harper's Bazaar* (June 1906): 496.

"Prisons, Convicts, and Women Voters." *Forerunner* 4 (1913): 92.

"Progress through Birth Control." *North American Review* 224 (1927): 622–629.

"Sex and Race Progress." In *Sex in Civilization*, ed. V. F. Calverton and Samuel D. Schmalhausen, 109–126. New York: Macaulay, 1929.

"She Who Is To Come." In *In This Our World: Poems*, 143. 3rd ed. Boston: Small, 1899.

"A Small God and a Large Goddess." *Forerunner* 1 (1909): 1–4.

Social Ethics. Serialized in *Forerunner* (1914).

"Socialist Psychology." Unpublished article or lecture, 5 March 1933. Rpt. in *Charlotte Perkins Gilman: A Nonfiction Reader*, ed. Larry Ceplair, 302–312.

"Something to Vote For." *Forerunner* 2 (1911): 143–153. Rpt. in *On to Victory: Propaganda Plays of the Woman Suffrage Movement*, ed. Bettina Friedl. Boston: Northeastern University Press, 1989.

"The Spirit of the Movement." *Vote* 14 (1911): 140–141.

"A Suggestion on the Negro Problem." *American Journal of Sociology* 14 (1908): 78–85. Rpt. in *Charlotte Perkins Gilman: A Nonfiction Reader*, ed. Larry Ceplair, 176–183.

"Teaching the Mothers." *Forerunner* 3 (1912): 73–75.

Three Women. Floor plan. Ellen Terry Memorial Museum, Tenterden, Kent, UK.

Three Women. Play programme fragment. Ellen Terry Memorial
   Museum, Tenterden, Kent, UK.

Three Women. Prompt copy. Ellen Terry Memorial Museum, Tenterden,
   Kent, UK.

Three Women. Props list. Ellen Terry Memorial Museum, Tenterden,
   Kent, UK.

"Three Women." *Success* 11 (August 1908): 490–491, 522–526.

"Three Women: A One-Act Play." *Forerunner* 2 (1911): 115–123, 134.

"Toward Monogamy." Rpt. in *Our Changing Morality: A Symposium,* ed.
   Freda Kirchwey, 53–68. New York: Boni, 1924.

"Two Storks." *Forerunner* 1 (1910): 12.

Unpunished: A Mystery. 1929. Ed. and with an afterword by Denise D.
   Knight and Catherine Golden. New York: Feminist, 1997.

"The Vintage." *Forerunner* 7 (1916): 253–257. Rpt. in *"The Yellow Wall-
   Paper,"* ed. Denise D. Knight, 104–111.

What Diantha Did. New York: Charlton, 1910.

"What May We Expect of Eugenics?" *Physical Culture* 31 (1914): 219–
   222.

"What Our Children Might Have." *Century* 110 (1925): 706–711.

"Where Are All the Pre-War Radicals?" *Survey* 55 (1926): 564.

"Who Owns the Children?" Unpublished lecture, 1891. Box XIII, Folder
   165. Charlotte Perkins Gilman Collection, Schlesinger Library,
   Radcliffe College, Cambridge, Massachusetts.

"Why Women Do Not Reform Their Dress." *Woman's Journal* (October
   1886): 338.

"The Widow's Might." 1911. Rpt. in *The Charlotte Perkins Gilman
   Reader,* ed. Ann J. Lane, 98–106.

"With Her in Ourland." Serialized in *Forerunner* 7 (1916).

*Women and Economics: A Study of the Economic Relation between Men
   and Women as a Factor in Social Evolution.* Boston: Small, 1898. Ed.
   and introd. Carl N. Degler. New York: Harper, 1966.

"The Yellow Wallpaper." 1892. Rpt. as *The Yellow Wallpaper.* New York:
   Feminist Press, 1973. Rpt. in *The Charlotte Perkins Gilman Reader,*
   ed. Ann J. Lane, 3–20.

OTHER WORKS

Allen, Judith A. "The Making of a Prostitute Proletariat in Early
   Twentieth Century New South Wales." In *So Much Hard Work:
   Women and Prostitution in Australian History,* ed. Kay Daniels, 192–
   232. Sydney: Fontana, 1984.

————. *Rose Scott: Vision and Revision in Feminism*. Melbourne: Oxford University Press, 1994.

————. *Sex and Secrets: Crimes Involving Australian Women Since 1880*. Melbourne: Oxford University Press, 1990.

Allen, Polly Wynn. *Building Domestic Liberty: Charlotte Perkins Gilman's Architectural Feminism*. Amherst: University of Massachusetts Press, 1988.

Antler, Joyce, and Sari Knopp Biklen. *Changing Education: Women as Radicals and Conservators*. Albany: State University of New York Press, 1990.

Asser, J. *Historic Hairdressing*. London: Pitman, 1966.

Atwood, Margaret. *The Handmaid's Tale*. London: Virago, 1987.

Baker, Michael. *Our Three Selves: A Life of Radclyffe Hall*. London: Hamilton, 1985.

Bederman, Gail. *Manliness and Civilization*. Chicago: University of Chicago Press, 1995.

Bellamy. Edward. *Looking Backward: 2000–1887*. New York: Ticknor, 1888. New York: Viking Penguin, 1960, 1982.

Berkeley, Ellen Perry. "Architecture: Toward a Feminist Critique." In *New Space for Women*, ed. Gerda R. Wekerle, Rebecca Peterson, and David Morley, 205–218. Boulder: Westview, 1980.

Berkin, Carol Ruth. "Private Woman, Public Woman: The Contradictions of Charlotte Perkins Gilman." In *Critical Essays on Charlotte Perkins Gilman*, ed. Joanne B. Karpinski, 17–42. New York: G. K. Hall, 1992.

Best, Joel. "Careers in Brothel Prostitution: St. Paul, 1865–1883." *Journal of Interdisciplinary History* (Spring 1982): 597–619.

Bingham, Edwin R. *Charles F. Lummis: Editor of the Southwest*. San Marino: Huntington Library, 1955.

Blackburn, George M., and Sherman L. Richards. "The Prostitutes and Gamblers of Virginia City, Nevada: 1879." *Pacific Historical Review* 48 (1979): 239–258.

Brandt, Allan. *No Magic Bullet: A History of Venereal Disease in the United States since 1880*. New York: Oxford University Press, 1985.

Brownmiller, Susan. *Femininity*. New York: Simon and Schuster, 1984.

Burnham, John C. "Medical Inspection of Prostitutes in America in the Nineteenth Century: The St. Louis Experiment and Its Sequel." *Bulletin of the History of Medicine* 45 (1971): 203–218.

Butler, Anne M. *Daughters of Joy, Sisters of Misery: Prostitutes in the American West, 1865–90*. Urbana: University of Illinois Press, 1985.

Butler, Judith. *Gender Trouble: Feminism and the Subversion of Identity*. London: Routledge, 1990.

Calverton, V. F. "Are Women Monogamous?" In *Woman's Coming of Age: A Symposium*, ed. Samuel D. Schmalhausen and V. F. Calverton, 475–488. New York: Liveright, 1931.

Carlisle, Marcia. "Disorderly City, Disorderly Women: Prostitution in Ante-bellum Philadelphia." *Pennsylvania Magazine of History and Biography* 110 (1986): 549–568.

Carpenter, Edward. *Love's Coming of Age: A Series of Papers on the Relations of the Sexes*. New York: Mitchell Kennerly, 1911.

Ceplair, Larry, ed. *Charlotte Perkins Gilman: A Nonfiction Reader*. New York: Columbia University Press, 1991.

Chapkis, W. *Beauty Secrets: Women and the Politics of Appearance*. London: Women's Press, 1986.

Chase, Allen. *The Legacy of Malthus: The Social Costs of the New Scientific Racism*. New York: Knopf, 1977.

Chic (first issue: November/December 1993).

Cockin, Katharine. *Edith Craig: Dramatic Lives*. London: Cassell, 1998.

———. "New Light on Edith Craig." *Theatre Notebook* 55:3 (1991): 132–143.

———. "The Pioneer Players (1911–1925): A Cultural History." Diss., Leicester University, 1994.

———. "The Pioneer Players: Plays of/with Identity." In *Difference in View: Women in Modernism*, ed. Gabriele Griffin, 142–154. London: Taylor, 1994.

Colmore, Gertrude. "The Nun." *Vote* (29 June 1912): 175.

Cooper, Wendy. *Hair: Sex, Society and Symbolism*. New York: Stein, 1971.

Corson, R. *Fashions in Hair: The First Five Thousand Years*. London: Owen, 1980.

Cott, Nancy F. *The Grounding of Modern Feminism*. New Haven: Yale University Press, 1987.

Cowan, Ruth Schwartz. *More Work for Mother: The Ironies of Household Technology from the Open Hearth to the Microwave*. New York: Basic Books, 1983.

Cremin, Lawrence A. *Traditions of American Education*. New York: Basic Books, 1977.

Daniels, Kay. "Prostitution in Tasmania from Penal Settlement to Civilized Society." In *So Much Hard Work: Women and Prostitution in Australian History*, ed. Kay Daniels, 15–86. Sydney: Fontana, 1984.

Darwin, Charles. *On the Origin of Species by Natural Selection, or The*

Preservation of Favoured Races in the Struggle for Life. 1859.
Cambridge: Harvard University Press, 1964.

D. B. M. "The New Woman." In *The New Woman*, ed. Juliet Gardiner,
15. London: Collins, 1993.

de Cortais, G. *Women's Headdress and Hairstyles in England from AD 600
to the Present Day.* London: Batsford, 1973.

Degler, Carl. "Charlotte Perkins Gilman on the Theory and Practice of
Feminism." *American Quarterly* 7 (1956): 21–39.

———. Introduction. In *Women and Economics: A Study of the
Economic Relation between Men and Women as a Factor in Social
Evolution* by Charlotte Perkins Gilman, ed. Carl Degler, vi–xxxv.
New York: Harper-Torchbooks, 1966.

Dell, Floyd. "Can Men and Women Be Friends?" In *Our Changing
Morality: A Symposium*, ed. Freda Kirchwey, 235–239. New York:
Boni, 1924.

Dinnerstein, Leonard. *Uneasy at Home.* New York: Columbia University
Press, 1987.

Dixson, Miriam. *The Real Matilda: Women and Identity in Australia,
1788–1975.* Ringwood: Penguin, 1976.

Docker, John. *The Nervous Nineties.* Melbourne: Oxford University
Press, 1991.

Donawerth, Jane L., and Carol A. Kolmarten, eds. *Utopian and Science
Fiction by Women: Worlds of Difference.* Liverpool: Liverpool
University Press, 1994.

Dorynne, Jess. "The Surprise of His Life." TS. Ellen Terry Memorial
Museum, Tenterden, Kent, UK.

Doyle, William T. "Charlotte Gilman and the Cycle of Feminist
Reform." Diss., University of California, 1960.

Dubois, Ellen C., and Linda Gordon. "Seeking Ecstasy on the Battlefield:
Danger and Pleasure in Nineteenth-Century Sexual Thought."
Feminist Studies 9 (1983): 7–23.

Dymkowski, Christine. "Entertaining Ideas: Edy Craig and the Pioneer
Players." In *The New Woman and Her Sisters: Feminism and Theatre
1850–1914*, ed. Viv Gardner and Susan Rutherford, 221–233. Hemel
Hempstead: Harvester Wheatsheaf, 1992.

Eddy, Mary Baker. *Science and Health with Key to the Scriptures.* Boston:
Trustees under the Will of Mary Baker G. Eddy, 1922.

Ehrenreich, Barbara, and Deirdre English. *For Her Own Good.* Garden
City: Anchor-Doubleday, 1978.

Eichorn, Jill. "Working Bodies, Working Minds: The Domestic Politics of

American Women in Labor 1896–1940." Diss., Miami University of Ohio, 1995.

Engels, Frederick. "The Origin of the Family, Private Property, and the State." In *Karl Marx and Frederick Engels: Selected Works, 1884*, 468–593. New York: International Publishers, 1984.

Erskine, Thomas L., and Connie L. Richards, eds. *"The Yellow Wallpaper": Charlotte Perkins Gilman.* New Brunswick, N.J.: Rutgers University Press, 1993.

Evans, Sara M. *Born for Liberty: A History of Women in America.* New York: Free Press; London: Collier Macmillan, 1989.

Faderman, Lillian. *Surpassing the Love of Men: Romantic Friendship and Love between Women from the Renaissance to the Present.* New York: Morrow, 1981.

Faludi, Susan. *Backlash: The Undeclared War against American Women.* New York: Crown, 1991.

Featherstone, M. *Consumer Culture and Postmodernism.* London: Sage, 1991.

Feldman, Egal. "The Prostitute, the Alien Woman, and the Progressive Imagination, 1910–1915." *American Quarterly* 30 (1967): 192–206.

Felt, Jeremy. "Vice Reform as a Political Technique: The Committee of Fifteen in New York, 1900–1901." *New York History* 54 (1973): 24–51.

Fetterly, Judith. "Reading about Reading: 'A Jury of Her Peers,' 'The Murders in the Rue Morgue,' and 'The Yellow Wallpaper.' " In *The Captive Imagination*, ed. Catherine Golden, 253–260. New York: Feminist, 1992.

Finkelstein, J. *The Fashioned Self.* London: Polity, 1991.

Fishkin, Shelley Fisher. " 'Making a Change': Strategies of Subversion in Gilman's Journalism and Short Fiction." In *Critical Essays on Charlotte Perkins Gilman*, ed. Joanne B. Karpinski, 234–248. New York: G. K. Hall, 1992.

Foucault, Michel. *The History of Sexuality: Volume I, An Introduction.* Trans. Robert Hurley. Harmondsworth: Penguin, 1976; reprint 1990.

Frampton, Kenneth. "Reflections on the Autonomy of Architecture: A Critique of Contemporary Production." In *Out of Site: A Social Criticism of Architecture*, ed. Diane Ghirado, 13–26. Seattle: Bay Press, 1991.

Franck, Karen A. "A Feminist Approach to Architecture: Acknowledging Women's Ways of Knowing." In *Architecture: A Place for Women*, ed. Ellen Perry Berkeley and Matilda McQuaid, 201–216. Washington, D.C., and London: Smithsonian Institution, 1989.

Frank, A. "For a Sociology of the Body: An Analytical Review." In *The Body: Social Process and Cultural Theory*, ed. M. Featherstone, M. Hepworth, and B. Turner, 42–51. London: Sage, 1991.

Friedl, Bettina, ed. *On to Victory: Propaganda Plays of the Woman Suffrage Movement*. Boston: Northeastern University Press, 1989.

Gale, Zona. Foreword. In *The Living of Charlotte Perkins Gilman* by Charlotte Perkins Gilman, ed. Ann J. Lane, xxvii–lii.

Gardiner, Juliet, ed. *The New Woman*. London: Collins and Brown, 1993.

Gardner, Viv, ed. *Sketches from the Actresses' Franchise League*. Nottingham: Nottingham Drama Texts, 1985.

Gardner, Viv, and Susan Rutherford, eds. *The New Woman and Her Sisters: Feminism and Theatre 1850–1914*. Hemel Hempstead: Harvester Wheatsheaf, 1992.

Ghirado, Diane. "Introduction." In *Out of Site: A Social Criticism of Architecture*, ed. Diane Ghirado, 2–12. Seattle: Bay Press, 1991.

Giddens, A. *Modernity and Self-Identity*. London: Polity, 1991.

Gilbert, Sandra, and Susan Gubar. "The Madwoman in the Attic: The Woman Writer and the Nineteenth-Century Literary Imagination." In *The Captive Imagination*, ed. Catherine Golden, 145–148. New York: Feminist, 1992.

———. *The Madwoman in the Attic: The Woman Writer and the Nineteenth-Century Literary Imagination*. New York: Yale University Press, 1979.

Gilligan, Carol. *In a Different Voice: Psychological Theory and Women's Development*. Cambridge: Harvard University Press, 1982.

Gilligan, Carol, and Lyn Mikel Brown. *Meeting at the Crossroads: Women's Psychology and Girl's Development*. New York: Ballantine, 1992.

Glaspell, Susan. "Trifles." 1916. In *Fifty One Act Plays*, ed. Constance M. Martin, 641–660. London: Gollancz, 1934.

———. *The Verge*. Boston: Small, Maynard, 1922.

Glover, Evelyn. "A Chat with Mrs. Chicky." In *How the Vote Was Won and Other Suffragette Plays*, ed. Dale Spender and Carole Hayman, 17–33. London: Methuen, 1985.

Golden, Catherine, ed. *The Captive Imagination: A Casebook on "The Yellow Wallpaper."* New York: Feminist Press, 1992.

Goldman, Marion S. *Golddiggers and Silverminers: Prostitution and Society on the Comstock Lode*. Ann Arbor: University of Michigan Press, 1981.

Gough, V., and J. Rudd. *A Very Different Story: Studies on the Fiction of Charlotte Perkins Gilman*. Liverpool: Liverpool University Press, 1998.

Gray, Delphine. "The Conference." TS. Ellen Terry Memorial Museum, Tenterden, Kent, UK.

Greer, Germaine. *The Female Eunuch*. London: MacGibbon, 1970.

Griffin, Gabriele, ed. *Difference in View: Women in Modernism*. London: Taylor, 1994.

Gronlund, Laurence. *The Co-operative Commonwealth*. Ed. George Bernard Shaw. London: Modern Press, 1885.

Grossman, Herbert, and Suzanne H. Grossman. *Gender Issues in Education*. Boston: Allyn, 1994.

Gutmann, Amy. *Democratic Education*. Princeton: Princeton University Press, 1987.

Halttunen, Karen. *Confidence Men and Painted Women: A Study of Middle-Class Culture in America, 1830–1870*. New Haven: Yale University Press, 1982.

Hamilton, Cicely. *Jack and Jill and a Friend*. London: Lacy's Acting Edition, 1911.

———. *Marriage as a Trade*. 1909. London: Women's Press, 1981.

Hamilton, G. V. "The Emotional Life of Modern Woman." In *Woman's Coming of Age: A Symposium*, ed. Samuel D. Schmalhausen and V. F. Calverton, 207–229. New York: Liveright, 1931.

Haney-Peritz, Janice. "Monumental Feminism and Literature's Ancestral House: Another Look at 'The Yellow Wallpaper.'" In *Charlotte Perkins Gilman: The Woman and Her Work*, ed. Sheryl L. Meyering, 95–107. Ann Arbor: UMI, 1989.

Haug, F., ed. *Female Sexualization*. London: Verso, 1987.

Hayden, Dolores. "The Feminist Paradise Palace." *Heresies* 3:3 (1981): 56–58.

———. *The Grand Domestic Revolution: A History of Feminist Designs for American Homes, Neighborhoods, and Cities*. Cambridge, Mass.: MIT Press, 1981.

———. *Redesigning the American Dream: The Future of Housing, Work, and Family Life*. New York: Norton, 1984.

H.D. *Collected Poems 1912–1944*. Ed. Louis L. Martz. New York: New Directions, 1983.

Heijermans, Herman. *The Good Hope*. Trans. Christopher St. John. London: Hendersons, 1921.

Heilbrun, Carolyn. "The Politics of Mind: Women, Tradition and the University." *Papers on Language and Literature* 24:3 (1988): 231–244.

Hennessy, Rosemary. *Materialist Feminism and the Politics of Discourse*. London: Routledge, 1993.

Herald, J. *Fashions of a Decade: The Twenties*. London: Batsford, 1991.

Hill, Mary A. *Charlotte Perkins Gilman: The Making of a Radical Feminist, 1860–1896*. Philadelphia: Temple University Press, 1980.

———, ed. *Endure: The Diaries of Charles Walter Stetson*. Philadelphia: Temple University Press, 1980.

———, ed. *A Journey from Within: The Love Letters of Charlotte Perkins Gilman*. Lewisberg: Bucknell University Press, 1995.

Hinkle, Beatrice M. "Women and the New Morality." In *Our Changing Morality: A Symposium*, ed. Freda Kirchwey, 183–196. New York: Boni, 1924.

Hobson, Florence Edgar. *A Modern Crusader*. London: Fifield, 1912.

———. "Woman and the House." *Freewoman* 2:29 (6 June 1912): 56.

Hofstadter, Richard. *Social Darwinism in American Thought*. Philadelphia: University of Pennsylvania Press, 1944. Boston: Beacon, 1955.

Holledge, Julie. *Innocent Flowers: Women in Edwardian Theatre*. London: Virago, 1981.

Housman, Laurence. *Pains and Penalties*. London: Sidgwick, 1911.

Howells, William Dean, ed. *The Great Modern American Stories*. New York: Boni and Liveright, 1920.

Humphrey, David C. "Prostitution and Public Policy in Austin, Texas, 1870–1915." *Southwestern Historical Quarterly* 86 (1983): 473–516.

Irigaray, Luce. "Women, the Sacred and Money." In *Psychoanalytic Criticism: A Reader*, ed. Sue Vice, 182–193. London: Polity, 1996.

Jackson, Deidra. "Cooperative Community Has Spirit to Share with Close-Living Neighbors." *News and Observer* (2 July 1995): A1, A14.

Jelliffe, Smith Ely. "The Theory of the Libido." In *Sex in Civilization*, ed. V. F. Calverton and Samuel D. Schmalhausen, 456–471. New York: Macaulay, 1929.

Joannou, Mary, and June Purvis, eds. *New Feminist Essays on Women's Suffrage*. Manchester, Eng.: Manchester University Press, 1996.

Jones, L. *Bulletproof Diva: Tales of Race, Sex, and Hair*. Harmondsworth: Penguin, 1995.

Kann, Mark E. "Character Education for Democratic Citizenship." *Moral Education Forum* 18 (1993): 24–28.

Karpinski, Joanne B., ed. *Critical Essays on Charlotte Perkins Gilman*. New York: G. K. Hall, 1992.

Kent, Susan Kingsley. *Sex and Suffrage in Britain, 1860–1914*. Princeton: Princeton University Press, 1987.

Keohane, Nannerl O. "Educating Women Students for the Future." In

Changing Education: Women as Radicals and Conservators, ed. Joyce Antler and Sari Knopp Biklen, 68–83. Albany: State University of New York Press, 1990.

Kessler, Carol Farley. "Brittle Jars and Bitter Jangles: Light Verse by Charlotte Perkins Gilman." *Regionalism and the Female Imagination* 4:2 (1978): 35–43. Reprinted in *Charlotte Perkins Gilman: The Woman and Her Work*, ed. Sheryl L. Meyering, 133–143.

———. *Charlotte Perkins Gilman: Her Progress toward Utopia with Selected Writings*. New York: Syracuse University Press, 1995.

———. "Consider Her Ways: The Cultural Work of Charlotte Perkins Gilman's Pragmatopian Stories 1908–1913." In *Utopian and Science Fiction by Women: Worlds of Difference*, ed. Jane L. Donawerth and Carol A. Kolmarten, 126–136. Syracuse: Syracuse University Press/Liverpool: Liverpool University Press, 1994.

Knight, Denise D. *Charlotte Perkins Gilman: A Study of the Short Fiction*. New York: Twayne, 1997.

———, ed. *The Diaries of Charlotte Perkins Gilman*. 2 vols. Charlottesville: University of Virginia Press, 1994.

———, ed. *The Later Poetry of Charlotte Perkins Gilman*. Newark: University of Delaware Press, 1996.

———. "'With the First Grass-Blade': Whitman's Influence on the Poetry of Charlotte Perkins Gilman." *Walt Whitman Quarterly* (Summer 1993): 18–29.

———, ed. *"The Yellow Wall-Paper" and Selected Stories of Charlotte Perkins Gilman*. Newark: University of Delaware Press, 1994.

Lane, Ann J., ed. *The Charlotte Perkins Gilman Reader*. New York: Pantheon, 1980.

———. Introduction. In *The Living of Charlotte Perkins Gilman* by Charlotte Perkins Gilman, xi–xxiv. Madison: The University of Wisconsin Press, 1991.

———. *To Herland and Beyond: The Life and Work of Charlotte Perkins Gilman*. New York: Pantheon, 1990; Meridian, 1991.

Lanser, Susan S. "Feminist Criticism, 'The Yellow Wallpaper,' and the Politics of Color in America." *Feminist Studies* 15:3 (1989): 415–441. Rpt. in *The Yellow Wallpaper*, ed. Thomas L. Erskine and Connie L. Richards, 225–256. New Brunswick: Rutgers University Press, 1993.

Leonard, Carol, and Isidor Wallimann. "Prostitution and Changing Morality in the Frontier Cattle Towns of Kansas." *Kansas History* 2 (1979): 34–53.

Lickona, Thomas. "The Return of Character Education." *Educational Leadership* 51 (1993): 3–9.

Light, Ivan. "The Ethnic Vice Industry, 1880–1944." *American Sociological Review* 42 (1977): 464–479.

———. "From Vice District to Tourist Attraction: The Moral Career of American Chinatowns, 1880–1940." *Pacific Historical Review* 43 (1974): 367–394.

London Feminist Group, ed. *The Sexual Dynamics of History*. London: Pluto, 1983.

Lubove, Roy. "The Progressives and the Prostitute." *Historian* 24 (May 1962): 308–330.

Lyttelton, Edith. "The Thumbscrew." *Nineteenth Century* (1911): 938–960.

Maglin, Nan Bauer. "Kitchen Dramas." *Heresies* 3:3 (1981): 42–46.

Magner, Lois N. "Women and the Scientific Idiom: Textual Episodes from Wollstonecraft, Fuller, Gilman, and Firestone." *Signs* 4 (1978): 61–80.

Martin, Jane Roland. *Reclaiming a Conversation: The Ideal of the Educated Woman*. New Haven: Yale University Press, 1985.

Marx, Karl. *Das Capital*. 1867. New York: Vintage, 1976.

———. *Economic and Philosophic Manuscripts of 1844*. 1932. Trans. Rodney Livingstone and Gregor Benton. New York: Vintage, 1974.

Marx, Karl, and Frederick Engels. *The German Ideology*. 1932. Ed. C. J. Arthur. New York: International Publishers, 1970.

McGrath, Ann. "'Black Velvet': Aboriginal Women and Their Relations with White Men in the Northern Territory, 1910–1940." In *So Much Hard Work: Women and Prostitution in Australian History*, ed. Kay Daniels, 233–297. Sydney: Fontana, 1984.

Mercer, K. "Black Hair/Style Politics." *New Formations* 3 (1987): 33–54.

Metzger, Walter. "A Spectre Haunts American Scholars: The Spectre of 'Professionalism.'" *Educational Researcher* 16 (1987): 5–9.

Meyering, Sheryl L., ed. *Charlotte Perkins Gilman: The Woman and Her Work*. Ann Arbor: UMI, 1989.

Michaels, Walter B. *The Gold Standard and the Logic of Naturalism*. Berkeley: University of California Press, 1987.

Millett, Kate. *The Prostitution Papers*. New York: Ballantine, 1976.

Mills, C. Wright. Introduction. In *The Theory of the Leisure Class*, by Thorstein Veblen, vi–xix. New York: New American Library, 1953.

Morantz-Sanchez, Regina. *Sympathy and Science: Women Physicians in American Medicine*. Oxford: Oxford University Press, 1985.

Morton, Marian J. "Seduced and Abandoned in an American City: Cleveland and Its Fallen Women, 1869–1936." *Journal of Urban History* 11 (1985): 443–469.

Murphy, Mary. "The Private Lives of Public Women: Prostitution in Butte, Montana, 1878–1917." In *The Women's West*, ed. Susan Armitage and Elizabeth Jameson, 193–206. Norman: University of Oklahoma Press.

Nash, Stanley. "Prostitution and Charity: The Magdalen Hospital, A Case Study." *Journal of Social History* (1984): 617–628.

Nevinson, Margaret Wynne. *In the Workhouse*. London: International Suffrage Shop, 1911.

Nies, Judith. "Charlotte Perkins Gilman." In *Seven Women: Portraits from the Radical American Tradition*. New York: Viking, 1977.

Noddings, Nel. *Caring: A Feminine Approach to Ethical and Moral Education*. Berkeley: University of California Press, 1984.

Noyes, John Humphrey. *History of American Socialisms*. 1871. New York: Dover, 1966.

O'Brien, Mary. *The Politics of Reproduction*. London: Routledge, 1981.

Oram, Alison. "Serving Two Masters? The Introduction of a Marriage Bar in Teaching in the 1920s." In *The Sexual Dynamics of History*, ed. London Feminist History Group, 134–148.

Pateman, Carole. "Defending Prostitution: Charges against Ericsson." *Ethics* 93 (1982): 557–562.

———. *The Sexual Contract*. Cambridge: Polity, 1988.

Patterson, Marjory. *Pan in Ambush*. Baltimore: Norman Remington, 1921.

Piercy, Marge. *Circles on the Water*. New York: Knopf, 1982.

———. *Woman on the Edge of Time*. New York: Random, 1976.

Rakatansky, Mark. "Spatial Narratives." *Harvard Architecture Review* 8 (1992): 102–121.

Rich, Adrienne. "Compulsory Heterosexuality and Lesbian Existence." In *Adrienne Rich's Poetry and Prose*, 203–204. New York: Norton, 1975.

Richards, J. Radcliffe. *The Sceptical Feminist: A Philosophical Enquiry*. London: Routledge, 1980.

Riviere, Joan. "Womanliness as a Masquerade." *International Journal of Psychoanalysis* 10 (1929): 303–313.

Romines, Ann. *The Home Plot: Women, Writing and Domestic Ritual*. Amherst: University of Massachusetts Press, 1992.

Rosen, Ruth. *The Lost Sisterhood: Prostitution in America, 1900–1918*. Baltimore: Johns Hopkins University Press, 1983.

Rottenberg, Lori. "The Wayward Worker: Toronto's Prostitute at the

Turn of Century." In *Women at Work – Ontario, 1850–1930*, ed. Janice
Acton, Penny Goldsmith, and Bonnie Shepard, 121–136. Toronto:
Canadian Women's Educational Press, 1974.

Sartre, Jean-Paul. *Critique de la raison dialectique*. Paris: Gallimard, 1960.

Scharnhorst, Gary. *Charlotte Perkins Gilman*. Boston: Twayne, 1985.

————. *Charlotte Perkins Gilman: A Bibliography*. Metuchen, N.J.:
Scarecrow, 1985.

————. "Making Her Fame: Charlotte Perkins Gilman in California."
California History 64 (1985): 192–201.

Schmalhausen, Samuel D. "The Sexual Revolution." In *Sex in
Civilization*, ed. V. F. Calverton and Samuel D. Schmalhausen, 349–
436. New York: Macaulay, 1929.

Schwartz, Lynne Sharon, ed. *The Yellow Wallpaper and Other Writings
by Charlotte Perkins Gilman*. New York: Bantam, 1989.

Scott, Clifford H. *Lester Frank Ward*. Boston: Twayne, 1976.

Scott, Rose. Correspondence, "Miscellaneous." Mitchell Library
Manuscripts A2283. Sydney, State Library of New South Wales.

Shryrock, Richard Harrison. "Women in American Medicine." In
Medicine in America: Historical Essays, 177–202. Baltimore: Johns
Hopkins University Press, 1966.

Shulman, Robert, ed. *The Yellow Wall-Paper and Other Stories*. Oxford:
Oxford University Press, 1996.

Shumsky, Neil Larry. "San Francisco's Zone of Prostitution, 1880–1934."
Journal of Historical Geography 7 (1981): 71–89.

————. "Tacit Acceptance: Respectable Americans and Segregated
Prostitution, 1870–1910." *Journal of Social History* 19 (1986):
665–679.

Smith-Rosenberg, Carroll. "The Hysterical Woman: Sex Roles and Role
Conflict in Nineteenth-Century America." *Social Research* (1972):
652–678.

Solomon, Barbara H., ed. *Herland and Selected Stories by Charlotte
Perkins Gilman*. New York: Penguin, Signet, 1992.

Spain, Daphne. *Gendered Spaces*. Chapel Hill: University of North
Carolina Press, 1992.

Spender, Dale, and Carole Hayman, eds. *How the Vote Was Won and
Other Suffragette Plays*. London: Methuen, 1985.

Stansell, Christine. "Women, Children, and the Uses of the Streets: Class
and Gender Conflict in New York City, 1850–1860." *Feminist Studies*
8 (1982): 309–335.

St. John, Christopher. *The First Actress*. London: Utopia, n.d.

————. "Macrena." TS. Ellen Terry Memorial Museum, Tenterden, Kent, UK.

Stowell, Sheila. *A Stage of Their Own: Feminist Playwrights of the Suffrage Era.* Ann Arbor: University of Michigan Press, 1992.

Strasser, Susan. "The Business of Housekeeping." *Insurgent Socialist* 8 (1978): 147–163.

Sullivan, Barbara. "Rethinking Prostitution." In *Transitions: New Australian Feminism,* ed. Barbara Caine and Rosemary Pringle, 184–197. Sydney: Allen, 1995.

Summers, Anne. *Damned Whores and God's Police: The Colonization of Women in Australia.* Ringwood: Penguin, 1975.

Susman, Warren. *Culture as History.* New York: Pantheon, 1984.

Synnott, A. *The Body Social: Symbolism, Self and Society.* London: Routledge, 1993.

Tansey, Richard. "Prostitution and Politics in Antebellum New Orleans." *Southern Studies* 18 (1979): 449–479.

Trodd, Anthea. *A Reader's Guide to Edwardian Literature.* Hemel Hempstead: Harvester Wheatsheaf, 1991.

Turner, Frederick Jackson. "The Significance of the Frontier in American History." In *American Historical Association, Annual Report,* 199–226. Washington, D.C., 1893.

Valverde, Mariana. *The Age of Light and Soap and Water: Moral Reform in English Canada, 1880–1925.* Toronto: McClelland Stewart, 1991.

Veblen, Thorstein. *The Theory of the Leisure Class.* 1899. New York: New American Library, 1953.

Vice, Sue, ed. *Psychoanalytic Criticism: A Reader.* London: Polity, 1996.

Vicinus, Martha. *Independent Women: Work and Community for Single Women 1850–1920.* London: Virago, 1985.

Walker, Cheryl. *American Women Poets of the Nineteenth Century: An Anthology.* New Brunswick: Rutgers University Press, 1992.

Walsh, Mary Roth. *"Doctors Wanted: No Women Need Apply": Sexual Barriers in the Medical Profession, 1835–1975.* New Haven: Yale University Press, 1977.

Ward, Lester. *Dynamic Sociology or, Applied Social Science, as Based upon Statical Sociology and the Less Complex Sciences.* Vols. 1 and 2. New York: Appleton, 1883, 1907.

————. "Our Better Halves." *Forum* 6 (November 1888): 266–275.

————. *Pure Sociology: A Treatise on the Origin and Spontaneous Development of Society.* 1903. 2nd ed. New York: Macmillan, 1916.

Wearing, J. P. *The London Stage 1910–1919: A Calendar of Plays and Players*. Metuchen, N.J.: Scarecrow, 1982.

Weisman, Leslie Kanes. *Discrimination by Design: A Feminist Critique of the Man Made Environment*. Urbana: University of Illinois Press, 1992.

———. "A Feminist Experiment: Learning from WSPA, Then and Now." In *Architecture: A Place for Women*, ed. Ellen Perry Berkeley and Matilda McQuaid, 125–133. Washington, D.C.: Smithsonian Institution Press, 1989.

West, Rebecca. "A Modern Crusader." *Freewoman* 2:27 (May 1912): 8–10.

Wigley, Mark. "Untitled: The Housing of Gender." In *Sexuality and Space*, ed. Beatriz Colomina, 327–389. New York: Princeton Architectural Press, 1992.

Wilson, E. *Adorned in Dreams: Fashion and Modernity*. London: Virago, 1985.

Wolf, Laurie. "Suffragettes of the Edwardian Theatre: Edith Craig and the Pioneer Players." Diss., University of California, 1989.

Wolf, Naomi. *The Beauty Myth*. Toronto: Random, 1990.

Wollstonecraft, Mary. *A Vindication of the Rights of Woman*. Ed. M. Krammick. Harmondsworth: Penguin, 1975.

Woolf, Virginia. "A Higher Court." *New Statesman* (17 April 1920). Rpt. in *Essays of Virginia Woolf*, ed. Andrew McNeillie, 207–210. London: Hogarth, 1988.

Young, David. *The Discovery of Evolution*. Cambridge: Cambridge University Press, 1992.

Zangrando, Joanna. "Work, Class, and Domestic Ideology: Charlotte Perkins Gilman and the Home Economists at the Turn-of-the-Century." American Studies Association Conference, Baltimore, October 1991.

Zaretsky, Eli. "Socialism and Feminism III: Socialist Politics and the Family." *Socialist Revolution* 4 (1974): 83–98.

INDEX

Works are referred to by short title; full details appear in the bibliography.